UNITED NATIONS CONFERENCE ON TRADE AND DEVELOPMENT
Geneva

THE LEAST DEVELOPED COUNTRIES
REPORT 2008

Prepared by the UNCTAD secretariat

UNITED NATIONS
New York and Geneva, 2008

Note

Symbols of United Nations documents are composed of capital letters with figures. Mention of such a symbol indicates a reference to a United Nations document.

The overview of this report can also be found on the Internet, in all six official languages of the United Nations, at www.unctad.org.

UNCTAD/LDC/2008

UNITED NATIONS PUBLICATION

Sales No. E.08.II.D.20

ISBN 978-92-1-112751-5

ISSN 0257-7550

What are the Least Developed Countries?

Fifty countries are currently designated by the United Nations as "least developed countries" (LDCs): Afghanistan, Angola, Bangladesh, Benin, Bhutan, Burkina Faso, Burundi, Cambodia, Cape Verde (until December 2007), Central African Republic, Chad, Comoros, Democratic Republic of the Congo, Djibouti, Equatorial Guinea, Eritrea, Ethiopia, Gambia, Guinea, Guinea-Bissau, Haiti, Kiribati, Lao People's Democratic Republic, Lesotho, Liberia, Madagascar, Malawi, Maldives, Mali, Mauritania, Mozambique, Myanmar, Nepal, Niger, Rwanda, Samoa, Sao Tome and Principe, Senegal, Sierra Leone, Solomon Islands, Somalia, Sudan, Timor–Leste, Togo, Tuvalu, Uganda, United Republic of Tanzania, Vanuatu, Yemen and Zambia. The list of LDCs is reviewed every three years by the Economic and Social Council (ECOSOC) in the light of recommendations by the Committee for Development Policy (CDP).

The following criteria were used by the CDP in the 2006 review of the list of LDCs:

(a) A "low-income" criterion, based on the *gross national income (GNI) per capita* (a 3-year average, 2002–2004), with thresholds of $750 for cases of addition to the list, and $900 for cases of graduation from LDC status;

(b) A "human assets" criterion, involving a composite index (the *Human Assets Index*) based on indicators of (i) nutrition (percentage of the population undernourished); (ii) health (child mortality rate); (iii) school enrolment (gross secondary school enrolment rate); and (iv) literacy (adult literacy rate); and

(c) An "economic vulnerability" criterion, involving a composite index (the *Economic Vulnerability Index*) based on indicators of (i) natural shocks (index of instability of agricultural production; share of population displaced by natural disasters); (ii) trade shocks (index of instability of exports of goods and services); (iii) exposure to shocks (share of agriculture, forestry and fisheries in GDP; merchandise export concentration index); (iv) economic smallness (population in logarithm); and (v) economic remoteness (index of remoteness).

For all three criteria, different thresholds are used for addition to, and graduation from, the list of LDCs. A country will qualify to be added to the list if it meets the three criteria and does not have a population greater than 75 million. A country will normally qualify for graduation from LDC status if it has met graduation thresholds under at least two of the three criteria in at least two consecutive reviews of the list. However, if the GNI per capita of an LDC has risen to a level at least double the graduation threshold, this country will be deemed eligible for graduation regardless of its performance under the other two criteria. After a recommendation to graduate a country has been made by the CDP and endorsed by ECOSOC and the General Assembly, the graduating country will be granted a three-year grace period before actual graduation takes place. In accordance with General Assembly resolution 59/209, this standard grace period is expected to enable the relevant country and its development partners to agree on a "smooth transition" strategy, so that the loss of LDC-specific concessions at the end of the grace period does not disturb the socioeconomic progress of the country.

Acknowledgements

The Least Developed Countries Report 2008 was prepared by a team consisting of Charles Gore (team leader), Alberto Amurgo Pacheco (from March 2008), Lisa Borgatti, Agnès Collardeau-Angleys, Junior Davis (from March 2008), Zeljka Kozul-Wright, Madasamyraja Rajalingam, Rolf Traeger and Stefanie West. Yan Shen participated in the final stages of the preparation of the Report from May 2008. Michael Herrmann and Nguyuru Ibrahim Lipumba were part of the team until December 2007 and March 2008, respectively. The work was carried out under the overall supervision of Habib Ouane, Director, Division for Africa, Least Developed Countries and Special Programmes.

An ad hoc expert group meeting was organized as part of the preparations for the report. Entitled "Managing structural transformation in least developed countries", it was held in Geneva on 8 and 9 November 2007. It brought together specialists in the fields of official development assistance, agricultural development, mineral development, urban management, development planning, governance, state capability and finance. The participants in the meeting were: Debapriya Bhattacharya, Marquise David, John Di John, Gerald Epstein, Shenggen Fan, Samuel Gayi, Padmashree Gehl Sampath, Paul Jourdan, William Kalema, Mushtaq Khan, Tony Killick, Ibrahim Lipumba, Richard Marshall, Banji Oyelaran-Oyeyinka, Alice Sindzingre, Morris Teubal, Ole Therkilsson, Brian Van Arkadie, Meiner Pieter van Dijk and Robert Wade.

The report draws on background papers prepared by Shenggen Fan, Massoud Karshenas, Tony Killick and Richard Marshall.

We are grateful for comments on an earlier draft of Chapter 1 from Marquise David and also for advice on aid statistics from Yasmin Ahmad and Ann Zimmerman. We would also like to thank Adam Prakash and Paul Racionzer for kindly providing FAO data on food and agriculture.

Secretarial support was provided at different times by Sylvie Guy, Stefanie West and Cora Yance Roberts. Sophie Combette designed the cover. The overall layout, graphics and desktop publishing were done by Madasamyraja Rajalingam.

The financial support of donors to the UNCTAD LDC Trust Fund, particularly the Governments of Norway and Finland, is gratefully acknowledged.

Contents

List of Boxes

List of Charts

Annex Charts

List of Tables

Box Tables

Explanatory Notes

The term "dollars" ($) refers to United States dollars unless otherwise stated. The term "billion" signifies 1,000 million.

Annual rates of growth and changes refer to compound rates. Exports are valued f.o.b. (free on board) and imports c.i.f. (cost, insurance, freight) unless otherwise specified.

Use of a dash (–) between dates representing years, e.g. 1981–1990, signifies the full period involved, including the initial and final years. An oblique stroke (/) between two years, e.g. 1991/92, signifies a fiscal or crop year.

The term "least developed country" (LDC) refers, throughout this report, to a country included in the United Nations list of least developed countries.

In the tables:

Two dots (..) indicate that the data are not available, or are not separately reported.

One dot (.) indicates that the data are not applicable.

A hyphen (-) indicates that the amount is nil or negligible.

Details and percentages do not necessarily add up to totals, because of rounding.

Abbreviations

AFRODAD	African Forum and Network on Debt and Development
AIDS	acquired immunodeficiency syndrome
AR	antiretroviral (drugs)
CPIA	country policy and institutional assessment
CRS	creditor reporting system
DAC	Development Assistance Committee
DC	developed country
DFID	Department for International Development
DOTS	directly observed treatment short
ESAF	Enhanced Structural Adjustment Facility
EURODAD	European Network on Debt and Development
FAO	Food and Agriculture Organization of the United Nations
FDI	foreign direct investment
GDP	gross domestic product
GER	gross enrolment ratio
GFCF	gross fixed capital formation
GNI	gross national income
GPI	Gender Parity Index
HIPC	heavily indebted poor country
HIV	human immunodeficiency virus
IAEG	Inter-Agency and Expert Group
ICP	International Comparison Programme
IDA	International Development Association
IEG	Independent Evaluation Group
IEO	Independent Evaluation Office (of the IMF)
IFAD	International Fund for Agricultural Development
IFI	international financial institution
IMF	International Monetary Fund
IMG	independent monitoring group
LDC	least developed country
M&E	monitoring and evaluation
MDG	Millennium Development Goal
MDRI	Multilateral Debt Relief Initiative
NGO	non-governmental organization
ODA	official development assistance
ODC	other developing country
ODP	ozone depletion potential
ODS	ozone-depleting substance
OD-RO	operational development strategies and result-oriented framework

OECD	Organisation for Economic Co-operation and Development
PAF	performance assessment framework
PIU	project implementation unit
PPP	purchasing power parity
PRGF	Poverty Reduction and Growth Facility
PRS	poverty reduction strategy
PRSC	poverty reduction strategy credit
PRSP	poverty reduction strategy paper
R&D	research and development
S&T	science and technology
SAG	Sector Advisory Group
SIDS	small island developing State
SITC	Standard International Trade Classification
SME	small and medium-sized enterprise
T/A	technical assistance
TAS	Tanzania Assistance Strategy
TB	tuberculosis
TNC	transnational corporation
TRTA	trade-related technical assistance
UNCTAD	United Nations Conference on Trade and Development
UNDP	United Nations Development Programme
UNDESA	United Nations Department of Economic and Social Affairs
UNESCAP	United Nations Economic and Social Commission for Asia and the Pacific
UNESCO	United Nations Educational, Scientific and Cultural Organization
UNRISD	United Nations Research Institute for Social Development
UNSTAT	United Nations Statistics Division
WFP	World Food Programme

Country classification used in this Report

The least developed countries covered in this report consist of all the countries in that category in 2007. Cape Verde is therefore included even though it has now graduated (see box below). The 50 LDCs covered are subdivided, for the purpose of analysis, according to (a) geographical groups and (b) export specialization.

Geographical classification

African LDCs (and Haiti): Angola, Benin, Burkina Faso, Burundi, Central African Republic, Chad, Democratic Republic of the Congo, Djibouti, Equatorial Guinea, Eritrea, Ethiopia, Gambia, Guinea, Guinea-Bissau, Haiti, Lesotho, Liberia, Madagascar, Malawi, Mali, Mauritania, Mozambique, Niger, Rwanda, Senegal, Sierra Leone, Somalia, Sudan, Togo, Uganda, United Republic of Tanzania, Zambia (32).

Asian LDCs: Afghanistan, Bangladesh, Bhutan, Cambodia, Lao People's Democratic Republic, Myanmar, Nepal, Yemen (8).

Island LDCs: Cape Verde, Comoros, Kiribati, Maldives, Samoa, Sao Tome and Principe, Solomon Islands, Timor-Leste, Tuvalu, Vanuatu (10).

Some of the island LDCs are geographically in Africa or Asia, but they are grouped together with the Pacific islands due to their structural similarities. Similarly, Haiti and Madagascar are grouped together with African LDCs.

Classification according to export specialization

UNCTAD has classified the LDCs into six export specialization categories, namely, agriculture, fuels, manufacture, mining, mixed and services. They are classified in these categories according to which export category accounts for at least 45 per cent of the total exports of merchandise goods and services (see table A). Mineral exports from Burundi and Mali do not quite meet the required thresholds but since they account for over 40 per cent of those countries' total exports and play a major role in their economies, they are classified as mineral exporters.

The data used for this analysis are taken from the United Nations Commodity Trade Statistics Database (UN Comtrade), the Balance of Payments and International Investment Position Statistics of the International Monetary Fund (IMF), and the UNCTAD Handbook of Statistics 2007. The classification involves some degree of arbitrariness: the LDCs have been classified using their average merchandise export and service data for the period 2003–2005, except for Sierra Leone, for which only the estimates for the period 2004–2005 were available.

The merchandise exports of individual LDCs have been divided, using SITC Rev. 3 codes, into: agriculture (sections 0, 1, 2 and 4, excluding divisions 27 and 28), fuels (section 3), minerals (divisions 27, 28 and 68, and groups 667 and 971), manufactures (sections 5–8, excluding division 68 and group 667). With the exception of group 971 (non-monetary gold), SITC Rev. 3 section 9 (commodities and transactions not classified elsewhere in the SITC) has been included only in the total export of goods and services. It follows that the export shares of table B do not necessarily add up to 100.

Data for Afghanistan, Chad, Liberia, Somalia, Togo and Tuvalu have been estimated using mirror statistics. The unavailability of services data for Afghanistan, Liberia, Somalia and Tuvalu limit the exercise to merchandise exports in these countries. Merchandise export data for Liberia and Togo exclude re-export of ships, boats and floating structures (SITC Rev. 3 group 793).

Six LDCs have been classified as oil exporters, 11 as agricultural exporters, 10 as mineral exporters, 6 as manufactures exporters, 12 as services exporters, and 5 as mixed exporters (see table B). Madagascar, Senegal and Togo also export services, agricultural goods and manufactured goods. The Lao People's Democratic Republic also exports manufactured and agricultural goods. Myanmar has become an exporter of fuels and agricultural goods.

The Least Developed Countries Report 2002 (p. 131) classified 21 LDCs as agricultural exporters on the basis of their export structure in the late 1990s. Of these, only 11 are still exporting mostly agricultural products. Two (Chad and Sudan) have become oil exporters, three (Burundi, Mali and Mauritania) have become mineral exporters, five have become service exporters (Eritrea, Ethiopia, Rwanda, Sao Tome and Principe, and the United Republic of Tanzania), one (Togo) is also exporting manufactures and services, and one (Bhutan) is re-classified as manufactures exporter.

Graduation of Cape Verde from the group of LDCs

Cape Verde graduated from the group of LDCs on 21 December 2007. In the 2006 review of the list of least developed countries, Cape Verde met, for the second time, two of the three indicators required for graduation: it had a GNI per capita in 2004 of $1,487 (with the graduation threshold set at $900) and a human assets indicator of 82.1 (with the graduation threshold set at more than 64). However, Cape Verde did not meet the third indicator: its economic vulnerability indicator stood at 57.9, with the graduation threshold set at less than 38.

The analysis contained in this report covers Cape Verde as one of the least developed countries as the data in this report do not refer beyond the year 2006, when Cape Verde was still part of the group of LDCs.

Table A. Classification of LDCs according to their export specialization, 2003–2005

Oil exporters	Agricultural exporters	Mineral exporters	Manufactures exporters	Services exporters	Mixed exporters
Angola	Afghanistan	Burundi	Bangladesh	Cape Verde	Lao People's Dem. Republic
Chad	Benin	Central African Republic	Bhutan	Comoros	Madagascar
Equatorial Guinea	Burkina Faso	Dem. Republic of the Congo	Cambodia	Djibouti	Myanmar
Sudan	Guinea Bissau	Guinea	Haiti	Eritrea	Senegal
Timor-Leste	Kiribati	Mali	Lesotho	Ethiopia	Togo
Yemen	Liberia	Mauritania	Nepal	Gambia	
	Malawi	Mozambique		Maldives	
	Solomon Islands	Niger		Rwanda	
	Somalia	Sierra Leone		Samoa	
	Tuvalu	Zambia		Sao Tome and Principe	
	Uganda			United Republic of Tanzania	
				Vanuatu	

Source: UNCTAD secretariat estimates based on United Nations COMTRADE data; IMF, B*alance of Payments and International Investment Position Statistics*, online, December 2007; and UNCTAD, *Handbook of Statistics 2007*.

Table B. Shares in total merchandise goods and services exports for the LDCs, by country and main sectors, 2003–2005
(Per cent)

Country	Export specialization	Agriculture	Minerals	Fuels	Manufactures	Services
Afghanistan	A	65.0	7.5	10.1	17.4	..
Angola	O	0.1	2.2	95.8	0.3	1.5
Bangladesh	MF	6.6	0.1	0.3	80.8	12.2
Benin	A	51.1	1.1	0.2	6.5	40.4
Bhutan	MF	12.6	15.8	0.5	47.6	21.6
Burkina Faso	A	74.4	0.8	1.2	8.3	13.9
Burundi	MN	37.8	41.8	0.1	2.4	17.9
Cambodia	MF	3.1	0.4	0.0	73.0	23.5
Cape Verde	S	1.9	0.0	5.0	7.1	86.0
Central African Republic	MN	30.2	58.0	0.2	1.5	8.3
Chad	O	6.9	0.0	86.3	2.5	4.2
Comoros	S	19.7	0.0	0.0	3.7	76.5
Democratic Republic of the Congo	MN	5.7	71.9	10.2	2.3	8.5
Djibouti	S	1.7	1.0	0.2	1.2	94.5
Equatorial Guinea	O	2.3	0.0	90.8	4.1	2.4
Eritrea	S	3.5	0.2	0.0	2.0	94.0
Ethiopia	S	36.2	2.8	0.0	2.6	57.5
Gambia	S	6.8	0.1	0.0	3.7	89.3
Guinea	MN	4.3	71.8	2.0	10.8	10.8
Guinea-Bissau	A	70.2	0.6	7.4	14.2	7.2
Haiti	MF	4.6	0.5	0.0	70.2	24.0
Kiribati	A	77.8	1.1	0.5	16.3	0.0
Lao People's Democratic Republic	MX: A, MF	29.6	5.9	3.6	32.4	27.4
Lesotho	MF	7.4	14.1	0.0	69.3	8.8
Liberia	A	76.2	9.3	6.1	8.3	..
Madagascar	MX: A, MF, S	29.6	2.6	2.9	29.1	30.9
Malawi	A	78.3	0.3	0.1	13.2	8.1
Maldives	S	15.9	0.1	4.2	5.4	74.3
Mali	MN	32.2	42.7	0.4	5.2	19.1
Mauritania	MN	25.6	56.3	0.0	1.5	10.8
Mozambique	MN	15.6	48.5	11.3	5.6	17.2
Myanmar	MX: A, O	36.7	3.7	31.8	18.8	7.8
Nepal	MF	13.8	2.5	0.0	48.5	35.2
Niger	MN	24.1	44.7	1.2	7.1	22.2
Rwanda	S	28.4	11.7	1.7	4.4	53.0
Samoa	S	9.7	0.1	0.1	36.9	52.9
Sao Tome and Principe	S	20.8	0.0	0.0	1.1	78.1
Senegal	MX: A, MF, S	23.9	2.3	13.4	26.6	33.8
Sierra Leone	MN	6.5	52.8	0.4	8.2	31.3
Solomon Islands	A	70.0	0.3	0.0	1.4	27.6
Somalia	A	89.3	4.0	0.3	6.4	..
Sudan	O	13.1	2.7	78.8	2.9	1.8
Timor-Leste	O	17.7	1.1	70.0	10.7	0.0
Togo	MX: A, MF, S	25.9	7.9	0.6	37.9	26.5
Tuvalu	MF	11.1	1.7	0.0	87.2	..
Uganda	A	44.8	6.0	3.8	9.1	36.2
United Republic of Tanzania	S	24.5	26.4	0.1	3.5	45.5
Vanuatu	S	14.1	0.0	0.3	8.3	77.1
Yemen	O	4.5	0.5	84.9	2.8	7.3
Zambia	MN	17.8	51.9	1.1	16.0	13.3

Source: UNCTAD Secretariat estimates based on UN Comtrade; IMF, *Balance of Payments and International Investment Position Statistics*, online, December 2007; UNCTAD, *Handbook of Statistics, 2007.*

Note: A: agricultural exporter, **MF**: manufactures exporter, **MN**: mineral exporter, **MX**: mixed exporter, **O**: oil exporter, **S**: services exporter. For the SITC codes, Rev. 3 used for the classification, see text.
The country shares do not add up to 100 as SITC Rev. 3, section 9, except group 971 (non-monetary gold), has not been included.
Data on services were not available for Afghanistan, Liberia, Somalia and Tuvalu.

Overview

The strong growth performance of the least developed countries (LDCs) as a group has been one of the most encouraging features of the global economy in the current decade. Economic growth since 2000 has been higher than in the 1990s. In 2005 and 2006, there was further growth acceleration and the LDCs together achieved their strongest growth performance in 30 years. Their average growth rate in both these years exceeded the 7 per cent target set by the LDCs and their development partners as a key goal in the Brussels Programme of Action for the Least Developed Countries for the Decade 2001–2010, agreed at the Third United Nations Conference on the Least Developed Countries in 2001. It is estimated that, in 2007, there was only a slight slowdown, to 6.7 per cent.

Against this background, this Report considers three issues. Firstly, it assesses how sustainable economic growth is in the LDCs and examines how many LDCs are participating in the growth surge. Secondly, it considers the extent to which economic growth is leading to improvements in human well-being, and in particular to accelerated poverty reduction and improved progress towards the Millennium Development Goals. Thirdly, it assesses progress towards country-owned development strategies in LDCs and the role of recipient-led aid management policies at the country level as a practical policy mechanism to strengthen country ownership. These are central aims of the Paris Declaration on Aid Effectiveness, adopted in March 2005, whose implementation status will be assessed in Accra, Ghana, in September 2008.

There are major downside risks to the sustainability of rapid growth. This reflects the fact that the type of growth which is occurring in most LDCs is strongly affected by trends in international markets and, in particular, commodity prices. On top of this, the LDCs depend heavily on external sources of finance, particularly official development assistance (ODA), rather than domestically-generated resources. The LDCs are growing rapidly, but without a positive process of diversification and structural change. As a result, they are very vulnerable to trade shocks due to the volatility of commodity prices, affecting both exports and imports. But the aid inflows which provide their major source of external finance are mainly directed towards improving social services and social infrastructure, including governance mechanisms, rather than increasing their productive capacities and promoting structural change and diversification.

The expectation implicit in the prevailing development policy paradigm was that investment in productive sectors would be taken care of by the international private sector, through access to international capital markets or inflows of foreign direct investment (FDI). But this has proved to be an illusion in the former case, as LDCs remain almost entirely marginalized from this source of finance. As for FDI, inflows have concentrated on a few LDCs and have often been weakly linked with the rest of the economy. Workers' remittances are growing and — while playing a role in directly alleviating poverty for those who receive them — their contribution to development by financing investment remains to be proven. They should not be seen as a substitute for long-term capital inflows, and deliberate policies are required to enhance their developmental impact.

The relationship between economic growth and human well-being is a complex issue. Rapid economic growth in the LDCs has been associated with a slow rate of poverty reduction and human development, as gauged by their progress towards the Millennium Development Goals. In 2005, 36 per cent of the total population of the LDCs lived in extreme poverty — that is to say on less than $1 a day — and 76 per cent subsisted on less than $2 a day. Although the incidence of poverty (i.e. the share of the population living in poverty) is falling slowly, the number of people living on less than $1 a day or on less than $2 a day was larger in 2005 than in 2000.

The LDCs as a group are off track to achieve the goal of reducing the incidence of poverty by half between 1990 and 2015, and there is no evidence of a significant change in the trend since 2000, after the adoption of the Millennium Declaration and more socially-oriented policy reforms. For most human development indicators for which data are available for a wide sample of LDCs, less than half the countries are on track to achieve the Millennium Development Goals, and for some indicators, only one third of the countries or even less are on track. The effects of soaring international food prices in 2007 and early 2008 are likely to be more severe in the LDCs than in other developing countries. Rising international prices are already being transmitted to national markets, and rising food prices will have negative effects on poverty trends in the LDCs, further slowing progress towards the Millennium Development Goals.

The weak correlation between growth and improvements in human well-being arises because of the type of economic growth which is occurring. This can not generally be equated with an inclusive process of development. In most LDCs, the majority of the population is employed in agriculture, but agricultural labour productivity is very low and growing very slowly. As it is difficult to make a living in agriculture, more and more people are seeking work in other sectors of the economy. However, remunerative employment opportunities are not being generated quickly enough to meet this growing demand for non-agricultural work. With this accelerating process of "deagrarianization", poverty in LDCs now has two faces. One face is low-productivity, small-scale agriculture; the other is low-productivity, urban, informal-sector activities in petty trade and services.

As discussed in the last three *Least Developed Countries Reports* — on *Knowledge, Technological Learning and Innovation for Development* (2007), *Developing Productive Capacities* (2006) and *Linking International Trade with Poverty Reduction* (2004) — the trends which are occurring are related to policy choices, in particular the development model which has been pursued in most LDCs. This model has sought to deepen the integration of the LDCs into the world economy, increase the efficiency of resource allocation and free markets. Global integration is vital for development and poverty reduction in LDCs. However, without the development of productive capacities and associated employment, external integration does not lead to inclusive development. Export-led growth without associated expansion of sectors serving domestic markets often leads to an exclusive pattern of economic growth. The impact of the soaring international food prices illustrates the vulnerability of LDCs following the current approach, and underlines the need for a policy change towards more sustained and inclusive development. As UNCTAD said at the High-level Conference on World Food Security in June 2008 in Rome, the food crisis is a development crisis.

With the global economic outlook worsening, most LDCs will face major challenges in the period ahead. This will require renewed efforts by both the LDCs and their development partners to develop the productive base of LDCs and address their structural weaknesses. Otherwise, the marginalization of the LDCs in the global economy is likely to deepen. Most of them are highly vulnerable to rising oil and food prices. Their export performance depends heavily on volatile commodity prices or on low-skills manufactures in which global competition is intensifying. In addition, as the reaction to the recent food price increases shows, with the high levels of poverty in LDCs, external shocks can easily lead to social unrest and conflict. To build economic resilience, they need to improve agricultural productivity and diversify their economies to create non-agricultural employment opportunities. As argued in earlier *Least Developed Countries Reports*, this requires a new development model focused on building productive capacities and shifting from commodity-price-led growth to catch-up growth.

Achieving a more sustainable type of economic growth and better poverty reduction and social outcomes in LDCs requires effective national development strategies, effective development aid and development-friendly international regimes for trade, investment and technology. The fundamental priority for LDC Governments is to formulate and implement national development strategies that promote sustained development and poverty reduction. Their development partners need to: (a) scale up aid flows to meet their commitments; (b) align aid flows to the priorities expressed in LDCs' national development strategies; and (c) deliver aid in ways which respect country leadership in the formulation and implementation of their national development strategies and help to strengthen their capacity to exercise such leadership.

Unfortunately, the Report finds that there are still major constraints on the ability of LDC Governments to exercise effective leadership in the design and implementation of their national development strategies and policies. This arises because of very high levels of dependence on donor finance, weak technical capacities, the continuing bark and bite of policy conditionality, the slow progress in aid alignment with country plans and budgets, and donor financing choices.

Weak country ownership has negative consequences for governance. When politicians and policymakers feel inhibited from saying and doing certain things because of a sense of aid dependence, the political qualities of a free-thinking society atrophy. The Report shows that weak country ownership is also having adverse consequences for development effectiveness. This is particularly due to: (a) the weak integration of the macroeconomic framework with sectoral and trade policies; (b) the downscaling of ambition in relation to increased aid inflows; and (c) the low financing of productive sector development.

Increasing country ownership should be a major priority for both LDC Governments and their development partners in order to improve development effectiveness. This will involve action on a range of fronts, which include in particular further consideration of the issues of policy conditionality and aid predictability, and the building of local research and policy analysis capacity which can support the generation of policy alternatives and in particular home-grown solutions.

However, one of the principal recommendations of the Report is that a first step towards improving country ownership could be to adopt recipient-led aid management policies within LDCs. The Paris Declaration encourages countries to do this. Moreover, some LDCs are global pioneers in the introduction of country-level aid management policies. The report urges other LDCs to follow their lead.

How sustainable is LDCs' growth?

THE IMPORTANCE OF TRADE

The record rates of economic growth achieved by the LDCs as a group in 2005 and 2006 were underpinned by a record of level of exports — which was particularly associated with high commodity prices for oil and minerals — and record levels of capital inflows, particularly aid.

The export performance of the LDCs as a group was particularly remarkable. In nominal terms, the value of merchandise exports from LDCs rose by some 80 per cent from 2004 to 2006, reaching $99 billion in 2006. This aggregate picture is being driven to a large degree by the enhanced export performance of oil-exporting LDCs (Angola, Chad, Equatorial Guinea, , Sudan, Timor-Leste and Yemen), as well as by mineral exporters (Democratic Republic of the Congo, Guinea, Mali, Mauritania, Mozambique and Zambia). Seventy-six per cent of the total increase in LDCs' merchandise exports from 2004 to 2006 can be attributed to these countries. The increase is largely explained by rising international commodity prices.

For the LDCs as a group, dependence on commodities has increased since 2000, along with the growth acceleration. Primary commodities increased from 59 per cent of total merchandise exports in 2000–2002 to 77 per cent in 2005–2006. Within this overall pattern, however, there was considerable divergence between African, Asian and island LDCs. The Asian LDCs continued to diversify their economies away from commodities towards manufacturing, while African LDCs increased dependence on primary commodities. Island LDCs remained primarily dependent on service exports, which also exhibit high levels of volatility.

The widening regional divergence between African and Asian LDCs in terms of the form of their integration into the global economy is evident in their different export structures. In the period 2005–2006, over 92 per cent of all exports from African LDCs consisted of primary commodities, including fuels, while in Asian LDCs, this figure was less than half (44 per cent). This type of specialization rendered Asian LDCs much less vulnerable to external fluctuations. Some of them also achieved high rates of export growth based on manufactures. However, the share of medium- and high-tech manufactures exports originating from LDCs remained very small (8.4 per cent). The slowness of the process of export upgrading, even in Asian LDCs, remains an issue of concern.

The ability to compete in global markets and increase manufactures exports has helped Asian LDCs promote a limited degree of structural transformation in which manufacturing is increasing as a share of gross domestic product (GDP). However, for the LDCs as a group, the recent growth surge is not generally associated with a structural transition in which the share of manufacturing in total output is growing. In fact, compared to ten years ago, half of the LDCs have experienced deindustrialization as measured by a declining share of manufacturing in GDP.

Whilst exports have boomed in LDCs, imports have also surged. In 2006, 42 LDCs had trade deficits and, in 37 of them, this deficit was higher in 2006 than it was in 2003–2004. The merchandise trade deficit of oil-importing LDCs has increased from $25 billion in 2005 to $31 billion in 2006. By contrast, the merchandise trade surplus of the oil-exporting LDCs rose from $11 billion in 2004 to $29 billion in 2006. Together, oil and food constituted 30 per cent of LDCs' merchandise imports in 2006.

Most LDCs are highly dependent on food imports. In 2005–2006, the food import bill of the LDCs as a group reached $14.6 billion, which was equivalent to 4.4 per cent of their GDP. This is $6.1 billion higher than in 2000–2002, an increase equivalent to some 2 per cent of their GDP in 2005–2006. It is against this background that soaring food prices in 2007 and early 2008 are having such a negative impact on LDCs.

CONTINUING HIGH DEPENDENCE ON EXTERNAL FINANCE

Despite the record rates of economic growth, LDCs remain highly dependent on external finance. The level of domestic savings continues to be low in many LDCs, including good performers, which have achieved rapid economic growth. In 2006, only one third of the LDCs had gross domestic savings rates above 15 per cent of GDP. Fifteen LDCs had negative domestic savings rates, meaning that they were relying on foreign savings not only to finance domestic investment but also their domestic consumption.

ODA inflows are particularly important. In this regard, it is encouraging to note that net aid disbursements reached the record level of $28 billion in 2006. Sixteen LDCs also received significant debt relief in 2006, with $27 billion ODA principal being forgiven for 16 of them through the Multilateral Debt Relief Initiative. However, only eight Organisation for Economic Co-operation and Development (OECD) Development Assistance Committee members (Luxembourg, Norway, Denmark, Sweden, Ireland, Netherlands, Belgium and United Kingdom) met the Brussels Programme of Action target of making net ODA disbursements equal to or higher than 0.15 per cent of their gross national income (GNI), whilst six of these countries (the above countries minus Belgium and the United Kingdom) met the higher target of 0.20 per cent of GNI.

Multilateral and bilateral aid commitments are increasingly concentrated on social infrastructure and services. ODA commitments to social infrastructure and services constituted 42 per cent of total ODA commitments to LDCs in 2006, up from an average of 34 per cent during the period 2000–2004 and 31 per cent in the second half of the 1990s. In 2006, the share of aid going to education, health, population programmes, water supply and sanitation, Government and civil society all were higher than during the period 2000–2004. This reflects the impact of the focus on the Millennium Development Goals as well as the concern to improve governance. In contrast, aid to build productive sectors and economic infrastructure has continued to receive less priority. The share of aid committed to economic infrastructure and production sectors (including multisector) constituted just 25 per cent of total ODA commitments to LDCs in 2006. This was similar to the level during the period 2000–2004.

Despite all the rhetoric of a renewed interest in economic infrastructure, the share of aid committed to transport, storage and energy was less in 2006 than it was in 2000–2004, and the portion committed to agriculture (including forestry and fishing) and industry (including mining and construction) also declined over that period. The share of aid committed to economic infrastructure and production sectors was also much lower than in 1995–1999, when it had been 38 per cent. Aid commitments to improve economic infrastructure decreased from 18 per cent of total commitments to LDCs in 1995–1999 to 12 per cent in 2006. Commitments to transport and storage infrastructure decreased from 11 per cent of total commitments to LDCs in 1995–1999 to 6 per cent in 2006, and disbursements to energy-related sectors shrunk from 5 per cent to 2 per cent in 2006.

These trends perhaps reflect the assumption that the international private sector can take over from official finance in these sectors. In practice, however, this assumption has proved flawed. LDCs remain marginalized from international capital markets. There has been a trend towards increased FDI inflows, which reached a level of $9 billion in 2006 after faltering in the previous years. Moreover, manufactures-exporting LDCs are now also attracting more FDI. Nevertheless, most FDI still remains concentrated on natural resource extraction, particularly of oil and minerals, and profit remittances on FDI are rising rapidly.

Migrant remittances reached the record level of $13 billion in 2006 and are particularly important for a few Asian countries. However, channelling these resources to finance long-term development rather than just short-term poverty alleviation remains a challenge to policymakers.

To sum up, the record rates of economic growth are welcome, but LDCs remain locked into a pattern of economic growth which makes them highly vulnerable to external shocks and in particular international commodity price volatility. Given the high levels of poverty, there is little surplus to deal with shocks, and domestic savings are very low. The development of productive capacities and diversification thus depends heavily on external finance. ODA is particularly important because LDCs have very limited access to international capital markets and FDI is mainly resource-seeking and focused on a few countries. However, ODA is mainly directed towards social sector development rather than building economic infrastructure and productive capacities. The allocation of ODA to health, education and other social purposes is of course important, and in itself makes a partial contribution to building productive capacities, but the key to strengthening the resilience of LDC economies is to build the capabilities of domestic producers and to diversify and strengthen linkages.

Trends in poverty and progress towards the Millennium Development Goals

Trends in terms of poverty reduction and progress towards the Millennium Development Goals have not been as apparently positive as the economic growth trends. Indeed, improvements in human well-being on these dimensions have been quite slow.

TRENDS IN POVERTY

The incidence of extreme poverty (measured as the proportion of the people living on less than $1 a day) has decreased from a peak of 44 per cent in 1994 to 36 per cent in 2005. But the absolute number of extremely poor people continued to rise in the LDCs until 2003, when the upward trend leveled off. Poverty reduction has been much faster in Asian LDCs than in African LDCs, where the absolute number of extremely poor people continues to rise. In 2005, we estimate that 277 million people lived on less than $1 a day in all LDCs, including 206 million in African LDCs, 71 million in Asian LDCs and 1 million in island LDCs. Classifying LDCs according to their export specialization, poverty incidence is highest in commodity exporters, i.e. those for which petroleum, mineral and agricultural products account for the majority of their exports.

Although the incidence of extreme poverty is declining, the proportion of the population living on more than $1 a day but less than $2 a day has remained constant, at approximately 40 per cent of the population. The population living on less than $2 a day has been declining only very slowly. In 2005, 581 million people lived under these conditions in the LDCs. This corresponds to three quarters of the population, which shows that poverty continues to be pervasive in these countries.

GROWTH AND POVERTY IN THE LDCs

The relationship between economic growth and human well-being is a controversial subject with many different viewpoints. This Report finds that the recent period of rapid economic growth in the LDCs has been associated with a slow rate of poverty reduction and progress towards the Millennium Development Goals because of the type of economic growth that is occurring and the development model in place in the LDCs.

Since 2000, economic growth has accelerated sharply in the LDCs, but this has been accompanied by only a marginal increase in the pace of poverty reduction, contrary to expectations. Thus, the relationship between economic growth and poverty reduction has weakened in the LDCs since then. This is explained by five main reasons:

(a) **Private consumption has been growing at a lower rate than total GDP.** Private consumption provides the link between macroeconomic growth and well-being at the household level. Standards of living can only improve if private consumption is rising. Conventionally, private consumption growing by less than GDP frees more resources to finance investment and the provision of public services. However, in a context of widespread poverty, there may be a conflict between the objectives of domestic resource mobilization and poverty reduction, which can only be lessened through foreign savings;

(b) **The population of the LDCs has been growing faster than in any other large groups of countries.** Reducing poverty under these circumstances requires that the economy create productive jobs and livelihoods at a very fast pace in order to absorb the rapidly growing working-age population. Economic growth in most LDCs, however, has not led to a hefty expansion of employment, and the jobs that are being created are mostly low-productivity and low-paying jobs. This reduces their contribution to poverty reduction;

(c) **Economic growth in LDCs has mostly been led by the expansion of exports.** This type of growth dynamic is often concentrated within an externally oriented enclave, such as capital-intensive natural resource extraction sites or export-processing zones, with few linkages with the rest of the economy. Such a pattern of growth generally benefits limited segments of the population (those somehow linked to export activities), while leaving the majority excluded. This is particularly the case for those earning their livelihoods from agriculture. They are almost 70 per cent of the population and their earnings depend on agricultural productivity. This has traditionally been low in most LDCs and — more worryingly — it has been growing only very slowly since the early 1990s. This situation tends to perpetuate pervasive poverty in the LDCs;

(d) **A more recent development has compounded the difficulties in combating poverty in these countries, namely deagrarianization.** This refers to a process in which more and more people from rural areas seek work outside agriculture. It could be positive if people were pushed out of agriculture by rising productivity and pulled into other sectors by the new employment opportunities being created outside agriculture. There are signs of such a structural transformation in a few Asian LDCs, which have combined rising food productivity based on a "Green Revolution" with steady industrialization founded on expansion of manufacturing exports. However, for most LDCs, deagrarianization is a negative process in which people are pushed out because they cannot make a living in agriculture. Even worse, they cannot find remunerative work elsewhere. As a result, there are now two faces of poverty in LDCs: poverty associated with long-standing agricultural neglect; and urban poverty, most dramatically evident in growing numbers of unemployed youth; and

(e) **Income inequality is hindering poverty reduction in many LDCs.** Worsening income distribution — i.e. increasing inequality — can slow the shrinking of poverty, even in countries experiencing strong economic growth. This has been the case in recent years in a majority of LDCs for which data are available.

PROGRESS TOWARDS THE MILLENNIUM DEVELOPMENT GOALS

Very low material living standards are associated with very low levels of well-being in terms of a broad range of social indicators. As with the analysis of poverty trends, lack of data availability seriously hampers analysis of progress towards the achievement of the Millennium Development Goals that deal with human development. However, for the few indicators for which it is possible to get information for a wide range of countries, a clear pattern is emerging. This pattern has four basic features:

(a) Some LDCs are making significant progress towards achieving some specific Millennium Development Goals, but there are very few LDCs that are making progress on a broad front encompassing more than three targets;

(b) More progress is being made on targets which depend primarily on the level of public service provision, and Governments and donors are committed to increasing public expenditure and implementing well-targeted programmes. In this regard, progress towards universal primary school enrolment shows what can be done in quantitative terms;

(c) There is a distinct hierarchy of achievement which reflects two factors: the priorities of Governments and donors who are funding the scale-up, and the magnitude and time-scale of investments required to meet the targets. The conjunction of these two factors largely explains why achievements in increasing primary education enrolment outstrip progress in improving access to water, which in turn outstrips achievements in improving sanitation; and

(d) Progress towards targets that depend more on household incomes rather than mainly on public service provision has been slowest. In this regard, progress has been slow in reducing the incidence of extreme poverty and hunger. It has also proved difficult to maintain progress in reducing child mortality, where trends reflect the effects of both private incomes and public services.

The overall implication of these trends is that broad-based success in achieving progress towards the Millennium Development Goals is as yet elusive in the LDCs. It is likely to remain so unless the achievement of the Millennium Development Goals is placed in an economic development framework and efforts focus on generating productive jobs and livelihoods, rather than just increasing the provision of public services directly linked to the Millennium Development Goals. An outcome in which the education targets were achieved but school leavers were left without the employment opportunities to exercise their skills and meet the new expectations would be tragic and dangerous.

The impact of the global food crisis on LDCs

Rapidly rising international food prices in 2007 and early 2008 will have negative effects on poverty trends in LDCs and slow progress towards the achievement of the Millennium Development Goals. The negative effects will arise for the following reasons:

(a) Rising food prices are restricting the ability of households to meet essential subsistence needs, given that their budget constraints were very tight even before the soaring prices;

(b) The large increases in food prices threaten economic growth through rising import bills in countries that already face rising trade and current account deficits;

(c) Rising food prices will have second-round effects on economic growth but farmers may not be able to adequately take advantage of rising prices because of their limited access to land, weak productive capabilities and a production and marketing cost squeeze associated with rising input and transport costs; and

(d) Dynamic growth forces can be stalled, given that these prices will compress profits in formal businesses — as subsistence wages adjust to higher food prices — and the available resources of the self-employed, whose accumulation activity, to the extent that it occurs, is directly related to their food consumption costs.

The overall effects are likely to be particularly severe in the LDCs, because most of them are net food importers and they already have large trade deficits. Levels of poverty and food insecurity in LDCs are already high, and many people spend as much as 50–80 per cent of their household income on food. Moreover, for 20 LDCs, the price rises will exacerbate already-existing food emergencies, which require external assistance, owing to such factors as natural disasters, concentrations of internally displaced persons and localized crop failures. Food price riots had already occurred in eight LDCs by June 2008.

THE NEED FOR A PARADIGM SHIFT IN DEVELOPMENT POLICY

The trends in economic growth, poverty, human development and food security that are taking place in LDCs and that are analysed in the preceding section are related to policy choices and to the development model which has been pursued in most LDCs. The current pattern of economic growth is neither robust nor inclusive enough. A basic message of this Report, therefore, is that it is time for a paradigm shift in development policy.

For some observers, the policy shift now required is a return to agricultural development. Indeed, as shown in *The Least Developed Countries Report 2007*, there has been a serious neglect of agricultural research and development, which is so important for increasing agricultural production and improving the living standards of small-scale producers. However, whilst improving agricultural productivity is vital, it is also important to improve productive employment activities outside agriculture, particularly in view of the process of deagrarianization which is occurring. What is therefore required is not a shift in sectoral focus, but rather a deeper change in approach which puts production, productive capacities and productive employment opportunities at the heart of policies to promote development and poverty reduction.

The nature of this paradigm shift is discussed in some detail in *The Least Developed Countries Report 2006,* and its policy implications in relation to knowledge, technological learning and innovation are set out in *The Least Developed Countries Report 2007*. In brief, what we have been advocating has three elements:

• Policy should focus on production, productivity and productive capacities rather than global integration and international trade *per se*. International trade is essential for productive development and productive development is essential for international trade. But policy should start at the development end, rather than the trade end, of the relationship between trade and development;

• Policy should recognize the primary importance of productive employment as the basis for substantial poverty reduction. This does not mean that social sector spending and human development goals are unimportant. Improved health and education standards are essential in the LDCs. However, there is a need for a better balance between the roles of private incomes (based on employment) and public services (through which health and education are primarily provided) in poverty reduction; and

• There is a need for a better balance between States and markets in promoting development and reducing poverty. The persistence of pervasive poverty and the food price bubble indicates massive market failure. Whilst Governments are not omnipotent, there is need for creative solutions based on public action which mobilizes key stakeholders, including in particular the private sector, to resolve development problems and create development opportunities.

Making such a change towards a more sustainable and inclusive development model depends on the decisions and political will of LDC Governments. However, they are also engaged in a development partnership for poverty reduction with donors. The terms of this development partnership affect both the nature of the current strategic approach and policies, and also the potential to change them.

Changes in the terms of development partnership

IMPORTANCE OF COUNTRY OWNERSHIP

Since 2000, development cooperation has been based on a partnership approach. The roots of the approach can be traced to the OECD report, *Shaping the Twenty-first Century: The Contribution of Development Co-operation* (1996). That report not only argued that aid should be focused on achieving a limited set of international poverty reduction and human development targets (a list that later formed the basis for the Millennium Development Goals), but also stated that the key to making a difference in achieving those targets was the establishment of development partnerships between donor and recipient Governments. The basic principle, according to the OECD report, was that "locally-owned country development strategies should emerge from an open and collaborative dialogue by local authorities with civil society and with external partners, about shared objectives and their respective contributions to the common enterprise. Each donor's contributions should then operate within the framework of that locally-owned strategy in ways that respect and encourage strong local commitment, participation, capacity development and ownership".

The idea of country ownership of national development strategies is at the heart of the partnership approach to development cooperation. Its importance was affirmed by the then President of the World Bank, James Wolfensohn, who made "ownership" one of the four key principles of the Comprehensive Development Framework, and in 1999 said that: "Countries must be in the driver's seat and set the course. They must determine the goals, and the phasing, the timing and sequencing of programs". Country ownership is also one of the key operational elements in the preparation of poverty reduction strategy papers (PRSPs). It was also part of the Monterrey Consensus on Financing for Development agreed in 2002, which states that "effective partnerships among donors and recipients are based on the recognition of national leadership and ownership of development plans". It was reaffirmed at the G8 summit at Gleneagles in 2005, where, as well as bold commitments to cancel debt and scale up aid, it was agreed that: "It is up to developing countries themselves and their governments to take the lead on development. They need to decide, plan and sequence their economic policies to fit with their own development strategies, for which they should be accountable to all their people" (Gleneagles Communiqué, "Africa", para. 31). Moreover, enhanced country ownership is one of the main components of the 2005 Paris Declaration on Aid Effectiveness, the implementation of which will be assessed in Accra, Ghana, in September 2008.

Within the LDCs, PRSPs are the main operational instrument of the partnership approach to development and the key locus where country ownership is being forged. This Report assesses progress towards country ownership in the formulation and implementation of recent PRSPs in LDCs using evidence from case studies to be found in the literature. It focuses in particular on progress towards the exercise of leadership in the design and implementation of their development strategies and in coordinating development actions. This is one of the key commitments of the Paris Declaration but it is not the aspect of ownership that is currently being monitored.

Defined in these terms, the notion of country ownership is very difficult to monitor. However, the case studies enable the identification of some ways in which the nature of the aid relationship is working to strengthen or weaken country ownership. They also enable the identification of some of the adverse consequences of weak country ownership.

PROGRESS TOWARDS COUNTRY OWNERSHIP

The Report finds that in the context of the PRSP approach, significant steps have been taken to enhance country ownership. Donors and international financial institutions are making major efforts to stand back and give country authorities greater space for formulating and implementing their development strategies and policies. However, it also finds that various processes continue to weaken country ownership in LDCs and this is having adverse consequences for development effectiveness and aid effectiveness. These processes cannot be attributed to the practices of donors *per se* or recipients *per se*, but rather depend on the nature of aid relationships. Ensuring that high levels of aid dependence do not result in donor domination is a complex challenge for both aid donors and aid recipients.

The processes weakening country ownership come into play at the level of policy formulation or at the level of policy implementation. The latter may arise because donors deliver part of their aid in ways which are off-plan, off-budget or simply unknown, or because, even when aid is integrated with government priorities, processes and systems, the way in which PRSPs are implemented is strongly influenced by policy conditionality, monitoring benchmarks or donor financing choices.

The Report shows that although progress is being made in the context of the drive to improve aid effectiveness, there is a continuing problem of poor alignment and harmonization of aid with Government plans, budgets and processes. Some LDCs are caught in what the OECD has called a "low ownership trap", where there is low capacity in Government and donors fear aid will be mismanaged and so set up parallel systems, which in turn undermine government capacity. There are also continuing problems of predictability that disrupt planning and budgeting, and Governments have incomplete information on how much aid money is entering the country and what it is used for. These widely recognized problematic features of aid delivery continue to undermine ownership in LDCs. Progress in this regard will be a key consideration at the meeting to assess the status of implementation of the Paris Declaration in Accra, Ghana, in September 2008.

The ability of countries to exercise effective leadership in the process of policy formulation is undermined by weak technical capacities. As a result, countries sometimes have to rely heavily on donor support in the design of national strategies. Freedom of action in policy design can also be constrained by the need to mobilize aid inflows and the sense, justifiable or not, that signs of lack of commitment to the types of policies that donors and international financial institutions believe are the best ones can work against aid mobilization. Second-generation PRSPs are now very broad documents that include an amalgam of elements, including: (a) a core policy agenda which is strongly owned by the national Government; (b) a policy agenda that is directly or indirectly negotiated with donors and around which there is broad consensus and agreement; and (c) a policy agenda that is more closely aligned with donor preferences and that enjoys very little or very narrow country ownership. There is thus an ownership frontier *within* the PRSPs. It is possible, therefore, for aid to be aligned and harmonized with the document but for this to be done in a way that is more focused on donor priorities within the national plan.

A consequence of this is that the processes of policy implementation are now a very important mechanism through which country ownership can be strengthened or weakened. The Report shows that there have been major shifts in the practice of policy conditionality. There is an increasing tendency for policy conditionalities to be drawn from Government documents and there has also been a shift towards administrative benchmarks rather than legally binding conditionality. However, macroeconomic stabilization, privatization and liberalization are still important types of conditionality. Policy conditionality has not been conducive to policy pluralism.

Given the broad policy agenda contained in PRSPs, donor financing choices are also an important determinant of how PRSPs work out in practice. This is the case even when donors give budget support, as this support usually involves performance assessment frameworks that are negotiated to set priorities. Donors are particularly oriented towards financing social sectors and social infrastructure.

CONSEQUENCES OF THE WEAKENING OF COUNTRY OWNERSHIP

The second-generation poverty reduction strategies in LDCs are quite different from the early PRSPs. They seek to place poverty reduction and the achievement of the Millennium Development Goals within a broad economic development framework. In many LDCs these strategies have the potential to become effective development strategies. However, realizing this potential depends on meeting a broad range of development governance challenges, rather than merely focusing on poverty-oriented public expenditure and budgeting, which have been the key concerns in the first-generation poverty reduction strategies up to now. The weakening of country ownership is having adverse consequences for addressing these challenges and also development effectiveness.

There are three major adverse outcomes that are related to weak country ownership.

Firstly, the macroeconomic framework of poverty reduction strategies is weakly integrated with sectoral policies and trade policies. This lack of integration is problematic because the parameters of macroeconomic responses, such as the impact of public spending, depend on sector-level issues (costs and consequences). It also means that there has been a failure to properly integrate trade into poverty reduction strategies as the macroeconomic forecasts of exports and imports are divorced from the actual trade policies within the strategies.

Secondly, there is a downscaling of ambition in relation to increased aid inflows. It is clear that most LDC Governments want increased aid inflows, but there is a fundamental mismatch between this desire and the way in which PRSPs are written. This arises because the macroeconomic framework is usually based on modest projections of future aid inflows. In fact, with these forecasts the PRSPs are downscaled to be realistic in terms of past aid inflows rather than upscaled to explore how increased aid inflows can be effectively used to promote economic growth, poverty reduction and the achievement of the Millennium Development Goals. This results in minimalist poverty reduction strategies rather than poverty reduction strategies that explore the effects of the scaling-up of aid.

Thirdly, there is a low level of financing of productive sectors. One of the hallmarks of the second-generation PRSPs is that they are no longer narrowly focused on increased social expenditure but also include the development of productive sectors. However, as noted above, there has been no change in the relative share of aid disbursements going to productive sectors over the last few years. This mismatch between the change in the policy content of PRSPs and the lack of change in the composition of aid is a primary indicator of weak country ownership in the implementation of poverty reduction strategies. The low financing of productive sector development means that although PRSPs aspire to place poverty reduction and the achievement of the MDGs within a broad economic development framework, in practice they do not succeed. Moreover, the combination of policy conditionality geared to stabilization, liberalization and privatization, with donor financing oriented towards social sectors, ends up giving a specific strategic thrust to PRSPs. The evidence discussed earlier in this overview shows that this development model is unlikely to result in either sustained or inclusive development.

WHAT CAN BE DONE?

Increasing country ownership should be a major priority for improving development effectiveness in LDCs. This involves action on a range of fronts. One of the principal recommendations of the Report is that a first step towards improving country ownership could be to adopt aid management policies within LDCs. The Paris Declaration encourages countries to do this. Moreover, some LDCs, such as Mozambique, Rwanda, Uganda and the United Republic of Tanzania, are pioneers in this innovative practice.

Initial experience indicates that country-level aid management policies can provide a powerful bottom–up approach to better aid management. The improvements observed include: better data on aid inflows; increased levels of trust; increasing assertiveness on the part of the Government in expressing its preferences; greater rationalization and harmonization of processes and procedures among donors; increased predictability of aid, with donors making multi-year aid commitments; reduced transaction costs as donors support a joint assistance strategy; and increased mutual accountability, as performance indicators relate not only to government actions but also to donor actions in relation to aid disbursements. The introduction of jointly agreed monitoring indicators at the country level in relation to donor practices seems to be a particularly powerful way to reduce transaction costs and promote alignment and harmonization. However, it is important that country-level efforts to improve aid management do not crowd out thinking and action on the design of effective development strategies.

The purpose of a country-level aid management policy is to ensure that development assistance is of such a type, and is so deployed, as to maximize its contribution to the priorities set out in its development strategy. Together, a country-level aid management policy and country-owned development strategy can work as important instruments through which the terms of development partnership can be made more effective. The aid management policy can help to build trust and develop more balanced partnership, but in itself it will not be sufficient.

In the end, enhanced country ownership will depend on systemic measures as well as country-level action. Given the new focus of the second-generation PRSPs, it is necessary to rebuild State capacities for promoting growth and development. Renewed attention needs to be given to the nature of policy conditionality and the problem of aid predictability and volatility. It is also necessary to assess whether there are systemic biases against using aid in a catalytic way to develop productive sectors. Action to build local policy analysis capacity in LDCs and to generate alternative perspectives, especially from developing countries and LDCs, in the production of knowledge about development will also be important.

Dr. Supachai Panitchpakdi
Secretary-General of UNCTAD

How Sustainable is LDCs' Growth?

A. Introduction

In 2005 and 2006, the least developed countries (LDCs) as a group achieved their highest rates of gross domestic product (GDP) growth in 30 years. This chapter examines the factors behind this growth performance and assesses its sustainability.

The chapter shows that the LDCs are highly integrated into the global economy through international flows of goods, services, capital and people (i.e. migrant workers and their remittances). Strong economic growth has been driven by record levels of exports, particularly associated with high commodity prices for minerals and oils, and record levels of capital inflows, especially aid. However, despite their high GDP growth, LDCs are still characterized by low levels of domestic resource mobilization and investment, very weak development of manufacturing industries, high levels of commodity dependence, weak export upgrading, worsening trade balances, and rising food and energy import bills. These conditions imply that LDCs are very vulnerable to growth slow-downs, or even growth collapses, arising from external sources. Despite their high level of integration, the LDCs remain marginalized in terms of their share of global output and global trade.

The easing of the debt burden in a number of LDCs through the Multilateral Debt Relief Initiative (MDRI) in 2006 opened a window of opportunity for 16 LDCs that were eligible. However, aid disbursements are still below donor commitments. Moreover, aid is focused on social sectors and social infrastructure, notably education, health and good governance, rather than on increasing investment in economic infrastructure and the development of productive sectors. Increased foreign direct investment (FDI) inflows are now associated with rapidly increasing profit remittances. With the global economy slowing and the downside risks of the global outlook worsening, LDCs will face major challenges in the period ahead. This will require renewed efforts by both the LDCs and their development partners to develop their productive base and address structural weaknesses. Otherwise, the marginalization of the LDCs in the global economy is likely to deepen.

This chapter is organized into five substantive sections, each of which identifies: (a) the overall pattern for the LDCs as a group; (b) regional differences between African, Asian and island LDCs; and (c) variations amongst individual LDCs. Section B describes trends in economic growth and sectoral growth rates, whilst section C focuses on trends in domestic savings and investment. Section D highlights trends in international trade, including commodity prices, the extent of export upgrading and the level of participation of the LDCs in world trade. Section E focuses on trends in external finance — including trends in official development assistance (ODA) and FDI inflows — whilst section F discusses trends in external debt, including the impact of the MDRI. The conclusion summarizes the major findings and policy implications.

In 2005 and 2006, the least developed countries as a group achieved their highest rates of GDP growth in 30 years.

Strong economic growth has been driven by record levels of exports and of capital inflows.

LDCs remain very vulnerable to growth slow-downs, or even growth collapses, arising from external sources.

B. Trends in economic growth

1. OVERALL GDP AND GDP PER CAPITA GROWTH RATES

The growth rate of the LDCs surpassed the goal of the Brussels Programme of Action for LDCs — namely a GDP growth rate of 7 per cent.

In 2005, the real GDP of the LDCs as a group grew by 7.9 per cent, which was the strongest growth performance since 1972. There was a slight slowdown of the growth rate in 2006 to 7.5 per cent.[1] But this was still the second highest growth rate in more than three decades. The average annual growth rate in 2005–2006 was almost 2 percentage points higher than the 5.9 per cent per annum achieved during 2000–2004, and almost double the average annual rate of 4 per cent achieved during the 1990s (table 1). The growth rate of the LDCs as a group achieved in 2005 and 2006 surpassed the goal of the Brussels Programme of Action for LDCs — namely a GDP growth rate of 7 per cent (United Nations, 2001).[2] But estimates suggest that the growth rate of the LDCs slowed down further to 6.7 per cent in 2007. This was mainly due to slower growth projected for oil-importing LDCs.

Despite the record GDP growth performance, the LDCs as a group continue to diverge from the other developing countries in terms of income per capita.

The high growth rates of the LDCs in 2005 and 2006 coincided with robust growth in the global economy. Other developing countries also experienced very high growth rates during these years. It is notable that the LDC growth rate exceeded the average for other developing countries in both 2005 and 2006, and that this situation also prevailed during 2000–2004. However, population growth rates are high in the LDCs — 2.5 per cent per annum — almost double the average rate in other developing countries. Thus, even though the GDP growth rate in LDCs as a group exceeded the average in other developing countries, the GDP per capita growth rate of the former has continued to lag behind that of the latter in all years except 2005. This implies that, despite the record GDP growth performance, the LDCs as a group continue to diverge from the other developing countries in terms of income per capita.

Table 1. Real GDP and real GDP per capita growth rates of LDCs, by country groups, other developing countries and OECD high-income countries, 1990–2007 *(Annual weighted averages, per cent)*										
	Real GDP					**Real GDP per capita**				
	1990–2000	2000–2004	2005	2006	2007 proj.[a]	1990–2000	2000–2004	2005	2006	2007 proj.[a]
LDCs	**4.0**	**5.9**	**7.9**	**7.5**	**6.7**	**1.3**	**3.4**	**5.3**	**5.0**	**4.3**
African LDCs (and Haiti)	3.4	5.6	7.9	8.2	8.9	0.6	2.7	5.0	5.3	6.2
African LDCs less African oil exporters	2.5	4.4	6.1	6.5	6.2	-0.2	1.6	3.3	3.7	3.4
Asian LDCs	5.1	6.5	7.9	6.4	6.0	2.6	4.4	5.8	4.3	4.1
of which: Bangladesh	4.9	5.4	6.7	6.5	6.2	2.8	3.4	4.8	4.7	4.5
Island LDCs	4.3	3.6	2.4	7.5	6.9	2.3	0.5	-0.6	4.6	4.3
Other developing countries	5.0	4.9	6.5	6.9	6.4	3.4	3.5	5.2	5.6	5.2
OECD high-income countries	2.6	1.8	2.4	3.0	2.3	1.8	1.2	1.8	2.5	1.8
Memo items:										
Oil-exporting LDCs	5.1	7.4	10.5	10.6	12.4	2.1	4.6	7.6	7.8	9.7
Oil-importing LDCs	3.7	5.4	7.0	6.5	6.1	1.1	2.9	4.5	4.0	3.7

Source: UNCTAD secretariat calculations based on data from United Nations/DESA Statistics Division; United Nations Population Unit; and UNCTAD estimates.

Note: Data are available for all 50 LDCs, including Cape Verde. Data for Timor-Leste have been estimated backward and is available from 1990.

a Growth rates for the year 2007 are taken from the Link Project Global Economic Outlook, Regional Data, online, January 2008; United Nations ESCAP data, direct communication; and OECD, *African Economic Outlook 2007.*

2. Differences in economic performance amongst LDCs

African LDCs did particularly well in both 2005 and 2006, after Asian LDCs had outperformed African LDCs during the period 2000–2004. The real GDP growth rates in African and Asian LDCs were the same in 2005 (7.9 per cent), while in 2006 the real GDP growth rate in African LDCs exceeded that in Asian LDCs by 1.7 percentage points. African oil exporters pulled up the regional average. But an important feature of economic trends in 2005 and 2006 was the continued improvement in the growth performance of oil-importing African LDCs. Their average annual real GDP growth rate was only 2.5 per cent in the 1990s, but was 4.4 per cent in 2000–2004, and is estimated to have exceeded 6 per cent in 2005, 2006 and 2007. The GDP growth rates of the island LDCs appear to be highly volatile, as low as 2.4 per cent in 2005 and as high as 7.5 per cent in 2006. The big increase is mainly due to the exceptional growth performance of the Maldives in 2006.

All the Asian LDCs were in the very high growth group with the exception of Nepal and Yemen.

A closer look at growth performance on a country-by-country basis shows that there are large variations amongst the LDCs. In 2006, the real GDP grew by 6 per cent or more in 19 LDCs; between 3 and 6 per cent in 20 LDCs; by less than 3 per cent in 9 LDCs; and it declined in two LDCs (table 2). It is notable that all the Asian LDCs were in the very high growth group (i.e. the first group), with the exception of Nepal — which experienced a major armed conflict over the period 2002–2005 and continuing political instability in 2006 — and Yemen. Apart from Afghanistan, which received large aid inflows, the very high-growth Asian countries either specialized in manufactures exports or such exports constituted a significant component in a mixed export basket. Twelve of the 34 African LDCs were in the very high growth group, and eight of them were oil or mineral exporters, indicating the importance of buoyant oil or mineral prices. None of the francophone African LDCs was in the very high growth group, a trend perhaps related to the problems associated with their currencies being pegged to the appreciating euro. Amongst the island LDCs, only the Maldives was in the very high growth group. Its good performance reflects the bounce-back after the tsunami, helped by high levels of aid inflows.

Despite the record overall GDP growth performance, GDP per capita grew by less than 1 per cent or declined in 16 LDCs (almost one third of the sample).

If these growth rates can be sustained in the future, a few LDCs can be expected to reach the threshold to graduate from LDC status (box 1). However, even supposing that the high growth rates of 2004–2006 would continue, only 15 LDCs would have reached the graduation threshold by 2020, including eight which have already reached it.

To put the overall performance in a comparative perspective, only 11 LDCs were growing at such a pace that their GDP per capita was converging with the average of other developing countries in 2006. Despite the record overall GDP growth performance, GDP per capita stagnated or declined in nine LDCs, and grew by less than 1 per cent or declined in 16 LDCs (almost one third of the sample) (table 2).

During the period 2000–2006, the highest growth rate was evident in mining industries, the exploitation of crude oil, and construction.

3. Sectoral growth rates

During the period 2000–2006, the highest growth rate in the LDCs as a group was evident in non-manufacturing industries — including, in particular, mining industries, the exploitation of crude oil, and construction activities (chart 1). But there were significant differences amongst the sectoral growth rates in African, Asian and island LDCs. In African LDCs, the leading sector was non-manufacturing industrial activities, with an average annual growth rate of 10.3 per cent during the present decade. The leading sector in terms of growth rate in Asian LDCs was manufacturing industries, which is estimated to have grown by 8 per cent per annum from 2000 to 2006. In island LDCs, services emerged as the leading sector, growing at 10.2 per cent per annum over the same period. On average, agricultural growth rates lagged behind the growth rates in other sectors in the major groups of LDCs during the period 2000–2006 (chart 1).

For LDCs as a group, the structure of production is changing, but only very slowly.

The sectoral pattern of growth implies that, for LDCs as a group, the structure of production is changing, but only very slowly. Agriculture contributed 33 per cent of total GDP in 2005–2006, compared with 36 per cent 10 years earlier (table 3). The share of manufacturing in total value added only increased marginally — from 10 per cent to 11 per cent of total GDP over this period — whilst the share of services declined marginally, from 42 to 40 per cent. Non-manufacturing industries (especially oil extraction and mining) are of increasing importance, particularly within African LDCs, where they are estimated to account for 19 per cent of total GDP.[3]

The share of agriculture in GDP actually increased from 1995–1996 to 2005–2006 in 18 LDCs.

Within this overall pattern of sluggish structural change, there are significant differences amongst LDCs, and the share of agriculture in GDP actually increased from 1995–1996 to 2005–2006 in 18 LDCs. Only four of these LDCs were in the group of the 19 LDCs which achieved very high growth in 2006. At the other end of the spectrum, there were 18 LDCs where the share of agriculture in GDP declined by more than 5 percentage points, in some cases much more, over the 10-year period. In most cases, the decline in the economic importance of agriculture has been accompanied by a sharp increase in the relative importance of services (as in the cases of Afghanistan, Ethiopia, Liberia, Burundi, Mauritania, Samoa and Tuvalu) or non-manufacturing industries (as in the cases of Equatorial Guinea,

---

Box 1. Growth and graduation from LDC status

The recent high rates of the LDCs' GDP growth raise the issue of how this affects their graduation prospects. This box makes a simulation of the likely future dates of graduation of LDCs if current growth rates were sustained in the future.

It must be stressed that decisions about graduation from the LDC category — which the United Nations Economic and Social Council reviews every three years based on recommendations provided by the Committee for Development Policy — are based on three criteria: (a) low income; (b) human assets; and (c) economic vulnerability. A country needs to meet at least two of the three graduation thresholds to qualify for graduation. The focus on the first criterion is thus a partial analysis.

It should also be noted that the thresholds for graduation are reassessed from time to time. The present simulation is based on a low-income graduation threshold equal to $1,040 per capita GNI. This corresponds to the average for the low-income countries during the period 2004–2006 plus the customary extra 20 per cent.

Under the assumption that the annual GNI per capita (assumed to grow at the same rate of GDP per capita) growth rates of the individual LDCs during the period 2004–2006 will continue in the future, it is possible to estimate the number of years that it will take them to reach the estimated income graduation threshold.

Box table 1 lists the average GNI per capita of the LDCs, and the estimates of the number of years needed by each LDC to reach the graduation threshold if the current average annual growth rates are maintained.

From the table, it is apparent that eight LDCs already meet the income threshold for graduation, while another three are close. Amongst the countries that have reached the graduation threshold, there are two oil-exporting LDCs and five island LDCs. Cape Verde has already graduated from the group, while the Maldives and Samoa are scheduled to graduate in 2011.

The remaining 30 LDCs have been divided into two sub-groups: Countries that would reach the income graduation threshold in the medium term and those that would reach it in the long term. Twenty-one of the 28 oil-importing African LDCs are included in these last two sub-groups. The group of countries that would reach the income threshold in the long term includes thirteen countries that would reach the income graduation level in less than 50 years and another twelve that have been estimated as taking more than 50 years. Within the first sub-group, there are large differences among countries. On the one hand, Senegal, Solomon Islands and Zambia would reach the graduation threshold in 20 years, Ethiopia in 25 years, and the United Republic of Tanzania in 30 years; on the other hand, Uganda and Mali would reach the income graduation level in 45 years. Since the estimation of the time period required to reach the income graduation threshold is based on the countries' performance during the period 2004–2006, a worsening of the economic performance will increase the estimated number of years necessary to meet the income threshold level.

Box 1 (contd.)

Box table 1. Estimation of the number of years needed to meet the graduation threshold for LDCs, by country, 2004-2006

	GNI per capita[a]	Years[b]
Countries that have reached the income threshold		
Equatorial Guinea	5 620	Achieved
Vanuatu	1 580	Achieved
Kiribati	1 157	Achieved
Cape Verde	1 913	Achieved
Samoa	2 017	Achieved
Maldives	2 480	Achieved
Bhutan	1 253	Achieved
Angola	1 443	Achieved
Countries that are close to reaching to income threshold[c]		
Djibouti	1 013	1
Sudan	660	6
Mauritania	610	8
Countries that should reach the income threshold in the medium term[c]		
Lesotho	893	10
Cambodia	430	11
Sao Tome and Principe	780	11
Lao People's Democratic Republic	457	15
Bangladesh	463	17
Countries that should reach the income threshold in the long term[c]		
Zambia	510	20
Senegal	683	20
Solomon Islands	630	20
Mozambique	307	24
Ethiopia	157	25
Sierra Leone	223	29
United Republic of Tanzania	337	30
Burkina Faso	413	34
Yemen	660	38
Chad	417	40
Guinea	430	40
Uganda	277	45
Mali	383	45
Gambia	290	> 50
Democratic Republic of the Congo	120	> 50
Rwanda	230	> 50
Madagascar	287	> 50
Malawi	163	> 50
Liberia	123	> 50
Niger	237	> 50
Central African Republic	340	> 50
Guinea-Bissau	177	> 50
Haiti	453	> 50
Nepal	270	> 50
Benin	500	> 50

Source: UNCTAD secretariat calculations based on World Bank, *World Development Indicators*, online data, March 2008.

Note: No data for Afghanistan, Myanmar, Somalia and Tuvalu.
Burundi, Comoros, Eritrea, Timor-Leste and Togo have been excluded from the computation as their real average annual growth rates are negative.
Countries have been ranked according to the number of years necessary to reach the income threshold of $1,040. See box text for an explanation of how the threshold was calculated.
a   Calculated with the World Bank Atlas method.
b   The years have been estimated using the formula $\ln(1,040) - \ln(\text{GNI pc}_0)/(\text{GDP pc growth rate})$. It is assumed that real GNI pc and real GDP pc grow at the same rate.
c   Assuming that the LDCs will grow at the same average annual growth rate as in 2004-2006 and that everything else stays constant.

Table 2. Real GDP and real GDP per capita growth rates of LDCs, by country, 2000–2007
(Annual averages, per cent)

	Export specialization	Real GDP				Real GDP per capita			
		2000–2004	2005	2006	2007 proj.	2000–2004	2005	2006	2007 proj.
Countries with real GDP growth > 6% in 2006									
Maldives	S	7.5	-4.0	21.7	6.6	5.8	-5.6	19.7	4.8
Angola	O	8.1	20.6	14.3	21.0	5.0	17.2	11.1	18.2
Mauritania	MN	3.6	5.4	14.1	6.3	0.6	2.5	11.1	3.7
Sudan	O	6.5	7.9	12.1	11.0	4.4	5.7	9.7	8.7
Afghanistan	A	14.8	14.5	11.1	13.0	10.6	10.0	6.8	8.9
Ethiopia	S	3.3	10.3	10.6	9.5	0.7	7.5	7.9	6.9
Sierra Leone	MN	14.2	7.5	9.7	6.5	9.3	3.7	6.8	4.4
Mozambique	MN	8.9	6.2	8.5	7.5	6.3	3.8	6.3	5.5
Malawi	A	2.9	1.9	8.5	4.8	0.3	-0.7	5.8	2.2
Bhutan	MF	8.0	6.5	8.5	17.1	5.1	4.2	6.5	15.6
Lao People's Democratic Republic	MX	6.0	7.3	7.3	7.4	4.3	5.6	5.5	5.7
Cambodia	MF	7.7	13.4	7.2	8.5	5.8	11.5	5.4	6.8
Liberia	A	-8.7	5.3	7.0	9.5	-10.6	2.4	2.9	4.7
Myanmar	MX	12.7	13.2	7.0	4.2	11.7	12.3	6.1	3.3
Bangladesh	MF	5.4	6.7	6.5	6.2	3.4	4.8	4.7	4.5
Democratic Republic of the Congo	MN	3.6	6.5	6.5	6.5	0.7	3.2	3.2	3.2
Uganda	A	5.7	6.5	6.2	6.0	2.4	3.1	2.8	2.7
Burundi	MN	2.3	0.9	6.1	3.2	-0.9	-2.9	2.0	-0.9
Zambia	MN	4.5	5.1	6.0	5.5	2.5	3.2	4.1	3.6
Countries with real GDP growth between 3% and 6% in 2006									
United Republic of Tanzania		6.9	6.9	5.9	7.0	4.2	4.3	3.3	4.5
Burkina Faso	A	6.3	5.9	5.9	6.0	2.9	2.6	2.7	3.0
Gambia	S	3.2	5.0	5.6	7.0	0.0	2.0	2.7	4.3
Sao Tome and Principe	S	4.0	3.0	5.5	5.5	2.2	1.3	3.8	3.9
Cape Verde	S	5.1	5.8	5.5	7.0	2.6	3.3	3.1	4.7
Guinea	MN	3.0	3.3	5.0	5.0	1.1	1.4	3.0	2.9
Solomon Islands	A	0.9	5.0	5.0	5.4	-1.7	2.4	2.5	3.0
Madagascar	MX	0.9	4.6	4.7	6.4	-1.9	1.7	1.9	3.7
Guinea-Bissau	A	-1.5	3.5	4.6	5.2	-4.5	0.4	1.5	2.2
Mali	MN	6.3	6.1	4.6	5.4	3.2	3.0	1.5	2.3
Djibouti	S	2.8	3.2	4.2	5.0	0.8	1.4	2.4	3.2
Togo	MX	2.4	0.8	4.2	5.5	-0.5	-1.9	1.4	2.8
Senegal	MX	4.2	5.5	4.0	5.4	1.5	2.8	1.4	2.9
Samoa	S	3.4	5.1	4.0	3.0	2.6	4.4	3.1	2.1
Yemen	O	3.8	4.6	3.9	3.7	0.8	1.5	0.9	0.7
Benin	A	4.4	2.9	3.6	5.0	1.0	-0.4	0.4	1.9
Niger	MN	4.1	7.1	3.5	4.0	0.5	3.4	0.0	0.4
Vanuatu	S	-0.5	3.1	3.4	2.5	-3.0	0.5	0.9	0.1
Central African Republic	MN	-2.2	2.2	3.2	4.0	-3.8	0.5	1.4	2.2
Rwanda	S	5.1	6.0	3.0	4.8	2.5	3.9	0.5	2.0
Countries with real GDP growth < 3% in 2006									
Chad	O	15.5	8.6	2.9	2.5	11.3	5.0	-0.3	-0.5
Somalia	A	2.9	2.4	2.4	-3.5	-0.1	-0.6	-0.6	-6.5
Haiti	MF	-0.9	1.8	2.3	3.5	-2.5	0.2	0.7	1.9
Eritrea	S	3.5	4.8	2.0	2.0	-0.7	0.8	-1.6	-1.4
Nepal	MF	2.7	2.7	1.9	2.6	0.5	0.7	-0.1	0.6
Lesotho	MF	2.9	2.9	1.6	1.4	1.8	2.2	0.9	0.8
Comoros	S	2.2	2.8	1.2	1.0	-0.5	0.2	-1.3	-1.5
Tuvalu	A	6.2	2.0	1.0	2.5	5.7	1.6	0.6	2.1
Kiribati	A	2.9	3.6	0.8	1.0	1.0	1.8	-0.9	-0.6
Equatorial Guinea	O	28.3	9.3	-1.0	10.0	25.4	6.8	-3.3	7.6
Timor-Leste	O	-0.8	2.2	-1.6	32.1	-6.1	-2.9	-5.7	28.4

Source: UNCTAD secretariat estimates based on United Nations/DESA Statistics Division; United Nations/DESA *Link Global Economic Outlook*, online, January 2008; United Nations ESCAP data and estimates; and OECD, *African Economic Outlook* 2006/07.

Note: **A**=agricultural exporter, **MF**=manufactures exporter, **MN**=mineral exporter, **MX**=mixed exporters, **O**=oil exporter, **S**=services exporter. Countries are ranked in decreasing order according to the real GDP growth rate in 2006.

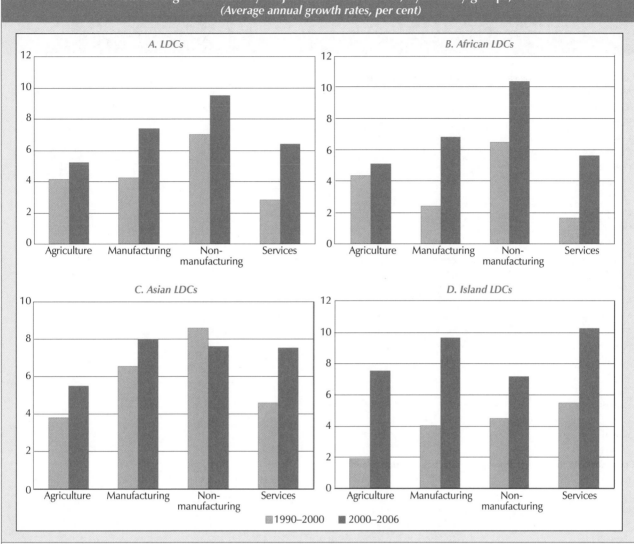

Chart 1. Real GDP growth rates by major economic sectors, by country groups, 1990–2006
(Average annual growth rates, per cent)

Source: UNCTAD secretariat calculations based on United Nations/DESA Statistics Division.

Note: Non-manufacturing includes mining, utilities and construction.

United Republic of Tanzania, Bhutan, Chad and Mali). The relative decline in the importance of agriculture is associated with a significant rise in the importance of manufacturing in only three LDCs — Cambodia, the Lao People's Democratic Republic and Mozambique. Both Burkina Faso and Uganda exhibited a more balanced pattern of structural change, with the relative share of manufacturing, non-manufacturing industries and services all increasing while the relative share of agriculture in GDP declines.

The share of manufacturing in GDP during 2005–2006 for the LDCs as a group (11 per cent) continues to lag far behind the average in other developing countries (24 per cent). Indeed, this gap is widening. Moreover, from 1995–1996 to 2005–2006, half of the LDCs experienced de-industrialization reflected in the declining importance of manufactures in GDP. These trends suggest that the recent growth surge in LDCs is not generally associated with a structural transition in which the share of manufactures in total output is growing (except for most Asian LDCs). It also indicates the failure to develop productive capacities in LDCs and the weak development of the productive base of their economies, irrespective of strong GDP growth.

The share of manufacturing in GDP for the LDCs as a group continues to lag far behind the average in other developing countries and this gap is widening.

Table 3. Share of value added in main economic sectors in LDCs, by country and country groups, 1995–2006
(Per cent of value added)

| | Agriculture | | Industry | | | | Services | |
| | | | Manufacturing | | Non-manufacturing[a] | | | |
	1995–1996	2005–2006	1995–1996	2005–2006	1995–1996	2005–2006	1995–1996	2005–2006
Countries with increasing share of manufacture in value added								
Afghanistan	50.4	24.1	4.1	8.9	0.6	2.3	45.0	64.7
Bangladesh	27.1	22.9	15.9	17.4	9.6	11.9	47.4	47.8
Burkina Faso	36.2	26.5	12.1	15.2	5.3	8.5	46.4	49.8
Cambodia	46.8	33.4	8.2	18.8	6.8	10.3	38.2	37.6
Central African Republic	43.5	50.9	10.2	11.1	7.2	7.9	39.1	30.1
Djibouti	3.4	3.7	2.7	2.8	12.7	14.4	81.2	79.1
Equatorial Guinea	43.1	6.9	1.2	10.5	35.1	75.2	20.6	7.4
Eritrea	19.4	19.8	9.3	9.3	9.7	14.3	61.6	56.5
Ethiopia	59.0	53.0	3.5	3.6	4.8	6.0	32.7	37.4
Gambia	22.6	24.5	5.1	5.2	5.1	5.3	67.3	65.0
Guinea	23.6	25.0	4.5	4.7	29.2	31.2	42.6	39.1
Haiti	32.7	30.7	7.5	7.8	11.3	16.2	48.5	45.3
Lao People's Democratic Republic	54.5	45.9	15.0	20.4	5.2	8.1	25.3	25.6
Liberia	86.1	63.6	1.9	9.1	1.9	5.2	10.2	22.1
Madagascar	30.3	27.5	11.8	11.9	1.2	2.9	56.7	57.7
Mozambique	34.1	27.5	8.2	16.7	6.9	10.6	50.7	45.3
Myanmar	54.7	49.5	8.0	9.8	4.9	7.5	32.4	33.3
Sao Tome and Principe	31.4	32.6	4.1	4.1	13.4	13.4	51.1	49.9
Somalia	58.7	56.1	2.3	2.6	4.8	5.4	34.2	35.9
Sudan	42.3	49.6	7.9	8.2	7.7	16.9	42.1	25.2
Togo	42.4	43.8	6.2	6.4	16.4	16.7	35.0	33.1
Uganda	45.2	36.7	9.1	10.8	8.0	10.0	37.7	42.5
United Republic of Tanzania	46.3	41.3	7.9	8.7	8.0	12.0	37.7	38.1
Yemen	21.2	21.3	9.1	9.7	22.1	16.6	47.6	52.5
Zambia	26.7	23.2	35.4	39.9	5.2	-1.5	32.8	38.4
Countries with decreasing share of manufacture in value added								
Angola	7.3	7.8	3.7	3.6	64.5	62.8	24.6	25.8
Benin	39.3	40.3	8.7	8.6	4.7	4.8	47.3	46.3
Bhutan	30.4	16.6	10.2	6.5	27.8	42.2	31.6	34.8
Burundi	54.4	46.9	13.1	7.5	4.2	3.8	28.4	41.8
Cape Verde	10.5	8.7	8.9	5.4	15.0	13.9	65.6	72.0
Chad	51.5	35.1	9.3	7.9	1.6	25.3	37.7	31.7
Comoros	39.9	48.8	4.5	4.2	7.8	6.8	47.9	40.2
Democratic Republic of the Congo	41.8	44.5	8.7	5.7	17.6	19.1	31.8	30.7
Kiribati	13.1	12.2	1.3	1.1	4.4	10.9	81.2	75.8
Lesotho	15.8	12.3	17.4	16.8	22.2	25.0	44.7	46.0
Malawi	52.7	54.3	15.9	12.3	9.6	13.0	21.7	20.5
Maldives	10.6	9.0	7.2	6.9	5.4	10.1	76.7	74.0
Mali	40.7	35.3	10.0	9.0	8.8	17.2	40.5	38.5
Mauritania	39.3	20.6	8.2	6.6	15.1	18.3	37.3	54.5
Nepal	42.5	41.0	9.0	8.3	10.8	11.3	37.7	39.4
Niger	37.9	41.8	7.0	6.0	8.4	7.0	46.7	45.2
Rwanda	43.9	46.4	14.3	12.1	5.8	10.4	36.0	31.1
Samoa	21.3	12.4	17.6	14.2	10.0	12.1	51.2	61.4
Senegal	18.4	14.4	15.7	15.2	7.2	8.4	58.7	62.0
Sierra Leone	39.5	44.9	3.7	3.0	7.9	10.9	48.9	41.2
Solomon Islands	46.3	45.8	4.1	4.0	6.1	3.7	43.5	46.5
Timor-Leste	25.2	36.5	3.3	2.7	23.7	14.2	47.8	46.6
Tuvalu	22.6	14.0	2.1	1.7	11.7	13.8	63.6	70.5
Vanuatu	15.7	16.3	3.3	2.7	5.8	5.2	75.2	75.8
Guinea-Bissau	46.4	52.7	..	..	..	..	31.7	27.9
LDCs	**35.9**	**33.2**	**10.4**	**11.2**	**12.1**	**16.0**	**41.6**	**39.6**
African LDCs	*37.7*	*35.9*	*8.9*	*9.1*	*13.5*	*19.2*	*39.8*	*35.8*
Asian LDCs	*33.2*	*29.1*	*13.0*	*14.7*	*9.6*	*11.1*	*44.1*	*45.2*
Island LDCs	*23.2*	*20.9*	*6.3*	*5.4*	*10.8*	*10.4*	*59.8*	*63.3*

Source: UNCTAD secretariat calculations based on United Nations/DESA Statistics Division.
Note: The group averages are weighted averages.
  a Includes mining, utilities and construction.

C. Trends in investment and savings

For the LDCs as a group, gross capital formation increased from 20 per cent of GDP in 2000–2002 to 22 per cent in 2006, and over the same period, gross domestic savings increased from 13 per cent of GDP to 21 per cent. However, a closer look at the trends country-by-country shows that the overall averages for the LDCs as a group mask a very mixed picture, with many of these countries unable to raise domestic savings, increasing their reliance on foreign savings (table 4).

From 2000 to 2006, gross capital formation actually declined as a share of GDP in 17 LDCs, and domestic savings also declined over that period in almost half of the LDCs, some 22 countries. The big jump in the domestic savings rates over this period were found in the oil- and mineral-exporting LDCs — Angola, Chad, Equatorial Guinea, Mauritania, Mozambique and Sudan — plus the Lao People's Democratic Republic.

In 2006, the highest domestic savings rates were found in Equatorial Guinea (91 per cent of GDP), Chad (52 per cent), Angola (41 per cent), Lao People's Democratic Republic (33 per cent), Maldives (32 per cent), Bhutan (29 per cent), Mozambique (28 per cent), Sudan (26 per cent), Yemen (24 per cent) and Mauritania (23 per cent). Oil- and mineral-exporting LDCs — in which the growth of domestic savings was highly correlated with rents from extractive activities — are prominent in this list. Fifteen LDCs — mostly small countries — had negative domestic savings rates in 2006 and thus were relying on foreign savings to finance not only domestic investment but also their domestic consumption. These countries included five very high-growth countries — Afghanistan, Burundi, Malawi, Liberia and Sierra Leone. Only one third of the LDCs had gross domestic savings above 15 per cent of GDP and savings rates remained very low in a number of African LDCs which have had relatively sustained growth performance over a number of years, including Burkina Faso, Ethiopia, Uganda, the United Republic of Tanzania and Senegal.

The overall trends of gross capital formation and gross domestic savings for the LDCs as a group suggest that the resource gap, which indicates reliance on foreign resources, has fallen quite significantly since 2000. It declined from 7 per cent of GDP in 2000–2002 to 1.6 per cent in 2006. However, the resource gap exceeded 10 per cent of GDP in 33 LDCs in 2006 and in 17 of these it exceeded 20 per cent of GDP. The resource gap also increased by more than 1 percentage point in half the LDCs (25 countries), and by more than 5 percentage points in 15 of these countries from 2000–2002 to 2006. The supply of external financial resources thus remains critical for capital formation (and in some cases even for consumption) in most LDCs, and the dependence on external sources of capital has also been increasing for many of them in recent years.

D. Trends in international trade

International trade is equivalent to over 50 per cent of the GDP of the LDCs as a group, and high rates of export growth have been a key driver of their strong GDP growth performance. However, their export structure remains concentrated on primary commodities and low-skill labour-intensive manufactures. Most LDCs are net food importers. Trade performance is highly dependent on commodity price trends. Trade deficits are increasing in most LDCs, particularly those which specialize in agricultural exports. Despite a high level of integration with the global

For the LDCs as a group, the resource gap, which indicates reliance on foreign resources, has fallen from 7 per cent of GDP in 2000–2002 to 1.6 per cent in 2006, but...

...fifteen LDCs — mostly small countries — had negative domestic savings rates in 2006 and thus were relying on foreign savings to finance domestic investment and consumption.

From 2000 to 2006, gross capital formation declined as a share of GDP in 17 LDCs.

LDCs' export structure remains concentrated on primary commodities and low-skill manufactures, and most of them are net food importers.

Table 4. Gross domestic savings, gross capital formation and resource gap in LDCs, by country and ODCs, 2000–2006

(Per cent of GDP)

	Gross capital formation			Gross domestic savings			Resource gap[a]		
	2000–2002	2005	2006	2000–2002	2005	2006	2000–2002	2005	2006
Countries with real GDP growth > 6% in 2006									
Maldives	26.6	61.3	55.6	45.2	28.1	32.3	18.5	-33.2	-23.3
Angola	13.6	7.5	13.1	26.8	32.0	40.5	13.2	24.5	27.4
Mauritania	21.8	44.5	29.0	1.5	-14.9	23.1	-20.3	-59.4	-5.9
Sudan	18.5	22.4	23.8	12.9	18.2	26.2	-5.6	-4.1	2.3
Afghanistan	12.6	21.3	17.3	-24.1	-24.8	-30.8	-36.7	-46.1	-48.1
Ethiopia	20.4	20.5	19.8	3.8	6.4	7.6	-16.6	-14.1	-12.1
Sierra Leone	-15.9	18.6	16.5	-48.7	-6.0	-5.5	-32.7	-24.6	-22.1
Mozambique	29.8	20.4	24.8	16.6	18.3	27.7	-13.2	-2.1	3.0
Malawi	13.6	11.0	10.5	1.0	-22.9	-20.6	-12.6	-33.9	-31.0
Bhutan	55.8	51.4	53.5	33.9	39.1	29.2	-21.9	-12.3	-24.3
Lao People's Dem. Republic	17.0	32.0	30.7	12.1	28.2	33.2	-4.9	-3.7	2.5
Cambodia	18.6	19.7	19.3	9.2	11.1	7.5	-9.5	-8.5	-11.8
Liberia	5.5	15.9	12.3	-1.1	2.3	-0.4	-6.6	-13.6	-12.7
Myanmar	11.2	12.6	15.2	11.2	12.7	15.3	0.0	0.1	0.1
Bangladesh	23.2	24.9	25.6	18.3	20.6	21.0	-4.9	-4.3	-4.6
Democratic Republic of the Congo	9.5	14.2	16.7	10.0	6.5	5.4	0.5	-7.7	-11.2
Uganda	19.7	23.8	24.8	5.3	8.7	8.2	-14.4	-15.1	-16.6
Burundi	8.2	15.5	23.2	-7.0	-11.9	-10.0	-15.3	-27.4	-33.2
Zambia	20.6	25.6	25.9	14.7	17.7	18.3	-6.0	-7.9	-7.6
Countries with real GDP growth between 3% and 6% in 2006									
United Republic of Tanzania	17.9	22.2	22.5	11.6	12.4	11.0	-6.4	-9.7	-11.4
Burkina Faso	25.8	22.7	24.5	10.6	8.5	9.6	-15.2	-14.3	-14.8
Gambia	20.9	26.0	24.1	13.6	7.8	5.7	-7.3	-18.2	-18.4
Sao Tome and Principe	34.8	34.5	67.6	-18.3	-24.9	-24.7	-53.0	-59.4	-92.3
Cape Verde	32.9	37.9	38.7	-6.1	3.9	3.2	-38.9	-34.0	-35.5
Guinea	21.0	17.4	21.5	17.3	7.5	10.6	-3.6	-10.0	-10.9
Solomon Islands	19.6	19.6	19.6	19.6	19.6	19.6	0.0	0.0	0.0
Madagascar	16.0	21.5	21.7	10.4	13.0	9.0	-5.6	-8.6	-12.7
Guinea-Bissau	17.8	14.6	15.7	5.3	-2.8	1.5	-12.5	-17.4	-14.2
Mali	20.0	21.4	22.5	14.3	18.0	17.4	-5.7	-3.4	-5.1
Djibouti	19.4	20.2	19.7	7.6	9.6	8.7	-11.8	-10.7	-11.0
Togo	16.8	19.7	20.8	1.7	1.0	3.7	-15.1	-18.7	-17.1
Senegal	18.6	25.7	25.6	9.0	9.9	8.6	-9.6	-15.8	-17.0
Samoa	13.8	10.4	9.8	-12.7	-14.0	-13.9	-26.5	-24.4	-23.7
Yemen	19.0	21.9	21.5	21.3	21.4	23.8	2.3	-0.5	2.3
Benin	18.9	18.2	21.0	11.6	11.2	11.7	-7.3	-7.0	-9.3
Niger	15.1	19.3	22.8	6.5	8.0	9.1	-8.6	-11.4	-13.7
Vanuatu	21.1	20.4	20.2	18.5	15.8	15.9	-2.6	-4.6	-4.3
Central African Republic	8.4	6.0	5.7	0.9	-4.2	-4.9	-7.5	-10.2	-10.6
Rwanda	17.7	21.1	20.8	0.4	-1.4	-4.2	-17.3	-22.5	-25.0
Countries with real GDP growth < 3% in 2006									
Chad	40.3	26.7	23.6	4.8	54.5	51.9	-35.5	27.8	28.3
Somalia	20.3	20.3	20.3	19.0	19.0	18.9	-1.4	-1.4	-1.4
Haiti	12.3	13.0	28.6	-9.5	-9.5	-0.3	-21.9	-22.5	-28.9
Eritrea	25.2	19.0	18.1	-31.7	-30.2	-19.0	-56.9	-49.2	-37.1
Nepal	24.2	28.9	30.3	14.1	12.4	11.1	-10.1	-16.5	-19.2
Lesotho	41.4	35.1	41.1	-20.0	-1.5	-2.0	-61.4	-36.6	-43.1
Comoros	12.4	10.9	13.8	-1.6	-6.9	-6.8	-14.0	-17.8	-20.6
Tuvalu	55.6	55.8	55.7	-45.3	-45.3	-45.3	-100.9	-101.2	-101.1
Kiribati	43.5	43.7	43.6	2.1	1.8	1.9	-41.4	-41.8	-41.6
Equatorial Guinea	53.0	36.0	33.2	80.1	88.9	90.7	27.1	52.9	57.4
Timor-Leste	29.2	19.1	19.0	-38.7	-17.3	-18.6	-67.9	-36.4	-37.6
LDCs	**19.8**	**21.2**	**22.2**	**12.8**	**17.5**	**20.7**	**-7.0**	**-3.7**	**-1.6**
ODCs	**25.0**	**27.7**	**27.5**	**27.9**	**33.3**	**33.4**	**2.9**	**5.6**	**5.9**

Source: UNCTAD secretariat calculations based on United Nations/DESA Statistics Division.
   a   Measured as the difference between gross domestic savings and gross capital formation.

economy and good export performance, the marginalization of the LDCs in global trade has declined only slightly if oil is excluded. Marginalization is rooted in the continuing failure of export upgrading.

1. OVERALL TRENDS IN MERCHANDISE TRADE

In nominal terms, the value of LDCs' merchandise exports has more than doubled since 2003, reaching a record level of $99.3 billion in 2006. This was $23 billion above the level in 2005 and $43 billion above the value in 2004 (table 5). This improved export performance was largely attributable to rising international commodity prices. With oil and mineral prices rising, exports from the African LDCs almost doubled from 2004 to 2006, whilst they increased by 53 per cent in the Asian LDCs.

Despite a high level of integration with the global economy and the good export performance, the marginalization of the LDCs in global trade has declined only slightly if oil is excluded.

LDCs' improved export performance was largely attributable to rising international commodity prices.

Table 5. LDCs' exports, imports and balance of merchandise trade, by country groups, 2003–2006					
	2003	2004	2005	2006	2004–2006
	\$ million				% change[a]
Merchandise exports					
LDCs total	***43 535***	***55 878***	***76 514***	***99 295***	***77.7***
African LDCs	27 078	36 288	51 874	69 448	91.4
Asian LDCs	16 078	19 118	24 098	29 244	53.0
Island LDCs	380	472	542	603	27.6
Oil exporters	17 007	23 837	38 301	51 731	117.0
Non-oil exporters	26 528	32 041	38 212	47 564	48.4
Agricultural exporters	2 984	3 236	3 977	4 413	36.4
Mineral exporters	5 942	7 741	9 192	13 000	67.9
Manufactures exporters	10 133	13 026	14 701	18 256	40.1
Services exporters	1 978	2 410	3 004	3 297	36.8
Mixed exporters	5 491	5 628	7 338	8 599	52.8
Merchandise imports					
LDCs total	***59 871***	***69 418***	***86 282***	***100 464***	***44.7***
African LDCs	36 170	43 412	55 110	65 362	50.6
Asian LDCs	22 150	24 192	29 107	32 658	35.0
Island LDCs	1 551	1 814	2 065	2 443	34.7
Oil exporters	11 176	12 658	19 006	22 348	76.6
Non-oil exporters	48 694	56 760	67 276	78 116	37.6
Agricultural exporters	10 444	11 699	15 284	17 733	51.6
Mineral exporters	8 115	10 782	12 540	14 304	32.7
Manufactures exporters	16 179	18 358	20 666	23 858	30.0
Services exporters	7 055	8 113	10 406	13 244	63.2
Mixed exporters	6 901	7 809	8 380	8 976	14.9
Merchandise trade balance					
LDCs total	***-16 335***	***-13 540***	***-9 769***	***-1 169***	***-91.4***
African LDCs	-9 092	-7 125	-3 237	4 086	N/A
Asian LDCs	-6 073	-5 074	-5 009	-3 414	-32.7
Island LDCs	-1 171	-1 342	-1 523	-1 841	37.2
Oil exporters	5 831	11 180	19 295	29 383	162.8
Non-oil exporters	-22 166	-24 720	-29 064	-30 552	23.6
Agricultural exporters	-7 460	-8 463	-11 306	-13 321	57.4
Mineral exporters	-2 173	-3 041	-3 348	-1 304	-57.1
Manufactures exporters	-6 046	-5 332	-5 966	-5 602	5.1
Services exporters	-5 077	-5 703	-7 402	-9 947	74.4
Mixed exporters	-1 410	-2 181	-1 042	-377	-82.7

Source: UNCTAD secretariat calculations based on UNCTAD, *Handbook of Statistics 2007* and UNCTAD estimates.

Note: Data for Afghanistan, Chad, Liberia, Somalia and Tuvalu have been estimated using mirror trade data.

   a Percentage change in trade values between initial and end year.

As much as 64 per cent of the total increase in LDCs' merchandise exports from 2004 to 2006 was attributable to oil exporters, and a further 12 per cent to mineral exporters. Manufactures exporters also managed to increase exports significantly over this period, contributing to a 12 per cent increase in LDCs' total merchandise export revenues. But export growth was comparatively slow in LDCs agricultural exporters, constituting only 3 per cent of the increase in merchandise export revenues from 2004 to 2006. The latter group of countries achieved only a marginal expansion of $400 million in their merchandise exports between 2005 and 2006, in sharp contrast with the booming export performance of other LDCs.

The evidence suggests that most of the LDCs' merchandise exports came from a few countries and that the level of geographical concentration of exports is increasing. The top five LDC exporters — Angola, Bangladesh, Myanmar, Sudan and Yemen — doubled their merchandise exports from 2004 to 2006, and in the latter year, they accounted for 63 per cent of the total merchandise exports of the LDCs. The exports of the 30 LDCs that exported least accounted for only 7 per cent of LDCs' total merchandise exports in 2006, down from 10 per cent in 2004 (table 6).

Although imports have also been increasing, the merchandise trade balance of the LDCs as a group has improved significantly. Indeed, for the first time in over 30 years, their merchandise trade balance was close to equilibrium in 2006 (table 5). However, this result masks large differences amongst the LDCs. The merchandise trade surplus of oil-exporting LDCs rose from $11 billion in 2004 to $29 billion in 2006, whilst the merchandise trade deficit of oil-importing LDCs increased from $25 billion to $31 billion. The majority of the LDCs — 42 of the 50 — had a merchandise trade deficit during the period 2005–2006; that deficit was greater than in 2003–2004 for 37 LDCs (chart 2).

Amongst the oil-importing LDCs, there were also significant differences. Mineral exporters reduced their merchandise trade deficit from 2004, and the deficit did not worsen by much in the manufacture exporters taken as a group. However, the merchandise trade deficit of the LDCs which specialize in agricultural exports considerably worsened in 2005 and 2006, when the deficit reached a record high of $13 billion. Their average merchandise trade deficit in 2005–2006 was equivalent to 18 per cent of their GDP.

Rising trade deficits are also evident in trade in services, despite healthy service export growth (box 2).

2. TRENDS IN INTERNATIONAL COMMODITY PRICES

The improved export performance of a large number of LDCs in 2005 and 2006 has been driven by increased international demand for commodities, which is leading to much higher international commodity prices.[4] The prices of some commodities of particular importance for the LDCs rose strongly in 2006, following another increase in 2005. However, there is notable difference between the price trends during this period for food and agricultural raw materials on the one hand, and mineral, ores, metals and crude petroleum on the other. Moreover, within each broad category, the prices of some commodities rose much more than others.

The difference between agricultural products and minerals is evident both in 2005 and 2006 (table 7). From 2004 to 2005, the average price indices of food and agricultural raw materials only increased by 6 per cent and 4 per cent

---

64 per cent of the total increase in LDCs merchandise exports from 2004 to 2006 was attributable to oil exporters, and a further 12 per cent to mineral exporters.

The merchandise trade surplus of oil-exporting LDCs rose from $11 billion in 2004 to $29 billion in 2006, whilst the merchandise trade deficit of oil-importing LDCs increased from $25 billion to $31 billion.

The improved export performance of a large number of LDCs in 2005 and 2006 has been driven by much higher international commodity prices.

Table 6. LDCs' merchandise exports and imports, by country, 2004–2006

	Export specialization	Exports				Imports			
		$ million	Annual percentage change			$ million	Annual percentage change		
		2006	2004	2005	2006	2006	2004	2005	2006
Largest 5 exporters									
Angola	O	33 795.0	40.5	78.9	45.6	6 908.9	4.9	43.2	35.0
Bangladesh	MF	11 962.6	29.1	14.0	26.9	15 279.4	12.1	15.3	16.6
Yemen	O	6 264.0	8.5	38.5	11.7	4 935.1	1.6	30.2	1.5
Sudan	O	5 478.7	45.6	24.7	21.6	8 844.5	39.2	82.6	20.1
Myanmar	MX	4 863.3	3.5	60.2	18.0	2 155.2	7.8	-12.3	9.0
Middle 15 exporters									
Cambodia	MF	3 990.5	32.1	12.4	26.9	2 996.2	16.2	20.1	20.9
Equatorial Guinea	O	3 804.3	31.5	55.3	29.7	1 098.7	34.8	34.6	-3.3
Zambia	MN	3 770.4	60.7	14.9	108.3	3 074.3	36.7	18.9	20.2
Mozambique	MN	2 381.1	44.1	18.6	33.5	2 869.3	28.8	18.4	19.1
Democratic Republic of the Congo	MN	2 300.2	34.6	18.4	5.0	2 799.5	24.6	14.3	23.3
Chad	O	2 274.7	1 293.3	55.9	16.0	456.4	2.4	17.5	8.4
United Republic of Tanzania	S	1 689.9	17.5	16.1	9.4	4 439.5	17.9	28.3	35.6
Senegal	MX	1 491.6	13.9	11.8	1.4	3 671.0	18.4	23.2	5.0
Liberia	A	1 490.2	15.6	42.0	3.7	6 446.3	8.1	15.7	30.7
Mali	MN	1 476.6	-2.0	16.2	28.7	1 990.3	7.3	24.8	16.8
Mauritania	MN	1 258.7	35.7	27.8	126.2	1 073.3	246.8	0.2	-20.0
Ethiopia	S	1 043.0	19.9	50.7	12.6	5 207.3	7.0	42.5	27.2
Madagascar	MX	1 008.2	-0.8	-13.9	20.6	1 760.3	25.3	2.1	4.4
Guinea	MN	976.2	3.0	22.7	1.1	807.7	2.8	18.8	9.8
Uganda	A	962.2	22.9	24.4	18.4	2 557.3	25.1	19.4	24.5
Smallest 30 exporters									
Lao People's Democratic Republic	MX	876.5	-4.5	52.2	59.5	752.3	-3.4	23.7	20.1
Nepal	MF	759.7	15.8	9.7	-8.4	2 098.9	3.8	-0.6	12.9
Lesotho	MF	671.9	36.9	-7.3	10.3	1 535.3	40.2	2.7	4.5
Malawi	A	668.4	-8.7	8.0	34.9	1 209.2	18.2	25.5	3.8
Haiti	MF	522.6	13.9	20.2	10.4	1 637.3	10.9	11.3	11.7
Burkina Faso	A	482.9	23.2	-2.4	25.7	1 419.1	33.8	10.1	1.9
Togo	MX	359.7	-17.4	-11.9	-0.1	637.4	-1.9	6.2	7.6
Niger	MN	355.7	22.3	24.7	2.3	688.0	19.1	10.3	-6.5
Bhutan	MF	348.2	15.8	41.0	60.3	310.4	22.1	-6.0	8.6
Benin	A	283.1	9.9	-3.4	-1.8	1 011.3	0.2	0.5	12.5
Sierra Leone	MN	216.6	51.1	14.4	36.3	388.9	-5.6	20.3	13.0
Afghanistan	A	179.6	-8.5	25.4	-10.1	4 130.9	10.6	87.2	5.7
Somalia	A	160.8	-41.1	107.7	-11.1	602.2	-28.7	101.0	5.4
Central African Republic	MN	144.3	53.8	15.2	24.0	198.7	59.6	17.2	6.6
Maldives	S	135.6	50.3	-9.2	-12.0	926.5	36.3	16.1	24.4
Rwanda	S	135.4	94.6	27.8	8.1	496.4	8.8	41.7	23.3
Burundi	MN	120.1	25.5	41.6	2.6	414.4	19.4	48.8	61.2
Timor-Leste	O	114.1	84.1	47.1	45.3	104.6	-48.7	-10.5	2.9
Cape Verde	S	110.3	21.9	488.4	23.3	538.2	21.0	2.1	22.8
Solomon Islands	A	91.5	-3.9	8.2	14.3	165.3	21.9	51.6	8.9
Samoa	S	84.9	-1.9	-0.6	0.0	275.0	39.5	13.9	15.1
Guinea-Bissau	A	83.9	15.9	18.2	-11.3	91.4	18.8	27.4	-12.5
Vanuatu	S	44.9	37.1	2.6	18.3	159.7	21.9	16.7	6.8
Djibouti	S	18.9	0.0	4.0	39.7	215.8	1.8	6.1	21.1
Gambia	S	11.5	256.3	-71.8	125.0	259.3	45.6	9.7	-0.1
Eritrea	S	11.2	66.4	-4.2	5.6	552.7	9.1	3.1	13.5
Comoros	S	7.5	16.6	-35.5	-17.4	102.5	24.5	15.4	16.8
Kiribati	A	6.3	38.5	-80.1	77.3	61.4	21.3	29.8	-17.0
Sao Tome and Principe	S	3.9	-46.4	-3.9	13.4	71.1	1.5	20.3	42.7
Tuvalu	A	3.5	-24.9	-37.3	194.4	39.0	-3.5	73.5	34.4

Source: UNCTAD secretariat calculations based on UNCTAD, *Handbook of Statistics 2007* and UNCTAD estimates.

Note: **A**=agricultural exporter, **MF**=manufactures exporter, **MN**=mineral exporter, **MX**=mixed exporters, **O**=oil exporter, **S**=services exporter. Countries have been ranked in decreasing order according to the value of their exports in 2006.

Chart 2. LDCs' merchandise trade balance, 2003–2006
($ million, period averages)

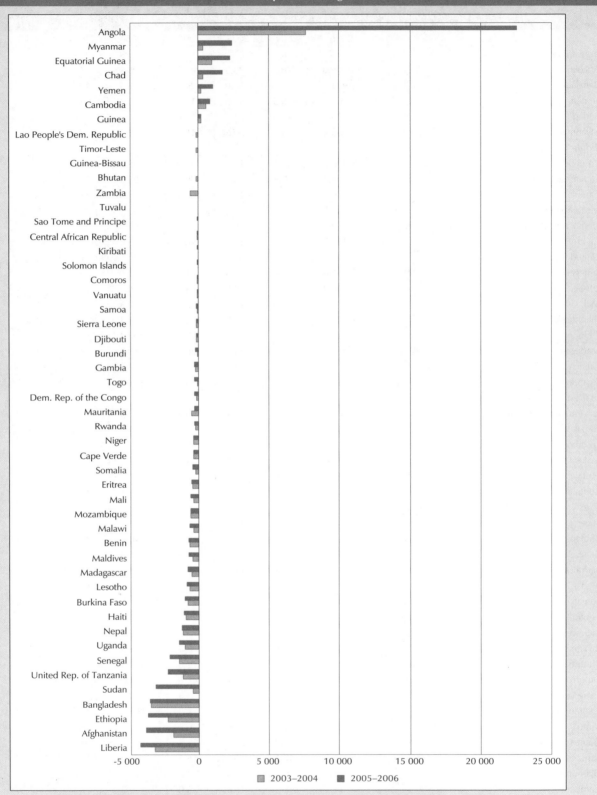

Angola
Myanmar
Equatorial Guinea
Chad
Yemen
Cambodia
Guinea
Lao People's Dem. Republic
Timor-Leste
Guinea-Bissau
Bhutan
Zambia
Tuvalu
Sao Tome and Principe
Central African Republic
Kiribati
Solomon Islands
Comoros
Vanuatu
Samoa
Sierra Leone
Djibouti
Burundi
Gambia
Togo
Dem. Rep. of the Congo
Mauritania
Rwanda
Niger
Cape Verde
Somalia
Eritrea
Mali
Mozambique
Malawi
Benin
Maldives
Madagascar
Lesotho
Burkina Faso
Haiti
Nepal
Uganda
Senegal
United Rep. of Tanzania
Sudan
Bangladesh
Ethiopia
Afghanistan
Liberia

-5 000   0   5 000   10 000   15 000   20 000   25 000

■ 2003–2004   ■ 2005–2006

Source: UNCTAD secretariat estimates based on UNCTAD, *Handbook of Statistics 2007.*

Note: Data for Afghanistan, Chad, Liberia, Somalia and Tuvalu have been estimated using mirror data.

Box 2. Trends in trade in services

Data on trade in services are much less reliable and complete than data on merchandise trade. However, the available data indicate that the LDCs' exports are at record levels and the balance of services trade is negative and worsening, as it is for most countries in merchandise trade.

Exports of commercial services from LDCs have been increasing rapidly in recent years. In 2006, they amounted to $14 billion (box table 2). This was equivalent to about 12 per cent of total exports of goods and services for the LDCs as a group. But service exports are particularly important for island LDCs; services are estimated to be equivalent to 67 per cent of their total exports of goods and services.

The service exports of LDCs in 2006 were $2 billion higher than in 2005 and $3.2 billion higher than in 2004. Two thirds of the increase in service export revenue is attributable to increases in commercial services exports from African LDCs. Although service exports are of crucial significance for island LDCs, they have been growing at a lower rate than in the African LDCs.

Tourism is the most important service export of the LDCs. It constituted 33 per cent of the total service export receipts in 2006 for the LDCs as a group. Tourism is even more important for the island LDCs, accounting for 65 per cent of the services exports for this group of countries in 2006.

In spite of the large increase in total service exports, the LDCs remain net service importers. In 2006, LDCs spent an estimated $33 billion to finance their imports of services. Island LDCs export more services than they import, and their service trade surplus reached a record $546 million in 2006. On the other hand, the Asian and the African LDCs experienced a worsening of their service trade deficit between 2004 and 2006, from $1.2 billion to $1.7 billion and from $10.9 billion to $17.7 billion respectively. Payments for service imports absorbed 34 per cent of the total export revenue of the African LDCs from goods and services in 2006. Such payments are particularly high for the landlocked African LDCs, as shown in *Least Developed Countries Report 2004* (UNCTAD, 2004:113).

Box table 2. Export and import of services in LDCs, by country groups, 2003–2006
($ million, per cent)

	Total services ($ million)				Tourism[a] (%)			
	2003	2004	2005	2006	2003	2004	2005	2006
Exports					*% of total exports of services*			
LDCs	8 959.0	10 747.3	11 855.2	13 985.0	36.6	38.2	35.3	33.2
African LDCs and Haiti	5 422.9	6 508.0	7 279.7	8 629.1	34.9	34.9	33.0	28.5
Asian LDCs	2 655.6	3 195.2	3 636.1	4 104.2	31.9	35.2	33.7	33.1
Island LDCs	880.5	1 044.1	939.3	1 251.7	61.4	67.8	59.8	65.4
Imports					*% of total imports of services*			
LDCs	17 936.0	22 405.0	27 833.2	32 856.3	9.1	9.9	10.4	11.4
African LDCs and Haiti	13 556.9	17 403.2	22 134.6	26 330.9	8.1	8.8	9.7	11.3
Asian LDCs	3 912.1	4 448.9	5 065.6	5 819.2	10.2	11.8	11.2	10.2
Island LDCs	467.0	552.8	633.0	706.2	28.0	27.5	25.0	25.3
Net exports								
LDCs	-8 977.1	-11 657.7	-15 978.0	-18 871.3				
African LDCs and Haiti	-8 134.0	-10 895.2	-14 854.9	-17 701.8				
Asian LDCs	-1 256.5	-1 253.7	-1 429.5	-1 715.0				
Island LDCs	413.5	491.2	306.4	545.5				

Source: IMF, *Balance of Payments and International Investment Positions Statistics*, CD-ROM, December 2007 and UNCTAD estimates.
Note: No data for Afghanistan, Bhutan, Liberia, Somalia and Tuvalu.
    a   Includes travel and personal, cultural and recreational activities.

respectively, whilst the average price indices of minerals, ores and metals rose by 26 per cent. Between 2005 and 2006, the average price index of food and agricultural raw materials increased by more than the previous year — 16 per cent and 15 per cent respectively — but the average price index of minerals, ores and metals soared by 60 per cent. The crude petroleum price index increased by 41 per cent and 21 per cent, respectively, during the same years.

Underlying these broad trends, particular commodities of importance to LDCs behaved differently. The largest nominal price increases from 2004 to 2006 occurred for copper, with grade A copper 135 per cent higher in 2006 than in 2004. But strong hikes in iron ore and gold, and to a lesser extent aluminium, also

Table 7. Price indices of selected primary commodities of importance to LDCs, 1995–2006 *(Index, 2000=100)*								
	1995	2003	2004	2005	2006	Standard deviation[a]	% change	
						1995–2006	1995–2006	2000–2006
All food	139	107	121	128	149	..	8	49
Wheat	139	127	115	109	129	23	-8	29
Rice	158	98	121	141	149	57	-6	49
Sugar	162	87	88	121	181	3	11	81
Fish meal	120	148	157	172	282	199	135	182
Coffee, Arabicas	174	74	93	132	132	39	-24	32
Coffee, Robustas	303	88	86	120	162	29	-47	62
Cocoa beans	161	198	174	173	179	13	11	79
Tea	71	78	80	87	97	29	37	-3
Agricultural raw materials	153	112	127	132	152	..	-1	52
Tobacco	88	89	92	93	99	273	12	-1
Cotton	164	107	104	92	97	15	-41	-3
Non-coniferous woods	108	118	136	144	165	21	53	65
Minerals, ores and metals	128	98	137	173	278	..	117	178
Iron ore	97	112	132	226	269	16	176	169
Aluminium	117	92	111	123	166	346	42	66
Copper, grade A	162	98	158	203	371	748	129	271
Copper, wire bars	158	97	153	198	361	68	128	261
Gold	138	130	147	159	217	95	57	117
Memo items:								
Crude petroleum	60	102	134	189	228	15	280	128
Unit value index of manufactured goods exported by developed countries	123	111	121	125	130	..	6	30

Source: UNCTAD secretariat calculations based on UNCTAD, *Commodity Price Bulletin*, various issues.

a Based on annual averages of free market prices.

drove up the average price index of minerals, metals and ores. The price of fish meat also rose by almost 80 per cent over this period. Coffee prices recovered, with Robustas up by 89 per cent and Arabicas up 42 per cent. Sugar prices increased by 106 per cent. But cotton prices were marginally lower in 2006 than in 2004, and tobacco prices were only marginally higher. The prices of tea, tobacco and cotton — key commodities for the LDCs which specialize in exporting agricultural commodities — were lower in 2006 than in 2000 (even in nominal terms). The price of coffee (both Arabicas and Robustas) was higher, but still lower than in 1995.

Despite the trend towards higher commodity prices, the prices for most commodities over the period 1995–2006 showed a high degree of variability, gauged by the standard deviation of annual free market prices (table 7). The highest variability is evident in some of the commodities — namely copper, fish meat, gold, aluminium and tobacco — that are important to those LDCs which experienced the highest price increases in 2005 and 2006. The variability of commodity prices remains a critical problem for the LDCs, affecting macroeconomic stability, and also threatening debt sustainability and sustained growth.

3. THE LEVEL OF COMMODITY DEPENDENCE

The latest UNCTAD data show that in 2005–2006, primary commodities constituted 77 per cent of the merchandise exports of the LDCs as a group (table

8). Fuel exports accounted for 53 per cent of total LDCs' exports in those years, followed by manufactured goods, which made up 22 per cent, and minerals, ores and metals, which amounted to 11 per cent. A comparison with estimates for 2000–2003 shows a significant shift, with fuel exports rising in relative importance, up from 38 per cent of total LDCs' exports in 2000–2003, and manufactures exports decreasing in relative importance, down from 34 per cent of total LDCs' exports during that period. These shifts resulted mainly from the relative expansion of fuel exports prices (affecting all fuels exporters) and volumes (the latter particularly in Angola, Chad and Equatorial Guinea).

There is, however, a significant difference between the African and the Asian LDCs in terms of the composition of their exports. Fuels constituted 64 per cent of the exports of the African LDCs in 2005–2006, whilst manufactured goods accounted for only 8 per cent. This was almost a mirror image of the exports of the Asian LDCs, where manufactured goods made up 55 per cent, whilst fuels were 28 per cent.

With a 10-year perspective, it is apparent that the Asian LDCs as a group continue to diversify their export structure away from primary commodities into manufactures, whilst the African LDCs are increasingly commodity-dependent, owing to increasing commodity prices and — to a lesser extent — to expanding volumes. During 2005–2006, 75 per cent of LDCs' total exports of manufactured goods were from the Asian LDCs. Bangladesh alone exported an average of $7.3 billion of manufactured goods per year, equivalent to 7.4 per cent of the LDCs' total merchandise exports and 34 per cent of the LDCs' total manufactured exports. Similarly, 83 per cent of LDCs' total exports of fuel were from the African LDCs, and a similar 79 per cent of LDCs' total primary commodity exports *excluding fuels* was also from the African LDCs.

In 2003–2005, commodities constituted over 50 per cent of total exports of goods and services for over half of the LDCs for which data are available (24 of 45 countries). Moreover, they accounted for 25 to 50 per cent of total export

In 2005–2006, fuel exports accounted for 53 per cent of total LDCs' exports, followed by manufactured goods, which made up 22 per cent.

Asian LDCs continue to diversify their export structure away from primary commodities into manufactures, whilst the African LDCs are increasingly commodity-dependent.

Table 8. Composition of merchandise exports and imports in LDCs, African and Asian LDCs, 2005–2006
(Per cent)

	Merchandise exports			Merchandise imports		
	LDCs	African LDCs	Asian LDCs	LDCs	African LDCs	Asian LDCs
	% of country group exports					
Total all products	100.0	100.0	100.0	100.0	100.0	100.0
All food items	8.6	8.3	8.6	15.6	15.4	15.8
Agricultural raw materials	4.8	4.7	4.7	1.8	1.2	3.0
Mineral, ores and metals	11.0	14.9	2.4	1.1	0.8	1.7
Fuels	52.7	63.7	28.4	13.6	12.9	14.9
Manufactured goods	22.4	8.0	55.3	66.0	67.7	63.4
Chemical products	0.9	0.8	1.1	8.8	8.5	9.4
Machinery and transport equipment	2.6	3.1	1.2	33.0	38.4	22.7
Primary commodities, including fuels	77.0	91.5	44.1	32.2	30.3	35.3
Primary commodities, excluding fuels	24.3	27.9	15.7	18.6	17.4	20.4

Source: UNCTAD secretariat calculations based on UNCTAD, *Handbook of Statistics 2007* and UNCTAD estimates.

Note: Data for Afghanistan, Chad, Liberia, Somalia and Tuvalu have been estimated based on mirror data.
Goods categories according to SITC, rev. 3: All food items (0+1+22+4); agricultural raw materials (2-22-27-28); mineral, ores and metals (27+28+68+667+971); manufactures (5 to 8 less 68 and 667); fuels (3); chemical products (5); machinery and transport equipment (7); primary commodities including fuels (0+1+2+3+4+68+667+971).

earnings in a further nine countries. Commodity export dependence was stronger in the African LDCs, where they constituted over 25 per cent of total exports of goods and services in 23 of the 33 countries for which data are available.

4. TECHNOLOGY CONTENT OF EXPORTS

The Least Developed Countries Report 2007 stresses the importance of technological progress and of catching up for the LDCs' effort to develop their productive capacities (UNCTAD, 2007). The evolution of export patterns also depends on the technological level of the countries. Clearly, an export structure that is more technology-intensive is also more dynamic, and volumes and values tend to grow faster, while exports that use basic technologies tend to have more slowly-growing markets, as well as a smaller scope for technological upgrading (Lall, 2000). The technological content of exports is also likely to affect the current and future economic growth performance. Technology-intensive products offer better prospects for growth, not only because their products tend to be more dynamic in trade, but there are also more opportunities for dynamic productivity gains and externalities. Although basic technologies tend to be associated with more slowly-growing products and markets, they can still experience rapid trade growth, which could lead to high economic growth. This form of growth is not, however, likely to be sustainable in the long term, as it involves limited learning, technological upgrading and spillovers. Once its growth benefits are exhausted, countries should target other products with a higher technological content (Lall, 2000).

Using the taxonomy provided by Lall (2000), manufactured exports are classified according to technological content into the following categories[5]:

(a) Resource-based, including simple and labour-intensive products that are applied to the production of processed agricultural goods and minerals;

(b) Low-technology, including those products that rely on basic and well-diffused technology;

(c) Medium-technology, including those products that use more complex, skill-intensive technologies; and

(d) High-technology, including those products that use advanced, research and development-based, fast-changing technologies.

This classification is used to highlight whether there has been technological upgrading of the export composition for the LDCs, and the extent of such upgrading compared with other developing countries and developed countries during 1995–2006. Data show that the export structure of the LDCs experienced a small shift away from resource-based into low-technology labour-intensive manufactures (chart 3). In 1995–1996, resource-based manufactures accounted for 58 per cent of LDCs' total manufactures exports, against some 33 per cent for the low-technology manufactures. By 2005–2006, the latter category increased to 41 per cent of the manufactures, while the share for resource-based manufactures decreased to 52 per cent. The share of medium- and high-technology manufactures declined slightly.

In the case of the other developing countries as a group, the evidence of a technology-related change taking place is more evident. While the shares of resource-based and medium-technology manufactures remained stable over time at 18 per cent and 24 per cent of total manufactured exports of the group respectively, the share of low-technology manufactures decreased (from 30 per cent in 1995–1996 to 23 per cent in 2005–2006). This development has been to

A more technology-intensive export structure is more dynamic, while exports that use basic technologies tend to have more slowly-growing markets and a smaller scope for technological upgrading.

The export structure of the LDCs experienced a small shift away from resource-based into low-technology labour-intensive manufactures.

Chart 3. Distribution of manufactured exports of LDCs, other developing and developed countries according to technological categories, 1995–2006
(Per cent of total manufactured exports of the country groups)

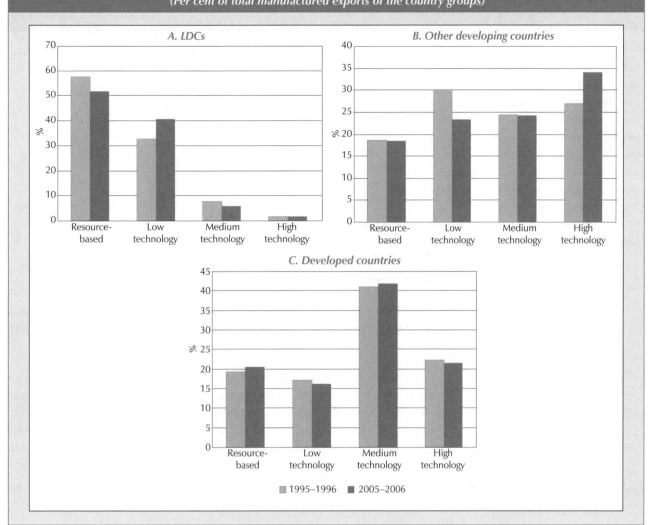

Source: UNCTAD secretariat calculations based on UNCTAD, *Handbook of Statistics 2007* and estimates. No data available for Afghanistan, Chad, Liberia, Somalia and Tuvalu.

Note: The division according to technological categories is drawn from Lall (2000). Data are grouped by 3-digit SITC, revision 3. The manufactured category is larger than in the usual classification as processed foods like sugar, cheese and vegetables are classified as resource-based manufactures (rather than commodities).

the benefit of high-technology exports, whose share increased by 7 per cent during the 11 years considered. On the other hand, the technology-mature developed countries experienced no technology-related change in their composition of manufactured exports over the period.

Using a more detailed classification of technology-based manufactured exports, the LDCs as a group have switched their manufacture exports into resource-based mineral manufactures and low-technology textile, garment and footwear. Together, these two categories accounted for 78 per cent of the LDCs' total manufactured exports in 2005–2006, up from 69 per cent in 1995–1996. These averages mask the large difference that exists between African and Asian LDCs. Table 9 shows that the former have increased their technological specialization in the exports of resource-based minerals, driven by the buoyant international prices, while the latter have increased their specialization in low-technology manufactures, namely textiles, garments and footwear. Among the LDC sub-groups, the island LDCs have experienced the most upgrading of their manufactured exports. They have been the only group to experience a strong increase in their share of medium-technology manufactures (from 15 per cent of total manufactured exports in

LDCs as a group have switched their manufactured exports into mineral manufactures and low-technology textile, garment and footwear.

Table 9. Distribution of manufactured exports according to technological categories for LDCs and country groups, 1995–2006

(Per cent of total manufactured exports)

	LDCs		African LDCs		Asian LDCs		Island LDCs	
	1995–1996	2005–2006	1995–1996	2005–2006	1995–1996	2005–2006	1995–1996	2005–2006
Resource-based manufactures: Agro-based	19.1	11.1	16.2	8.7	19.2	13.2	62.6	36.8
Resource-based manufactures: Mineral	38.7	40.7	65.6	70.3	9.0	5.6	7.9	24.4
Low technology manufactures: Textile, garment and footwear	29.9	37.2	6.6	8.4	59.4	73.0	7.4	3.0
Low technology manufactures: Other products	2.9	3.4	2.3	4.4	3.6	2.4	4.3	2.5
Medium technology manufactures: Automotive	1.8	1.0	2.4	1.1	1.3	0.8	0.5	3.1
Medium technology manufactures: Process	3.8	2.6	3.0	2.7	4.6	2.4	7.0	5.4
Medium technology manufactures: Engineering	2.2	2.3	2.3	2.8	1.7	1.4	7.4	16.5
High technology manufactures: Electronic and electrical	0.7	1.0	0.8	1.1	0.4	0.8	2.1	2.8
High technology manufactures: Other	0.9	0.6	0.9	0.7	0.8	0.4	0.8	5.4

Source: UNCTAD secretariat calculations based on UNCTAD, *Handbook of Statistics 2007* and estimates.

Note: No data for Afghanistan, Chad, Liberia, Somalia and Tuvalu.
The classification by technological categories is drawn from Lall (2000). Data are grouped by 3-digits SITC, revision 3.
The manufactured category is larger than in the usual classification as processed foods like sugar, cheese and vegetables are classified as resource-based manufactures (rather than commodities).

1995–1996 to 25 per cent in 2005–2006). But this is mainly attributable to one investment project in one country — exports of engineering manufactures from Samoa.

Although export diversification in some LDCs is welcome, there is no room for complacency regarding the trade prospects of those LDCs which have managed to reduce commodity dependence and increase manufactures exports. Given the high degree of competition in global markets for low-technology, low-skill manufactures, these countries remain vulnerable. The recent erratic growth experience of manufactures exporters such as Lesotho, Haiti and Nepal shows that export upgrading is critical to sustained competitiveness.

In 2005–2006, manufactured goods constituted 66 per cent of the merchandise imports of the LDCs. But both food and fuel are also important components of the LDCs' import bill.

5. COMPOSITION OF MERCHANDISE IMPORTS

In 2005–2006, manufactured goods constituted 66 per cent of the merchandise imports of the LDCs. But both food and fuels are also important components of the LDCs' import bill, accounting for 16 per cent and 14 per cent of total merchandise imports respectively (table 8).

Because they are net food importers, most LDCs are particularly vulnerable to swings in the prices of food items and to the financial terms attached to food imports.

The position of food imports in LDCs' trade structure bears close attention, given its potential importance for food security and poverty. Because they are net food importers, most LDCs are particularly vulnerable to swings in the prices of food items and to the financial terms attached to food imports (i.e. their concessionality level). In 2005–2006, the food import bill of the LDCs as a group reached $14.6 billion, which was equivalent to 4.4 per cent of their GDP. This was $6.1 billion higher than in 2000–2002, an increase equivalent to some 2 per cent of their GDP in 2005–2006. During 2005–2006, the LDCs' net food trade deficit was equivalent to $7.1 billion. African, Asian and island LDCs, considered as groups, were all net food importers. But two thirds of the total food trade deficit was attributable to the African LDCs. The majority (36) of LDCs were net food importers and net food imports increased in 40 LDCs between 2004 and 2006 (table 10).

The high level of food import dependence is a major feature of the vulnerability of LDCs and this issue, including the poverty impact of the rising prices in 2007 and 2008, will be examined in more detail in the next chapter.

Table 10. Food imports and exports in LDCs, by country, 2000–2006
($ million, per cent)

| | Food exports | | | Food imports | | | | | | Food balance | |
| | $ million | | | $ million | | | % of total imports | | | $ million | |
	2000	2005	2006	2000	2005	2006	2000	2005	2006	2000	2006
Net food importers											
Afghanistan	52.7	89.0	85.7	294.9	827.6	965.4	37.0	21.2	23.4	-242.2	-879.7
Angola	42.7	24.6	28.2	825.8	941.2	1 305.8	27.2	18.4	18.9	-783.1	-1 277.6
Bangladesh	418.2	636.5	807.2	1 254.0	1 712.4	2 185.2	16.5	13.1	14.3	-835.9	-1 378.0
Benin	37.8	69.6	58.0	119.6	268.1	281.4	21.9	29.8	27.8	-81.9	-223.5
Burkina Faso	34.5	89.4	145.8	91.0	208.7	181.9	12.6	15.0	12.8	-56.5	-36.0
Cambodia	13.3	146.2	146.0	136.8	225.8	237.7	9.5	9.1	7.9	-123.4	-91.6
Cape Verde	2.0	12.4	15.6	73.6	133.7	157.0	31.0	30.5	29.2	-71.6	-141.4
Central African Republic	8.4	0.9	1.6	20.7	31.9	39.8	29.3	17.1	20.0	-12.2	-38.2
Chad	4.2	0.2	0.2	22.9	55.4	73.3	16.8	13.2	16.1	-18.8	-73.1
Comoros	6.1	7.3	6.1	15.7	30.9	33.9	21.9	35.2	33.0	-9.6	-27.8
Dem. Rep. of the Congo	25.9	34.4	29.3	192.2	601.3	729.1	27.6	26.5	26.0	-166.3	-699.8
Djibouti	4.2	5.5	8.2	38.2	40.0	46.7	24.5	22.4	21.6	-34.0	-38.5
Equatorial Guinea	36.4	1.0	1.2	44.1	170.4	169.0	9.8	15.0	15.4	-7.7	-167.8
Eritrea	12.7	2.8	3.1	122.6	162.7	132.6	37.4	33.4	24.0	-109.9	-129.6
Gambia	13.1	4.0	9.3	65.4	97.9	80.9	34.5	37.7	31.2	-52.3	-71.6
Guinea	13.1	69.8	72.5	148.0	159.5	136.2	24.2	21.7	16.9	-135.0	-63.7
Haiti	31.1	23.1	24.0	350.2	394.7	428.9	33.7	26.9	26.2	-319.2	-404.9
Kiribati	10.2	2.9	4.6	14.4	27.0	20.7	36.7	36.4	33.7	-4.2	-16.2
Lao People's Dem. Republic	25.7	33.3	37.6	74.5	87.5	93.4	13.9	14.0	12.4	-48.7	-55.7
Lesotho	16.7	2.5	2.3	108.0	358.2	362.9	17.6	24.4	23.6	-91.4	-360.6
Liberia	3.8	7.5	7.9	77.6	161.9	172.6	1.4	3.3	2.7	-73.8	-164.7
Maldives	40.9	102.9	133.6	91.8	115.9	147.9	23.6	15.6	16.0	-50.9	-14.3
Mali	8.2	55.4	103.1	121.9	219.5	275.8	15.1	12.9	13.9	-113.7	-172.7
Mozambique	156.2	208.5	376.0	162.4	347.4	398.7	14.0	14.4	13.9	-6.2	-22.6
Nepal	70.6	162.1	133.5	184.7	251.6	312.0	11.9	13.5	14.9	-114.2	-178.5
Niger	127.7	67.1	87.1	135.1	251.6	224.8	35.1	34.2	32.7	-7.4	-137.7
Samoa	4.5	17.5	18.5	25.9	43.5	51.0	24.4	18.2	18.6	-21.4	-32.6
Sao Tome and Principe	2.7	3.2	3.7	9.2	19.2	21.8	30.8	38.5	30.6	-6.5	-18.1
Senegal	363.3	423.9	495.4	361.9	984.2	858.4	23.3	28.1	23.4	1.4	-363.0
Sierra Leone	11.9	14.2	16.5	33.6	53.8	80.3	22.5	15.6	20.6	-21.7	-63.8
Somalia	100.5	128.7	97.9	153.4	257.2	303.1	47.3	45.0	50.3	-52.9	-205.2
Sudan	272.9	299.2	298.6	360.0	921.7	1 053.0	21.7	12.5	11.9	-87.1	-754.3
Timor-Leste	0.0	8.0	9.0	24.5	17.9	19.2	19.5	17.6	18.4	-24.5	-10.2
Togo	37.5	77.2	79.7	59.5	92.0	99.7	18.4	15.5	15.6	-21.9	-20.0
Tuvalu	0.2	0.0	0.0	2.4	3.8	3.1	34.2	13.0	8.0	-2.2	-3.1
Yemen	87.5	247.2	273.5	829.1	1 154.5	1 044.1	35.6	23.7	21.2	-741.6	-770.6
Net food exporters											
Bhutan	13.7	32.8	79.3	31.4	29.6	26.1	17.9	10.4	8.4	-17.6	53.2
Burundi	36.8	52.8	53.7	34.5	16.6	31.0	22.9	6.5	7.5	2.3	22.6
Ethiopia	320.7	680.7	735.8	88.1	435.9	443.9	7.0	10.6	8.5	232.6	291.9
Guinea-Bissau	31.7	76.6	67.9	12.1	25.8	24.6	24.7	24.7	26.9	19.5	43.3
Madagascar	273.4	244.4	330.0	130.6	259.0	255.4	13.2	15.4	14.5	142.8	74.5
Malawi	331.1	393.9	551.3	52.3	212.5	183.2	9.8	18.2	15.1	278.8	368.2
Mauritania	71.2	137.7	356.4	66.1	137.2	268.6	18.7	10.2	25.0	5.1	87.7
Myanmar	330.1	746.9	935.4	278.5	274.9	301.6	11.6	13.9	14.0	51.6	633.8
Rwanda	29.7	74.8	79.6	44.0	42.8	61.6	20.8	10.6	12.4	-14.3	18.0
Solomon Islands	21.7	20.3	17.2	12.8	17.9	18.6	13.0	11.8	11.3	9.0	-1.4
Uganda	242.5	473.4	523.2	134.1	308.1	348.0	14.1	15.0	13.6	108.4	175.2
United Republic of Tanzania	359.5	574.0	585.4	231.6	331.7	542.5	14.6	10.1	12.2	127.9	42.9
Vanuatu	17.9	23.3	34.2	20.8	18.0	21.4	23.9	12.0	13.4	-2.8	12.8
Zambia	83.6	239.4	226.1	71.8	159.0	233.5	8.1	6.2	7.6	11.9	-7.3
LDCs	**4 261.0**	**6 849.0**	**8 196.0**	**7 853.9**	**13 699.6**	**15 487.3**	**17.3**	**15.9**	**15.4**	**-3 592.9**	**-7 291.3**

Source: UNCTAD secretariat calculations based on United Nations/DESA Statistics Division and UNCTAD estimates.

Note: Countries have been classified according to a three-year (2004–2006) average of food balance.
For SITC codes for food, see note to table 8.

6. THE CONTINUING MARGINALIZATION OF LDCs IN WORLD TRADE

The net result of all the recent trends identified previously is that the LDCs are in a situation where they are highly integrated with the global economy through trade, but at the same time, their marginalization, as measured by their level of participation in world trade, remains significant.

In 2006, LDCs generated only 0.8 per cent of world merchandise exports, but excluding fuels, this share was only 0.5 per cent.

Total merchandise trade (including both exports and imports) of the LDCs as a group amounted to 56 per cent of their GDP in 2006. This was up from 44 per cent in 2000. But the share of the LDCs in world merchandise trade continued to remain tiny despite the recent export boom for the group as a whole. In 2006, LDCs generated only 0.8 per cent of world merchandise exports. Although this represented an important increase with respect to the 0.5 per cent of world merchandise exports in 2000, it was mainly driven by fuel exports. Excluding fuels, the share of LDCs' exports in world exports only grew from 0.4 per cent in 2000 to 0.5 per cent in 2006.

Chart 4 shows the evolution of the share in world merchandise exports, by sectors, of the LDCs, the other developing countries (ODCs) and developed countries. Over the period considered, the LDCs increased their world share in fuels, from 2 per cent in 2000 to 2.5 per cent in 2006. Their world share of

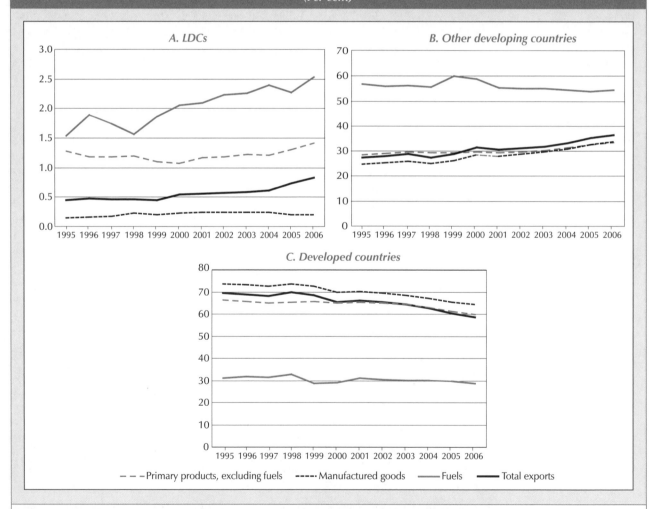

Chart 4. Shares in world merchandise exports of LDCs, ODCs and developed countries, total and by sectors, 1995–2006
(Per cent)

Source: UNCTAD secretariat estimates based on UNCTAD, *Handbook of Statistics 2007*. No data available for Afghanistan, Chad, Liberia, Somalia and Tuvalu.

Note: The world shares do not add up to 100 as the economies in transition are not shown in a separate chart.
For the SITC classification by products, refer to table 8.

primary products excluding fuels also increased over time, from 1.1 per cent in 2000 to 1.4 per cent in 2006. On the other hand, in spite of the rapid increase in manufactured exports of the Asian LDCs, the LDCs' total share in world manufactured exports has stagnated over time at around 0.2 per cent. This is a major area where most LDCs are lagging behind other developing countries. The latter together accounted for 34 per cent of world manufactured exports, up from 27 per cent in 2000.

LDCs' total share in world manufactured exports has stagnated over time at around 0.2 per cent.

E. Trends in external finance[6]

The strong economic performance of the LDCs in recent years has been underpinned not only by record exports, but also by higher levels of long-term capital inflows than during the late 1990s and during the early part of the present decade. These capital inflows include both private capital inflows and official flows, mostly ODA. But whereas exports continued to surge between 2004 and 2006, the increase in long-term capital inflows slowed significantly during this period. International reserves have also increased significantly, reducing the availability of external resources for development and poverty reduction. The slowdown in the increase in long-term capital inflows also occurred along with increasing profit remittances on FDI and interest payment on long-term debt. As a consequence, aggregate net transfers to the LDCs actually declined over the period 2004–2006.[7] This trend has been partially offset by rising workers' remittances to the LDCs, though the developmental impact of remittances versus other type of inflows remains unclear.

Whereas exports continued to surge between 2004 and 2006, the increase in long-term capital inflows slowed significantly during this period.

1. OVERALL PICTURE

Excluding debt forgiveness grants, aggregate net foreign resource flows increased during the period 2000–2003 from an annual average of $17.3 billion to $27 billion in 2004 (table 11). This was more than double the average level of long-term capital inflows of the second half of the 1990s. But the strong upward trend was broken in 2004 and these flows only increased marginally in 2005 and reached $28.9 billion in 2006.

As in earlier years, the increase in aggregate net resource flows to the LDCs from 2004 to 2006 was mainly attributable to grants disbursements, which increased by $2.1 billion over this period (excluding debt forgiveness and technical cooperation), and also FDI inflows, which increased by about $3 billion. But as the more detailed analysis of ODA flows and FDI later in this section shows, both of these types of capital inflows are highly concentrated geographically. Moreover, ODA inflows are not oriented to building up the productive base of the economy which is essential for future growth sustainability.

The increase in aggregate net resource flows to the LDCs from 2004 to 2006 was mainly attributable to grants disbursements and FDI inflows.

Official net resource flows continue to be the main source of long-term capital inflows to the LDCs. Excluding debt forgiveness grants, they accounted for 61 per cent of aggregate net resource flows to the LDCs in 2006, up from an average of 57 per cent during 2000–2003. Grants (excluding technical cooperation and debt forgiveness) constituted 50 per cent of aggregate net resource flows to LDCs in 2006. Portfolio equity flows remained of marginal significance and the main source of debt flows was from multilateral creditors, whose net loans to the LDCs were equivalent to $3.7 billion in 2006, 13 per cent of aggregate net resource flows.

Table 11. Long-term net capital flows and transfers to LDCs, 1995–2006 ($ million)					
	1995–1999	2000–2003	2004	2005	2006
A. Aggregate net foreign resource flows	**13 788**	**20 087**	**30 850**	**29 886**	**59 364**
A'. Aggregate net foreign resource flows, excluding debt forgiveness grants[a]	13 788	17 321	27 087	27 413	28 864
Official net resource flows	9 947	12 692	20 057	20 075	48 131
Official net resource flows, excluding debt forgiveness grants[a]	9 947	9 926	16 295	17 602	17 630
Grants, excluding technical cooperation	7 586	10 018	16 270	16 421	45 134
Official debt flows	2 361	2 675	3 787	3 654	2 997
Bilateral	-208	-545	-191	-590	-668
Multilateral	2 569	3 220	3 978	4 244	3 666
Private net resource flows	3 842	7 395	10 793	9 811	11 233
Foreign direct investment	3 744	7 040	9 331	7 783	12 334
Portfolio equity flows	-6	16	18	55	42
Private debt flows	104	339	1 444	1 973	-1 143
Private, non-guaranteed	-11	123	480	252	467
Private, guaranteed	115	216	964	1 720	-1 610
B. Aggregate net transfers (A–C–D)	**11 260**	**15 328**	**22 960**	**18 650**	**45 171**
B'. Aggregate net transfers, excluding debt forgiveness grants[a] (A'–C–D)	11 260	12 561	19 198	16 177	14 671
C. Interest payments on long-term debt	1 131	1 058	1 276	1 399	1 914
D. Profit remittances on FDI	1 398	3 701	6 613	9 838	12 279
Memo item:					
International reserves[b]	-696	-2 882	-5 517	-2 976	-10 115
International reserves as % GDP	7.1	9.9	11.9	11.1	12.4

Source: UNCTAD secretariat estimates based on World Bank, *Global Development Finance*, online, April 2008.

Note: No data available for Afghanistan, Kiribati, Timor-Leste and Tuvalu.
   a From 2000 onwards. b Year-to-year change. A negative figure implies an increase in international reserves.

An important development in 2006 was that net debt flows from private creditors, which had always been small for the LDCs as a group, turned negative, and the negative net debt flows from bilateral creditors increased. Net debt flows to LDCs from both official and private creditors actually fell by $3.4 billion over the period 2004–2006. Excluding debt forgiveness grants, the slowdown in the increase in aggregate net resource flows to LDCs since 2004 was mainly attributable to the smaller increase in ODA grants to LDCs, as well as the already mentioned decline in net debt flows.

Aggregate net transfers to the LDCs declined by almost one quarter between 2004 and 2006.

The reliance of LDCs on external finance as measured by the ratio of aggregate net resource flows to GDP has declined somewhat in recent years (chart 5). Excluding debt forgiveness grants, this ratio was 8 per cent in 2006, down from 11 per cent in 2004. But the reliance on external finance remains much higher than in other developing countries, for which the average ratio was 3 per cent in 2006. A regional breakdown shows that African and island LDCs were particularly reliant on external finance. Aggregate net resource flows were equivalent to 11 per cent of GDP in African LDCs and 12 per cent of GDP in island LDCs in 2006.

Profit remittances on FDI soared and exceeded net FDI inflows in both 2005 and 2006.

A very significant emerging trend during the period 2004–2006 is the fall in aggregate net transfers to the LDCs. Excluding debt forgiveness grants, such transfers declined from $19.2 billion in 2004 to $14.7 billion in 2006 — this is a fall of almost one quarter. Given the high level of dependence of LDCs on external finance, this trend does not bode well for the future if it continues.

The fall in aggregate net transfers is due to a combination of tendencies. However, it is striking that profit remittances on FDI have soared. They almost doubled between 2004 and 2006, from $6.6 billion to $12.4 billion. Interest payments on long-term debt also rose. The increase in interest payments on long-term debt and profit remittances is such that for the LDCs group as a whole, the

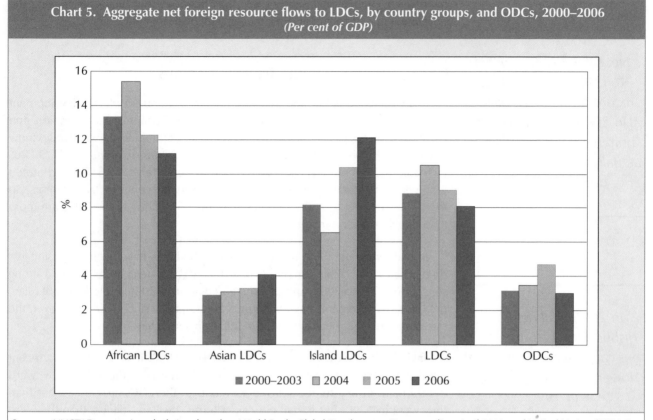

Chart 5. Aggregate net foreign resource flows to LDCs, by country groups, and ODCs, 2000–2006
(Per cent of GDP)

Source: UNCTAD secretariat calculations based on World Bank, *Global Development Finance*, online, April 2008; and United Nations/DESA Statistics Division for GDP.

sum of these outflows was almost equivalent to ODA grants (excluding technical cooperation and debt forgiveness) to LDCs in 2006. Moreover, profit remittances on FDI actually exceeded net FDI inflows in 2005 and were more or less equal to them in 2006.

The rise in profit remittances was apparent between 2000 and 2004, but did not lead to declining aggregate net transfers to the LDCs because long-term capital inflows were rising sharply over this period, driven by increased aid inflows. However, with a pause in the sharp upswing of capital inflows, and also the rise in interest payments in spite of debt relief, aggregate net transfers have fallen significantly.

Finally, an important emerging trend in the LDCs is that international reserves have increased markedly (table 11). According to available data, international reserves reached a record level of $43 billion in 2006, up from $15 billion in 2000. International reserves increased by 17 per cent per annum between 2000 and 2004, and at an accelerated rate of 20 per cent per annum from 2004 to 2006. In 2006, the international reserves of the LDCs as a group were equivalent to 12.4 per cent of GDP, up from an annual average of 7.1 per cent during 1995–1999.

These trends mirror those in other developing countries. However, whilst the increase in international reserves in other developing countries has been prompted by the objective of avoiding the financial crises which were such a significant feature of the 1990s, the increase in such reserves in the LDCs is more associated with macro-economic advice and conditionality and as a buffer against aid volatility (see chapter 3 of this Report). The right level of international reserves for the LDCs, which face volatility of official flows more than volatility of private flows, is a complex issue. However, the build-up in international reserves means that the availability of external financial resources for promoting economic development and poverty reduction has been less than it could have been. The

International reserves increased from from $15 billion in 2000 to a record level of $43 billion in 2006.

The increase in such reserves in the LDCs is associated with macro-economic advice, conditionality and aid volatility.

increase in international reserves has thus been another factor attenuating the developmental impact of increased capital inflows in recent years.

2. TRENDS IN AID FLOWS

It is possible to get a more detailed picture of trends in official development assistance from the data of the Organisation for Economic Co-operation and Development (OECD)/Development Assistance Committee (DAC). These show that net ODA disbursements to the LDCs from all donors reporting to OECD/DAC increased to a record level of $28.1 billion in 2006 (table 12).[8] This constituted 26.7 per cent of total ODA disbursed to all developing countries by all donors, up from 25.3 per cent in 2000. In nominal terms, aid inflows to the LDCs are more than double the level in 2000.

Net ODA disbursements to LDCs increased to a record level of $28 billion in 2006, but the recent nominal doubling of aid is actually reversing the 1990s downward trend.

In real terms, net ODA disbursements to the LDCs have been increasing less dramatically. Real disbursements actually reached a plateau in 2003 after a strong surge from 1999 to 2003, and only increased again in 2006. Excluding debt relief, net ODA disbursements have been increasing steadily since 1999. However, the rate of increase has been slower from 2003 onward (chart 6).

In 2006, real net ODA disbursements to the LDCs per capita were 17 per cent lower than they had been in 1990.

Taking a long-term view which goes back to 1990, it is clear that the recent nominal doubling of aid to the LDCs is actually reversing the 1990s downward trend in aid. In real terms, aid disbursements to the LDCs are now higher than they were in 1990. But in real per capita terms, they are still less than the 1990 level. Indeed, in 2006, real net ODA disbursements to the LDCs per capita stood at $35, which was 17 per cent lower than it had been in 1990.

(a) Geographical distribution of aid amongst the LDCs

Aid constituted 9.3 per cent of GDP in the African LDCs compared with 4.8 per cent of GDP in the Asian LDCs (or 2.7 excluding Afghanistan).

A regional comparison shows that, in 2006, 74 per cent of aid inflows went to the African LDCs, which was roughly the same proportion as in 2000. Indicators of the economic importance of aid show that the African LDCs are much more aid-dependent than the Asian LDCs. In 2006, aid constituted 9.3 per cent of GDP in African LDCs, compared with 4.8 per cent of GDP in the Asian LDCs (or 2.7 per cent if Afghanistan is excluded). Moreover, in 2006, aid inflows per capita to the African LDCs were double those to the Asian LDCs ($43 versus $20). But it is also clear that the island LDCs as a group are the most aid dependent of all LDCs. Although aid flowing to the island LDCs has been decreasing over time, in 2006 it still was equivalent to $181.9 per capita and 17 per cent of GDP.

Within these overall regional patterns, there are significant differences amongst the LDCs in terms of ODA trends. In 2006, 17 LDCs experienced a decrease in

Table 12. Net ODA disbursements to LDCs from all donors[a], by country groups, 2000–2006									
($ million, per cent, $ per capita)									
	$ million			% of GDP			$ per capita		
	2000	*2005*	*2006*	*2000*	*2005*	*2006*	*2000*	*2005*	*2006*
LDCs	**12 621.4**	**25 882.0**	**28 181.3**	**7.2**	**8.5**	**7.9**	**18.6**	**33.8**	**35.9**
Excluding Afghanistan	12 485.4	23 129.9	25 181.5	7.1	7.8	7.2	19.0	31.2	33.2
Excluding Afghanistan, Dem. Rep. of the Congo and Sudan	12 087.9	19 470.3	21 067.6	7.6	7.4	6.9	21.0	30.1	31.9
African LDCs	9 061.7	18 651.7	20 915.7	9.8	10.2	9.3	22.2	39.8	43.5
Asian LDCs	2 790.0	5 920.2	6 155.0	3.9	5.1	4.8	10.4	20.1	20.5
Excluding Afghanistan	2 654.0	3 168.1	3 155.3	3.5	2.8	2.7	10.8	11.7	11.5
Island LDCs	561.3	799.1	709.3	21.5	21.2	17.0	172.3	210.6	181.9

Source: UNCTAD secretariat calculations based on OECD/DAC, online data, March 2008, and United Nations/DESA Statistics Division for GDP and population.

a This includes multilateral and bilateral aid from OECD/DAC member countries and non-DAC members reporting to OECD/DAC (see endnote 8).

Chart 6. Real net ODA disbursements to LDCs including and excluding debt relief, 1990–2006
(Million of 2006 dollars, $ per capita)

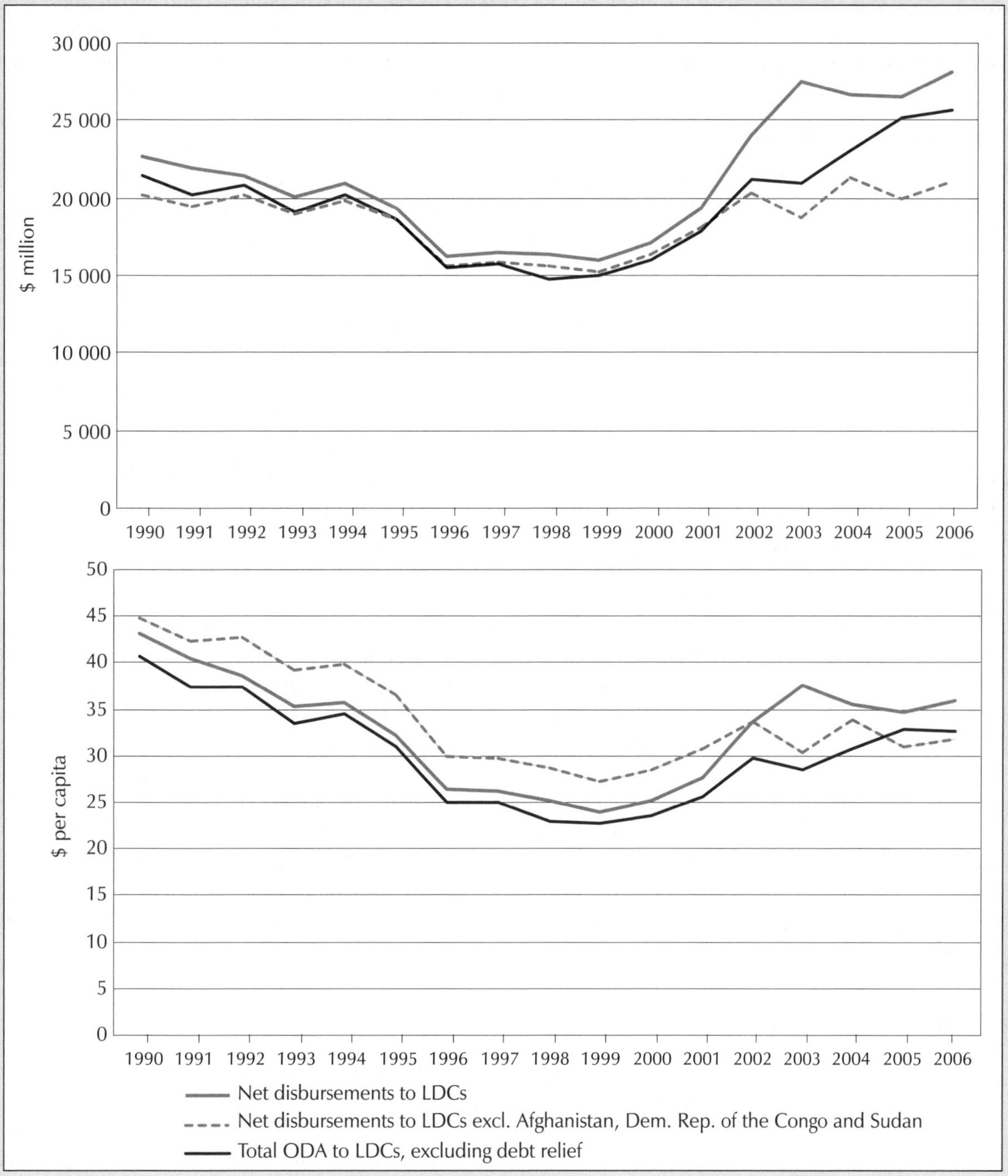

Net disbursements to LDCs
Net disbursements to LDCs excl. Afghanistan, Dem. Rep. of the Congo and Sudan
Total ODA to LDCs, excluding debt relief

Source: UNCTAD secretariat calculations based on OECD/DAC online, April 2008; and United Nations/DESA Statistics Division for population.

real aid disbursements, while for 10 LDCs aid disbursements increased by 20 per cent or above. Of the 17 LDCs receiving less aid, 15 had increasing aid in the period 2000–2004. This is indicative of the instability in aid disbursements which Governments have to cope with.

One important feature of the geographical distribution of aid is the high level of concentration in ODA inflows for a few countries. In 2006, Afghanistan, the Democratic Republic of the Congo and Sudan accounted for one fourth of total net ODA disbursements going to the LDCs, while the Democratic Republic of the Congo and Sudan accounted for one fourth of total nominal ODA going to the African LDCs.

Three countries accounted for one fourth of total net ODA disbursements to the LDCs in 2006.

A second important feature is that from 2000 to 2006, real ODA disbursements flowed into post-conflict and post-disaster countries at a faster pace than in the other LDCs. ODA inflows to Afghanistan, Burundi, the Democratic Republic of the Congo, Ethiopia, Haiti, Liberia, Maldives, Somalia and Sudan, most of whom are in this category, increased at an average annual growth rate of 10 per cent or higher during this period. These nine countries, which in 2000 were receiving only 13.6 per cent of total ODA disbursements, received 38.1 per cent in 2006. During the same period, 2000–2006, ODA inflows into 19 LDCs were declining. In 2000, these countries (Angola, Bangladesh, Cambodia, Comoros, Eritrea, Gambia, Guinea, Guinea-Bissau, Kiribati, Lao People's Democratic Republic, Mauritania, Mozambique, Nepal, Samoa, Sao Tome and Principe, Timor-Leste, Togo, Vanuatu and Yemen) were receiving 37.4 per cent of total disbursements; by 2006, they only received 20.4 per cent (table 13).

A third important feature of the geographical distribution of aid is that ODA disbursements seem to be inversely correlated with export performance. On the one hand, net ODA inflows to oil-exporting and manufactures-exporting LDCs, which are achieving stronger export growth, are falling. On the other hand, aid per capita to the LDCs which specialize in exporting agricultural commodities, where export growth has been sluggish, increased in real terms, from an annual average of $36 per capita in 2000 to $67 per capita in 2006. Aid as a share of GDP also rose for this group of countries over the same dates, from 13.5 per cent to 21.4 per cent. This has certainly helped the LDCs which specialize in agricultural exports to sustain their growth in spite of weak trade performance. But the fact that decisions on aid allocation, may be responding to the trade performance of countries suggests that LDCs' development partners are not facilitating mutual synergies between aid and trade in supporting development in the LDCs. In effect, a good export performance is associated with falling aid receipts rather than aid and trade working together to reinforce development.

Finally, it is worth noting that a large number of the very high-growth LDCs in 2006 received significant aid inflows in the previous year. Of the 19 very high-growth LDCs in 2006, aid constituted over 10 per cent of GDP in 14 of them in 2005. The only exceptions to this pattern were two oil exporters (Angola and Sudan), two successful Asian manufactures exporters (Bangladesh and Cambodia) and Myanmar.

(b) Type and purpose of aid

The type and purpose of aid has a strong influence on the impact of aid inflows on long-term growth. Table 14 shows a breakdown of ODA disbursements into grants and loans, and also indicates the allocation of grants between technical cooperation, debt relief, humanitarian aid and development food aid. In interpreting the table, it is important to note that the bulk of debt forgiveness grants in 2006 was due to the writing-off of ODA principal, in effect converting past ODA loans into grants. In order to avoid double counting, such ODA principal forgiveness is included as an offsetting entry for debt relief under net ODA loans. It is not new aid and, as is standard practice, is thus not included in the analysis of the composition of aid below. The remainder of debt forgiveness grants includes ODA interest forgiven and also the use of ODA for other debt forgiveness. It is this sum which is counted here as new aid and is used in estimating the share of aid going to debt relief.

With this in view, four important features are clear from the table:

(a) The proportion of net ODA disbursements provided in the form of grants continues to rise. It constituted 87 per cent of net ODA disbursements in 2006, up from an annual average of 80 per cent during 2000–2004;

ODA disbursements flowed into post-conflict and post-disaster countries at a faster pace than in the other LDCs.

ODA disbursements seem to be inversely correlated with export performance negating synergies between aid and trade in supporting development.

A large number of the very high-growth LDCs in 2006 received significant aid inflows in the previous year.

The proportion of net ODA disbursements provided in the form of grants rose to 87 per cent in 2006.

Table 13. Real net ODA disbursements to LDCs, by country and country groups, 2000–2006

	Average annual growth rates			$ per capita			% of real GDP		
	2000–2004	2004–2005	2005–2006	2000	2005	2006	2000	2005	2006
Countries with real GDP growth > 6% in 2006									
Maldives	0.5	178.5	-50.8	83.7	260.6	126.2	3.9	10.3	4.1
Angola	27.6	-62.8	-62.1	29.3	27.1	10.0	2.0	1.3	0.4
Mauritania	-11.2	6.5	-6.4	109.9	66.2	60.3	18.4	10.5	8.6
Sudan	41.3	79.1	8.9	9.0	49.7	52.9	1.7	7.4	7.1
Afghanistan	82.1	23.7	5.9	9.2	109.8	111.7	5.1	40.2	38.4
Ethiopia	17.5	3.1	-0.8	13.0	24.2	23.4	10.4	16.8	15.1
Sierra Leone	4.5	-4.9	4.4	54.4	61.6	62.6	29.5	22.6	21.5
Mozambique	-0.1	0.7	23.2	66.4	62.2	75.0	27.4	19.2	21.8
Malawi	-1.8	12.2	12.4	49.8	43.7	47.8	31.4	27.8	28.8
Bhutan	2.5	13.2	4.5	126.8	140.7	144.4	12.2	10.7	10.3
Lao People's Democratic Republic	-3.5	8.4	21.7	63.8	52.2	62.5	15.8	10.3	11.7
Cambodia	0.4	9.6	-3.0	38.7	38.7	36.9	12.4	8.7	7.9
Liberia	31.1	6.1	12.9	28.4	67.6	73.4	12.6	42.4	44.7
Myanmar	0.5	14.6	0.2	2.6	3.0	3.0	1.8	1.2	1.1
Bangladesh	1.0	-7.7	-11.3	10.6	8.7	7.6	3.0	2.1	1.7
Democratic Republic of the Congo	99.5	-1.8	9.4	4.9	31.1	33.0	4.2	25.7	26.4
Uganda	1.9	-3.8	28.0	45.3	40.7	50.4	16.2	12.8	15.4
Burundi	26.8	-1.4	10.8	19.1	46.5	49.5	17.7	45.8	47.9
Zambia	4.9	-18.8	48.5	102.2	81.5	118.7	18.4	12.8	17.9
Countries with real GDP growth between 3% and 6% in 2006									
United Republic of Tanzania	7.7	-17.3	19.9	38.9	38.5	45.0	14.6	11.8	13.3
Burkina Faso	6.9	6.9	24.7	39.3	48.9	59.1	11.7	12.6	14.9
Gambia	-2.6	8.7	19.3	45.9	37.9	44.0	16.6	13.3	15.0
Sao Tome and Principe	-9.8	-6.6	-34.4	356.6	209.0	134.9	84.9	44.9	27.9
Cape Verde	6.5	10.7	-17.3	287.9	319.9	258.4	17.0	16.5	12.9
Guinea	3.7	-28.3	-19.3	23.8	22.1	17.5	7.8	6.8	5.2
Solomon Islands	3.5	51.5	1.6	246.0	419.6	416.1	29.4	53.0	51.3
Madagascar	27.5	-28.2	-19.2	25.6	49.0	38.5	8.8	17.3	13.4
Guinea-Bissau	-1.4	0.5	1.0	84.6	49.5	48.6	38.2	26.3	25.4
Mali	6.2	19.9	15.1	48.3	60.2	67.2	12.0	12.7	14.0
Djibouti	-5.9	17.2	49.9	125.9	94.9	139.8	15.0	10.8	15.6
Togo	-7.4	25.2	-7.5	17.4	13.3	11.9	4.9	3.9	3.5
Senegal	11.7	-36.4	19.8	55.3	57.1	66.7	8.3	7.8	9.0
Samoa	-7.3	35.8	9.3	212.9	239.1	259.1	11.0	10.5	11.1
Yemen	-13.2	30.8	-17.5	18.7	15.9	12.8	2.6	2.1	1.7
Benin	2.3	-12.2	5.6	45.7	40.8	41.8	9.3	7.9	8.1
Niger	19.0	-7.3	-23.5	25.0	38.5	28.5	10.7	15.7	11.6
Vanuatu	-10.7	-0.9	22.5	335.3	183.3	219.0	18.7	11.4	13.5
Central African Republic	-1.0	-14.8	36.0	24.5	22.8	30.5	6.8	7.2	9.5
Rwanda	1.7	14.9	-0.3	53.6	61.8	60.2	27.2	27.4	26.5
Countries with real GDP growth < 3% in 2006									
Chad	14.3	13.8	-27.4	20.9	37.7	26.5	6.0	6.5	4.6
Somalia	7.1	13.9	59.8	20.4	28.9	44.9	7.1	10.2	16.0
Haiti	1.7	86.2	11.8	30.0	53.9	59.3	6.3	12.6	13.7
Eritrea	1.8	30.4	-64.6	64.0	78.4	26.8	29.7	36.6	12.7
Nepal	-1.8	-2.6	18.4	19.6	15.7	18.2	7.4	5.7	6.6
Lesotho	14.6	-29.9	2.2	28.1	34.6	35.1	4.2	4.7	4.7
Comoros	-4.0	-4.3	18.8	38.5	31.2	36.1	7.9	6.5	7.6
Tuvalu	1.5	6.5	76.3	587.1	860.1	1 509.6	31.6	36.1	62.9
Kiribati	-3.4	59.4	..	266.6	302.6	..	34.9	37.3	..
Equatorial Guinea	0.4	26.2	-32.9	76.7	79.5	52.1	1.5	0.5	0.4
Timor-Leste	-16.1	10.0	11.2	410.3	173.1	184.5	100.5	52.8	59.7
LDCs by export specialization									
Oil	14.4	7.4	-8.2	21.2	37.4	33.5	2.8	3.7	3.1
Agricultural	15.9	11.7	13.7	35.9	61.1	67.2	13.5	20.1	21.4
Mineral	19.1	-4.1	14.6	33.5	44.4	49.5	14.3	16.9	18.2
Manufactures	0.9	4.9	-0.8	15.1	14.4	14.0	4.3	3.5	3.3
Services	8.5	-0.1	0.8	28.3	35.6	35.0	14.4	15.5	14.6
Mixed	13.0	-24.6	0.7	18.4	23.4	23.1	6.9	6.9	6.5

Source: UNCTAD secretariat calculations based on OECD/DAC online, March 2008, and United Nations/DESA Statistics Division for population and GDP.

Note: Real GDP figures have been re-based to 2005 using an implicit GDP deflator. Country ranking as in table 2.

Table 14. Net ODA disbursements from all donors to LDCs, by aid type, 2000–2006

(Million 2006 dollars)

	2000–2004	2005	2006
ODA total net	22 919.2	26 588.9	28 181.3
ODA grants, total	19 172.0	23 825.3	52 707.9
Of which:			
Technical cooperation	4 119.5	5 151.2	5 438.6
Debt forgiveness grants	3 508.3	2 461.3	30 500.5
Of which:			
ODA principal forgiven	694.7	1 449.0	28 267.2
Other	2 813.5	1 012.4	2 233.4
Humanitarian aid	2 266.7	4 114.7	3 555.9
Development food aid	719.7	679.1	587.6
ODA loans total net	3 747.2	2 763.7	-24 526.6
Of which:			
Net loans[a]	4 437.0	4 212.8	3 740.6
Offsetting entry for debt relief	-694.7	-1 449.0	-28 267.2

Source: UNCTAD secretariat calculations based on OECD/DAC online, April 2008.

a Represents the difference between loans extended and loans received.

Only 58 per cent of ODA disbursements were available as financial resources for development projects and programmes within the LDCs.

(b) Technical cooperation grants amounted to almost a fifth of net ODA disbursements to LDCs in 2006;

(c) Humanitarian aid and food aid are also important components of aid to LDCs. They together accounted for as much as 18 per cent of net ODA disbursements in 2005 and 15 per cent in 2006; and

(d) Debt relief was a lower share of net ODA disbursements in 2005 and 2006 than in the period 2000–2004, falling to 8 per cent in 2006.[9]

Together, grants for technical cooperation, debt relief (excluding ODA principal forgiveness), humanitarian aid and food aid absorbed 42 per cent of net ODA disbursements in 2006. This was around the same share as during 2000–2004. But it meant that only 58 per cent of ODA disbursements were available as financial resources for development projects and programmes within the LDCs. In 2006, this was equivalent to $16.4 billion out of net ODA disbursements of $28.2 billion.

Multilateral and bilateral aid commitments are increasingly concentrated on social infrastructure and services.

It is possible to get an idea of the trends in the sectoral distribution of aid using OECD/DAC data on ODA commitments. These clearly show that multilateral and bilateral aid commitments are increasingly concentrated on social infrastructure and services. ODA commitments to social infrastructure and services constituted 42 per cent of net ODA disbursements to the LDCs in 2006, up from an average of 34 per cent during the period 2000–2004 and 31 per cent in the second half of the 1990s. In 2006, the share of aid going to education, health, population programmes, water supply and sanitation, Government and civil society all were higher than during the period 2000–2004. This reflects the impact of the focus on Millennium Development Goals (MDGs) as well as the concern to improve governance.

The share of aid committed to economic infrastructure and production sectors (including multisector) constituted just 25 per cent of total ODA commitments to LDCs in 2006.

In contrast, aid to build productive sectors and economic infrastructure has continued to receive less priority. The share of aid committed to economic infrastructure and production sectors (including multisector) constituted just 25 per cent of total ODA commitments to the LDCs in 2006. This was similar to the level during the period 2000–2004. Despite all the rhetoric of a renewed interest in economic infrastructure, the share of aid committed to transport and storage and energy was less in 2006 than in 2000–2004. The share committed to agriculture (including forestry and fishing) and industry (including mining and construction) also declined over that period. The share of aid committed to economic infrastructure and production sectors was also much lower than during 1995–1999, when it was 38 per cent. Aid commitments to improve economic infrastructure decreased from 18 per cent of total commitments to the LDCs in 1995–1999 to 12 per cent in 2006. Commitments to transport and storage infrastructure decreased from 11 per cent of total commitments to the LDCs in 1995–1999 to 6 per cent in 2006, and disbursements to energy-related sectors shrank from 5 per cent to 2 per cent in 2006 (table 15). Earlier estimates in the *Least Developed Countries Report 2006* showed that economic infrastructure and production sectors constituted as much as 48 per cent of total aid commitments during 1992–1994 (UNCTAD, 2006: 16–20).

It is impossible to get a clear picture of the sectoral composition of aid disbursements before 2002, owing to data unreliability. However, the recent data show that the share of aid disbursements to economic infrastructure and production sectors is even lower than the commitments data indicate. In 2006, just 19 per cent of net ODA disbursements to the LDCs went to economic infrastructure and production sectors.

To conclude, it is apparent that the upsurge in aid to the LDCs since 1999 has been associated with a major shift away from production sectors and economic infrastructure to social infrastructure and services. The support to sectors that could best facilitate the economic capability-building process in the LDCs has been drastically downsized in relative terms. The increased share of aid going to social sectors reflects donors' approach to poverty reduction. But poverty reduction depends on both private incomes and public services. The focus on improving and extending public services in health and education is certainly important. But sustainable poverty reduction also requires the expansion of employment

The support to sectors that could best facilitate the economic capability-building process in the LDCs has been drastically downsized in relative terms.

Table 15. Total sectoral allocation of nominal ODA disbursements and commitments to LDCs, bilateral and multilateral, 1995–2006
(Per cent)

	Commitments				Disbursements	
	1995–1999	2000–2004	2005	2006	2005	2006
Total	100.0	100.0	100.0	100.0	100.0	100.0
Social infrastructure and services	31.0	33.7	35.0	42.3	36.4	41.0
Education	7.7	8.3	6.8	9.4	7.5	8.0
Health	6.6	5.1	8.0	7.4	6.4	7.7
Water supply and sanitation	5.2	3.9	2.9	5.6	2.3	2.6
Government and civil society	6.7	9.4	10.4	11.5	10.2	13.5
Commodity aid	12.9	15.2	12.5	13.1	10.0	11.4
Action relating to debt	10.0	13.6	11.0	7.4	11.6	11.2
Emergency assistance and reconstruction	7.2	10.5	14.8	11.6	18.2	15.6
Sub-total	61.4	73.7	73.3	74.4	76.2	79.2
Economic infrastructure	18.7	12.9	12.5	11.6	8.8	8.9
Transport and storage	10.8	7.0	8.1	6.3	5.6	5.0
Communications	0.7	0.4	0.2	0.4	0.3	0.2
Energy	5.1	3.3	3.0	1.9	1.7	0.9
Banking and financial services	1.0	0.9	0.5	0.8	0.4	0.4
Production sectors	10.7	6.6	6.7	6.8	4.1	4.0
Multisector	8.1	5.9	5.8	6.4	4.2	5.7
Sub-total	37.3	24.7	25.0	24.7	17.1	18.6

Source: UNCTAD secretariat calculations based on OECD, *Creditor Reporting System,* online, May 2008.

Note: The shares do not add up to 100 as aid in support to NGOs, administrative costs of donors, support for refugees and unallocated aid are not shown.

and income-earning opportunities, and for this, aid for productive sectors and economic infrastructure is vital (see chapter 2 of this Report).

(c) Progress on aid commitments of the Brussels Programme of Action

The aid effort of all DAC member countries, as measured by the ODA to gross national income (GNI) ratio, stood at 0.09 per cent in 2006, up from 0.08 per cent in 2005 and 0.06 per cent in 2002. In 2006, more DAC member countries met the Brussels Programme of Action targets for aid. Eight DAC members (Luxembourg, Norway, Denmark, Sweden, Ireland, Netherlands, Belgium and United Kingdom) met the programme target of making net ODA disbursements equal to or higher than 0.15 per cent of their GNI, whilst six of these countries (the above countries except Belgium and United Kingdom) met the higher target of 0.20 per cent of GNI. Belgium and the United Kingdom both managed to increase their net ODA disbursements as shares of GNI between 2005 and 2006. Of the countries that did not meet the target, Spain and Italy decreased their net aid disbursements as a share of GNI between 2005 and 2006.

Among the DAC member countries, the United States is still the largest donor to the LDCs in absolute terms. In 2006, its net aid disbursements amounted to $6.4 billion, which accounted for 21.8 per cent of total DAC donors' aid. With $3.8 billion, the United Kingdom became the second largest donor to the LDCs in absolute terms in 2006, up from $2.7 billion in 2005. The European Union as a whole provided aid disbursements equivalent to $16.3 billion in 2006, 56 per cent of total DAC disbursements to the LDCs in 2006 and 28 per cent of their total aid (table 16).

One of the important commitments of the Brussels Programme of Action was the 2001 DAC Recommendation on Untying Official Development Assistance to the Least Developed Countries. OECD progress reports on the implementation of this recommendation indicate that substantial progress has been made in implementing the recommendation. However, progress with expanding the coverage of the recommendation to include food aid and technical cooperation has been limited (OECD, 2008a). Moreover, a large proportion of contracts financed by untied aid are still going to donor country suppliers (OECD, 2008b). This is mainly because of practical constraints on local firms' participation in donor-funded procurement, including weak supply capacities and limited knowledge of international tendering. There are still gaps in data availability which limit analysis of progress on untying. But OECD/DAC statistics on the tying status of bilateral aid show that over 90 per cent of aid commitments (excluding technical cooperation and administrative costs) were untied in 2006 in all DAC members except Austria, where the untying ratio stood at 89.5 per cent, Greece, Italy, Portugal and Spain (OECD 2008b: 187). No data were reported to the DAC statistical reporting system for Australia and the United States, though the United States Millennium Challenge Account provides aid in untied form.

3. TRENDS IN FOREIGN DIRECT INVESTMENT

UNCTAD data show that FDI inflows into the LDCs fell in 2004 and 2005 after reaching a peak of $10.6 billion, but subsequently jumped again to $9.4 billion in 2006. Despite this recovery, the share of world FDI inflows going to the LDCs fell from 1.9 per cent in 2003 to 0.7 per cent in 2006 (chart 7). In contrast, 27 per cent of world FDI inflows went to developing countries.

Of the total FDI inflows to the LDCs, 88 per cent went to African LDCs in 2006. There has been little change in this proportion since 2000–2003 (table

Sustainable poverty reduction requires the expansion of employment and income-earning opportunities, and for this aid for productive sectors and economic infrastructure is vital.

The European Union provided 56 per cent of total of total DAC disbursements to LDCs in 2006 and the United States 21.8 per cent.

Over 90 per cent of aid commitment were untied in 2006, but a large proportion of contracts financed by untied aid are still going to donor country suppliers.

Table 16. Net aid disbursements from OECD/DAC member countries to LDCs[a], 2005–2006
($ million, per cent)

	$ million		% of total DAC		LDCs' share (%)		% of donor's GNI	
	2005	*2006*	*2005*	*2006*	*2005*	*2006*	*2005*	*2006*
Countries meeting the Brussels aid target in 2006								
Luxembourg	105.6	123.4	0.4	0.4	42.4	45.2	0.35	0.38
Norway	1 029.1	1 128.6	4.2	3.8	38.6	40.1	0.35	0.34
Denmark	814.1	878.4	3.3	3.0	41.6	42.1	0.31	0.32
Sweden	1 100.6	1 151.7	4.5	3.9	34.0	30.1	0.31	0.30
Ireland	364.7	524.5	1.5	1.8	53.8	54.6	0.21	0.28
Netherlands	1 657.5	1 394.7	6.7	4.7	33.2	26.3	0.26	0.21
Belgium	609.3	729.3	2.5	2.5	31.5	37.5	0.16	0.18
United Kingdom	2 709.2	3 827.2	11.0	13.0	25.8	31.4	0.12	0.16
Countries not meeting the Brussels aid target in 2006								
Finland	245.4	296.0	1.0	1.0	28.2	38.3	0.13	0.14
Portugal	209.7	240.2	0.9	0.8	56.9	62.2	0.12	0.13
France	2 392.3	2 624.0	9.7	8.9	23.6	23.6	0.11	0.12
Switzerland	404.9	452.6	1.6	1.5	23.6	28.5	0.10	0.11
Canada	1 047.8	1 243.5	4.3	4.2	30.0	36.4	0.09	0.10
Germany	1 883.5	2 641.7	7.7	9.0	19.0	25.7	0.07	0.09
Austria	244.6	252.3	1.0	0.9	15.7	17.0	0.08	0.08
New Zealand	69.6	74.0	0.3	0.3	27.6	31.6	0.07	0.08
Japan	2 326.1	3 340.1	9.5	11.3	18.5	31.1	0.05	0.07
Spain	816.6	767.0	3.3	2.6	27.6	21.7	0.07	0.06
Australia	419.0	451.5	1.7	1.5	25.6	21.6	0.06	0.06
United States	4 661.1	6 416.2	18.9	21.8	18.2	27.9	0.04	0.05
Italy	1 406.8	789.0	5.7	2.7	29.2	22.5	0.08	0.04
Greece	79.5	102.7	0.3	0.3	21.3	25.2	0.03	0.03
Total DAC	**24 597.2**	**29 448.5**	**100.0**	**100.0**	**24.0**	**28.9**	**0.08**	**0.09**
Of which: EU-15	14 639.5	16 342.0	59.5	55.5	26.8	28.2	0.11	0.12

Source: UNCTAD secretariat calculations based on OECD/DAC, online, March 2008, and United Nations/DESA Statistics Division for GNI.

Note: The countries have been ranked according to their aid as share of donor's GNI for the year 2006.
  a   Includes imputed multilateral flows.

17). However, the share of FDI inflows to the LDCs going to oil-exporting LDCs actually declined between 2004 and 2006, from 56 per cent to 47 per cent of total LDC inflows over that period. This reflects the volatility of FDI inflows for natural resource extraction. In contrast, the share of the LDCs' FDI inflows going to manufacture-exporting LDCs increased considerably over this period, mainly due to increasing FDI inflows to Bangladesh, Cambodia and Lao People's Democratic Republic.

The share of FDI inflows to LDCs going to oil-exporting LDCs declined between 2004 and 2006, while that going to manufactures-exporting LDCs increased.

The five LDCs receiving the greatest volume of FDI inflows in 2006 are three oil-exporting LDCs, namely Sudan, Equatorial Guinea and Chad, followed by two manufactured-good exporting LDCs, namely Bangladesh and Cambodia. Together, these five countries received 75 per cent of the total FDI inflows to the LDCs in 2006.

FDI inflows were equivalent to about 15 per cent of gross fixed capital formation of LDCs as a group in 2006. But it constitutes around 23 per cent of such capital formation in the African and island LDCs. Moreover, it accounted for over 50 per cent of gross fixed capital formation in 2006 in seven LDCs — Burundi, Chad, Djibouti, Guinea-Bissau, Gambia, Sudan and Vanuatu. Given the low levels of investment by private domestic investors, FDI contributes a significant share of gross fixed capital formation even in LDCs where FDI inflows are small.

FDI inflows were equivalent to 23 per cent of gross fixed capital formation in the African and island LDCs.

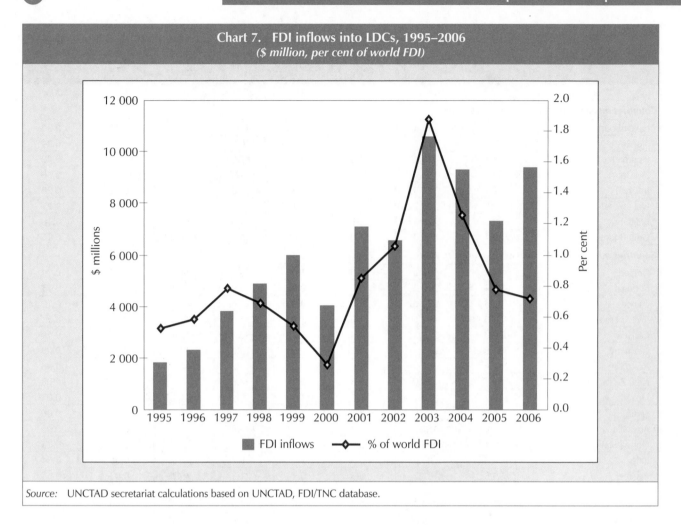

Chart 7. FDI inflows into LDCs, 1995–2006
($ million, per cent of world FDI)

Source: UNCTAD secretariat calculations based on UNCTAD, FDI/TNC database.

The increasing flow of FDI into some LDCs which specialize in manufactures exports is a positive trend, as FDI in extractive industries has tended to be focused on enclaves with weak linkages to the rest of the economy and few spillovers into it. However, the balance of FDI inflows into the LDCs in the form of cross-border mergers and acquisitions on the one hand, and in the form of greenfield investment on the other hand, has also shifted considerably in recent years. Cross-border mergers and acquisitions accounted for 42 per cent of FDI inflows into the LDCs in 2006, up from 15 per cent over 2000–2003. Whilst the ownership changes associated with cross-border mergers and acquisitions can have a beneficial impact on productivity and links along value chains, their overall developmental impact, particularly on the development of productive capacities, may be less than FDI which involves greenfield investment.

Cross-border mergers and acquisitions accounted for 42 per cent of FDI inflows into the LDCs in 2006. Their overall developmental impact may be less than that of greenfield FDI.

4. Trends in workers' remittances

Workers' remittances to the LDCs continuously increased over the recent period. The precise situation is difficult to gauge, owing to the fact that many of these private transfers were unrecorded. The available evidence shows that, in nominal terms, workers' remittances reached a record of $13.2 billion in 2006, compared with average annual remittances of $4.8 billion during 1995–1999 (table 18). As a share of GNI, workers' remittances to the LDCs increased from 2.9 per cent during 1995–1999 to 3.8 per cent in 2004, and have stayed around that level since. This was about twice as important as they were in other developing countries, where workers' remittances constituted 1.7 per cent of GNI on average.

Workers' remittances to the LDCs increased from 2.9 per cent of GNI during 1995–1999 to 3.8 per cent in 2004, twice as much as in other developing countries.

Table 17. FDI inflows into LDCs, by country and by country groups, 2000–2006
($ million, per cent of GFCF)

	$ million				% of GFCF			
	2000–2003	*2004*	*2005*	*2006*	*2000–2003*	*2004*	*2005*	*2006*
Sudan	757	1 511	2 305	3 541	29.2	39.7	44.8	65.3
Equatorial Guinea	705	1 651	1 873	1 656	56.0	91.5	125.7	105.5
Chad	553	495	613	700	56.1	32.5	50.5	54.7
Bangladesh	403	460	692	625	3.4	3.0	4.6	3.9
Cambodia	132	131	381	483	17.8	11.4	32.3	38.9
United Republic of Tanzania	325	331	448	377	18.3	13.6	15.8	12.6
Ethiopia	301	545	221	364	24.4	30.1	8.9	13.9
Zambia	112	364	380	350	14.7	27.3	21.2	18.5
Uganda	180	222	257	307	15.1	12.2	12.7	14.3
Burundi	3	0	1	290	4.2	0.0	0.5	127.8
Madagascar	83	95	86	230	11.5	11.3	7.0	17.8
Lao People's Dem. Republic	26	17	28	187	9.1	3.9	5.8	37.1
Mali	145	101	224	185	22.7	9.5	19.1	15.0
Dem. Rep. of the Congo	95	10	-79	180	17.9	0.8	-9.5	20.5
Haiti	9	6	26	160	2.3	1.3	5.2	30.4
Mozambique	270	245	108	154	28.4	19.6	7.1	9.6
Myanmar	221	251	236	143	22.8	22.3	18.8	10.8
Cape Verde	19	20	76	122	10.1	6.5	22.4	26.7
Djibouti	6	39	22	108	8.0	28.0	23.2	107.6
Guinea	31	98	102	108	6.8	18.1	23.2	23.3
Somalia	0	-5	24	96	0.0	-1.1	5.4	20.6
Gambia	34	49	45	70	46.0	49.5	38.2	56.8
Benin	40	64	53	63	8.2	8.1	6.3	7.1
Vanuatu	17	18	13	61	32.5	27.9	19.8	86.2
Senegal	56	77	45	58	5.4	4.2	2.3	2.8
Lesotho	32	53	57	57	8.6	9.6	11.0	10.4
Togo	48	59	77	57	17.1	13.6	17.3	12.1
Sierra Leone	17	61	59	43	31.5	29.1	24.4	16.9
Guinea-Bissau	2	2	9	42	5.0	3.1	14.3	65.7
Malawi	28	22	27	30	13.3	12.5	13.5	14.4
Burkina Faso	18	14	34	26	2.4	1.2	2.7	1.9
Central African Republic	7	25	29	24	11.5	45.3	39.8	32.0
Niger	11	20	30	20	4.1	4.3	5.6	3.6
Solomon Islands	-3	6	19	19	-6.1	10.9	32.6	31.3
Rwanda	5	8	11	15	1.6	2.1	2.3	3.1
Maldives	13	15	9	14	7.3	5.4	4.6	6.4
Kiribati	16	19	1	12	73.8	65.6	2.5	36.7
Bhutan	1	3	9	6	0.3	0.8	1.4	0.9
Eritrea	20	-8	-3	4	11.1	-3.7	-1.2	1.4
Timor-Leste	30	3	0	3	20.1	3.0	0.1	2.4
Afghanistan	1	1	4	2	0.1	0.1	0.3	0.2
Comoros	1	1	1	1	2.6	2.1	2.8	2.2
Tuvalu	6	0	0	0	74.7	0.3	-0.1	0.1
Sao Tome and Principe	3	-2	-1	0	16.3	-7.3	-2.4	-1.7
Samoa	0	2	-4	-2	-0.1	5.5	-7.6	-3.3
Mauritania	72	392	864	-3	52.5	220.4	392.8	-1.5
Nepal	7	0	2	-7	0.7	0.0	0.2	-0.4
Liberia	101	237	-479	-82	269.6	355.4	-951.7	-153.9
Yemen	62	144	-302	-385	3.3	5.3	-11.5	-13.9
Angola	2 050	1 449	-1 303	-1 140	139.4	80.4	-40.1	-33.3
LDCs	**7 064**	**9 320**	**7 326**	**9 375**	**17.9**	**17.5**	**12.5**	**15.1**
African LDCs and Haiti	*6 141*	*8 251*	*6 238*	*8 212*	*29.7*	*28.1*	*18.2*	*22.6*
Asian LDCs	*875*	*1 010*	*1 050*	*1 058*	*4.9*	*4.3*	*4.4*	*4.2*
Island LDCs	*48*	*59*	*39*	*104*	*14.0*	*12.6*	*9.1*	*23.3*

Source: UNCTAD secretariat calculations based on UNCTAD FDI/TNC database.

Note: Negative FDI flows indicate that one of the three components of FDIs (equity capital, reinvested earnings, intra-company loans) is negative and not offset by the positive amounts of the remaining components.
Countries have been ranked in decreasing order according the value of FDI inflows in 2006.

Table 18. Workers' remittances to LDCs, by country, and to the other developing countries, 1995–2006

($ million, per cent)

	$ million				% of GNI				% of LDC remittances
	1995–1999	2000–2002	2005	2006	1995–1999	2000–2002	2005	2006	2006
Countries with remittances >10% of GNI									
Haiti	253.2	626.0	985.0	985.0	8.1	18.8	24.7	21.3	7.4
Lesotho	349.8	218.3	327.0	327.0	28.1	23.0	18.6	18.7	2.5
Nepal	60.2	312.0	1 211.0	1 211.0	1.3	5.5	15.9	16.2	9.1
Cape Verde	87.0	84.3	137.0	137.0	16.9	14.9	15.2	12.6	1.0
Gambia	11.6	9.3	58.0	58.0	2.9	2.5	13.0	12.0	0.4
Countries with remittances between 5% and 10% of GNI									
Guinea-Bissau	2.0	10.0	28.0	28.0	0.9	5.2	9.7	9.2	0.2
Uganda	233.0	333.7	450.0	845.0	3.8	5.8	5.0	8.7	6.4
Togo	22.4	69.0	179.0	179.0	1.5	5.0	8.2	7.9	1.4
Bangladesh	1 497.2	2 310.3	4 314.0	5 485.0	3.2	4.4	6.3	7.6	41.4
Yemen	1 161.6	1 292.3	1 283.0	1 283.0	18.9	13.8	8.8	7.5	9.7
Senegal	155.8	294.0	633.0	633.0	3.0	5.9	7.3	6.8	4.8
Kiribati	7.0	7.0	7.0	7.0	7.9	7.6	5.4	5.4	0.1
Countries with remittances < 5% of GNI									
Cambodia	52.4	131.3	200.0	200.0	1.6	3.5	3.4	3.2	1.5
Vanuatu	22.8	32.0	11.0	11.0	9.6	13.7	3.3	3.2	0.1
Mali	97.0	99.3	177.0	177.0	3.5	3.5	3.4	3.1	1.3
Comoros	12.0	12.0	12.0	12.0	5.4	5.4	3.2	3.0	0.1
Sudan	468.0	786.3	1 016.0	1 016.0	4.7	6.4	4.3	3.0	7.7
Sao Tome and Principe	1.0	1.0	1.0	1.0	2.5	2.2	1.9	1.8	0.0
Niger	12.6	18.3	60.0	60.0	0.7	1.0	1.9	1.8	0.5
Guinea	2.8	8.3	42.0	42.0	0.1	0.3	1.5	1.5	0.3
Benin	84.8	82.4	63.0	63.0	3.7	3.3	1.5	1.4	0.5
Ethiopia	22.6	34.7	174.0	172.0	0.3	0.5	1.5	1.3	1.3
Mozambique	53.6	44.0	57.0	80.0	1.7	1.2	0.9	1.2	0.6
Rwanda	8.2	7.3	21.0	21.0	0.5	0.4	1.0	0.9	0.2
Myanmar	125.4	109.0	117.0	117.0	1.7	1.3	1.0	0.9	0.9
Burkina Faso	80.0	55.7	50.0	50.0	2.6	2.0	0.9	0.8	0.4
Solomon Islands	2.0	2.0	2.0	2.0	0.5	0.6	0.5	0.5	0.0
Samoa	43.8	30.3	1.0	1.0	19.6	12.8	0.3	0.2	0.0
Maldives	2.2	2.0	2.0	2.0	0.5	0.3	0.3	0.2	0.0
Madagascar	12.0	13.0	11.0	11.0	0.3	0.3	0.2	0.2	0.1
United Rep. of Tanzania	8.2	11.7	16.0	16.0	0.1	0.1	0.1	0.1	0.1
Sierra Leone	19.4	12.0	2.0	2.0	1.9	1.1	0.1	0.1	0.0
Mauritania	3.2	2.0	2.0	2.0	0.3	0.2	0.1	0.1	0.0
Malawi	1.0	1.0	1.0	1.0	0.1	0.1	0.0	0.0	0.0
Lao People's Dem. Rep.	31.8	1.0	1.0	1.0	2.0	0.1	0.0	0.0	0.0
Djibouti	12.0	..	..	..	2.4	..	..	..	..
Eritrea	3.5	3.0	..	..	0.4	0.4	..	..	..
LDCs	**4 823.4**	**7 064.1**	**11 651.0**	**13 238.0**	**2.9**	**3.8**	**4.0**	**3.9**	**100.0**
ODCs	**62 552.0**	**90 998.5**	**171 971.0**	**189 090.4**	**1.1**	**1.4**	**1.8**	**1.7**	**..**

Source: UNCTAD secretariat calculations based on World Bank, *Global Development Finance*, online, March 2008 and United Nations/DESA Statistics Division for GNI.

Note: Data not available for Afghanistan, Angola, Bhutan, Burundi, Central African Republic, Chad, Dem. Rep. of the Congo, Equatorial Guinea, Liberia, Somalia, Timor-Leste and Zambia.
Countries have been ranked according to their share of remittances in GDP (from the highest to the lowest) for the year 2006.

For the LDCs as a group, the scale of workers' remittances is such that they were 40 per cent higher than FDI inflows to the LDCs in 2006. This is a significant feature of the form of integration of the LDCs into the global economy. Whilst they are marginalized from private international capital markets, their integration through international labour markets is increasingly important for their economies.

As with FDI inflows, workers' remittances are highly concentrated in a few LDCs. Workers' remittances going to the Asian LDCs account for over 60 per cent of the total workers' remittances flowing to the LDCs. Bangladesh alone received 41 per cent of the total workers' remittances to the LDCs in 2006, and Yemen and Nepal together received a further 19 per cent. Workers' remittances accounted for more than 5 per cent of GNI in almost a third of the LDCs for which data were available (12 of the 38 countries). Moreover, they accounted for over 10 per cent of GNI in five countries — Haiti, Lesotho, Nepal, Cape Verde and Gambia. This highlights the high degree of dependency on workers' remittances that characterizes the economies of some LDCs. However, there are some LDCs for which workers' remittances do not play a significant role. For almost a third of LDCs for which data are available (once again 12 countries), workers' remittances accounted for less than 1 per cent of their GNI in 2006 (table 18).

Workers' remittances accounted for over 10 per cent of GNI in Haiti, Lesotho, Nepal, Cape Verde and Gambia.

The increasing dependence of LDCs on workers' remittances can be seen as offsetting the decline in aggregate net transfers discussed earlier in this chapter. However, the developmental, rather than poverty-alleviating, impact of workers' remittances remains to be proven, and the big differences amongst LDCs in terms of their significance implies that their role varies considerably amongst the countries in the group. They should not be seen as a substitute for long-term capital inflows and deliberate policies are required to enhance the development impact of remittances.

Workers' remittances are not a substitute for long-term capital inflows and deliberate policies are required to enhance their development impact.

F. Trends in external debt

The LDCs' total debt stock reached a record level of $163 billion in 2004, after three successive annual increases. As shown in previous *Least Developed Countries Reports*, most of these increases was attributable to an expansion in the multilateral debt stock. But the total debt stock fell moderately in 2005, to $157.4 billion, and more dramatically in 2006, to $131.5 billion.

Country data show that the debt stock fell in 17 out of 46 LDCs, including 16 of the 33 African LDCs for which data are available. African LDCs still accounted for 65 per cent of the total debt stock of the LDCs in 2006, but this was down from a high of 77 per cent in 1998. Both multilateral and bilateral debt fell between 2004 and 2006, but the former declined at a faster rate. Multilateral debt constituted 58 per cent of total LDC debt stock in 2004, but fell to 53 per cent in 2006.

In contrast to other developing countries, most of the debt of LDCs is owed to official creditors. In 2006, for example, debt arising from concessional loans constituted 73 per cent of the total debt stock in LDCs, as against 22 per cent in other developing countries. As a consequence, trends in debt stock are strongly influenced by official debt relief initiatives.

LDCs' total debt stock has fallen dramatically, reflecting the continued implementation of the Enhanced HIPC Initiative and also the adoption of the MDRI in 2006.

The recent debt stock trends in LDCs reflect, in particular, the continued implementation of the Enhanced Heavily Indebted Poor Countries (HIPC) Initiative and also the adoption of the MDRI in 2006. The latter Initiative goes further than the former by providing additional resources for the cancellation of multilateral debt contracted with the World Bank, International Monetary Fund (IMF) and African Development Bank for countries which have passed the completion point of the HIPC Initiative (see box 3). As a result of the MDRI, grants for ODA principal forgiveness increased from $1.5 billion in 2005 to $28.2 billion in 2006. In effect, such debt forgiveness retrospectively converted earlier concessional loans into grants (see subsection E.2 above). Of this sum ($26.9 billion), 97 per cent was related to the MDRI.

Box 3. The Multilateral Debt Relief Initiative

In 2005, the G-8 countries, during the summit in Gleneagles, proposed to cancel the entirety of the debt of the eligible heavily indebted poor countries (HIPCs) contracted with the International Development Association (IDA) — the concessional facility agency of the World Bank — before 1 January 2004, and with the IMF and the African Development Fund before 1 January 2005. The Inter-American Development Bank joined in 2007. Such an initiative led to the creation of the MDRI, whose objective is "to provide additional support to HIPCs to reach the MDGs while ensuring that the financing capacity of the IFIs is preserved" (World Bank, 2006b: 2). The MDRI became effective on 1 January 2006 for the IMF and the African Development Fund, and 1 July for the IDA.

Analysts have shown that, to preserve the IFI financing capacity, the MDRI applies the criterion of additionality in aid, which implies that debt cancellation will involve additional financing by the international community.

The MDRI is particularly important for LDCs because multilateral debt accounts for such a high level of their overall debt stock. LDCs which have received debt cancellation under MRDI have experienced major reductions in indicators of their debt burden. But the additionality of the debt relief is not as great as it might be because of how it works. The way in which the World Bank debt cancellation works is that if a country paid IDA debt service of $10 million, this would be cut by $10 million, but at the same time the country would receive an equivalent cut of $10 million in new finance from IDA. Donors would then compensate IDA for this $10 million write-off and this money would be distributed amongst all IDA-only countries according to their score on the Country Policy and Institutional Assessment index. For example, the country getting the debt relief might get $5 million back from this process. Analysis suggests that this considerably reduces the additionality of the MRDI (Hurley, 2007).

Countries become eligible for debt relief under the MDRI once they reach the HIPC completion point. This requires that they meet all of the following conditions:

(a) Satisfactory macroeconomic performance under an IMF poverty reduction and growth facility programme;

(b) Satisfactory progress in implementing a poverty reduction strategy; and

(c) An adequate public expenditure management system that meets minimum standards for governance and transparency in the use of public resources (World Bank, 2006a; World Bank, 2006b).

Furthermore, all post-HIPC completion point countries "will be required to maintain reasonable governance standards" (World Bank, 2006b: 6), as well as high standards for transparency and public expenditure management. MDRI recipient countries are subject to a three- to five-year assessment of their public financial management.

Source: Djoufelkit-Cottenet (2007), World Bank (2006a) and World Bank (2006b).

Table 19 shows the status of LDCs within the HIPC Initiative as of October 2007. Sixteen LDCs had reached completion point and were receiving irrevocable debt relief under the terms of the initiative. Of these countries, four LDCs — Malawi, Rwanda, Sierra Leone and Zambia — reached the HIPC completion point in 2005 or 2006 and Sao Tome and Principe in 2007. All of these 16 LDCs

Table 19. LDCs covered by the HIPC initiative
(As of October 2007)

Completion point (date of completion point)	Decision point (date of decision point)	Pre-decision point
Benin (2003)	Afghanistan (2007)	Comoros
Burkina Faso (2002)	Burundi (2005)	Eritrea
Ethiopia (2004)	Central African Rep. (2007)	Liberia
Madagascar (2004)	Chad (2001)	Nepal
Mali (2003)	Dem. Rep. of the Congo (2003)	Somalia
Malawi (2006)	Gambia (2000)	Sudan
Mauritania (2002)	Guinea (2000)	Togo
Mozambique (2001)	Guinea-Bissau (2000)	
Niger (2004)	Haiti (2006)	
Rwanda (2005)		
Sao Tome & Principe (2007)		
Senegal (2004)		
Sierra Leone (2006)		
Uganda (2000)		
United Rep. of Tanzania (2001)		
Zambia (2005)		

Source: World Bank.

have also benefited from MDRI debt cancellation. This has radically changed their debt burden and opens a window of opportunity.

Progress in debt relief remains slow for the other LDCs eligible for HIPC. Various conditions have to be met, both to reach the HIPC decision point and to proceed to completion point. The time between decision point and completion point has been increasing since the early batch of countries reached decision-point before end–2003. For the five LDCs which reached completion point in 2005 and 2006, the time between completion point and decision point was 4.3 years for Zambia and Rwanda, 4.7 years for Sierra Leone, 5.7 years for Malawi and 6.2 years for Sao Tome et Principe (IMF and World Bank, 2007: figure 1). Of the nine LDCs that have passed the decision point, but not reached completion point, four reached decision point in 2001 and one in 2003. These countries — Chad, Gambia, Guinea, Guinea-Bissau and Democratic Republic of the Congo — have all experienced interruptions in their IMF-supported programmes and have faced difficulties in meeting completion-point triggers. But Burundi, Chad, Democratic Republic of the Congo, Gambia, Guinea-Bissau and Guinea adopted a full Poverty Reduction Strategy Paper (PRSP) by the end of 2007, a condition for reaching the completion point.

Sixteen LDCs had reached completion point and were receiving irrevocable debt relief under the HIPC Initiative.

Of the seven LDCs which have been judged eligible for HIPC according to their debt sustainability criteria, but have not reached decision-point, four — Liberia, Somalia, Sudan and Togo — have large arrears to multilateral institutions and have not been able to engage in IMF- and IDA-supported programmes, three years' participation in which is a condition for reaching the decision point.[10] Moreover, other LDCs which are not judged eligible for the HIPC Initiative remain outside the debt forgiveness process.

For the LDCs as a group, the overall debt burden fell sharply from 86 per cent of GNI in 2000–2002 to 42 per cent in 2006.

The effect of these initiatives on the debt burden for the LDCs as a group and for individual LDCs is shown in table 20. For the LDCs as a group, there has been a major reduction in the overall debt burden since 2000–2002. LDCs' debt stocks fell from 86 per cent of GNI during 2000–2002 to 58 per cent in 2005, and then dropped further to 42 per cent in 2006. But within the overall trend, some countries are doing much better than others.

From the table, it is apparent that there has been a major improvement in the debt situation in those LDCs which have received debt cancellation under the MDRI. The debt stock in these countries was cut from $54.7 billion in 2005 to $25.7 billion in 2006. In almost all of these countries, the total debt stock as a share of GNI was halved between 2005 and 2006. Nevertheless, the debt service payments of these countries actually increased, from $1.1 billion in 2005 to $1.3 billion in 2006. As a ratio of exports of goods, services and workers' remittances, debt service payment for this group of countries fell marginally, from an average of 6.8 per cent in 2005 to 5.7 per cent in 2006.

LDCs which are not judged eligible for the HIPC Initiative remain outside the debt forgiveness process.

At the other end of the spectrum, it is clear that the debt burden remains very high in most of those LDCs which are eligible for HIPC debt relief, but have not reached the decision point or the completion point. The debt stock as a share of GNI is increasing in nine LDCs, including five LDCs which have reached the HIPC decision point — Burundi, Chad, Guinea, Guinea-Bissau and Haiti. Moreover, of the 45 LDCs for which data are available, the debt stock in 2006 was higher than the GNI in nine LDCs and over 50 per cent of GNI in a further 13 countries.

The debt stock in 2006 was higher than the GNI in nine LDCs and over 50 per cent of GNI in a further 13 countries.

Despite overall improvement in the debt situation, the debt burden for the LDCs as a group remains much higher than in other developing countries — on average 42 per cent of GNI in 2006 in the LDCs, compared with 26 per cent in other developing countries. Moreover, although the debt relief provides important breathing space for those countries which have reached HIPC completion point

Table 20. Selected indicators on debt burden in LDCs, by country, and ODCs, 2000–2006
(Per cent)

	Total debt stock as % GNI			Total debt stock as % exports[a]			Total debt service as % exports[a]		
	2000–2002	2005	2006	2000–2002	2005	2006	2000–2002	2005	2006
Coutnries with debt > 100% of GNI in 2006									
Liberia	524.5	619.2	541.3	..	..	..	..	..	..
Sao Tome and Principe*	..	..	295.8	1 819.5	1 540.6	..	25.5	..	..
Guinea-Bissau	374.7	239.6	241.2	959.3	564.2	..	22.0	..	..
Samoa	87.8	172.2	205.5	..	527.4	693.5	..	17.3	19.9
Burundi	172.1	170.3	179.7	2 493.8	1 440.9	1518.9	49.4	41.5	40.4
Gambia	136.8	150.0	145.2	..	459.1	..	..	11.8	12.4
Dem. Rep. of the Congo	253.1	156.8	137.5	..	484.0	487.0	..	..	..
Sierra Leone*	174.6	141.8	101.0	1 526.3	704.9	..	63.1	9.3	9.6
Guinea	109.8	98.9	100.2	419.8	..	..	16.0	..	..
Countries with debt between 50% and 100% of GNI in 2006									
Lao People's Dem. Republic	155.5	103.0	99.5	542.0	..	..	8.5	..	..
Togo	108.5	81.7	82.8	278.2	175.7	..	4.9	1.6	..
Bhutan	56.6	79.7	77.1	209.5	202.7	..	0.0	..	..
Eritrea	64.8	76.5	74.1	349.3	..	..	3.1	..	..
Comoros	112.8	75.6	70.3	538.7	423.6	410.7	..	..	..
Central African Republic	93.3	74.3	68.7	..	..	..	..	..	..
Mauritania*	201.7	121.8	58.9	570.5	346.3	..	..	..	..
Sudan	140.4	71.0	56.0	629.1	309.9	278.5	7.9	6.4	4.1
Djibouti	48.3	53.1	55.3	..	..	..	5.1	4.6	6.4
Cape Verde	65.7	56.3	54.7	162.9	125.9	108.3	6.6	6.5	4.7
Maldives	39.9	50.7	52.3	50.1	75.7	65.6	4.5	7.0	4.9
Solomon Islands	64.2	55.8	51.3	188.2	116.2	97.9	8.3	8.9	2.0
Cambodia	71.6	59.1	51.1	123.0	83.1	68.0	1.1	0.7	0.6
Countries with debt < 50% of GNI in 2006									
Mozambique*	159.4	72.3	47.1	584.3	216.2	114.7	9.1	3.8	1.9
Nepal	50.0	42.4	41.4	201.3	132.1	144.5	6.7	4.7	5.1
Malawi*	154.9	156.6	38.8	598.6	585.7	121.6	10.1	..	..
Lesotho	68.2	37.7	37.6	118.9	64.2	60.8	11.6	7.4	4.0
Haiti	33.5	30.3	34.7	114.6	83.5	88.2	3.0	3.2	3.2
Chad	73.1	33.6	34.2	488.5	51.7	..	..	..	..
United Rep. Tanzania*	71.8	62.8	33.3	395.4	262.8	130.3	8.9	4.3	3.4
Yemen	57.9	35.3	31.6	99.3	66.5	60.7	4.3	2.6	2.4
Bangladesh	32.6	30.0	31.4	171.9	127.4	110.5	7.8	5.4	3.7
Madagascar*	106.8	69.9	26.8	355.1	177.5	65.2	6.5	5.7	..
Angola	110.0	41.0	24.5	113.3	48.5	..	23.5	10.7	12.8
Vanuatu	34.6	24.0	24.1	47.8	45.8	42.5	1.1	1.3	1.7
Mali*	111.3	59.6	23.4	304.5	190.6	..	9.3	5.6	..
Zambia*	182.6	79.0	23.3	619.1	253.4	56.6	19.6	10.9	3.6
Senegal*	83.4	47.9	22.4	222.4	130.1	..	12.8	..	..
Niger*	86.5	58.3	22.1	488.1	307.0	..	7.6	5.9	..
Burkina Faso*	52.1	35.9	18.3	473.1	348.3	..	13.3	..	..
Ethiopia*	77.1	55.2	17.5	564.9	299.7	97.1	12.9	4.1	6.8
Benin*	69.2	43.5	17.5	268.2	222.1	..	9.5	7.4	..
Rwanda*	77.0	71.6	16.9	960.9	551.5	145.9	15.3	8.1	9.6
Uganda*	65.6	51.7	13.8	371.7	243.1	55.5	6.2	9.3	4.8
Equatorial Guinea	26.5	7.6	5.3	14.9	3.8	..	..	..	..
Myanmar	..	..	..	208.7	158.2	..	3.5	2.5	1.7
LDCs	**86.2**	**58.2**	**42.4**	**261.4**	**140.2**	**92.0**	**8.8**	**6.0**	**6.3**
ODCs	**37.3**	**27.6**	**25.7**	**94.8**	**61.5**	**56.2**	**16.6**	**12.8**	**13.2**

Source: UNCTAD secretariat calculations based on World Bank, *Global Development Finance*, online data, March 2008.

Note: Data not available for Afghanistan, Kiribati, Somalia, Timor-Leste and Tuvalu.
Group averages have been weighted according to the denominator and are subject to data availability.

a Includes all exports of goods and services, and workers' remittances.

* HIPC countries that have reached the completion point.

and have received debt cancellation under the MDRI, the long-term sustainability of debt remains a problem.

This point was clearly made by the evaluation update of the HIPC Initiative, which was undertaken before the MDRI. It pointed out the limits of debt relief as a means of assuring debt sustainability and showed that "debt ratios have deteriorated significantly since completion point in the majority of countries, with the increase in debt ratios correlated quite closely to the length of time since completion point" (IEG, 2006: 21). Before the MDRI, Burkina Faso, Ethiopia, Rwanda and Uganda were all expected to be unable to maintain debt sustainability above the HIPC thresholds in the nine years following completion point. Moreover, the evaluation found that the forecasts underlying predictions of future debt sustainability for these countries, and also those which were expected to remain below the sustainability threshold, continued to be based on forecasts of GDP and export growth which were far higher than historical trends.

Despite debt forgiveness, the debt burden for the LDCs (42 per cent of GNI) is much higher than in other developing countries (26 per cent).

The MDRI has improved this situation. However, according to the latest IMF-World Bank assessment of debt sustainability, debt distress is low in only seven post-completion point LDCs. It is moderate in Benin, Burkina Faso, Ethiopia, Malawi, Mauritania, Niger, Sao Tome and Principe and Sierra Leone, and remains high for Rwanda (IMF and World Bank, 2007). A simulation of the first 16 post-completion point HIPCs to participate in the MDRI also finds that, in the absence of MDRI, the net present value of the external debt stock of these countries is expected to rise from 74 per cent of exports in 2004 to 236 per cent by the end of 2015. With the MDRI, it is expected to rise much less, but — at 176 per cent of exports — still be unsustainable according to HIPC thresholds in 2015 (Nwachukwu, 2008).

Debt ratios have deteriorated significantly since completion point in the majority of countries.

These results reflect the assumption of the simulation. They depend on estimates of the grant component of new disbursements, as well as forecasts of domestic savings and foreign exchange receipts. However, the model also clarifies the key conditions for growth with external debt. These are that: (a) the projected marginal savings rate exceeds the fixed investment ratio required to achieve the target rate of growth; (b) the anticipated rate of growth of imports should not exceed the growth of exports; (c) the estimated growth of external debt and interest payments should not continuously exceed the real growth rate of exports; and (d) the marginal product of foreign capital should be greater than the cost of international borrowing.

Unless there is a shift in emphasis to building up the productive base of poor economies and to promote structural change, they will become unsustainably indebted again.

The key to ensuring debt sustainability is to develop productive capacities. The problem with the current situation and the focus on social sectors is that this is not being done. On the contrary, the MDGs build up fiscal obligations for Governments without generating at the same time a sound fiscal base to raise these revenues. Similarly, they increase import requirements without building up export receipts to pay for these imports. Unless there is a shift in emphasis to building up the productive base of poor economies and promote structural change to reduce vulnerability to commodity price shocks, they will inevitably become unsustainably indebted again.

G. Conclusion

LDCs as a group achieved the strongest growth performance in 30 years in 2005 and 2006, underpinned by record levels of exports and capital inflows.

This chapter has shown that the LDCs as a group achieved the strongest growth performance in 30 years in 2005 and 2006, with the average growth rate surpassing the Brussels Programme of Action growth target (7 per cent) in those years. Improvement in their growth performance was underpinned by a record of level of exports, which was particularly associated with high commodity prices for oil and minerals, and record levels of capital inflows, particularly aid. In nominal terms, the value of merchandise exports from the LDCs rose by some 80 per cent between 2004 and 2006, reaching $99 billion in the latter year. Annual long-term capital inflows excluding debt forgiveness grants were about 60 per cent higher than during 2000–2003, and double the level of the second half of the 1990s. Net aid disbursements reached the record level of $28.1 billion in 2006. Moreover, 16 LDCs also received significant debt relief in 2006, with $26.9 of ODA principal being forgiven for 16 of them through the MDRI. FDI inflows recovered to $9.4 billion in 2006, slightly down from the peak in 2003, whilst recorded migrant remittances reached the record level of $13.2 billion in 2006.

Growth sustainability is questionable due to: (a) feeble structural transformation; (b) rising trade deficits; and (c) falling net transfers.

Although the high GDP growth rates are very positive, the sustainability of the growth performance in 2005 and 2006 remains questionable. The recent growth surge is generally not associated with a structural transition in which the share of manufactures in total output is growing (except for most Asian LDCs). In fact, as compared with 10 years earlier, half of the LDCs have experienced de-industrialization, reflected in a declining share of manufacturing in GDP. The level of domestic savings continues to be low in many LDCs, including good performers. In 2006, only one third of the LDCs had gross domestic savings rates above 15 per cent and 15 LDCs had negative domestic savings rates, meaning that they were relying on foreign savings not only to finance domestic investment, but also their domestic consumption.

Even though LDCs' GDP growth rate outperformed other developing countries, their average per capita income has continued to diverge.

Other sources of vulnerability arise from: (a) increasing merchandise trade deficits in many LDCs, particularly those which specialize in exporting agricultural commodities; and (b) increasing pressures from rising oil and food prices. Oil and food together constituted 31 per cent of LDC merchandise imports by value in 2006. Another particularly disturbing trend is that aggregate net transfers (excluding debt forgiveness grants) to the LDCs declined by one third from 2004 to 2006. This was due to a slowdown in the rate of increase in capital inflows into the LDCs, as donors slowed the pace of aid scale-up and FDI inflows briefly faltered, at the same time as profit remittances soared and interest payments on loans also rose. This decline makes the LDCs particularly vulnerable to external prices shocks and interruptions to the commodity boom.

Dependence on commodities has increased since 2000, along with the growth acceleration.

The chapter also shows that there is a high degree of variation amongst the LDCs. Not all of them are experiencing rapid growth. In 2006, the real GDP grew by 6 per cent or more in 19 LDCs, by between 3 and 6 per cent in 20 LDCs, by less than 3 per cent in 9 LDCs, and declined in two LDCs. Most LDCs have high population growth rates (2.5 per cent per annum on average) and as a result, even though they outperformed other developing countries in terms of GDP growth rates, their average per capita income has continued to diverge from other developing countries in all years since 2000 except 2005. GDP per capita stagnated or declined in nine LDCs in 2006 and grew by less than 1 per cent in almost one third of the LDCs.

For the LDCs as a group, dependence on commodities has increased since 2000, along with the growth acceleration. Primary commodities increased from 59 per cent of total merchandise exports in 2000-2002 to 77 per cent in 2005-2006. But within this overall pattern, there is considerable divergence between the African, Asian and island LDCs. The Asian LDCs continue to diversify their economies away from commodities towards manufacturing, while the African LDCs increase dependence on primary commodities. The Island LDCs remain primarily dependent on service exports which also exhibit high levels of volatility.

The widening regional divergence between the African and Asian LDCs in terms of the form of their integration into the global economy is evident in their different export structure. In the 2005-2006 period, 92 per cent of all exports from the African LDCs consisted of primary commodities, including fuels, while in the Asian LDCs, this figure was 44 per cent. This type of specialization renders the Asian LDCs much less vulnerable to external fluctuations. Some of them have also achieved high rates of export growth based on manufactures. However, the share of medium and high tech manufactured exports originating from the LDCs remains very small (8.4 per cent). The slowness of the process of export upgrading in the Asian LDCs remains an issue of concern.

Accelerated growth underpinned by fluctuating prices of primary commodities cannot guarantee sustainable growth in an increasingly open, globalized economy. Those LDCs which have diversified into low-skill manufactures face increasing global competition. The LDCs must build economic resilience through diversification and technological upgrading. Otherwise, their growth will remain fragile. Investment in productive sectors remains the key lever for robust growth that increases domestic savings, creates employment opportunities and stimulates local demand. Only then can external risks be mitigated and growth made more sustainable.

A virtuous circle of sustained growth can be catalyzed by aid inflows. Even though they are rising, however, aid disbursements remain below donor commitments in the Brussels Programme of Action. Moreover, they are more focused on social sectors and social infrastructure than on increasing investment in economic infrastructure and developing productive sectors. In some LDCs, a good export performance is associated with falling aid receipts rather than aid and trade working together to reinforce development.

With the global economy slowing down and downside risks of the future outlook increasing, the LDCs will face major challenges in the period ahead. This will require renewed efforts to promote not simply accelerated GDP growth, but a type of economic growth which is sustainable. More attention needs to be given to the form of integration into the global economy, rather than the level of integration and the degree of openness *per se*. It is clear from recent experience that there is no automatic relationship between increasing exports, the development of productive capacities and structural change. Increasing dependence on primary commodities and low-skill manufactures has not translated into catch-up growth with other developing countries. More emphasis needs to placed in the future on efforts to develop the productive base of the LDC economies and to address their continuing structural weaknesses.

LDCs must build economic resilience through diversification and technological upgrading.

The LDCs will face major challenges in the period ahead as the global economy slows down and downside risks of the future outlook increase.

There is no automatic relationship between increasing exports and the development of productive capacities and structural change.

Notes

1 The figures in this section are based on data from the United Nations Department of Economic and Social Affairs (DESA) Statistics Division. World Bank data show slightly lower real GDP growth rates for the LDCs as a group — 7 per cent in 2005 and 6.8 per cent in 2006. But these are still the highest growth rates for over 30 years.

2 The Brussels Programme of Action for LDCs was agreed at the end of the Third United Nations Conference for LDCs, which was held in Brussels, Belgium, in May 2001.

3 These estimates are based on sectoral value added as a share of total value added of the economy.

4 For a discussion of the causes of the current upswing in the commodity prices cycle, see IMF, 2008 and UNCTAD, 2008.

5 Under this classification, the "manufactures" category is larger than in the trade classification used elsewhere in this report, as processed foods such as sugar, cheese and vegetables are classified as resource-based manufactures (rather than as commodities).

6 This section draws on three different data sources to identify trends in capital flows: (a) World Bank Global Development Finance Online for the overall picture; (b) Organization for Economic Cooperation and Development (OECD)/Development Assistance Committee (DAC) for aid flows; and (c) UNCTAD for FDI flows. These are not wholly consistent, but together they can provide the best overall picture of what is happening.

7 *Aggregate net resource flows* are the sum of net resource flows on long-term debt (excluding IMF) plus net direct foreign investment, portfolio equity flows and official grants (excluding technical cooperation). Net flows (or net lending or net disbursements) are disbursements minus principal repayments. *Aggregate net transfers* are equal to aggregate net resource flows minus interest payments on long-term loans and foreign direct investment profits. (Source: World Bank, *Global Development Finance*, online, April 2008).

8 This section refers to assistance from DAC member countries and also from a number of non-DAC donors, including Hungary, Iceland, Republic of Korea, Poland, Slovakia, Thailand, Turkey and Arab countries, for which data are also recorded by DAC. There are other donors to LDCs, including China, which is also rapidly expanding its development cooperation programme. The "Beijing Action Plan" of November 2006 calls for a doubling of aid to Africa from 2006 and 2009. Unfortunately, data on aid from China are not published and is therefore excluded from the discussion in this section.

9 This excludes the forgiveness of ODA principal, which is not counted as it has already been recorded as an aid disbursement at an earlier point in time and its inclusion would thus involve double-counting.

10 This condition has been relaxed for Liberia.

References

Djoufelkit-Cottenet, H. (2007). How to lend to African countries after a decade of debt relief? *OECD Policy Insight*, 36: 1–3.

Hurley, G. (2007). Multilateral debt: one step forward, how many back? HIPC & MDRI update, EURODAD, Brussels.

IMF (2008). *World Economic Outlook: Housing and the Business Cycle.* International Monetary Fund, Washington, DC.

IMF and World Bank (2007). The joint World Bank-IMF debt sustainability framework for low-income countries. Factsheet prepared by the staffs of the International Monetary Fund and World Bank, Washington DC.

Lall, S. (2000). The technological structure and performance of developing country manufactured exports: 1985–1998. *Oxford Development Studies*, 28 (3): 337–369.

Nwachukwu, J. (2008). The prospects for foreign debt sustainability in post-completion point countries: Implications of the HIPC-MDRI Framework.

OECD (2008a). Implementing the 2001 DAC recommendation on untying ODA to the LDCs: Comprehensive review, part I. document no. DCD/DAC(2008)13/REV 2, Organisation for Economic Co-operation and Development, Paris.

OECD (2008b). *OECD Journal on Development: Development Co-operation Report 2007.* Organisation for Economic Co-operation and Development, Paris.

United Nations (2001). Brussels Programme of Action for the least developed countries for the decade 2001–2010. United Nations document A/CONF. 191/11, Geneva and New York.

UNCTAD (2004). *The Least Developed Countries Report: Linking International Trade and Poverty Reduction*. United Nations publication, sales no. E.04.II.D.27, Geneva and New York.

UNCTAD (2006). *The Least Developed Countries Report: Developing Productive Capacities.* United Nations publication, sales no. E.06.II.D.9, Geneva and New York.

UNCTAD (2007). *The Least Developed Countries Report: Knowledge, Technological Learning and Innovation for Development.* . United Nations publication, sales no. E.07.II.D.8, Geneva and New York.

UNCTAD (2008). The changing face of commodities in the twenty-first century. Note prepared by the UNCTAD secretariat, UNCTAD 12th Session, Accra, 20–25 April 2008, TD/428, Geneva.

World Bank (2006a). The multilateral debt relief Initiative: Implementation modalities for IDA. International Development Association no. 35768, vol. I, Washington, DC.

World Bank (2006b). Multilateral debt relief Initiative: Country eligibility assessment. International Development Association no. 35768, vol. III, Washington, DC.

World Bank Independent Evaluation Group (2006). Debt relief for the poorest: An evaluation update of the HIPC Initiative. World Bank, Washington, DC.

Trends in Poverty and Progress Towards the MDGs

A. Introduction

It is clear from chapter 1 of this Report that since 2000, many least developed countries (LDCs) have achieved higher rates of economic growth than in the 1990s and even higher growth of exports. There is a widespread perception, however, that this is not translating effectively into poverty reduction and improved human well-being for the 785 million people who now live in LDCs. This chapter assesses the extent to which this is true and identifies some of the policy-related factors which influence the degree to which economic growth is translating into improvements in human well-being.

The chapter shows that the basic feature of poverty in most LDCs is that it is "generalized", that is to say, it is not something which affects a small section of the population. Rather, "a major part of the population lives at or below income levels sufficient to meet their basic needs and the available resources in the economy, even when equally distributed, are barely sufficient to cater for the basic needs of the population on a sustainable basis" (UNCTAD 2002: 40). This Report finds that 75 per cent of people in LDCs subsist on less than $2 a day and that average private consumption per capita per day in 2006 was just 76 cents per day (when estimated using market exchange rates).

Progress in reducing "$1-a-day poverty" (extreme or absolute poverty) and "$2-a-day poverty" ("total poverty" hereafter) in LDCs has been very slow and there has been very little improvement in the rate of progress since the adoption of the Millennium Declaration in 2000. The number of people living on less than $1 a day in LDCs was higher in 2005 than in 2000. The chapter also finds that although a few countries have made great progress in relation to some human development MDGs, particularly primary education and gender equality in education, most LDCs are off track to meet the MDGs on the majority of human development indicators for which data are available. The soaring food prices of 2007 and 2008 will have particularly adverse consequences for the LDCs and they are likely to slow down — and in some countries reverse — not only progress towards reducing hunger but also progress towards poverty reduction and the achievement of other human development goals.

The reasons why high GDP growth in LDCs is not translating very effectively into improvements in human well-being are complex. But the chapter is founded on what Graham Pyatt has called "a structuralist approach to poverty analysis" (UNCTAD, 2002: 192). This approach starts from the insight that household living standards depend primarily on the generation and sustainability of jobs and livelihoods. From this perspective, poverty trends are related to trends in income-generating and employment opportunities, which are in turn related to the changing structure of the economy and its relationship to the rest of the world. Locating livelihoods within the structure of the economy focuses attention on the influence on living standards of such factors as the sectoral and regional structure of the economy, the importance of, and connections between, formal and informal sector activities, the division of value added between capital and

There is a widespread perception that higher rates of economic growth are not translating effectively into poverty reduction and improved human well-being for the 785 million people who now live in LDCs.

75 per cent of people in LDCs subsist on less than $2 a day.

Most LDCs are off track to meet the MDGs on the majority of human development indicators.

labour, and the influence of macroeconomic policies. In this approach, both the level and distribution of living standards are jointly determined through the way in which production is organized. Moreover, the generation and sustainability of livelihoods and the structural dynamics of the economy are related to the form of the integration of the national economy into the global economy through trade, aid, private capital flows and debt dynamics. In this way, international economic relations are intimately linked to national poverty dynamics.

The level and distribution of living standards are jointly determined through the way in which production is organized and through the form of integration of the national economy into the global economy.

Using this structuralist approach, the chapter argues that the weak relationship between economic growth and improvements in human well-being in most LDCs is related to the type of growth which is occurring. The high rates of economic growth in LDCs cannot generally be equated with an inclusive process of development. In most of them, the majority of the population are employed in agriculture but agricultural labour productivity is very low and growing very slowly. As it is difficult to make a living in agriculture, more and more people are seeking work in other sectors of the economy, but remunerative employment opportunities are not being generated quickly enough to meet this growing demand for non-agricultural work.

The weak relationship between economic growth and improvements in human well-being in most LDCs is related to the type of growth which is occurring.

The trends which are occurring are related to policy choices and in particular the development model which has been pursued in most LDCs. This has sought to deepen the integration of the LDCs into the world economy, increase the efficiency of resource allocation and free markets. Global integration is vital for development and poverty reduction in LDCs. However, without the development of productive capacities and associated employment, external integration does not lead to inclusive development. Export-led growth by itself leads to an exclusive pattern of economic growth. The adverse impact of the soaring international food prices illustrates the vulnerability of LDCs following the current approach, underlining the need for a policy change towards inclusive development.

The chapter is organized in five substantive sections. Section B describes trends in average private consumption per capita. This is a very crude initial proxy for living standards which does not address the multidimensionality of poverty and ignores the effects of distribution on living standards. It does, however, provide an initial overview of material living standards in LDCs. Section C deepens the analysis by examining trends in income poverty, presenting the results of a new internationally comparable data set on income poverty in LDCs which uses both household surveys and national accounts data. This section updates and extends the analysis of poverty trends using the international $1-a-day and $2-a-day poverty lines in *The Least Developed Countries Report 2002* (UNCTAD, 2002). Section D discusses some reasons why the growth–poverty relationship is weak. Section E analyses progress towards achieving the human development goals which are part of the Millennium Development Goals (MDGs). It draws on the results of the United Nations system-wide effort to track progress towards the MDGs, presenting an overview of progress towards human development goals in LDCs for which data are available. Section F discusses the impact of rising food prices in 2007–2008 on LDCs and examines the policy implications of the food crisis which many are experiencing. Finally, the conclusion summarizes the major findings.

Without the development of productive capacities and associated employment, external integration does not lead to inclusive development.

B. Trends in private consumption

1. OVERALL TRENDS

If the real GDP of an economy grows at 7.2 per cent per year for 10 years, the value of goods and services produced in that economy should double in real terms. What this means at the household level and for individual lives depends critically on how economic growth translates first, into rising household incomes and consumption expenditure, and second, into improved supply of public services, particularly in education, health, water and sanitation.

Trends in average private consumption per capita, as recorded in the national accounts of all countries, provide a general indication of whether household consumption is rising or falling within a country and at what rate, offering a crude indicator of trends in living standards. However, some caution must be exerted, when analysing this variable. First, the national accounts provide aggregates, from which individual averages can be derived by using population data. They do not, however, provide information on the distribution of private consumption among households or within them. Neither do they — in the case of most LDCs — provide any information about the distribution of consumption among different geographical regions (e.g. rural vs. urban areas) within one country. Second, national accounts estimates of private consumption are, conceptually speaking, not exactly the same as those of household consumption expenditure, as they include spending by other institutions besides households, namely the non-profit institutions serving households. Third, private consumption is calculated as a residual from estimates of other macroeconomic aggregates, after the computation of aggregate output, imports, purchases by firms and Government and so on. It is thus far from an error-free number. Despite these shortcomings, trends in private consumption per capita do provide a crude, initial picture of how overall economic performance translates into changes in material well-being at the household level.

Trends in average private consumption per capita offer a crude indicator of trends in living standards.

Record growth performance of the LDCs has resulted in an increase in real private consumption per capita per day of only 5 cents per day.

Trends in GDP per capita per day and private consumption per capita per day in the LDCs are shown in table 21. The table shows that the record growth performance of the LDCs as a group in 2005 and 2006, with GDP growth exceeding 7 per cent per annum, has resulted in an increase in real private consumption per capita per day of only 5 cents per day ($0.05 in constant 2000 dollars) between 2004 and 2006. This increase has occurred in the LDCs as a group and also in African and Asian LDCs. However, private consumption per capita in island LDCs stagnated over those years, albeit at a higher level.

Table 21. Real GDP, private consumption and domestic resources available for finance, per capita, 1995–2006
(Constant 2000 dollars/day)

	Daily GDP per capita					Daily private consumption per capita					Daily domestic resources available for finance per capita				
	1995	2000	2004	2005	2006	1995	2000	2004	2005	2006	1995	2000	2004	2005	2006
LDCs	0.78	0.89	1.02	1.07	1.13	0.60	0.63	0.71	0.74	0.76	0.18	0.26	0.30	0.33	0.36
African LDCs	0.82	0.91	1.02	1.07	1.13	0.63	0.65	0.73	0.76	0.78	0.19	0.26	0.29	0.31	0.35
Asian LDCs	0.72	0.85	1.00	1.06	1.11	0.55	0.59	0.68	0.70	0.73	0.17	0.26	0.33	0.36	0.38
Island LDCs	1.69	1.87	1.92	1.91	2.00	1.19	1.30	1.33	1.34	1.33	0.50	0.57	0.60	0.58	0.66
Memo item:															
Mineral exporters	0.64	0.62	0.68	0.69	0.72	0.48	0.47	0.50	0.50	0.49	0.15	0.16	0.18	0.20	0.23

Source: UNCTAD secretariat calculations based on data from United Nations/DESA Statistics Division.

Note: Domestic resources available for finance per capita are estimated as the difference between GDP and private consumption per capita.

The growth of private consumption per capita in the LDCs as a group has certainly been much higher since 2000 than in the 1990s (chart 8). But these rates of growth are occurring from a very low base. The level of private consumption per capita remains pitifully low by international standards. In 2006, average daily private consumption per capita in the LDCs as a group was only $0.76. It was slightly higher in African LDCs ($0.78) and slightly lower in Asian LDCs ($0.73). But the island LDCs stand out as having a much higher level of private consumption per capita — $1.33 per day (table 21).

76 cents per day is an abject consumption standard and an increase of 5 cents per day is simply a slight improvement of this abject consumption standard.

These figures are based on market exchange rates rather than the purchasing power parity (PPP) exchange rates used in international comparisons of income and poverty. However, although prices for non-tradable goods and services may be cheaper in LDCs than in other countries, with the opening of their economies, more people in LDCs increasingly depend on imported goods and most local prices are affected by international fuel prices. Daily consumption figures give an indication of the real command of households over resources in an open economy setting where imports represent a rising share of GDP and consumption. From this perspective, 76 cents per day is an abject consumption standard and an increase of 5 cents per day is simply a slight improvement of this abject consumption standard.

The domestic resources available in LDCs to finance public and private investment and to pay to run all public services amounted to 36 cent per person per day.

It is also significant to note that the difference between average GDP per capita in LDCs and private consumption per capita, when measured at market exchange rates, was only 36 cents per person per day in 2006 (table 21). What this means is that the domestic resources which were on average available in LDCs to finance public and private investment, to pay to run all public services including health, education, the provision of water and sanitation and to finance good governance, including the maintenance of a civil service and the enforcement of law and order, amounted to 36 cents per person per day. It is clear therefore that not only are consumption standards very low in LDCs, but there are also very few domestic resources available to finance good governance, to provide the public goods which support the achievement of basic needs, and to invest in creating a better future. Moreover, there is little — if any — surplus to deal with economic shocks.

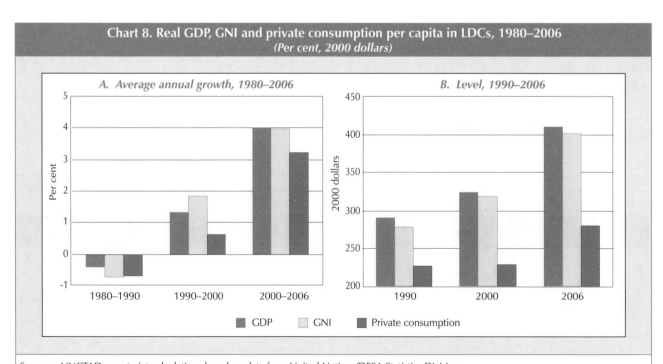

Chart 8. Real GDP, GNI and private consumption per capita in LDCs, 1980–2006
(Per cent, 2000 dollars)

A. *Average annual growth, 1980–2006*

B. *Level, 1990–2006*

GDP　　GNI　　Private consumption

Source:　UNCTAD secretariat calculations based on data from United Nations/DESA Statistics Division.

Note:　GDP – gross domestic product; GNI – gross national income.

2. Differences among LDCs

The relationship between private consumption per capita and GDP per capita varies between the LDCs (chart 9). Table 22 classifies the LDCs into four major groups according to whether the changes in GDP per capita and private consumption per capita in 2000–2006 were positive or negative. From the table, it is apparent that most LDCs (35 out of 50) are in the group which experienced both increasing GDP per capita and increasing private consumption per capita (group 3 in table 22). However, there are nine LDCs where both GDP per capita and private consumption per capita fell (group 1) and a further three (Chad, Lao People's Democratic Republic and Sierra Leone — group 4) where private consumption fell even though GDP per capita rose. The final three LDCs — Eritrea, Comoros and Madagascar (group 2) — had increasing private consumption per capita with decreasing GDP per capita, a pattern which is not sustainable without a continuing inflow of external resources. In all, there are 20 LDCs where private consumption per capita in 2006 was less than in 2000, or where private consumption per capita increased at less than 0.5 per cent per annum during that period.

Focusing on the largest of the four groups, there are 10 LDCs in which private consumption grew faster than GDP per capita (group 3b). This is not likely to be sustainable in the long run as the domestic resources available for financing development are diminishing in relative terms. There are 18 LDCs in which GDP per capita and private consumption per capita both rose, but the latter rose at a slower rate than the former so that domestic resources for financing development also expanded. However, private consumption grew quite slowly in most of these countries. Indeed, only 13 LDCs feature the virtuous combination of rising GDP per capita, private consumption per capita rising at more than 2 per cent per year and rising domestic resources available for finance per capita (estimated as the

Most LDCs experienced both increasing GDP per capita and increasing private consumption per capita.

Only 13 LDCs feature the virtuous combination of rising GDP per capita, private consumption per capita increasing at more than 2 per cent per year and expanding domestic resources available for finance per capita.

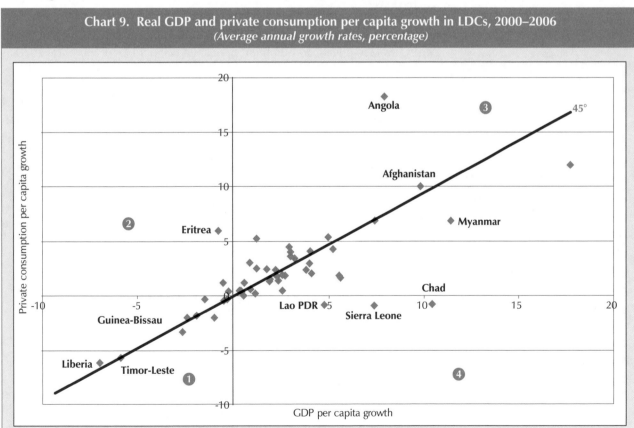

Chart 9. Real GDP and private consumption per capita growth in LDCs, 2000–2006
(Average annual growth rates, percentage)

Source: UNCTAD secretariat calculations based on data from United Nations/DESA Statistics Division.

Note: The numbers 1 to 4 refer to the country groups listed in table 22.

Table 22. Classification of countries according to GDP and private consumption per capita performance, 2000–2006

(Comparison between the average annual rate of growth of GDP and private consumption per capita in 2000-2006; the latter figure is provided in percentage)

Decreasing GDP per capita		Increasing GDP per capita				
		Increasing private consumption per capita (3)				
Decreasing private consumption per capita	Increasing private consumption per capita	Private consumption per capita increasing slower than GDP per capita	Private consumption per capita increasing faster than GDP per capita	Private consumption per capita increasing at the same rate as GDP per capita		Decreasing private consumption per capita
(1)	(2)	(3a)	(3b)	(3c)		(4)
Somalia −0.3	Eritrea 5.9	Equatorial Guinea 12.0	Angola 18.2	Afghanistan	10.0	Chad −0.8
Vanuatu −0.3	Comoros 1.2	Myanmar 10.1	Malawi 5.2	Bhutan	5.3	Lao People's Dem. Rep. −0.8
Togo −0.5	Madagascar 0.4	Cambodia 6.9	Burkina Faso 4.4	Tuvalu	4.0	Sierra Leone −0.9
Haiti −1.9		Sudan 4.2	Samoa 4.0	Ethiopia	3.4	
Burundi −2.0		Bangladesh 2.4	Zambia 3.6	Sao Tome & Principe	2.4	
Central African Rep. −2.0		United Rep. of Tanzania 2.0	Gambia 3.0	Solomon Islands	0.4	
Guinea-Bissau −3.3		Uganda 1.9	Guinea 2.5			
Timor-Leste −5.7		Cape Verde 1.9	Dem. Rep. of the Congo 2.4			
Liberia −6.1		Maldives 1.8	Nepal 1.2			
		Mauritania 1.8	Kiribati 0.4			
		Mozambique 1.7				
		Senegal 1.5				
		Rwanda 1.4				
		Lesotho 1.3				
		Yemen 0.6				
		Mali 0.4				
		Niger 0.3				
		Djibouti 0.2				
		Benin 0.0				

Source: UNCTAD secretariat calculations based on data from United Nations/DESA Statistics Division.

Note: Calculations are based on data in constant 2000 dollars.

difference between GDP and private consumption per capita).[1] If present trends persist, average private consumption per capita will double (or more) by 2020 as compared to 2000 in only nine LDCs.

In general, it is striking that if LDCs are classified according to their export specialization, private consumption per capita grew most slowly in mineral-exporting LDCs (at 1.2 per cent per annum). Despite their recent growth surge driven by high commodity prices, average private consumption per capita in mineral-exporting LDCs was actually lower in 2006 than in 2004, and in 2006 it was 36 per cent below the average of the LDCs as a group (table 21). This clearly illustrates that there is no automatic relationship between growth and rising consumption standards while indicating that the type of growth matters for the nature of the relationship.

Poverty reduction is at the heart of national and international development policies but internationally comparable data to identify and analyse poverty trends remains inadequate.

C. Poverty trends

1. NATURE OF POVERTY ESTIMATES

One of the paradoxical features of the current moment in development thinking and policy is that poverty reduction is at the heart of national and international development policies but internationally comparable data to identify and analyse poverty trends remains inadequate. This is particularly so in the case of the LDCs. The World Bank publishes internationally comparable poverty estimates based on household surveys of income or consumption for just 16 LDCs during the period 2000–2006. Within this sample, there are only 10 countries which have at least three household surveys enabling a description of trends over a 10-year period.

Because of the lack of available data, *The Least Developed Countries Report* has introduced innovations in the measurement of poverty in the LDCs, allowing it to provide insights into the dynamics of poverty in these countries. *The Least Developed Countries Report 2002: Escaping the Poverty Trap* used national accounts data to make the first internationally comparable estimates of $1-a-day and $2-a-day poverty in LDCs. The present Report updates and refines these estimates.

In *The Least Developed Countries Report 2002*, poverty estimates were made on the basis of the close cross-country relationship between the level of private consumption per capita measured in constant PPP dollars and the incidence of $1-a-day and $2-a-day poverty. The closeness of this statistical relationship enabled the generation of poverty estimates using national accounts data for countries in which there were estimates of private consumption in purchasing power dollars. The estimates in the current Report follow the same logic but refine the method by establishing the relationship between household survey estimates of private consumption per capita and national accounts estimates of private consumption per capita, seeking to base the poverty estimates on "calibrated survey means" (Karshenas, 2008).[2] Using this method, poverty estimates were made for 28 LDCs in Africa and Asia from 1980 to 2005.[3] The population of these countries accounts for 73 per cent of the population of all LDCs. The poverty estimates in these 28 countries is therefore representative of the trends in poverty for the LDC group as a whole.

It should be noted that because national accounts estimates of private consumption per capita deviate from household survey estimates of private consumption, this method results in international comparable poverty estimates which diverge from those of the World Bank. Table 23, which includes the UNCTAD and World Bank $1-a-day and $2-a-day estimates for selected LDCs, shows the magnitude of the divergence. In some cases, the UNCTAD estimates are higher than the World Bank estimates, while in other cases the reverse is true.

The discrepancies between the two sets of estimates arise because of the difference between the household survey means and the calibrated survey means of private consumption per capita. The latter are regarded as being as plausible as the household survey data. Indeed, they can be said to be more representative in the sense that they utilize all available information on private consumption, including both household survey and national accounts data. Significantly, however, as compared to household-survey based poverty estimates, the new method allows for a much wider coverage of internationally comparable poverty estimates, as well as estimates over time. Indeed, as stated in *The Least Developed Countries Report 2002* (UNCTAD, 2002: 45–51), it would be impossible to undertake the international comparative analysis of poverty in LDCs without such a method.

Finally, in reviewing the poverty trends described below, three features of the new estimates should be kept in mind.

First, these are internationally comparable estimates based on the international $1-a-day and $2-a-day poverty lines. They do not necessarily conform to poverty estimates based on national poverty lines. Moreover, in no sense is it argued here that these international estimates are more accurate than national

The Least Developed Countries Report has introduced innovations in the measurement of poverty in the LDCs, allowing it to provide insights into the dynamics of poverty in these countries.

Poverty estimates were made for 28 LDCs in Africa and Asia from 1980 to 2005 whose population accounts for 73 per cent of the population of all LDCs.

UNCTAD estimates can be said to be more representative than World Bank ones as they utilize all available information on private consumption, including both household survey and national accounts data.

Country	Year of latest household survey	Per capita consumption expenditure			Poverty rate			
					$1-a-day poverty line		$2-a-day poverty line	
		Survey	National accounts	Calibrated survey mean	New	World Bank	New	World Bank
		(1993 PPP dollars a day)			(Per cent of population)			
Bangladesh	2000	1.54	2.19	1.89	26.4	41.3	74.8	84.2
Benin	2003	1.96	2.76	2.21	24.0	30.8	65.8	73.0
Burkina Faso	2003	2.06	1.75	1.65	42.3	28.7	81.1	71.3
Burundi	1998	1.32	..	..	..	54.6	..	87.6
Cambodia	2004	1.19	..	..	..	66.0	..	89.8
Cape Verde	2001	7.29	7.84	5.16	8.6	1.9	32.3	19.0
Central African Republic	1993	1.35	2.45	2.04	52.7	66.6	73.9	84.0
Ethiopia	2000	1.83	0.86	1.14	60.6	21.6	94.0	76.6
Gambia	1998	3.04	2.98	2.33	38.6	27.9	65.6	55.9
Lao People's Dem. Republic	2002	1.90	..	..	..	27.4	..	74.2
Lesotho	1995	3.96	2.84	2.26	51.1	36.4	70.5	56.0
Madagascar	2001	1.32	2.44	2.03	41.6	61.0	71.4	85.1
Malawi	2004	2.36	2.00	1.79	36.8	20.8	77.6	63.0
Mali	2001	1.87	1.59	1.56	46.0	36.4	80.2	72.7
Mauritania	2000	2.23	1.26	1.37	51.5	25.9	85.1	63.1
Mozambique	2002	2.10	2.06	1.82	44.5	36.2	79.9	74.1
Nepal	2003	2.65	2.45	2.04	40.1	24.7	76.3	64.8
Niger	1994	1.36	1.71	1.62	45.0	54.8	80.4	86.1
Rwanda	2000	1.34	1.63	1.58	51.6	60.3	83.0	87.8
Senegal	2001	2.73	4.00	2.90	14.1	16.8	52.3	55.9
Sierra Leone	1989	1.61	1.27	1.37	60.7	57.0	78.6	74.4
Uganda	2002	1.88	3.04	2.37	42.1	82.3	77.7	95.7
United Republic of Tanzania	2000	1.20	1.04	1.24	54.4	57.0	89.8	90.2
Yemen	1998	2.84	..	..	..	9.4	..	43.5
Zambia	2004	1.35	1.52	1.52	54.6	60.0	81.8	84.9

Table 23. Private consumption per capita and poverty rates in LDCs

Source: UNCTAD secretariat compilation based on Karshenas (2008).

estimates of poverty. They are simply different types of estimates. The importance of the estimates on international poverty lines is that they enable international comparative analysis which can help us better understand the interplay between national and international factors in poverty dynamics. But national authorities should have discretion to define poverty lines in their own way.

Estimates on international poverty lines enable international comparative analysis and a better understanding of the interplay between national and international factors in poverty dynamics.

Second, the poverty estimates are based on estimates of private consumption using publicly available PPP exchange rates in constant 1993 dollars. Such rates are used to ensure that the purchasing power of a dollar is comparable between countries. The updated estimates do not take into account the revision of the PPP exchange rates (with base year 2005) published in early 2008 (when our estimates had already been made). These can have significant implications for poverty estimates in LDCs and in other countries. However, determining the consequences of the new set of PPPs will involve another round of calculations in which the poverty estimates are further updated and refined.

Third, the poverty estimates describe the two most usual poverty thresholds, namely $1 a day and $2 a day (in 1985 PPP dollars), which we refer to as the $1-a-day and $2-a-day poverty lines for brevity.[4] This does not imply, however, that higher standards should be excluded in the international analysis of poverty. With globalization, the consumption patterns to which people aspire are defined not simply by national norms but also by global norms. Thus, what people consider minimally acceptable is shifting with globalization. But this is not pointing downwards to the standards of living in the poorest countries, where $1 a day or $2 a day may be a poverty line, but rather upwards to the standards of living in the rich countries, where $10 a day or more may be the poverty line. In short, although we focus on $1-a-day poverty and $2-a-day poverty, these are actually minimal international standards to which we should be aspiring when we discuss poverty reduction.

2. LEVEL AND DYNAMICS OF POVERTY IN LDCs SINCE 1990

(a) Overall trends

The three basic features of the incidence of poverty in the LDCs since 1990 can be summarized as follows:

- The incidence of extreme poverty (measured by the proportion of the population living on less than $1 a day as a share of total population) has decreased continuously since 1994, reaching 36 per cent of the population in 2005 (chart 10A);

- Although the incidence of extreme poverty has been declining, the proportion of the population living on more than $1 a day but less than $2 a day has remained constant at around 40 per cent of the total population (chart 10B); and

The incidence of extreme poverty has decreased continuously since 1994, reaching 36 per cent of the population in 2005.

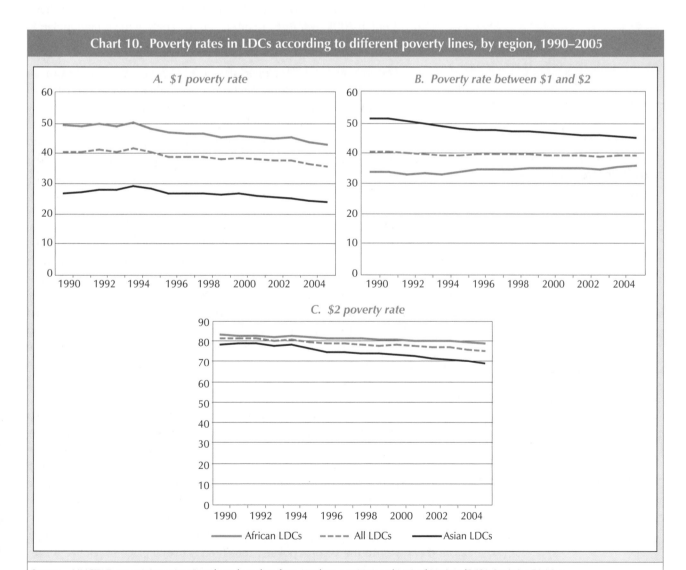

Chart 10. Poverty rates in LDCs according to different poverty lines, by region, 1990–2005

Source: UNCTAD secretariat estimations based on data from Karshenas (2008) and United Nations/DESA Statistics Division.

Note: Based on the sample of 28 LDCs mentioned in table 24.

Table 24. Poverty in LDCs, 1990–2005
(Percentage and million)

	Population living on:											
	less than $1 a day				between $1 and $2 a day				less than $2 a day			
	Percentage of total population[a]											
	1990	*1995*	*2000*	*2005*	*1990*	*1995*	*2000*	*2005*	*1990*	*1995*	*2000*	*2005*
LDCs	40.4	40.8	38.9	36.1	41.2	39.6	39.8	39.6	81.6	80.4	78.8	75.7
African LDCs[b]	49.7	49.3	46.9	43.9	34.2	33.7	35.3	36.0	83.9	83.1	82.2	79.9
Asian LDCs	26.9	28.3	26.9	24.0	51.4	48.1	46.7	45.2	78.3	76.4	73.6	69.2
	Million[c]											
LDCs	212.4	245.2	264.6	277.0	216.4	237.8	270.5	303.8	428.8	483.0	535.1	580.8
African LDCs[b]	154.9	176.1	192.0	205.6	106.5	120.5	144.4	169.0	261.4	296.5	336.4	374.6
Asian LDCs	56.9	68.4	71.9	70.6	108.7	116.1	124.8	133.3	165.6	184.5	196.7	203.9
Island LDCs[d]	0.6	0.7	0.8	0.8	1.2	1.3	1.3	1.5	1.8	2.0	2.1	2.3

Source: UNCTAD secretariat calculations based on data from Karshenas (2008) and United Nations/DESA Statistics Division.

a Percentage data refer to a sample of 28 LDCs: Angola, Bangladesh, Benin, Burkina Faso, Burundi, Cambodia, Cape Verde, Central African Republic, Chad, Ethiopia, Gambia, Guinea, Lesotho, Madagascar, Malawi, Mali, Mauritania, Mozambique, Nepal, Niger, Rwanda, Senegal, Sierra Leone, Togo, Uganda, United Republic of Tanzania, Yemen and Zambia.
b Includes Cape Verde.
c The total number of poor people in the LDCs has been estimated by assuming that the African LDCs for which data are not available have the same incidence of poverty as those for which data are available, and that the Asian and island LDCs for which data are not available have the same incidence of poverty as Asian LDCs for which data are available.
d Excludes Cape Verde.

• The proportion of the population living on less than $2 a day is declining slowly, but in 2005 over three quarters (76 per cent) of the total population was still living on less than $2 a day (chart 10C and table 24).

As indicated in past *Least Developed Countries Reports*, these figures mean that absolute poverty is not a marginal phenomenon. Rather, there is a situation of generalized poverty in the LDCs. A large share of the population lives at or below income levels sufficient to meet their basic needs, and in which the available resources in the economy, even when equally distributed, are barely sufficient to cater to the needs of the population on a sustainable basis. In this situation, the economic freedom of the majority of the population is seriously constrained by the inadequate purchasing power to meet basic needs.

In 2005 over three quarters of the population (581 million people) were still living on less than $2 a day.

Although the incidence of poverty has been falling, the high rate of population growth means that the number of people living in extreme poverty (i.e. on less than $1 a day) has increased over the long term. However, the *rate* of growth of the number of extremely poor people has been slowing, falling from 3.1 per cent per annum during the period 1990–1995 to 1.1 per cent per annum during 2000–2005. After 2003, the number of $1 poor people living in LDCs stopped rising (chart 11). However, the incidence of extreme poverty is much higher than in most other developing countries and the number of extremely poor people remains significant. It is estimated that 277 million people were living in extreme poverty in LDCs in 2005 (table 24).

277 million people were living in extreme poverty in LDCs in 2005.

While the number of people living in extreme poverty has stopped increasing, the rise in the number of people living above $1 a day but below $2 a day accelerated sharply during the second half of the 1990s and has decelerated only slightly since 2000. This pattern is similar to the one observed in other developing countries. There, most people who manage to escape extreme poverty situate themselves between the two poverty lines, thus swelling the figures of this second group (Chen and Ravallion, 2007). But leaving this second group is much more difficult than exiting from absolute poverty. In the case of the LDCs, the transfer from the lowest to the second poverty threshold is taking place in *relative* terms. Although the number of people living on less than $1 a day has not yet fallen (as has occurred in other developing countries) and stopped increasing only recently,

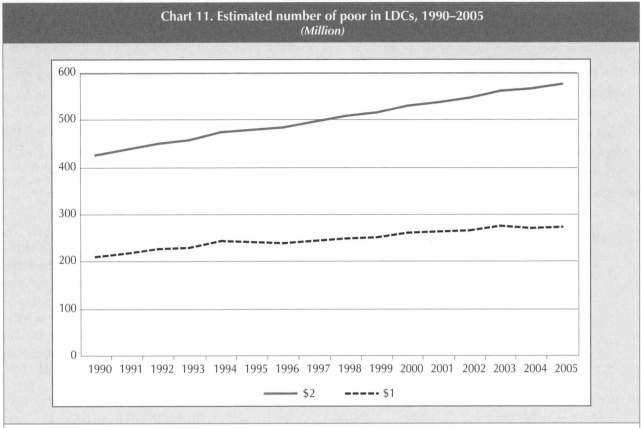

Chart 11. Estimated number of poor in LDCs, 1990–2005
(Million)

Legend: —— $2   ----- $1

Source: UNCTAD secretariat estimations based on data from Karshenas (2008) and United Nations/DESA Statistics Division.

Note: $1 - Number of people living on less than $1 a day.
$2 - Number of people living on less than $2 a day.
Based on the poverty rates of the sample of 28 LDCs mentioned in table 24.

the *rate* of growth of the population living on between $1 and $2 a day has exceeded the rate of growth of the extremely poor since the mid-1990s. Indeed, from 1995 onwards, the number of people living between the two poverty lines has grown at approximately the same pace as total population (table 25). As a consequence, the number of poor people between the two poverty lines continues to increase and largely exceeds the absolute increase in the number of the $1 poor. It is estimated that 304 million people in LDCs lived on between $1 and $2 a day in 2005 (table 24).

Trends in $2-a-day poverty are of course the combination of the trends in $1-a-day poverty and in poverty between the two ranges discussed above. The absolute number of $2-a-day poor continues to rise in LDCs, though the rate of growth slowed in 2000–2005 compared with 1990–1995. In 2005, it was estimated that 581 million people lived on less than $2 a day in the LDCs as a whole (table 24).

The incidence of extreme poverty is much higher in African LDCs than in Asian ones. Progress in reducing the incidence of poverty has been much faster in Asian LDCs than in African LDCs.

(b) Regional trends

The overall picture of the incidence and dynamics of poverty in the LDCs masks a sharp contrast between African and Asian countries.[5] First, the incidence of extreme poverty is much higher in African LDCs than in Asian ones. In 2005, the average incidence of extreme poverty in African LDCs was almost 20 percentage points higher than in Asian LDCs (chart 10A). Second, the ranking is the opposite in the case of the population living on between $1 and $2 a day, whose share of the total population is higher in Asia than in Africa. The gap has however been narrowing since the early 1990s (chart 10B). Third, progress in reducing the incidence of poverty (in both brackets) has been much faster in Asian LDCs than in African LDCs.

In African LDCs, the overall incidence of extreme poverty is estimated to have fallen from 50 per cent in the early 1990s to 44 per cent in 2005 (chart 10A). However, the number of extremely poor people continues to increase, though at a slowing rate of 1.5 per cent per annum in the period 2000–2005 compared with 2.8 per cent per annum in the period 1990–1995 (table 25). In 2005, an estimated 206 million people lived in extreme poverty in African LDCs. In Asian LDCs, by contrast, the pace of growth of the extremely poor population has declined sharply since the early 1990s, to the point that the absolute number of $1-a-day poor has stabilized since 2000. The incidence of extreme poverty fell continuously from 29 per cent in 1994 to 24 per cent in 2005 (chart 10A), when the number of extremely poor people is estimated to have been 71 million people.

The rate of growth of the contingent of people living on more than $1 a day but less than $2 a day accelerated in both African and Asian LDCs during the second half of the 1990s, but by much more in the former than in the latter. Since 2000, the population between the two poverty lines has been expanding by 3.2 per cent per annum in African LDCs, well above the pace of 1.4 per cent in Asian LDCs (table 25). The proportion of the total population living between the poverty lines continued to rise in African LDCs, reaching 36 per cent in 2005. In Asian LDCs, by contrast, the corresponding incidence fell by six percentage points between 1990 and 2005, when it reached 45 per cent (chart 10B and table 24).

The combination of divergent developments in the two brackets of poverty in African and Asian LDCs has resulted in different trends in total (i.e. $2-a-day) poverty. The incidence of $2-a-day poverty is declining faster in Asian LDCs than in African LDCs. In the former, an estimated 204 million lived under these conditions in 2005, whereas in Africa the corresponding figure was 375 million (table 24). As a result of contrasting developments in the level and trends of the two brackets of poverty, the gap between the total poverty rates is smaller than that within these brackets. In African LDCs, total poverty incidence was 80 per cent in 2005, while in Asia it was 69 per cent (chart 10C). Despite some reduction in incidence since the 1990s, this means that the vast majority of the population of LDCs in both regions continue to live in poverty.

(c) Poverty trends and export specialization

Apart from regional contrasts in patterns of poverty in the LDCs, there are also strong differences in the level and dynamics of poverty among these countries,

Table 25. Poverty and population dynamics in LDCs and country groups, 1990–2005
(Average annual growth rates of the number of people, per cent)

		1990–1995	1995–2000	2000–2005	1995–2005
A . $1-a-day poverty	LDCs	3.1	1.7	1.1	1.6
	African LDCs[a]	2.8	1.9	1.5	1.9
	Asian LDCs	3.9	1.4	-0.2	0.8
B. Poverty above $1 a day and below $2 a day	LDCs	1.7	2.7	2.4	2.5
	African LDCs[a]	2.4	3.8	3.2	3.3
	Asian LDCs	1.1	1.6	1.4	1.5
C. $2-a-day poverty (A+B)	LDCs	2.4	2.2	1.7	2.0
	African LDCs[a]	2.7	2.7	2.3	2.5
	Asian LDCs	2.1	1.5	0.8	1.2
D. Total population	LDCs	2.7	2.6	2.5	2.6
	African LDCs[a]	2.8	2.9	2.8	2.8
	Asian LDCs	2.6	2.2	2.0	2.1

Source: UNCTAD secretariat calculations based on data from Karshenas (2008) and United Nations/DESA Statistics Division.

Note: Sample composition as in table 24.   a Includes Cape Verde.

Table 26. Poverty and population dynamics in LDCs and country groups by export specialization, 1990–2005
(Average annual growth rates of the number of people, per cent)

	Export specialization	1990–1995	1995–2000	2000–2005	1995–2005
A. $1-a-day poverty	Oil	15.2	2.1	1.9	3.1
	Agricultural	0.7	1.1	2.5	2.1
	Mineral	4.1	1.8	1.7	1.9
	Manufactures	3.1	1.5	-0.2	0.6
	Services	2.1	2.0	0.8	1.5
	Mixed	0.9	1.4	2.4	3.5
B. Poverty above $1 a day and below $2 a day	Oil	3.1	2.8	3.2	3.1
	Agricultural	5.0	3.1	3.4	3.1
	Mineral	1.4	2.8	2.6	2.7
	Manufactures	0.7	1.5	1.2	1.3
	Services	0.6	5.5	4.0	4.7
	Mixed	6.7	2.5	1.3	1.1
C. $2-a-day poverty (A+B)	Oil	7.6	2.5	2.6	3.1
	Agricultural	2.5	2.0	2.9	2.6
	Mineral	3.0	2.3	2.1	2.2
	Manufactures	1.6	1.5	0.7	1.0
	Services	1.6	3.2	2.0	2.7
	Mixed	3.8	2.0	1.8	2.2
D. Total population	Oil	3.9	3.0	3.1	3.1
	Agricultural	2.9	3.0	3.1	3.1
	Mineral	2.9	2.6	2.7	2.6
	Manufactures	2.3	2.1	1.9	2.0
	Services	2.6	3.1	2.6	2.8
	Mixed	2.9	3.0	2.8	2.9

Source: UNCTAD secretariat calculations based on data from Karshenas (2008) and United Nations/DESA Statistics Division.

Note: As in table 24.

depending on export specialization. The categories of export specialization into which we have classified LDCs (table A) reflect different forms of insertion of these countries in the international economy, in particular the trade and investment links between their domestic economy and the international environment.[6] These international trade and investment linkages, in turn, are closely related to the productive structure of the domestic economy and the amount and quality of employment that it can generate. The productive structure and the patterns of employment generation determine the level and the distribution of income among domestic agents. Therefore, changes in production and employment through time have a direct impact on income distribution. By the same token, the dynamics of foreign trade and investment, together with those of domestic output and employment, determine the level of poverty in each country and its developments through time.

Specialization of production and trade in capital-intensive commodity-producing sectors typically tends to generate rising GDP and exports, particularly during periods of rising commodity prices — as has been the case for most of the present decade. However, this type of economic development tends also to increase income inequality within the country and can therefore have a limited poverty-reducing impact.[7] This is typically the case of specialization of trade and output in natural resource extraction.

The opposite case is that in which the international trade and investment links of a developing country are related to an output structure that leads to a virtuous circle of employment creation and income generation for a wider share of the population. This is typically the case of trade and output specialization in labour-intensive manufacturing. Given its employment-creating impact, this specialization pattern typically has a poverty-reducing impact, particularly at the

The dynamics of foreign trade and investment, together with those of domestic output and employment, determine the level of poverty in each country and its developments through time.

initial phases of development. Similarly, countries with a diversified trade and production structure tend to create jobs in a wider range of sectors, which mostly has a poverty-reducing impact.

Commodity-dependent countries typically have much higher rates of poverty than either manufactures or mixed exporters.

The different categories of LDCs according to export specialization have divergent levels and growth rates of poverty (table 26). Commodity-dependent countries typically have much higher rates of poverty than either those that are specialized in manufacturing or services or those that have a more diversified export structure. As chart 12 shows, in agricultural-, mineral- or oil-exporting LDCs, three-fourths or more of the population lives on less than $2 a day. This situation of generalized poverty in oil- and mineral-exporting countries is explained by their type of insertion in the international economy and by the domestic output and employment patterns, as mentioned in the preceding paragraphs. Poverty is also generalized in agriculture-exporting countries due to low and almost stagnant agricultural productivity and the incapacity of the agricultural sector to absorb gainfully the still rapidly increasing rural population (see sub-section D.3 of this chapter). In commodity-exporting countries, the poverty rate has been declining slowly since 1994, although the trend for oil-exporting countries has been somewhat erratic.

In manufactures and mixed exporters, the incidence of $2-a-day poverty was ten percentage points lower than in commodity-exporting LDCs in 2005.

In manufactures and mixed exporters, by contrast, the incidence of $2-a-day poverty was ten percentage points lower than in commodity-exporting LDCs in 2005 (chart 12). Moreover, it has been declining at a stronger pace than in the latter countries. Manufactures and mixed exporting LDCs have successfully diversified economic production, employment and exports out of the primary

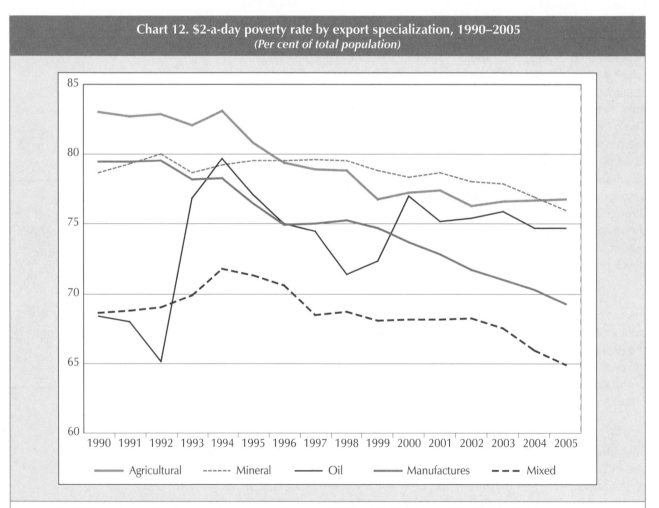

Chart 12. $2-a-day poverty rate by export specialization, 1990–2005
(Per cent of total population)

Source: UNCTAD secretariat estimations based on data from Karshenas (2008) and United Nations/DESA Statistics Division.
Note: Based on the sample of LDCs mentioned in table 24.

sector into industry and/ or services, allowing them to expand and widen the employment base. This has brought about a much steeper decline in poverty incidence than in commodity-producing LDCs. Moreover, these are the only two groups where the absolute number of extremely poor stopped growing, in 2000 (manufactures exporters) and 2003 (mixed exporters), respectively. The strongest decline in the incidence of poverty is in manufactures exporters. There, the activity of foreign investors in the garment and textile industry has led to a strong expansion of industrial employment and manufactured exports.[8] This is the only group of export specialization where the absolute number of the extremely poor has declined on average since 2000 and the one with the lowest rate of expansion of the $2-a-day poor population (table 26).

Divergent patterns of poverty levels and pace of change were already reflected in *The Least Developed Countries Report 2002* (UNCTAD 2002: 101-135). However, a major difference between the poverty estimates contained in that Report and those contained in the present Report is that the former reflected falling international commodity prices during the most recent years for which estimates had been made (i.e. the late 1990s). By contrast, the new set of estimates presented in this Report reflects rising international commodity prices in the most recent years for which estimates were made (i.e. up to 2005). It was expected that higher export prices would lead to stronger economic growth rates, and this has indeed been the case (see chapter 1 of this Report). It could additionally have been expected that stronger economic growth would have implied significant poverty reduction. The previous paragraphs have shown that this has not been the case. Section D of this chapter analyses the reasons for this.

It could have been expected that stronger economic growth would have implied significant poverty reduction, but this has not been the case.

D. The growth–poverty relationship in the LDCs

The rate of economic growth is an important determinant of poverty reduction in the LDCs, as in other developing countries. Indeed, the improved performance of LDCs in terms of poverty reduction since 1994 is related to the acceleration of economic growth. However, the continuing slow progress in poverty reduction despite very high growth rates implies that the type of growth which is occurring in most LDCs does not have a strong impact on poverty reduction.

The overall relationship between the annual percentage change in GDP per capita and in the incidence of $1-a-day and $2-a-day poverty during the period 1995–2005 is shown in chart 13. This covers the period in which the LDCs were most successful in reducing poverty (1995–2005). From the charts, it is apparent that:

- The incidence of poverty has generally risen when GDP per capita has declined. This is typically the case for $1-a-day poverty;

- In one-fourth of the countries in which GDP per capita increased during that period, the incidence of $1-a-day poverty also increased. The incidence of $2-a-day poverty generally fell when GDP per capita increased, but it rose in one-fifth of the GDP growth countries;

- Within the LDCs in which GDP per capita increased and the incidence of poverty fell, most were unable to raise the rate of poverty reduction above 2 per cent per year. Out of the sample of 28 countries, in only six of them did $1-a-day poverty fall at that pace or faster, and in only three countries did $2-a-day poverty fall at that rate or faster. If poverty continuously shrinks at 2 per cent per annum, it will take 34 years to halve the poverty rate.

Within the LDCs where GDP per capita increased and poverty fell, most were unable to raise the rate of poverty reduction above 2 per cent per year. At this rate, it will take 34 years to halve the poverty rate.

Chart 13. Economic growth and poverty in LDCs, 1995–2005

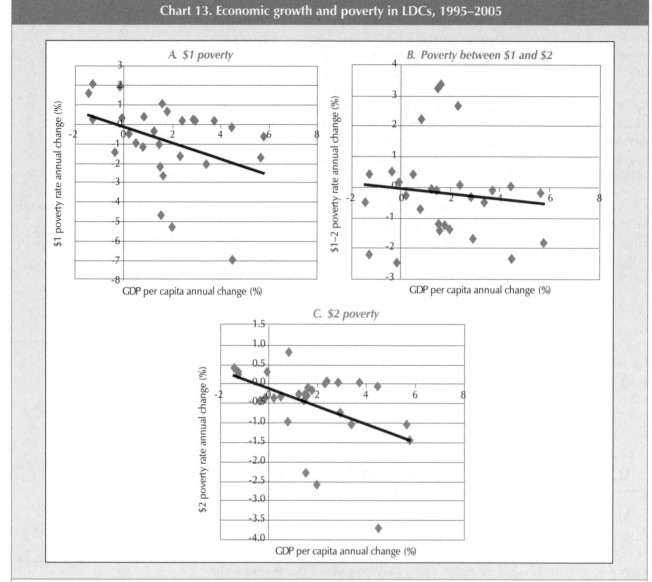

Source: UNCTAD secretariat estimations based on data from Karshenas (2008) and United Nations/DESA Statistics Division.

Note: Poverty rate is the number of people living in each threshold as a share of the total population.
$1 poverty refers to people living on less than $1 a day.
$1-2 poverty refers to people living on more than $1 a day, but less than $2 a day.
$2 poverty refers to people living on less than $2 a day.

The correlation between GDP growth and poverty reduction in our sample of LDCs has been weakening since the early 1990s.

The correlation between GDP growth and poverty reduction in our sample of LDCs has been weakening since the early 1990s. Moreover, economic growth has translated into falling poverty rates only for people living on less than $1 a day. It has not had an impact on the poverty incidence of those living on between $1 a day and $2 a day. In the 1990–1995 period the correlation between GDP per capita growth and the rhythm of reduction in $1-a-day poverty was -0.38 (and statistically significant), indicating that GDP growth led to a reduction in the extreme poverty rate. In the 2000-2005 period, by contrast, the correlation had fallen to -0.20 (and become statistically insignificant), pointing to a weakening of the economic growth–poverty reduction connection. In the case of poverty between the two poverty lines in our sample of LDCs, there has been no connection since 1990. The correlation is weak (less than 0.1), changes signs in different sub-periods and is never statistically significant. This is due to the already mentioned fact that in relative terms people transfer from the lower (below $1-a-day) to the higher bracket of poverty (between $1- and $2-a-day).

The weak correlation between growth in GDP per capita and poverty reduction in the LDCs can be attributed to a number of factors, notably: (1) the relationship between GDP growth and private consumption growth; (2) population growth and employment; (3) the patterns of economic growth; and (4) income distribution. Hereafter, we examine each one in turn.

1. Growth of GDP and private consumption

The immediate link between growth in GDP per capita and poverty reduction is that the former leads to higher household consumption per capita, which in turn is closely associated with poverty reduction (UNCTAD, 2002: 39–49). It is for this reason that the previous *Least Developed Countries Reports* have been arguing that what matters is not GDP growth *per se*, but a type of GDP growth which expands average household living standards. However, the acceleration of economic growth in the LDCs since the early 2000s has not been accompanied by a proportional strengthening of private consumption in most LDCs (see section B of this chapter).

In countries where the pace of private consumption increase lags behind the growth rate of GDP, the share of private consumption in GDP is shrinking. This is the case in more than half of the LDCs (table 27). However, this share fell particularly sharply between 2000 and 2006 in a number of countries, notably Chad, Equatorial Guinea, Lao People's Democratic Republic, Mozambique and Sierra Leone, where it declined by at least 20 percentage points. In three of these countries — Chad, Lao People's Democratic Republic and Sierra Leone — this shrinking share resulted from a combination of contracting private consumption with expanding GDP (group 4 in table 22), leading to a stagnation in the incidence of extreme poverty despite high economic growth.

Over the long run, the fall in the share of private consumption in GDP must be seen as a positive development if it results in the mobilization of domestic resources for financing development. In the short run, however, there is a trade-off between poverty reduction and increased domestic savings. It is this trade-off which makes the availability of external financial resources in the form of official development assistance (ODA) so important for starting a sustainable process of poverty reduction in very poor countries. There is certainly a stratum of rich people in very poor countries (see subsection 4 below) and they can play an important role in initiating a domestic accumulation process. However, in situations of generalized poverty where the majority of the population are very poor, the impact of the trade-off between using resources to meet immediate basic needs and mobilizing resources to invest in creating a better future can be considerably lessened through access to external resources. This is one reason why aid is so important for poverty reduction in the LDCs.

2. Population growth and labour force growth

Demographic growth is faster in the LDCs than in other developing countries. Between 1990 and 2005, total population of LDCs increased at an annual rate of 2.5 per cent, higher than that of other developing countries in Africa (the continent with strongest demographic growth), but also in the other regions. Population in all other developing countries grew by 1.5 per cent per annum during the same period. The higher rate of population growth means that in order to reduce poverty, LDC economies must not only grow at a sustained higher pace but also generate new jobs and remunerative income-earning opportunities at an accelerated rhythm. Increasing employment is therefore a precondition for

The acceleration of economic growth since the early 2000s has not been accompanied by a proportional strengthening of private consumption in most LDCs.

In the short run there is a trade-off between poverty reduction and increased domestic savings, which makes ODA so important for starting poverty reduction in very poor countries.

In order to reduce poverty, LDC economies must not only grow and increase labour productivity at a sustained higher pace, but also generate new jobs at an accelerated rhythm.

Table 27. Private consumption as a share of GDP in LDCs and country groups, 1995–2006
(Per cent)

	1995	2000	2004	2005	2006
Afghanistan	102	119	122	115	121
Angola	24	17	50	49	44
Bangladesh	74	67	64	63	62
Benin	79	81	80	79	78
Bhutan	41	49	47	45	54
Burkina Faso	67	51	53	54	55
Burundi	92	91	85	88	84
Cambodia	99	87	84	83	81
Cape Verde	93	98	98	93	92
Central African Republic	85	85	89	84	88
Chad	50	60	35	33	34
Comoros	83	80	88	88	88
Democratic Republic of the Congo	66	62	64	64	65
Djibouti	49	68	62	62	62
Equatorial Guinea	61	52	30	36	33
Eritrea	80	58	111	90	82
Ethiopia	89	81	82	84	82
Gambia	74	79	82	83	84
Guinea	85	88	98	95	94
Guinea-Bissau	71	59	59	57	58
Haiti	125	124	124	124	123
Kiribati	77	61	62	62	62
Lao People's Democratic Republic	93	85	69	65	59
Lesotho	128	87	91	83	82
Liberia	70	87	96	92	96
Madagascar	90	92	92	88	96
Malawi	87	102	117	126	124
Maldives	38	31	27	28	24
Mali	75	76	73	66	63
Mauritania	72	74	74	92	59
Mozambique	94	77	66	64	56
Myanmar	80	65	64	63	61
Nepal	76	76	77	77	79
Niger	73	72	74	68	72
Rwanda	71	62	58	59	59
Samoa	81	85	91	92	92
Sao Tome and Principe	95	102	88	108	102
Senegal	76	73	73	72	73
Sierra Leone	87	110	99	88	84
Solomon Islands	52	51	51	51	51
Somalia	72	73	73	73	73
Sudan	82	72	70	69	69
Timor-Leste	81	65	62	63	62
Togo	80	88	89	91	88
Tuvalu	91	91	91	91	91
Uganda	85	86	83	83	84
United Republic of Tanzania	84	79	72	69	69
Vanuatu	56	62	65	66	66
Yemen	64	58	61	60	57
Zambia	63	63	58	60	59
Total LDCs	**76**	**70**	**70**	**69**	**68**
African LDCs	76	71	72	71	69
Asian LDCs	77	69	67	66	66
Island LDCs	71	70	69	70	67
LDCs by export specialization:					
Oil	64	57	61	60	58
Agricultural	82	82	85	85	87
Mineral	76	75	74	72	68
Manufactures	78	71	68	67	67
Services	84	77	77	77	76
Mixed	81	74	71	70	69

Source: UNCTAD secretariat calculations based on data from United Nations/DESA Statistics Division.
Note: Calculations are based on data in constant 2000 dollars.

generating raising household incomes and consumption and hence a requisite of poverty reduction.

The working-age population of the LDCs has been increasing at an annual pace of 2.6 per cent since the 1980s, a rhythm that is projected to continue unabated until 2020. In order to bring about a significant dent in poverty, it is necessary to strongly increase employment opportunities and labour productivity. Yet in almost all LDCs there is an imbalance between the rate of growth of the labour force, which is very rapid, and the rate of capital accumulation and technological progress, which is generally slow. As a result, most workers have to earn their living using their raw labour, with rudimentary tools and equipment, little education and training, and poor infrastructure. Labour productivity is low and underemployment is widespread (UNCTAD, 2006: 167–192).

The impact of economic growth on poverty in LDCs has been seriously reduced because of the failure to generate sufficient employment opportunities (particularly in the formal sector) and to raise labour productivity, especially that of people working in informal sector activities both inside and outside agriculture.

In most LDCs there is an imbalance between the rapid growth of the labour force, and the slow rate of capital accumulation and technological progress.

3. PATTERN OF ECONOMIC GROWTH

(a) Export-led growth

Most LDCs since the 1990s have been following an export-led growth strategy of which an open trade regime is an important component. This strategy may be conducive to export expansion and overall economic expansion, which has actually taken place in LDCs in recent years (see chapter 1 of this Report). In *The Least Developed Countries Report 2004*, however, we showed that the pursuit of export-led growth in very poor countries is not generally inclusive (UNCTAD 2004: 123–160; 179–217).

One reason for this is that export sectors may have few linkages with the rest of the economy and therefore have limited multiplier and job-creating effects. In extreme cases, these sectors may develop as enclaves and therefore have little positive impact on other segments of the population and territory. This development pattern is typical where exports are based on natural resource extraction. But it may also be present in the development based on secondary sectors, for example in export processing zones, and tertiary sectors, for example tourism enclaves.

The failure of export-led economic growth to translate into significant poverty reduction is particularly evident in LDCs where growth has been propelled by the capital-intensive mining and oil industries.

The failure of export-led economic growth to translate into significant poverty reduction is particularly evident in those LDCs where growth has been propelled by investment in the capital-intensive mining and oil industries. It is striking that, in the oil-exporting LDCs of our sample, growth of private consumption per capita accelerated sharply between 1995–2000 and 2000–2005 from 0.4 per annum to 9.6 per cent per annum. By contrast, this was accompanied by an only marginally lower rhythm of expansion of the number of people living in extreme poverty, which changed from an annual rate of 2.1 per cent to 1.9 per cent during the same periods. Oil exporters experienced the fastest pace of expansion of total poverty between 1995 and 2005 (3.1 per cent per annum — table 26). Similar developments took place in the mineral-exporting countries of our sample: their private consumption per capita growth accelerated from an annual pace of 0.9 per cent to 1.6 per cent between those periods but the rhythm of expansion of absolute poverty remained almost unchanged, passing from 1.8 per cent per annum to 1.7 per cent per annum (table 26).

Oil exporters experienced the fastest pace of expansion of total poverty between 1995 and 2005.

The group with the second highest growth rates in per capita consumption is that of manufactures exporters. Given their specialization in low-skill but labour-intensive activities, economic growth has been accompanied by significant employment creation in industry. This largely explains why this group of countries has been the one most successful in curbing the expansion of poverty (both $1-a-day and $2-a-day) since the 1990s and the only one where the number of extremely poor stopped rising in 2000.

Manufactures exporters have been the most successful group in curbing the expansion of poverty.

As argued in both *The Least Developed Countries Report 2004* and *The Least Developed Countries Report 2006*, it is possible to see a more inclusive pattern of economic growth in countries where the demand-side sources of economic growth are more balanced between domestic demand and export expansion. This does not mean that exports do not matter. But what is required is adequate export growth along with expansion of domestic demand.

(b) Weak agricultural development

An important feature of the growth pattern in many LDCs is that agricultural growth has been very weak. This is important for poverty reduction trends, as agriculture is still the major source of employment in LDCs. As we shall see below, this situation is changing, quite rapidly in some countries. In 2004, however, 69 per cent of the economically active population was employed in the agricultural sector in the LDCs as a group.

A more inclusive pattern of economic growth occurs where the demand-side sources of economic growth are more balanced between domestic demand and export expansion.

Weak agricultural development is clearly reflected by a number of key trends. First, both food production and agricultural production have barely kept pace with population growth since the early 1990s (chart 14). The growth of food production per capita and agricultural production per capita has been much stronger in Asian LDCs than in African LDCs, where food production has actually declined since the early 1990s.

Second, agricultural productivity growth has been very slow. Estimates in fact suggest that the LDCs as a group experienced a decline of total factor productivity in agriculture of 0.1 per cent per annum between 1963 and 2001 (Nin Pratt quoted in Fan, 2008). Agricultural labour productivity, which is a major

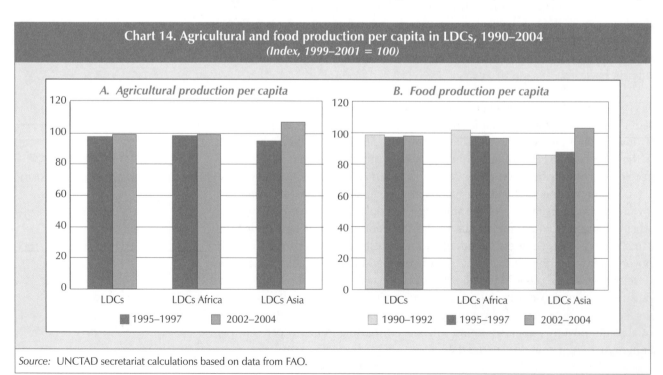

Chart 14. Agricultural and food production per capita in LDCs, 1990–2004
(Index, 1999–2001 = 100)

A. Agricultural production per capita

B. Food production per capita

Source: UNCTAD secretariat calculations based on data from FAO.

determinant of farm incomes, was just $380 per worker in 2003 (in constant 2000 prices). This was almost one-fifth of the average in other developing countries ($1,630 per worker). Moreover, it was only 20 per cent higher than the level in LDCs in 1981 ($319 per worker) (Fan, 2008). Generalized poverty in the LDCs is not surprising given that the majority of people work in agriculture and average agricultural labour productivity in LDCs was a little over $1 per day in 2003. The failure to achieve higher rates of poverty reduction in these countries is directly related to the failure to increase agricultural productivity more rapidly.

Third, frequently LDC farmers have been negatively affected by trade liberalization. As indicated in chapter 1 of this Report, the agricultural trade balance of the LDCs and also the food trade balance has been continually worsening since the mid-1970s. This, of course, is not bad in itself if LDCs can more effectively use their domestic resources to produce other products which they can trade internationally. In practice, however, most LDCs face increasing balance-of-payment problems, which are caused by the combination of worsening agricultural trade balances coupled with a failure to generate other internationally competitive activities except extractive industries and manufacturing in a few cases. The agricultural trade balance has worsened particularly strongly since the mid-1990s, as a high number of LDC producers have found it difficult to compete in their own markets for many key foodstuffs following trade liberalization.

These trends reflect policy decisions. In particular, public expenditure on agriculture has been neglected. Fan (2008) estimates that public spending on agriculture as a share of agricultural GDP was just 4.2 per cent in LDCs in 2004, less than half the level in other developing countries (10.7 per cent). Public expenditure on agricultural research and development (R&D) was also very low in most LDCs (UNCTAD, 2007: 174–177). Falling ODA for agriculture has been a critical element of the low levels of public expenditure on agriculture in LDCs in recent years. This trend runs counter to the findings of case studies, which show that better welfare indicators are prevalent in areas where farmers have higher adoption rates for improved technology (Minten and Barret, 2008).

(c) Urbanization and deagrarianization

The final and important aspect of the pattern of growth is that not only has agricultural development been weak, but more and more people are seeking work outside agriculture. This is evident in the accelerating trend towards urbanization. Although the share of the economically active population in agriculture is still high, it is declining sharply in a number of LDCs. As argued in *The Least Developed Countries Report 2006*, this reflects a situation in which it is increasingly difficult to make a living in agriculture, as average farm sizes are getting smaller and poor people cannot get access to the inputs which they need to increase productivity. Many children finish primary school, then seek work outside agriculture (UNCTAD, 2006: 167–189).

Some observers have described what is happening as "deagrarianization" (Bryceson, 1996). In this process, people living in rural areas increasingly survive through multiple activities, not simply farming, and more and more people also seek work outside agriculture. Like urbanization, this is occurring at an accelerating rate. Thus, even though agriculture is still the major employer in most LDCs, the annual increase in the number of people seeking work outside agriculture is starting to exceed the annual increase in the number of people seeking work within agriculture, marking a major change from the 1980s and 1990s. *The Least Developed Countries Report 2006* estimates that this employment transition will affect more than half the LDCs in the present decade and the rest during the next decade (UNCTAD, 2006: 167–189).

Generalized poverty in the LDCs is not surprising given that the majority of people work in agriculture, where labour productivity in LDCs was a little over $1 per day in 2003 (one-fifth of the average in other developing countries).

Since the mid-1990s, as a high number of LDC producers have found it difficult to compete in their own markets for many key foodstuffs following trade liberalization.

Public expenditure on agriculture has been neglected.

In "deagrarianization", people living in rural areas increasingly survive through multiple activities, not simply farming, and more and more people also seek work outside agriculture.

Such a transformation in the structure of employment could be seen as positive if people are pushed out of agriculture by rising productivity and pulled into other sectors by new employment opportunities being created outside agriculture. Yet only some Asian LDCs, which have managed to combine progress in the Green Revolution in agriculture with expansion of manufacturing exports, show signs of this kind of structural transformation. For most LDCs, however, deagrarianization is a negative process in which people are pushed out because they cannot make a living in agriculture or find remunerative work elsewhere. This is leading to the other face of poverty in LDCs — unemployed youth in the cities — which now coexists alongside the poverty associated with long-standing agricultural neglect.

Poverty in LDCs has now two faces: unemployed youth in the cities and poverty associated with long-standing agricultural neglect.

4. INCOME DISTRIBUTION

Finally, the relationship between economic growth and poverty reduction is mediated by the level of income distribution and the way in which it changes during the growth process. In turn, the level of inequality is related to the economic structures and patterns of specialization prevailing in each country (see subsection C.2(c) of this chapter).

Data on income inequality in LDCs is patchy. However, available estimates from household surveys indicate a mixed pattern: some LDCs have very high income inequality, while others have low inequality. Interestingly, the lower-income LDCs are at both ends of the spectrum. As table 28 shows, there are a few LDCs, including Sierra Leone, Central African Republic, Lesotho, Haiti, Zambia, Cape Verde and Gambia, where the Gini index (an indicator of inequality) is higher than 50. In these countries, the level of inequality is such that the growth impact on poverty is likely to be strongly attenuated.

The relationship between economic growth and poverty reduction is mediated by the level of income distribution and the way in which it changes during the growth process.

There are very few estimates of changes in inequality. However, in order to test whether the recent growth spurt has been accompanied by rising inequality with an adverse impact on poverty reduction, we have made two additional poverty estimates for our sample of countries, besides the main estimate. The first additional estimate is obtained by calculating what the poverty incidence would have been if each country had had a Gini index constant at the lowest level actually reached during the 1980–2005 period. This provides the lower bound of estimates (the "Minimum Gini" curve in chart 15). The second hypothetical

Table 28. Income inequality in LDCs, 2005 *(Gini index)*					
Low inequality *(Gini index < 30)*		**Medium inequality** *(40 < Gini index < 50)*		**High inequality** *(Gini index > 50)*	
Burkina Faso	39.5	Madagascar	47.5	Sierra Leone	62.9
Mauritania	39.0	Mozambique	47.3	Central African Rep.	61.3
Malawi	39.0	Nepal	47.2	Lesotho	60.0
Benin[a]	36.5	Rwanda	46.8	Haiti	59.2
Chad	35.0	Uganda	45.7	Zambia	50.8
Lao People's Dem. Rep.[b]	34.6	Burundi	42.4	Cape Verde	50.5
United Rep. of Tanzania	34.6	Cambodia	41.7	Gambia	50.2
Togo	33.8	Niger	41.5		
Bangladesh	33.4	Senegal	41.3		
Yemen	33.4	Guinea	40.4		
Ethiopia	30.0	Angola	40.2		
		Mali	40.1		

Source: UNCTAD secretariat compilation based on data from World Bank, *World Development Indicators,* online, May 2008.

a Data for 2003.
b Data for 2002.

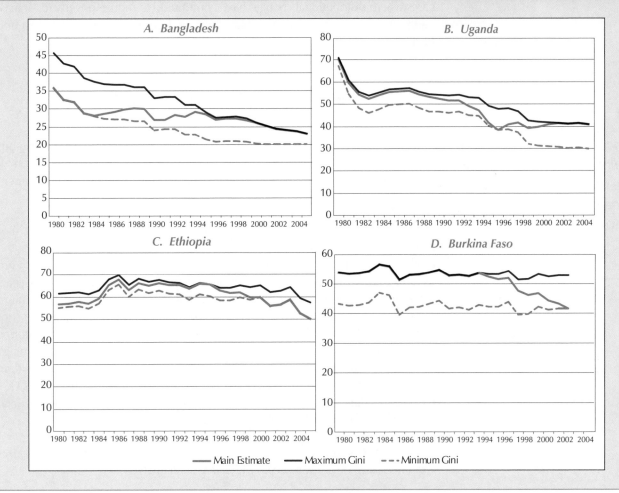

Chart 15. Absolute poverty rates under different income distribution assumptions in selected LDCs, 1980–2005
(Share of population living on less than $1 a day, per cent)

A. Bangladesh

B. Uganda

C. Ethiopia

D. Burkina Faso

—— Main Estimate   —— Maximum Gini   --- Minimum Gini

Source: Karshenas (2008).

Note: The main estimate was obtained according to the methodology explained in the Annex.

Maximum Gini is the poverty rate that would have prevailed if the Gini index had remained constant at its actual maximum level during the period. Minimum Gini is the poverty rate that would have prevailed if the Gini index had remained constant at its actual minimum level during the period.

poverty rate is obtained by keeping the Gini index constant at the highest level actually reached during that period. This yields the upper bound of poverty estimates (the "Maximum Gini" curve in chart 15). The main estimate fluctuates between these two bounds. If it converges towards the lower bound, this means that falling income inequality is contributing to poverty reduction. On the other hand, if it approaches the upper bound, this means that a worsening income distribution is slowing poverty reduction. These interpretations hold irrespective of whether poverty is increasing or falling.

Distributional factors have a relatively important effect on $1-a-day poverty, but not on $2-a-day poverty.

This analysis has yielded two types of findings. First, while distributional factors seem to have a relatively important effect on $1-a-day poverty, the effect in the case of $2-a-day poverty is not noticeable. This is explained by the fact that when total poverty reaches the 70 per cent to 90 per cent ranges (as is the case in most LDCs), it is clear that changes in the shape of the distribution curve cannot have much impact on poverty in either direction (Karshenas, 2003).

Income distribution has worsened along with growth, slowing down poverty reduction.

Second, in most countries of our sample, the main $1-a-day poverty estimates have moved from the lower bound towards the higher bound. The typical pattern is that income distribution has worsened along with growth, slowing down poverty reduction. This is exemplified by Bangladesh and Uganda, two of the countries with the steadiest and most sustained good growth performance during the period considered (charts 15A and 15B and table 21). There are a few exceptions — cases where distributional changes have contributed to reduce poverty (or at least partly offset other factors that would otherwise have worsened it). Ethiopia and Burkina Faso are the main examples (charts 15C and 15D).

E. Progress towards the MDGs

Income poverty is only one dimension of poverty, and the Millennium Development Goals target a broader range of human development indicators.

Income poverty is only one dimension of poverty, and this section extends the analysis by introducing a broader range of human development indicators. It assesses the extent to which LDCs are achieving selected Millennium Development Goals.

As with the analysis of poverty trends, there is a serious lack of data to monitor progress towards internationally agreed goals in LDCs. Chart 16 shows the availability of data on the status of LDCs with regard to 48 indicators which are used to monitor the MDGs. The indicators refer to 2004–2005, the latest years for which international data are available, and are taken from the Millennium Development Goals Indicators site of the United Nations Department of Economic and Social Affairs, Statistics Division,[9] the prime source for monitoring progress towards MDG achievement. From the chart, it is apparent that coverage of countries is woefully inadequate. There are only 13 targets for which more than 45 LDCs have recent data. For 32 out of the 48 indicators, less then ten LDCs have recent data. Moreover, for the 13 indicators for which there is recent data, there are only five which enable trend analysis back to 1990.

Given the dearth in data on both level and progress towards most MDGs, this section focuses on a few selected MDG targets, namely:

1. Halving, between 1990 and 2015, the proportion of people whose income is less than $1 a day (MDG 1);

Data coverage of MDG indicators in LDCs is woefully inadequate.

2. Halving, between 1990 and 2015, the proportion of people suffering from hunger (MDG 1);

3. Ensuring that, by 2015, children everywhere, boys and girls alike, are able to complete a full course of primary schooling (MDG 2);

4. Eliminating gender disparity in primary and secondary education, preferably by 2005, and at all levels of education no later than 2015 (MDG 3);

5. Reducing, by two thirds, between 1990 and 2015, the under-5 mortality rate (MDG 4);

6. Halving, by 2015, the proportion of people without access to safe drinking water (MDG 7); and

7. Halving the proportion of people without access to sanitation (MDG 7).

The assessment of progress towards the $1-a-day poverty target uses the new poverty estimates presented in section C of this chapter. The other indicators are based on a mix of sources. They mostly draw from the official MDG Indicators data set available on the United Nations Department of Economic and Social Affairs, Statistics Division website. This is the product of the Inter-agency and Expert Group (IAEG) on MDG Indicators, and it reports a mix of national level surveys, Government data and IAEG estimates. We have supplemented this with country-level "MDG Profile" narratives. These data are supplied by national Governments and UNDP country offices but cover only 40 out of 50 LDCs.

Chart 16. Number of LDCs with data on the MDG indicator, 2004–2005

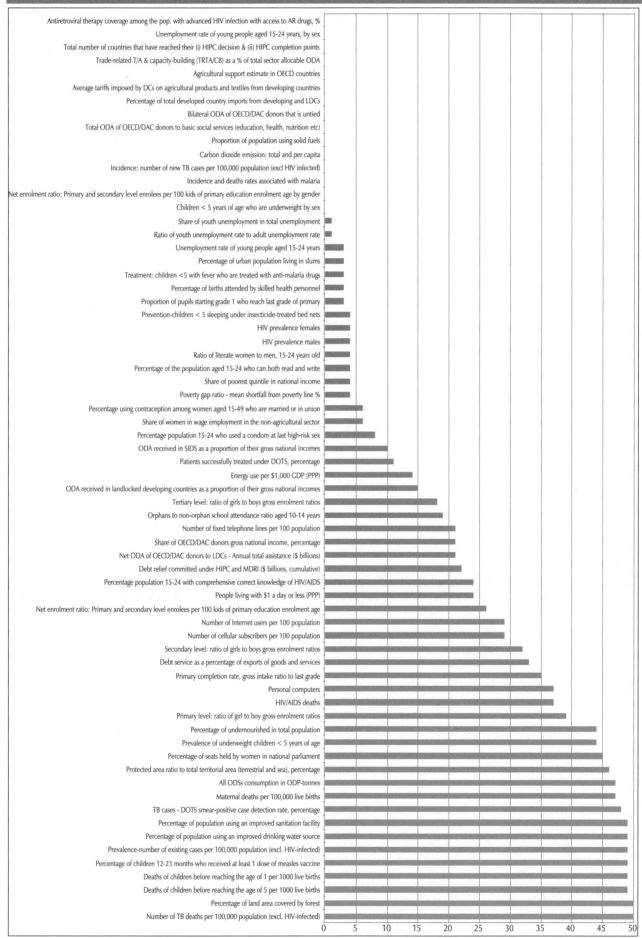

Source: UNCTAD secretariat calculations based on data from United Nations/DESA Statistics Division, *Millennium Development Goals Indicators* (unstats.un.org/unsd/mdg/default.aspx), downloaded in May 2008.

1. OVERALL PATTERN

LDCs are generally off track to achieve the few poverty and human development MDGs for which it is possible to monitor progress. This is exemplified by the progress they have achieved in poverty reduction and in combating child mortality. Chart 17 shows that there is a widening gap between the progress actually achieved by the LDCs and the path that they would have to follow in order to reach the respective MDGs by 2015.

With regard to $1-a-day poverty, it is apparent that the LDCs as a group are seriously off track to meet this goal. The critical date in the poverty trend is 1994, the year in which the incidence of extreme poverty started to slowly decline in LDCs. However, there has been only a marginal improvement in the rate of poverty reduction since the adoption of the Millennium Declaration. Moreover, even with the very high rates of economic growth achieved in recent years, the rate of poverty reduction is still much slower than that required to achieve the relevant MDG.

For the MDG target to be achieved, the incidence of extreme poverty in the LDCs must fall from 40.4 per cent in 1990 to 20.2 per cent in 2015. Yet if the incidence of extreme poverty declines from 2006 to 2015 at the same rate as during the period 1990–2005, it will only reach 33.4 per cent in 2015. Moreover, even if it declines at the higher rate achieved over the period 2000–2005, the incidence of extreme poverty is projected to reach only 31.7 per cent. This means that the extreme poverty rate will have decreased by 25 per cent rather than 50 per cent in 2015. Moreover, there will be 116 million more people living in extreme poverty in 2015 than there would have been had the MDG target been met.

Similarly, chart 17B indicates for child mortality that, for the LDCs as a group, there has been no change in the slow downward trend in child mortality rates. The overall child mortality rate fell from 167 per 1,000 live births in 1990 to 138 per 1,000 in 2005. If anything, however, the rate of progress towards this goal has slowed slightly since 2000.

LDCs are generally off track to achieve the few poverty and human development MDGs for which it is possible to monitor progress.

There is a widening gap between the progress actually achieved by the LDCs and the path that they would have to follow in order to reach the respective MDGs by 2015.

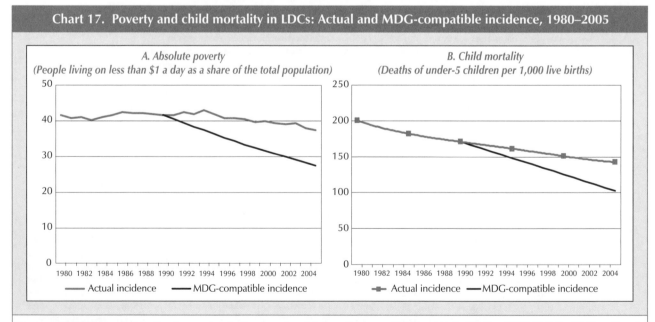

Chart 17. Poverty and child mortality in LDCs: Actual and MDG-compatible incidence, 1980–2005

Source: UNCTAD secretariat estimations and projections based on data from Karshenas (2008) and United Nations/DESA Statistics Division. Poverty data are based on the sample of LDCs mentioned in table 24. Child mortality data are the unweighted average for all the LDCs.

Note: The MDG-compatible incidence is the hypothetical path that poverty and child mortality incidence would need to follow if the LDCs were to achieve the respective MDG targets by 2015.

Still, there are a few countries which are making significant progress on specific indicators. However, the pattern is very mixed and only a handful of countries are making progress across a broad front.

In general, it is possible to see an emerging pattern in which significant progress is being made to achieve targets which depend primarily on public services and can be achieved with some increase in public expenditure. However, there is a distinct hierarchy in the rate of achievement which reflects the priorities of Governments and also donors who are funding the scale-up in provision. In this regard, achievements in increasing primary education enrolments outstrip progress in improving access to water, which in turn exceeds accomplishments in improving sanitation. Thus:

- More than half of the LDCs for which data are available are on track to achieve the primary education enrolment goal;

- Between one-third and half of the LDCs for which data are available are on track to achieve the goal of access to safe water; and

- Just one-third of the LDCs for which data are available are on track to achieve the sanitation goal.

Where progress also depends on cultural factors, such as the gender equality in education target, relative progress has also been slower. Between one-third and half of LDCs for which data are available are on track to achieve this goal.

Leaving aside quality-related issues, progress towards the primary education enrolment goal shows what is possible where government and donor policy commitment is combined with appropriate levels of financial and technical assistance in the cases of goals that depend primarily on public services and expenditure. However, progress towards targets that depend more on household incomes has been slower. In this regard, there is very slow progress in reducing the incidence of extreme poverty. Less than 15 per cent of the countries for which data are available are on track. In relation to the hunger target of MDG1, one-quarter of the LDCs are not simply off track but are experiencing reversal or stagnation. Moreover, this situation will certainly be exacerbated by recent food price increases. It is proving very difficult for LDCs to keep on track in reducing child mortality, which is affected by trends for both private incomes and public services. Only 20 per cent of the LDCs for which data are available are on track with regard to this indicator.

The following sections provide some details on these trends and identify some LDCs which have performed well with regard to progress towards MDG achievement.

2. PROGRESS IN REDUCING $1-A-DAY POVERTY

Country-level trends suggest that just four countries out of a total of 28 in our sample are likely to achieve the target on the basis of poverty reduction trends of 1990–2005, namely Cape Verde, Guinea, Malawi and Senegal. On the basis of poverty reduction trends of a more recent and generally more favourable period (2000–2005), Cambodia, Cape Verde, Guinea and Senegal are likely to achieve the goal.

The distance between projected achievements and the target is quite different between African and Asian LDCs, as are developments in their poverty trends. The goal for the African LDCs in the sample of countries for which we have made poverty estimates (table 24) is to reach a poverty rate of 24.7 per cent in 2015.

There are a few countries making significant progress on specific indicators. However, the pattern is very mixed and only a handful of countries are making progress across a broad front.

Significant progress is being made to achieve targets which depend primarily on public services and can be achieved with some increase in public expenditure.

Progress towards targets that depend more on household incomes has been slower.

Just four countries out of a total of 28 in our sample are likely to achieve the target on the basis of poverty reduction trends.

Our projections indicate that they will reach a poverty rate of 38.5 per cent even if poverty reduction occurs at the same rate as during the period 2000–2005. The projected poverty rate is just slightly higher if poverty reduction occurs at the same rate as in 1990–2005. The target of the Asian LDCs of our sample is to reduce extreme poverty to 13.5 per cent in 2015. Our projections indicate that they will also miss the target, but by a narrower margin than the African LDCs. The two alternative scenarios for Asian LDCs yield a greater variation than those for the African countries. Asian LDCs are projected to achieve rates of between 19.6 per cent in 2015 if they reduce poverty incidence at the same rate as in 2000–2005, and 23.2 per cent in 2015 if they reduce it at the same pace as in 1990–2005.

Asian LDCs will also miss the poverty target, but by a narrower margin than the African LDCs.

These outcomes are regarded as being representative for the LDCs as a group. However, the actual outcome in terms of poverty reduction is likely to be worse than those mechanically projected on the basis of past trends because of the impact of sharply rising food prices since 2007. This issue is discussed in section F of this chapter.

3. PROGRESS TOWARDS OTHER HUMAN DEVELOPMENT TARGETS

Most LDCs are also off track as a group to meet the Millennium human development targets for which it is possible to gather data for a wide group of countries (table 29). Nevertheless, some countries have made progress towards specific targets.

(a) Hunger

In one third of the LDCs, average food consumption is below the minimum adequate for proper bodily functioning.

Given the high incidence of extreme poverty in LDCs, the incidence of hunger is also high. In one third of the LDCs for which data are available (14 out of 42 countries), average food consumption is below 2,100 calories per day, which is considered the minimum adequate for proper bodily functioning. For the LDCs as a group, the share of the population which is estimated to be undernourished in 2002 was 31 per cent, compared with 17 per cent in other developing countries. In half of the LDCs for which data are available, over one-third of the population is estimated to be undernourished. The incidence of hunger is particularly high in conflict-affected countries (such as Democratic Republic of the Congo and Somalia), but it is also high in some countries which have sustained high growth rates since the mid-1990s. For example, it is estimated that over 40 per cent of the population was undernourished in 2002 in Angola, Mozambique and Tanzania. In Bangladesh, 30 per cent of the population is estimated to be undernourished despite steady growth since the early 1990s. In general, the incidence of hunger is highest in mineral-exporting LDCs.

The proportion of the population which is undernourished in the LDCs is declining very slowly from an average of 33 per cent in 1991 to 31 per cent in 2002.

The proportion of the population which is undernourished in the LDCs as a group is declining very slowly. It has decreased from an average of 33 per cent in 1991 to 31 per cent in 2002 (unweighted averages). Within the overall trends, however, the picture is mixed. Out of a sample of 42 LDCs, 19 countries are on track to achieve the hunger reduction target and three are projected to have achieved the target by 2007. The top best performers are indicated in chart 18A. Yet there is only slow progress in eight countries and reversal or stagnation in a further 12 countries. Of those on track to achieve the target in terms of the incidence of hunger, the average level of food consumption remains very low. It is close to the 2,100 calories threshold in seven out of the 19 on-track countries.

(b) Primary education

With regard to the target of ensuring that by 2015 children everywhere are able to complete a full course of primary schooling, the overall picture is more encouraging. According to "MDG Profile" data, 19 out of 35 LDCs are on track to achieve the target and Maldives has already achieved it (table 29). According to the MDG Indicators data of the United Nations Department of Economic and Social Affairs, Statistics Division, average net enrolment in primary education in LDCs jumped from 47 per cent in 1991 to 76 per cent in 2005. Net enrolment rates exceed 75 per cent in 18 out of 30 countries for which data are available. Particularly big leaps in net primary enrolment rates have been achieved in a few countries. Net enrolment rates increased by over 7 per cent per annum in Tanzania, Ethiopia and Benin, between 2000 and 2005. At the same time, however, Cape Verde, Malawi and Mauritania reported a decline in the annual rate of net enrolment in primary education over the same period. The top 10 best performers are shown in chart 18B.

Net enrolment in primary education in LDCs jumped from 47 per cent in 1991 to 76 per cent in 2005.

Primary school completion rates are also increasing, and were up from 34 per cent in 1991 to 57 per cent in 2005. Mozambique, Cambodia, Benin and Niger all achieved high rates of progress on raising primary school completion rates. The weakest performers were in Africa. The intractable groups to reach with primary education remain girls, particularly those from ethnic, religious or caste minorities.

Beyond these quantitative measurements, qualitative aspects should also be taken into account.[10]

The ratio of girls' to boys' enrolment in primary school increased from 0.79 in 1991 to 0.89 in 2005.

(c) Gender equality in education

It is estimated that for LDCs as a group, the ratio of girls' to boys' enrolment in primary school increased from 0.79 in 1991 to 0.89 in 2005. As increasing numbers of students finish primary education, demand for secondary education is growing in LDCs. LDC gender disparities in access to education at this level are also diminishing. For the LDCs as a group, the ratio of girls' to boys' enrolment in secondary school increased from 0.77 in 1999 to 0.81 in 2005 (UNESCO, 2007).

As with the primary education enrolment as a whole, it is clear that quick progress can be made on aspects of this indicator (chart 18C). For example, the ratio between girls' and boys' primary enrolment increased from 0.08 in 1999 to 0.59 in 2005 in Afghanistan and during the same period from 0.62 to 0.86 in Ethiopia (UNESCO, 2007). However, important disparities affecting girls still prevail in some countries.

The higher one goes up the education system, the greater the gender disparities.

The higher one goes up the education system, the greater the disparities. A third of the countries with data available in 2005 had achieved gender parity in primary education, compared with a fifth in secondary education and only a tenth in tertiary education.

(d) Child mortality

As with hunger, child mortality rates are much higher in LDCs than in other developing countries. In 2006, 14 out of every 100 children born alive in the LDCs died before their fifth birthday as against 8 out of every 100 in all developing countries. According to the MDG Indicators database of the United Nations Department of Economic and Social Affairs, Statistic Division, 26 LDCs are off track to achieve the child mortality target and child mortality is either going up or stagnant in a further 13 LDCs. During the period 1990 to 2005, impressive reductions in annual under-5 mortality rates were recorded in Timor-Leste, Maldives, Bhutan, Nepal, Lao People's Democratic Republic and Bangladesh (chart 18D). Yet child mortality increased in Lesotho and Cambodia despite

In 2006, 14 out of every 100 children born alive in the LDCs died before their fifth birthday as against 8 out of every 100 in all developing countries.

Table 29. Progress towards selected human development targets in LDCs

Target	LDC data availability	Achieved by 2007	Achievable by 2015	Low progress	Reversal/ stagnation
		3	**19**	**8**	**12**
Hunger (undernourished)	42	Djibouti Myanmar Samoa	Angola Benin Cambodia Chad Guinea Haiti Kiribati Lao PDR Lesotho Malawi Maldives Mauritania Mozambique Niger Sao Tome and Principe Solomon Islands Timor Leste Togo Uganda	Bangladesh Burkina Faso Central African Republic Mali Nepal Rwanda Sudan Zambia	Burundi Comoros Dem. Rep. of the Congo Gambia Guinea-Bissau Liberia Madagascar Senegal Sierra Leone United Rep. of Tanzania Vanuatu Yemen
		1	**19**	**15**	
Primary education	35	Maldives	Angola Bangladesh Bhutan Cambodia Chad Djibouti Equatorial Guinea Guinea-Bissau Lao PDR Lesotho Madagascar Mauritania Myanmar Senegal Sierra Leone Timor Leste Uganda Yemen Zambia	Benin Burkina Faso Central African Republic Comoros Gambia Guinea Haiti Liberia Malawi Mali Samoa Somalia Sudan United Rep. of Tanzania Togo	
		4	**6**	**10**	**4**
Gender equality in education[a]	24	Lesotho Malawi Mauritania Myanmar	Ethiopia Lao People's Dem. Rep. Nepal Senegal Solomon Islands Sudan	Afghanistan Benin Burkina Faso Burundi Chad Djibouti Guinea Mozambique Niger Togo	Eritrea Madagascar Mali United Rep. of Tanzania

Table 29 (contd.)

Target	LDC data availability	Achieved by 2007	Achievable by 2015	Low progress	Reversal/ stagnation
		1	**10**	**26**	**13**
Child mortality	50	Samoa	Bangladesh Bhutan Cape Verde Comoros Eritrea Lao People's Dem. Rep. Malawi Maldives Nepal Timor Leste	Afghanistan Benin Burkina Faso Djibouti Ethiopia Gambia Guinea Guinea-Bissau Haiti Kiribati Madagascar Mali Mauritania Mozambique Myanmar Niger Senegal Sierra Leone Solomon Islands Sudan Tanzania Togo Tuvalu Uganda Vanuatu Yemen	Angola Burundi Cambodia Central African Republic Chad Dem. Rep. of the Congo Equatorial Guinea Lesotho Liberia Rwanda Sao Tome and Principe Somalia Zambia
		4	**12**	**15**	**6**
Access to safe water	37	Guinea Malawi Nepal Tuvalu	Afghanistan Burkina Faso Burundi Central African Republic Chad Eritrea Kiribati Myanmar Rwanda Senegal Uganda United Rep. of Tanzania	Angola Bangladesh Benin Dem. Rep. of the Congo Djibouti Haiti Liberia Madagascar Mali Mauritania Mozambique Niger Sudan Togo Zambia	Comoros Ethiopia Maldives Samoa Vanuatu Yemen
		3	**9**	**19**	**5**
Access to improved sanitation	36	Myanmar Samoa Tuvalu	Afghanistan Bangladesh Benin Kiribati Madagascar Malawi Nepal Senegal Zambia	Angola Burkina Faso Central African Republic Chad Comoros Dem. Rep. of the Congo Djibouti Eritrea Ethiopia Guinea Haiti Mali Mauritania Mozambique Niger Rwanda Sudan Uganda Yemen	Burundi Lesotho Liberia Tanzania Togo

Source: UNCTAD secretariat calculations based on data from United Nations/DESA Statistics Division, *Millennium Development Goals Indicators* (unstats.un.org/unsd/ mdg/default.aspx) and UNDP, *UNMDG Monitor* (www.mdgmonitor.org), both downloaded in May 2008.

Note: An LDC has achieved the target when the actual value of the indicator has already met the MDG target. An LDC is considered to have stagnated (reversed) when the actual value is equal to (worse than) the value at the beginning of the period. An MDG target is considered achievable for an LDC when the average actual rate of progress experienced to date is equal to (or better than) the required rate to achieve the target. An LDC is considered to have made low progress towards a MDG target when the average actual rate of progress experienced to date is less than the required rate to achieve the target.

a Gender equality is measured using the Gender Parity Index (GPI) of the Gross Enrolment Ratio (GER) for primary level education in LDCs.

Chart 18. Top 10 LDC performers in terms of progress towards selected MDGs

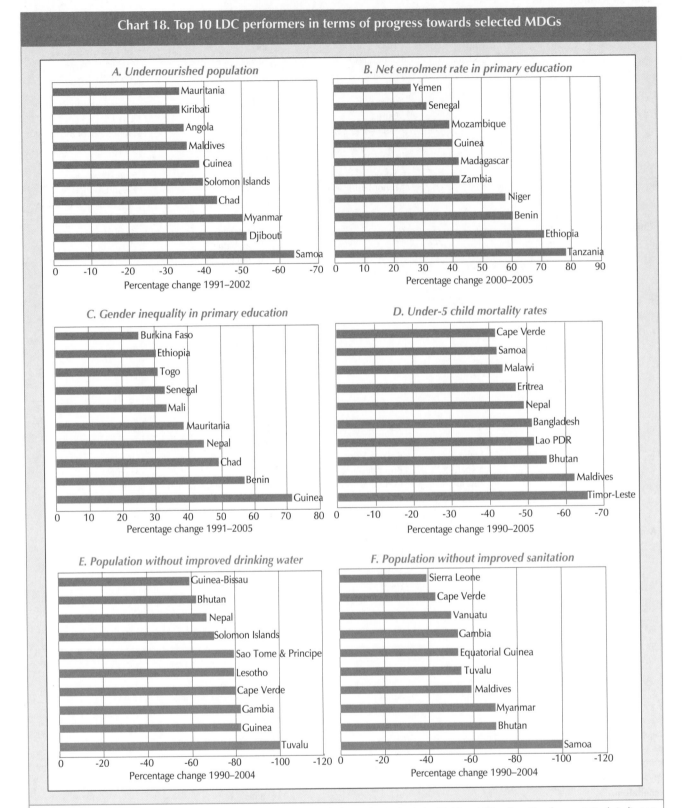

Source: UNCTAD secretariat calculations based on data from United Nations/DESA Statistics Division, *Millennium Development Goals Indicators*. (unstats.un.org/unsd/mdg/default.aspx), downloaded in May 2008.

high economic growth rates. The slow pace of progress reflects a combination of factors, including hunger and ill-health. Widespread malaria, the lack of basic health services and the prevalence of HIV/AIDS may in part explain the slow progress on average for LDCs.

(e) Drinking water and sanitation

During the period 1990 to 2004, there was steady progress towards halving the proportion of people without access to safe drinking water in LDCs. The proportion of people without such access fell from 47 per cent in 1991 to 37 per cent in 2004. Four LDCs have already met the drinking water target — Guinea, Malawi, Nepal and Tuvalu — and a further 12 countries are on track to achieve the goal in 2015. Tuvalu and Guinea have made the fastest progress of the 37 countries for which data are available (chart 18E). The LDCs that have performed poorly in trying to achieve this target include Ethiopia, which has significant water supply and climate-change-related problems.

Progress on sanitation, by contrast, has lagged. The proportion of the population without access to improved sanitation fell from 70 per cent in 1990 to 60 per cent in 2004. This is some 23 percentage points lower than the average rate of access to clean water, and is probably related to the fact that ODA for water supply and sanitation declined significantly from the mid-1990s to 2002 (World Bank, 2007). The top 10 performers in improving access to sanitation include Samoa, Bhutan, Myanmar and Maldives (chart 18F).

The share of people without access to safe drinking water fell from 47 per cent in 1991 to 37 per cent in 2004.

The proportion of the population without access to improved sanitation fell from 70 per cent in 1990 to 60 per cent in 2004.

F. Impact and policy implications of soaring international food prices

1. IMPACT OF RECENT FOOD PRICE INCREASES

As indicated in chapter 1 of this Report, the main surge in international commodity prices in the early part of this decade was for oil and minerals rather than agricultural commodities. International food prices rose sharply in 2006 and 2007, however, with a further price spike in the first half of 2008. The Food and Agriculture Organization of the United Nations (FAO) food price index was on average 8 per cent higher in 2006 than in 2005. Yet it was 24 per cent higher in 2007 than in 2006, and a further 53 per cent higher in the first three months of 2008 than the first three months of 2007 (FAO, 2008a). Particularly strong price surges have occurred in oils and fats and cereals. Price indices for these commodity groups in March 2008 were almost three times the level during the period 1998–2000. By March 2008, international prices of wheat and rice were twice their levels of a year earlier, while prices of maize were more than one third higher (FAO, 2008a).

International food prices rose sharply in 2006 and 2007, with a further price spike in the first half of 2008.

The global sharp increase in international food prices and the food riots that it provoked have given rise to an array of explanations for the current situation. The factors usually singled out to explain the price rises include growing food demand in emerging markets, the flow of speculative capital into commodity markets, increasing biofuel production, weather incidents and global warming. However, in order to understand the impact of the global food crisis on the LDCs and on their social developments, it is perhaps more important to examine the structural causes of the current crisis, the global interdependence that they highlight, and the type of insertion of these countries in the international economy. Using this perspective, the following factors become equally — if not more — important:

In order to understand the impact of the global food crisis on the LDCs and on their social developments, it is more important to examine the structural causes of the current crisis.

- The neglect of agriculture by public policies in many developing countries since the 1980s, resulting in underinvestment in infrastructure, withdrawal of domestic support measures to farmers, etc.;

- The adverse impact of trade liberalization on domestic farmers unable to cope with foreign competition, particularly smallholders producing staple food for local consumption;

- The negative impact of agricultural exports subsidies and domestic support policies in developed countries, which magnify the preceding factors; and

- The stark shrinkage of ODA financing for agricultural R&D.

The combination of these developments has resulted in low agricultural productivity level and growth in several developing countries, particularly in Africa (UNCTAD, 2008).

In the 1980s, LDCs as a group were net food exporters but became net food importers in the 1990s. The shift to food deficits was particularly marked in the African countries.

The above features apply to the majority of LDCs and are consistent with the policy model of outward orientation, trade openness and withdrawal of public support to production that LDCs have been following since the 1980s. In the 1980s, LDCs as a group were net food exporters but became net food importers in the 1990s, after the implementation of this policy package. The shift to food deficits was particularly marked in the African countries. LDCs as a group are still net food importers at present, as are almost three fourths of these countries (table 30). Current high international food prices are bringing about yet another episode of food import surges, which have become more frequent in the LDCs in the post-trade liberalization era (UNCTAD, 2004: 271-272).

Rising food prices will have negative effects on poverty trends in LDCs and also slow progress towards MDGs.

Rising food prices will have negative effects on poverty trends in LDCs and also slow progress towards MDGs. The negative effects will arise partly because the food price hikes threaten economic growth and partly because of the direct impact of rising domestic food prices on the ability of households to meet essential subsistence needs. These effects are likely to be more severe in the LDCs than in other developing countries. First, most LDCs are net food importers and already have large trade deficits. Second, levels of poverty and food insecurity are already high, and many people spend 50–80 per cent of their household income on food. Third, quite apart from generalized poverty, many LDCs are already dealing with food crises which require external assistance owing to such factors as natural disasters, concentrations of internally displaced persons and localized crop failures. These factors are analysed separately hereafter.

(a) Impact on food import bills

The bigger food import bills will widen further the already high trade deficits of the LDCs. The balance-of-payment impact will be accentuated as countries also have to deal with rising energy prices.

The immediate impact of the rising international food prices will be a worsening of the balance-of-payment problems of most LDCs. In 2004–2006, 36 out of 50 LDCs were net food importers (table 30). Moreover, using a narrow definition of food which excludes cash crops, processed food and seafood, only seven LDCs — Burkina Faso, Madagascar, Myanmar, Somalia, Tuvalu, Vanuatu and Zambia — were net food exporters in 2004–2005 (Ng and Aksoy, 2008).

Not only are most LDCs net food importers, but food imports constituted a significant share of total merchandise imports and total exports in many of them even before the recent international price spike. In 2006 food imports constituted over 20 per cent of total merchandise imports in 20 LDCs and more than 20 per cent of merchandise exports in 33 LDCs (table 30). Over half of total merchandise export earnings were used to purchase imported food in 17 LDCs in 2006, in 10 of them the totality of export earnings were not enough to meet the food import bill.

The aggregate food import bill of the LDCs as a group is estimated to have risen by 26 per cent between 2006 and 2007, much in line with the increase in the overall food price index. The increase in the food import bill was equivalent to 1 per cent of the GDP of the LDCs in 2006.[11]

Table 30. Indicators of food security in LDCs								
	Undernourished population	Food consumption	Change in per capita	Agricultural Production	Food aid	Food imports as % of:		
	%	Calories per capita/day	food consumption %	Instability Index[a]	% of total food imports	Total merchandise imports	Total merchandise exports	Food consumption
	2004	2002–2004	1995–1997 to 2002–2004	2004	2006	2006	2006	1996-2001
Net food importers and net importers of agricultural raw materials								
Angola	40	2 120	1.01	4.68	0.8	18.9	3.9	11.4
Bangladesh	30	2 200	0.97	3.47	2.2	14.3	18.3	7.8
Cape Verde	2.5	..	..	15.96	5.3	29.2	> 100	32.7
Comoros	62	1 770	-0.35	2.87	0.0	33.0	> 100	12.7
Djibouti	27	2 270	1.18	8.81	2.0	21.6	> 100	43.9
Eritrea	73	1 500	..	18.76	3.3	24.0	> 100	11.8
Gambia	27	2 240	0.23	18.42	7.2	31.2	> 100	38.1
Haiti	47	2 110	1.12	2.73	10.3	26.2	82.1	19.6
Kiribati	6	2 800	0.03	12.55	0.0	33.7	> 100	26.5
Maldives	11	2 600	0.64	4.00	1.1	16.0	> 100	31.0
Nepal	17	2 430	0.88	3.95	3.7	14.9	41.1	2.7
Niger	34	2 150	0.73	12.98	8.4	32.7	63.2	5.8
Samoa	4	2 930	1.31	7.52	0.0	18.6	60.1	18.5
Sao Time and Principe	13	2 490	1.08	7.03	0.0	30.6	> 100	14.9
Senegal	24	2 360	0.46	16.53	0.9	23.4	57.6	21.1
Sierra Leone	50	1 910	-0.61	5.46	11.8	20.6	37.1	10.0
Somalia	61	..	..	9.12	1.5	50.3	> 100	8.6
Tuvalu	3	..	..	21.10	0.0	8.0	88.5	24.7
Yemen	36	2 010	-0.08	5.21	2.1	21.2	16.7	31.2
Net food importers and net exporters of agricultural raw materials								
Afghanistan	56	..	..	15.36	5.5	23.4	> 100	6.1
Benin	15	2 590	0.59	6.48	1.9	27.8	99.4	5.3
Burkina Faso	19	2 500	0.39	7.76	14.7	12.8	37.7	10.4
Cambodia	33	2 070	1.13	8.01	0.2	7.9	6.0	3.4
Central African Republic	43	1 960	0.59	3.89	7.6	20.0	27.6	2.3
Chad	71	1 590	-1.08	3.72	0.0	26.0	31.7	2.2
Dem. Rep. of the Congo	9	0	0.00	6.78	2.0	15.4	4.4	5.6
Equatorial Guinea	26	..	..	3.48	0.0	16.9	14.0	8.7
Guinea	22	2 370	0.99	8.16	5.3	12.4	10.7	1.8
Lao People's Dem. Rep.	12	2 580	0.18	7.56	1.4	23.6	54.0	19.0
Lesotho	46	1 930	-0.66	11.28	0.0	2.7	11.6	12.9
Liberia	47	2 080	1.13	7.30	2.3	13.9	16.7	7.2
Mali	27	2 270	-0.25	8.42	4.6	11.9	19.2	4.7
Mozambique	34	2 130	1.06	7.81	9.2	16.1	3.2	2.0
Sudan	27	2 270	-0.25	8.42	3.9	11.9	19.2	4.7
Timor-Leste	7	2 750	0.22	4.88	9.8	18.4	16.9	..
Togo	29	2 200	0.20	6.13	0.1	13.9	18.7	3.7
Net food exporters and net exporters of agricultural raw materials								
Ethiopia	46	1 850	..	14.28	149.2	8.5	42.6	2.0
Guinea-Bissau	6	2 940	0.55	4.97	23.0	14.0	6.2	1.9
Madagascar	35	2 030	-0.66	4.26	15.4	26.9	29.4	11.4
Malawi	37	2 050	0.18	2.25	10.6	14.5	25.3	3.3
Myanmar	33	2 120	0.39	10.12	0.2	15.1	27.4	3.6
Solomon Islands	19	2 370	0.67	3.27	1.5	13.6	36.2	2.9
Tanzania	20	2 230	0.11	9.68	0.7	11.3	20.3	14.1
Uganda	44	1 960	0.44	3.97	6.5	12.2	32.1	4.6
Vanuatu	12	2 600	0.23	8.81	0.0	13.4	47.7	13.7
Zambia	49	1 950	0.14	9.86	1.4	7.6	6.2	4.5
Net food exporters and net importers of agricultural raw materials								
Bhutan	23	..	..	6.32	0.0	8.4	7.5	3.4
Burundi	68	1 660	-0.23	5.64	28.0	7.5	25.8	0.8
Mauritania	10	2 740	0.17	3.40	1.9	25.0	21.3	32.9
Rwanda	37	2 110	1.42	13.58	4.5	12.4	45.5	5.9
LDCs	**36**	**2 033**	**0.39**	**8.14**[b]	**3.7**	**15.4**	**15.6**	**23.6**

Source: UNCTAD secretariat calculations based on data from FAO, OECD/DAC and United Nations/DESA Statistics Division.

Note: The classification of LDCs according to their net exports of food and agricultural raw materials is based on a three-year (2004–2006) average of data from UNCTAD, *Handbook of Statistics 2007* and on UNCTAD estimates.
The definition of food and agricultural raw materials is the same as in table 8.
a Calculated according to the methodology of the Committee for Development Policy's Economic Vulnerability Index.   b Unweighted average.

| Table 31. Food insecurity in LDCs, by type of insecurity and region, 2008 ||
Country	Type of insecurity
Africa	
Lesotho	Multiple-year droughts until last season
Somalia	Conflict, adverse weather
Eritrea	IDPs, economic constraints
Liberia	Post-conflict recovery period
Mauritania	Several years of drought
Sierra Leone	Post-conflict recovery period
Burundi	Civil strife, IDPs and returnees
Central African Republic	Refugees, insecurity in parts
Chad	Refugees, conflict
Democratic Republic of Congo	Civil strife, returnees
Ethiopia	Insecurity in parts, localized crop failure
Guinea	Refugees
Guinea-Bissau	Localized insecurity
Sudan	Civil strife
Uganda	Civil strife in the north, localized crop failure
Asia	
Afghanistan	Conflict and insecurity
Bangladesh	Past floods and cyclone, avian influenza
Nepal	Poor market access, conflict and past floods
Timor-Leste	IDPs, past drought and floods
Latin America	
Haiti	Past floods

Source: Food and Agriculture Organization of the United Nations (http://www.fao.org/docrep/010/ai465e/ai465e02.htm). Data downloaded in May 2008.

> *The impact of rising international food prices on poverty depends on whether international price rises pass through to national markets and the extent to which households depend on purchased food.*

The bigger food import bills will widen further the already high trade deficits of the LDCs. This will affect all food-importing LDCs, and the balance-of-payment impact will be accentuated as countries also have to deal with rising energy prices. The countries which are particularly vulnerable are those in which food imports already constitute over 20 per cent of total merchandise imports and food imports also account for a high share of total food consumption, namely Cape Verde, Djibouti, Gambia, Haiti, Lesotho, Kiribati, Mauritania, Samoa, Senegal, Sao Tome and Principe and Yemen.

(b) Poverty and household food security

The impact of rising international food prices on poverty and household food security depends on whether price rises in international markets pass through to national markets and the extent to which households, particularly poor households, depend on purchased food.

> *One factor in favour of some LDCs is that imported food is not a significant proportion of total food consumption, but dependence of imported food products is increasing in many LDCs.*

In this regard, one factor which works in favour of some LDCs is that imported food is not a significant proportion of total food consumption. There are no up-to-date data on this. During the period 1996–2001, however, food imports represented less than 10 per cent of total food consumption in two-thirds of the LDCs. Part of total food consumption in rural areas is met from the household's own production. Moreover, in many African LDCs, a large share of staple food consumption is based on low-value, high bulk crops which are semi-tradable internationally, such as cassava, plantains, yams, millet, sorghum and white maize (UNCTAD, 1998: 141). At the same time, however, it is clear that dependence on imported food products is increasing in many LDCs. Moreover, even where imports are not a large proportion of total food consumption, local food prices are rising because of higher fuel and transport costs.

> *For cereals, rising international food prices are already being felt strongly in domestic markets in the LDCs.*

Chart 19. Domestic food prices in selected LDCs

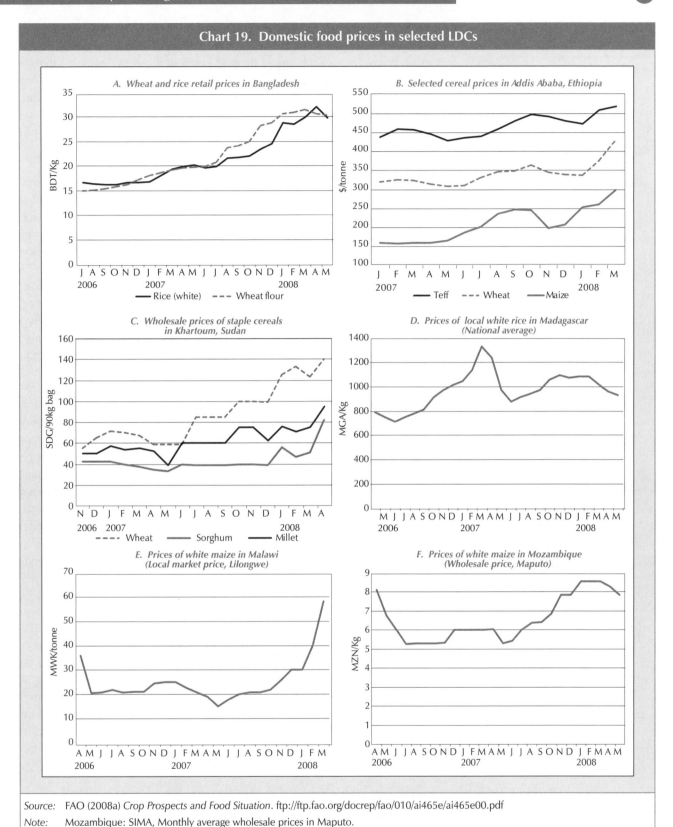

Source: FAO (2008a) *Crop Prospects and Food Situation.* ftp://ftp.fao.org/docrep/fao/010/ai465e/ai465e00.pdf

Note: Mozambique: SIMA, Monthly average wholesale prices in Maputo.
Malawi: Lilongwe local market price MoAFS & FEWSNet,
Madagascar: Observatoire du riz.
BDT=Bangladesh Taka; MGA=Malagasy Ariary; MWK=Malawi Kwacha; MZN=Mozambican Metical; SDG=Sudanese Pound; $=US dollar.

The available evidence indicates that for cereals, rising international food prices are already being felt strongly in domestic markets in the LDCs. The International Fund for Agricultural Development (IFAD) (2008) reports that in Senegal, wheat prices by February 2008 were twice the level of a year ago and sorghum was up 56 per cent. In Somalia, the price of wheat flour in the northern areas has almost tripled over twelve months, and in Sudan (Khartoum) it increased by 90 percent. The price of maize in Uganda (Kampala) was 65 percent higher in March 2008 than in September 2007. In March 2008, maize prices in Mozambique (Maputo) were 43 percent higher than a year ago. FAO (2008a) also reports that wheat and maize prices increased by more than 33 per cent in Addis Ababa in Ethiopia between March 2007 and March 2008, and that maize prices more than doubled over the same period in Dar es Salaam in Tanzania. In Malawi, the prices of white maize and rice almost tripled between mid-2007 and March 2008. Wheat and rice prices both increased by more than 50 per cent over this same period in Bangladesh (chart 19).

Not only are nutritional standards already low, but a number of LDCs already face complex food emergencies.

These rising food prices complicate an already precarious food security situation in the LDCs. Not only are nutritional standards already low, but a number of LDCs already face complex food emergencies associated with such factors as droughts and floods, or specific challenges of market access, such as the inability to circulate in a country owing to conflict, or severe localized food insecurity due to an influx of refugees or internally displaced people. Of the 37 countries which the FAO identifies as facing such complex food emergencies and thus requiring external assistance, 20 are LDCs (table 31). Significantly, in relation to the analysis of chapter 1 of this Report, nine of these countries are in the group of LDCs which achieved real GDP growth over 6 per cent in 2006. These are: Bangladesh, Liberia, Mauritania, Sierra Leone, Burundi, Ethiopia, Sudan, Uganda and Afghanistan.

Large shares of the population in LDCs spend 70–80 per cent of their income on food.

The countries with complex food emergencies may well be affected by the declining ability of the food aid system to meet needs. However, the food security of households in all LDCs will be affected in some way by the large price rises which are now occurring. The magnitude of this effect will be large because such a large share of the population is very poor and already faces food insecurity and hunger. In this regard, it is important to note that almost half of total individual consumption expenditure in the LDCs is intended for the acquisition of food, according to the World Bank's 2005 household survey for the International Comparison Programme (World Bank, 2008b). This share is double the share in other developing countries and more than five times as much as that of high-income OECD countries. In general, the poorer the household income, the higher the share that is devoted to food acquisition. FAO (2008b) argues that large shares of the population in LDCs spend 70–80 per cent of their income on food.

A high proportion of rural inhabitants are net food buyers in many LDCs.

A critical issue which affects the impact of the food price spike is whether or not households are net food buyers. In this regard, the negative impact on people living in urban areas will be greater than the impact on those living in rural areas. However, available evidence indicates that a large proportion of rural inhabitants are net food buyers in many LDCs. Estimates suggest that the share of rural households which are net staple food sellers is limited to 19 per cent in Bangladesh, 12 per cent in Malawi, 27 per cent in Ethiopia, 30 per cent in Zambia and 44 per cent in Cambodia (FAO, 2008a).

The supply response of LDC farmers is constrained by the weakness of agricultural development in the LDCs and by the consequences of long-standing neglect of agriculture by policy-makers.

The minority of households that are net sellers of staple food should benefit from higher domestic consumer prices provided these are passed through to farmgate prices. If this is the case, farmers should reap higher earnings from their produce. This should provide an incentive for rising output and/or productivity over the medium term. However, their supply response is constrained by the weakness of agricultural development in the LDCs and by the consequences of long-standing neglect of agriculture by policy-makers in these countries (see subsection D.3 of this chapter).

A number of simulations have been undertaken to estimate the impact of price increases on different income groups. These indicate that the poorest households are most vulnerable in all situations unless they are sellers of foodstuffs whose prices have risen. FAO simulations using household data from Malawi indicate that a 10 per cent increase in food prices leads to a 1.2 percent income loss for the poorest quintile in rural areas and a 2.6 percent income loss for the poorest urban quintile. According to this analysis, only the richest rural quintile gains from an increase in food prices. This will obviously have a negative impact on poverty. If the actual 200-per-cent increase in the white maize price in Malawi were representative of all food prices, this would imply an income loss of some 20 per cent. Ivanic and Martin (2008), using a sample of household data for nine low income countries analysing the impact of higher food prices of key staple foods on poverty, show that in Cambodia, Malawi, Zambia and Madagascar, the rise in food prices between 2005 and 2007 is estimated to have increased poverty by 3 percentage points. In the case of Yemen, World Bank estimates show that the doubling of wheat prices over the last year could reverse all gains in poverty reduction achieved between 1998 and 2005. Moreover, similar estimates of the impact of the rising food prices on poverty have been made by the United Nations Department of Economic and Social Affairs.

In the case of Yemen, the doubling of wheat prices could reverse all gains in poverty reduction achieved between 1998 and 2005.

(c) Second-round effects on economic growth

The immediate impact of rising food prices on poverty and food security is also likely to be compounded by second-round effects of these changes on economic growth. In this regard, the social unrest and riots associated with rising food prices have occurred in eight LDCs — Bangladesh, Burkina Faso, Guinea, Haiti, Mauritania, Mozambique, Senegal and Yemen — and this has already had a destabilizing effect. Yet rising food prices will also squeeze profits in formal businesses, as wage increases occur to maintain minimum subsistence living standards. In addition, a large proportion of the working population is self-employed, and its accumulation activity, to the extent that it occurs, is directly related to its food consumption costs (Wuyts, 2001). As the price of food rises, any dynamic momentum of economic growth can therefore stall.

It is possible that rising food prices offer an opportunity for renewed agricultural growth. It is debatable, however, if this can occur after such a long period of agricultural neglect. Widespread poverty in the agricultural sector is itself a major constraint on vigorous supply response, as poor farmers cannot command sufficient land, labour resources or modern inputs to increase production and productivity. The configuration of price changes, whereby not only food prices but also fuel prices and fertilizer prices are rising, may mean that even those farmers in a position to respond are also facing a production cost squeeze.

Rising food prices will squeeze profits in formal businesses, and dynamic momentums of economic growth can stall.

2. POLICY IMPLICATIONS

LDC Governments are responding to the rising food prices in different ways. Measures taken include the following:

- A two-month ban on rice exports (from 26 March 2008) and the release of rice stocks to curb rising domestic prices (Cambodia);

- The sale of rice at subsidized prices in urban areas (Bangladesh);

- Subsidies on wheat flour, tariff waivers and price controls (Senegal);

- Reinstatement of the export ban put in place last year, as well as large input subsidy schemes to foster cereal production (Zambia);

- Continuation of fertilizer and quality seed subsidies (Malawi);

- Wheat and fuel subsidies (Ethiopia); and

- Banning of exports of agricultural commodities and duty-free import of 300,000 tons of maize (Tanzania) (FAO, 2008a).

These are all stop-gap measures to deal with a short-term crisis in a situation to which there has been no strong international response as yet. From a long-term perspective, however, soaring food prices and their impact raise serious questions as to the advisability of the current development model being pursued in most LDCs and point to the need for a development policy paradigm shift. Earlier *Least Development Countries Reports* have argued that there is a need for such a shift. The unfolding events associated with soaring food prices bear out this view.

For some observers, the paradigm shift which is now required is a return to agricultural development. The earlier analysis in the chapter of the weaknesses of LDC agriculture reinforces this view. However, while this is part of the policy change required, a dynamic development perspective indicates that sustained and inclusive growth cannot be achieved without some form of structural transformation. It will be difficult to avoid balance-of-payment problems and achieve higher rates of economic growth unless there is a process of diversification in which new sectors and products which can accelerate capital accumulation and technological learning are introduced into economies. This can build on existing strengths in commodity production and major efforts should be made to increase agricultural productivity. With accelerating urbanization, however, there is also a need to generate productive employment opportunities outside agriculture as well as to improve agricultural performance.

Rather than a shift in sectoral focus, a deeper change in approach is required. In brief, there is a need for policy change in three dimensions (table 32).

First, policy should focus on production, productivity and productive capacities rather than international trade *per se*. International trade is essential for productive development, and productive development is essential for international trade. But policy should start at the development end, rather than the trade end, of the relationship between trade and development.

Second, policy should focus on employment rather than only social services as the royal road to poverty reduction. This does not mean that social sector spending and human development goals are unimportant. Improved health and education standards are essential in the LDCs. However, there is a need for a better balance between the role in private incomes (based on employment) and public services (through which health and education are still primarily provided) in poverty reduction.

Third, there is a need for a better balance between States and markets in promoting development and reducing poverty. The persistence of generalized poverty and the food price bubble indicate massive market failure. While Governments are not omnipotent, there is a need for creative solutions based on public action which mobilizes key stakeholders, including in particular the private sector, to resolve common development problems and create development opportunities.

Soaring food prices and their impact raise serious questions as to the advisability of the current development model being pursued in most LDCs and point to the need for a development policy paradigm shift.

Policy should focus on production, productivity and productive capacities rather than international trade per se and ...

... it should also focus on employment rather than only social services as the royal road to poverty reduction.

There is a need for a better balance between States and markets in promoting development and reducing poverty.

Table 32. Key dimensions of a paradigm shift in development policy

From	To
International trade	Production and international trade
Social services	Employment and social services
Markets	State and markets

Source: UNCTAD secretariat.

As chapter 3 of this Report shows, it is clear that LDC Governments are seeking to place poverty reduction and the achievement of MDGs within a broad economic development framework. However, there is a lack of development strategy, which is being reinforced by donor preferences and their tendency to favour the separate pursuit of individual MDG sectors.

To the extent that there is a coherent development strategy in place in the LDCs, it can be described as "export-led growth with a human face" (UNCTAD, 2004: 271–314). In this strategy, the export-led component is founded on trade liberalization and deepening behind-the-border measures, such as trade facilitation, to tackle internal rather than border constraints to international trade, and also to increase the export supply response to trade liberalization, which focuses on privatization and financial liberalization. Great emphasis is also placed on attracting FDI in order to break into international markets. At the same time, the basic needs part of the strategy concentrates on providing basic social services to the population and meeting the MDGs, and also ensuring that there is a minimal safety net to offset the heavier adjustment costs of liberalization borne by poor groups. This part of the strategy is financed by the LDC development partners, who are increasingly allocating development assistance to meet social needs.

This strategy is proving to be neither sustainable (as argued in chapter 1 of this Report) nor a guarantee of high rates of social progress (as argued in the present chapter). The current food crisis is revealing more clearly the weaknesses of the current approach. The basic policy implication is that it is high time for a change.

G. Conclusions

The main finding of this chapter is that although economic growth has accelerated in LDCs in recent years, the rate of progress in terms of poverty reduction and human development remains very low. The incidence of poverty and deprivation remains very high, and most LDCs are off track to meet the MDGs on indicators for which data are available. There is no evidence of a significant break in key trends since 2000 after the adoption of the Millennium Declaration and more socially oriented policy reforms. Moreover, soaring international food prices will have a particularly serious negative impact in the LDCs and are already jeopardizing recent progress in poverty reduction and human development in some LDCs.

The incidence of extreme poverty (measured as the proportion of the people living on less than $1 a day) has decreased from a peak of 44 per cent in 1994 to 36 per cent in 2005. Yet the number of extremely poor people continued to rise in the LDCs until 2003, when the upward trend levelled off. Poverty reduction has been much faster in Asian LDCs than African LDCs, and in the latter group of countries, the number of extremely poor people continues to rise. In 2005, it is estimated that there were 277 million people living on less than $1 a day in all LDCs, including 206 million in African LDCs, 71 million in Asian LDCs and 1 million in island LDCs.

Although the incidence of extreme poverty is declining, the proportion of the population living on more than $1 a day but less than $2 a day has remained the same. Moreover, the proportion of the population living on less than $2 a day has only been declining very slowly. In 2005, three-quarters of the population in the LDCs were living on less than $2 a day.

The development strategy in place in the LDCs is neither sustainable nor a guarantee of high rates of social progress.

Although economic growth has accelerated in LDCs in recent years, the rate of progress in terms of poverty reduction and human development remains very low.

There is no evidence of a significant break in key trends since 2000 after the adoption of the Millennium Declaration and more socially oriented policy reforms.

The relatively weak relationship between growth in GDP per capita and poverty reduction in LDCs can be attributed to a number of factors. The limited evidence suggests that economic growth has been associated with rising income inequality in the LDCs for which trends can be identified. However, the Report singles out the type of economic growth as the central reason why poverty reduction has been so slow. Agriculture is the major source of employment in LDCs, but agricultural productivity is very low and rising only slowly. On top of this, there are accelerating trends of urbanization and deagrarianization in which more and more people are seeking work outside agriculture. However, few LDCs have been able to generate sufficient productive employment opportunities for the growing numbers of young job-seekers. Because population growth is high, the expansion in the number of people seeking work either in agriculture or outside agriculture has been very rapid. Yet export-led growth has not generally been inclusive, owing to weak linkages between export sectors and the rest of the economy.

Few LDCs have been able to generate sufficient productive employment opportunities for the growing numbers of young job-seekers.

Deagrarianization, a process in which more and more people seek work outside agriculture, could be positive if people are pushed out of agriculture by rising productivity and pulled into other sectors by the new employment opportunities being created outside agriculture. There are signs of such a structural transformation in a few Asian LDCs, which have combined rising food productivity based on a Green Revolution with steady industrialization founded on expansion of manufacturing exports. For most LDCs, however, deagrarianization is a negative process in which people are pushed out because they cannot make a living in agriculture and they also cannot find remunerative work elsewhere. As a result, there are now two faces of poverty in LDCs — poverty associated with long-standing agricultural neglect and urban poverty, most dramatically evident in growing numbers of unemployed youth.

Very low material living standards are associated with very low levels of well-being in terms of a broad range of social indicators.

Very low material living standards are associated with very low levels of well-being in terms of a broad range of social indicators. As with the analysis of poverty trends, data availability seriously hampers analysis of progress towards human development MDGs. However, for the few indicators for which it is possible to get information for a wide range of countries, a clear pattern is emerging.

There is a distinct hierarchy of MDG achievement which reflects the priorities of Governments and also of those donors who are funding the scale-up.

This pattern has four basic features. First, some LDCs are making significant progress towards achieving some specific MDGs, but very few LDCs are making progress on a broad front encompassing more than three targets. Second, more progress is being made on targets which depend primarily on the level of public service provision, and Governments and donors are committed to increasing public expenditure. In this regard, progress towards universal primary school enrolment shows what can be done. But, third, there is a distinct hierarchy of achievement. This hierarchy reflects the priorities of Governments and also of those donors who are funding the scale-up. It also reflects the magnitude of the necessary investments in physical infrastructure and human capital, and the time scale for such investments. In this regard, achievements in increasing primary education enrolments outstrip achievements in improving access to water, which in turn outstrip progress in improving sanitation. Finally, progress towards targets that depend more on household incomes rather than mainly on public service provision has been slowest. In this regard, there is slow progress in reducing the incidence of extreme poverty and also of hunger. It has also proved difficult to keep on track in reducing child mortality, which reflects trends in both private incomes and public services.

Broad-based success in achieving progress towards the MDGs is as yet elusive in the LDCs.

The overall implication of these trends is that broad-based success in achieving progress towards the MDGs is as yet elusive in the LDCs. It is also likely to remain so unless the achievement of MDGs is placed in an economic development framework and efforts are focused on generating jobs and livelihoods as well as increasing the provision of public services directly linked to the MDGs.

Rising international food prices in 2007 and early 2008 will have negative effects on poverty trends in LDCs and slow progress towards the MDGs. These negative effects will arise partly because the large increases in food prices threaten economic growth through rising import bills, partly because of the direct impact of rising food prices on the ability of households to meet essential subsistence needs and partly because of the second-round effects of rising food prices on economic growth. The overall impact is likely to be particularly severe in the LDCs because most of them are net food importers and already have large trade deficits and because levels of poverty and food insecurity are already high, with many spending 50–80 per cent of their household income on food. Moreover, for 20 LDCs, the prices rises will exacerbate pre-existing food emergencies which require external assistance owing to such factors as natural disasters, concentrations of internally displaced persons and localized crop failures. Food price riots had already occurred in eight LDCs by June 2008.

Some LDC Governments are taking short-term measures to mitigate the impact of the food price shock. From a long-term perspective, however, soaring international food prices and their impact raise serious questions as to the advisability of the current development model being pursued in most LDCs and the need for a development policy paradigm shift. The food price shock reveals the weakness of the current development approach. The basic policy implication is that it is high time for a change.

For some observers, the paradigm shift which is required now is a return to agricultural development. However, whereas improving agricultural productivity is vital, it is also important to strengthen activities outside agriculture generating productive employment. What is required is not a shift in sectoral focus but rather a deeper change in approach, with a renewed focus on developing productive capacities and generating employment through a better balance between States and markets.

Making such a change towards a more sustainable and inclusive development model depends on the decisions and political will of LDC Governments. But they are also engaged in a development partnership for poverty reduction with donors. The terms of this development partnership affects both the nature of the current strategic approach and policies, and the potential to change it. This issue is taken up in chapter 3 of this Report.

The food price shock reveals the weakness of the current development approach.

What is required is a deeper change in approach, with a renewed focus on developing productive capacities and generating employment through a better balance between States and markets.

Annex:
Poverty estimates: Methodological updates and further considerations

The poverty estimates for 28 LDCs (24 African LDCs and 4 Asian LDCs) used in this chapter update the previous estimates described in the *Least Developed Countries Report 2002* (UNCTAD, 2002). The new estimates were calculated using a methodology different from the one discussed in *The Least Developed Countries Report 2002*. The estimates are also based on 1993 purchasing power parity (PPP) exchange rate estimates (not in the public domain when the previous estimates were made) rather than 1985 PPP estimates. In addition, they draw on more country-based household surveys. The new dataset is based on 408 observations, which make it four times larger than the one used in 2002. New 2005 PPP estimates became available in early 2008, but have not been incorporated into the analysis.

Unlike the 2002 estimation, where the distribution information contained in household surveys was combined with the scale variables from national accounts, the new poverty estimates were calculated by calibrating survey means using national accounts statistics. Survey means are calibrated to reduce the large measurements errors derived from different survey definitions and coverage across country and over time. In practice, this implies that a smooth curve is fitted to national accounts per capita household consumption data and that the calibrated survey means (for income and consumption surveys individually) are read off the fitted curve (annex chart 1).

This new estimation method was used since the previous national accounts-based method led to poverty reduction rates that overestimated the actual rates. The new poverty estimates for those countries where changes in poverty could be observed during a long period show more modest declines in poverty rates compared to the previous method. The empirical estimation technique has also improved its accuracy since the one used for *The Least Developed Countries Report 2002* (more details given below).

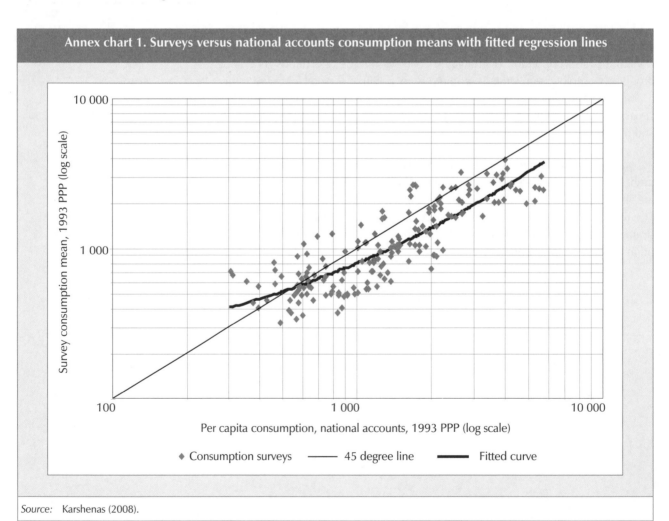

Annex chart 1. Surveys versus national accounts consumption means with fitted regression lines

Source: Karshenas (2008).

Some argue that poverty estimates should only be based on household survey data. However, as argued in *The Least Developed Countries Report 2002* (UNCTAD, 2002: 51), the use of national accounts information provides as plausible estimates as purely household survey-based estimates. The new poverty estimates deviate from those of the World Bank but are not systematically below them. Out of 56 comparable observations of $1-a-day headcount figures, the new estimates are lower in 32 cases and higher in 24 cases than those of the World Bank.

As in *The Least Developed Countries Report 2002*, poverty trends for those LDCs and those years where household surveys are not available have been estimated empirically using poverty curves. Such curves represent the relationship between poverty and mean income, which has been proxied by consumption expenditure (m), at different income levels (annex chart 2). Headcount poverty is estimated as the function, f(m/z), which represents the share of the population living below the poverty line, z. The shape of the poverty curve depends on how income distribution and per capita income change with respect to a country's development path. Poverty curves represent how poverty reduction occurs as a country moves along its development path as household consumption increases. They have been calculated on the basis of data available for 45 countries (low- and middle-income countries and LDCs).

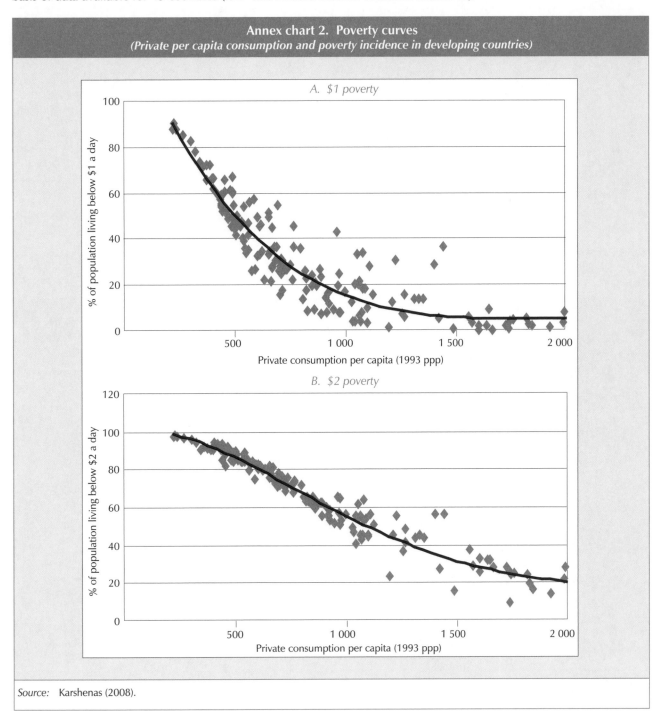

Annex chart 2. Poverty curves
(Private per capita consumption and poverty incidence in developing countries)

A. $1 poverty

B. $2 poverty

Source: Karshenas (2008).

Poverty estimates have been derived relying on a more sophisticated fixed-effect econometric model than the one used in *The Least Developed Countries Report 2002*. While the latter model only included household consumption data as well as a regional and a time dummy as independent variables, the new model includes Gini indices (g) and cross products of the income means and the Gini index. In the new formulation, consumption data has been normalized by the poverty line (m/z). The econometric model has a high explanatory power, which achieves almost perfect fit. Using the coefficients from the model, together with their Gini indices and their mean calibrated consumption, it is possible to calculate poverty trends for 28 LDCs from 1990 to 2005, and for 26 LDCs from 1980.

Source: Karshenas, 2008.

Notes

1 Angola, Bangladesh, Bhutan, Burkina Faso, Cambodia, Democratic Republic of the Congo, Equatorial Guinea, Ethiopia, Myanmar, Sudan, Tuvalu, United Republic of Tanzania and Zambia.

2 The annex to this chapter provides a more detailed explanation of the methodology used to estimate poverty.

3 We made poverty estimates for the 1990–2005 period for the following LDCs: Angola, Bangladesh, Benin, Burkina Faso, Cambodia, Burundi, Cape Verde, Central African Republic, Chad, Ethiopia, Gambia, Guinea, Lesotho, Madagascar, Malawi, Mali, Mauritania, Mozambique, Nepal, Niger, Rwanda, Senegal, Sierra Leone, Togo, Uganda, United Republic of Tanzania, Yemen and Zambia. Our estimates go back to 1980 for the sample, except for Cambodia and Yemen.

4 The actual threshold used is $1.08 and $2.17 in 1993 PPPs, as is standard practice to ensure comparability with the original $1-a-day and $2-a-day poverty lines, which were estimated in 1985 PPP dollars.

5 Poverty estimates for island LDCs have not been made due to lack of the necessary data, except for Cape Verde. For the current chapter, this country has been included in the African LDCs aggregate. This is different from what has been done elsewhere in this Report, where Cape Verde is part of the island LDCs group.

6 In the case of Africa, Geda (2006) claims that trade is the most significant channel through which global interdependence impacts the welfare of ordinary African citizens.

7 Specialization in capital-intensive commodity-producing sectors does not necessarily lead to income concentration if strong and effective policies of economic re-specialization towards other sectors and/or income redistribution are implemented. However, this has generally not been the experience of developing countries specialized in capital-intensive commodity production and trade.

8 The operations of TNCs in the garment and textile sector of LDCs have led to a strong expansion of employment and exports, but have generally not been accompanied by another expected benefit of FDI, namely technological learning and spillovers in the domestic economy (UNCTAD, 2007: 30-42).

9 http://unstats.un.org/unsd/mdg/default.aspx.

10 LDCs have achieved significant progress towards the quantitative MDG target on primary education, as mentioned in the text. However, concerns are being raised about the qualitative aspects of the education being provided to children. These arise from failings in several dimensions that contribute to the quality of education, particularly: pupil/teacher ratio, training of teachers, teacher's pay, learning materials (e.g. textbooks), school facilities and infrastructure, annual hours of teaching and functioning of school systems (UNESCO, 2004).

11 While rising food import bills have an adverse impact on countries' balance of payment, they do not necessarily mean that more food is being imported (which is especially true for grains) (FAO, 2008b). This is particularly the case if the food import bill has been increasing at the same pace as international food prices, as has been the case in the LDCs.

References

Bryceson, D.F. (1996). Deagrarianization and rural employment in sub-Saharan Africa: A sectoral perspective. *World Development*, 24 (1): 97–111.

Chen, S. and Ravallion, M. (2007). Absolute poverty measures for the developing world, 1981–2004. Policy Research Working Paper No. 4211, World Bank, Washington, DC.

Fan, S. (2008). How to promote agricultural growth in least developed countries through productive investment? Study prepared for UNCTAD as a background paper for *The Least Developed Countries Report 2008*. UNCTAD, Geneva.

FAO (2008a). Crop prospects and food situation: Number 2. Available on: ftp://ftp.fao.org/docrep/fao/010/ai465e/ai465e00.pdf.

FAO (2008b). Growing demand on agriculture and rising prices of commodities. Paper prepared for the Round Table organized during the Thirty-first session of IFAD's Governing Council, 14 February 2008, Rome.

IFAD (2008). High food prices: Impact and recommendations. Paper prepared by FAO, IFAD and WFP for the meeting of the Chief Executives Board for Coordination, 28–29 April 2008, Berne.

Ivanic, M. and Martin, W. (2008). Implications of higher global food prices for poverty in low-income countries. World Bank Research Policy Working Paper No. 4594, Washington, DC.

Geda, A. (2006). Openness, inequality and poverty in Africa. DESA Working Paper No. 25, New York.

Karshenas, M. (2003). Global poverty: National accounts based versus survey based estimates. *Development and Change*, 34 (4): 684–712.

Karshenas, M. (2008). Poverty trends in least developed countries. Study prepared for UNCTAD as a background paper for *The Least Developed Countries Report 2008*. UNCTAD, Geneva.

Minten, B. and Barrett, C. B. (2008). Agricultural technology, productivity and poverty in Madagascar. *World Development*, 36 (5): 797–822.

Ng, F. and Aksoy, M. (2008). Who are the net food importing countries? World Bank Policy Research Working Paper No. 4457, World Bank Development Research Group, Washington, DC.

UNCTAD (1998). *The Trade and Development Report: Regional Cooperation for Development*. United Nations publication, sales no. E.07.II.D.11, Geneva and New York.

UNCTAD (2002). *The Least Developed Countries Report: Escaping the Poverty Trap*. United Nations publication, sales no. E.02.II.D.13, Geneva and New York.

UNCTAD (2004). *The Least Developed Countries Report: Linking International Trade and Poverty Reduction*. United Nations publication, sales no. E.04.II.D.27, Geneva and New York.

UNCTAD (2006). *The Least Developed Countries Report: Developing Productive Capacities*. United Nations publication, sales no. E.06.II.D.9, Geneva and New York.

UNCTAD (2007). *The Least Developed Countries Report: Knowledge, Technological Learning and Innovation for Development*. United Nations publication, sales no. E.07.II.D.8, New York and Geneva.

UNCTAD (2008), *Addressing the Global Food Crisis: Key Trade, Investment and Commodity Policies in Ensuring Sustainable Food Security and Alleviating Poverty*. Note prepared by the UNCTAD secretariat for the High-Level Conference on World Food Security: The Challenges of Climate Change and Bioenergy (3-5 June 2008, Rome), Geneva.

UNESCO (2004). *EFA Global Monitoring Report 2005: Education for all: The Quality Imperative*. United Nations Educational, Scientific and Cultural Organization, Paris.

UNESCO (2007). *EFA Global Monitoring Report 2008: Education for all by 2015: Will we Make it? Regional Overview: Sub-Saharan Africa*. Oxford University Press, Oxford.

World Bank (2007). *Global Monitoring Report 2007: Confronting the Challenges of Gender Equality and Fragile States*. World Bank, Washington, DC.

World Bank (2008a). Rising food prices: policy options and World Bank response. Background Note prepared for the Development Committee Meeting on Recent Market Developments (unpublished mimeo), World Bank, Washington, DC.

World Bank (2008b). *2005 International Comparison Program. Tables of Final Results*. World Bank, Washington, DC.

Wuyts, M. (2001). Informal economy, wage goods and accumulation under structural adjustment: Theoretical reflections based on the Tanzanian experience. *Cambridge Journal of Economics,* 25(3): 417–438.

Changes in the Terms of Development Partnership

Chapter 3

A. Introduction

Achieving more sustainable economic growth, accelerated poverty reduction and better progress towards the Millennium Development Goals (MDGs) requires action by both the least developed countries (LDCs) and their development partners. The fundamental priority for LDC Governments is to formulate and implement national development strategies that effectively promote development and poverty reduction. Their development partners need to (a) scale up aid flows to meet their commitments within the Programme of Action for the Least Developed Countries for the Decade 2001–2010; (b) align aid flows with the priorities expressed in LDCs' national development strategies; and (c) deliver aid in ways which respect country leadership in the formulation and implementation of national development strategies and help to strengthen their capacity to exercise such leadership. Moreover, the international community needs to design international regimes for trade, investment and technology which address the special needs of the weakest members of the international community and which reinforce, rather than work against, the positive impact of national development strategies and official development assistance (ODA).

This chapter examines some recent policy trends in LDCs which are at the heart of balanced and effective development partnerships between LDCs and donor countries. It focuses in particular on progress towards country-owned development strategies in LDCs and seeks to identify ways to enhance country ownership.

The notion of country ownership is complex, and difficult to define and monitor. However, it is at the heart of the partnership approach to development cooperation which has been elaborated since 2000. There is a broad consensus amongst policy analysts that country ownership of development strategies and policies is essential for the effectiveness of those strategies and also for aid effectiveness. The principle of respecting country ownership has also received strong political support at the highest level. Thus, for example, at the G8 summit at Gleneagles in 2005, in addition to bold commitments to cancel debt and scale up aid, the following was agreed: "It is up to developing countries themselves and their Governments to take the lead on development. They need to decide, plan and sequence their economic policies to fit with their own development strategies, for which they should be accountable to all their people" (Gleneagles Communiqué, "Africa", para. 31). Moreover, enhanced country ownership is one of the main components of the 2005 Paris Declaration on Aid Effectiveness, the implementation of which will be assessed in Accra, Ghana, in September 2008.

This chapter contributes to the policy debate on country ownership in LDCs in three ways. Firstly, it focuses on aspects of progress towards country ownership which are contained within the Paris Declaration but which are not currently being assessed in the monitoring of its implementation. Secondly, it provides a brief overview of the second-generation poverty reduction strategy papers (PRSPs) and synthesizes evidence from case studies within the published literature which

Achieving more sustainable economic growth, accelerated poverty reduction and better progress towards the Millennium Development Goals requires action by both the least developed countries and their development partners.

The notion of country ownership is complex, and difficult to define and monitor. However, it is at the heart of the partnership approach to development cooperation which has been elaborated since 2000.

indicate processes through which PRSPs in LDCs are designed and implemented and how aid works. These studies, which cover 12 LDCs, were in all but one case not prepared specifically for UNCTAD, but together they enable the identification processes which are working to strengthen or weaken country ownership and their consequences.[1] Thirdly, it makes proposals to enhance country ownership, in particular through the introduction of recipient-led aid management policies at the country level.

This chapter shows that all parties agree that country ownership of development strategies is essential for development effectiveness and aid effectiveness, and significant steps are being taken to enhance country ownership within the partnership approach to development cooperation. However, its major message is that various processes continue to weaken country ownership in LDCs and that this is having adverse consequences for development effectiveness, but that there are practical measures which can rectify this situation.

The first part of the chapter — sections B and C — summarizes key features of the partnership approach to development cooperation and looks at the changes in the PRSPs written in LDCs, which are the main operational instrument of the partnership approach and the key locus where country ownership is being forged. The second part of the chapter — sections D, E, F and G — focuses on evidence relating to country ownership. Section D summarizes the assessment of country ownership in LDCs according to the monitoring process used in the Paris Declaration, as well as assessing the adequacy of the indicator used to monitor ownership. Sections E, F and G are based on a broader concept of country ownership, which is still compatible with the Paris Declaration, and uses the case studies to identify the major processes through which country ownership can be weakened in the formulation and implementation of the poverty reduction strategies. The next part of the chapter — section H — identifies some adverse outcomes of these processes, which are indicative of a malfunctioning of development partnership. Finally, section I discusses some possible ways to increase ownership, focusing in particular on country-level coordination of aid through recipient-led aid management policies, a policy innovation which is encouraged by the Paris Declaration. The conclusion summarizes the major messages of the chapter. The annex provides a road map, based on the innovative experience of a few LDCs, of the steps which other LDCs might take to introduce aid management policies at the country level.

Significant steps are being taken to enhance country ownership within the partnership approach to development cooperation...

... but various processes continue to weaken country ownership in LDCs, with adverse consequences for development effectiveness...

... but that there are practical measures which can rectify this situation.

B. Country ownership and the partnership approach to development

1. THE INTRODUCTION OF THE PARTNERSHIP APPROACH

Since 2000, a new approach to development cooperation has been introduced. The roots of the approach can be traced to the Organisation for Economic Co-operation and Development's (OECD's) report, *Shaping the Twenty-first Century: The Contribution of Development Co-operation*, which was published in 1996. That report not only argued that aid should be focused on achieving a limited set of international poverty reduction and human development targets (a list which later formed the basis for the Millennium Development Goals), it also stated that the key to making a difference in achieving those targets was the establishment of development partnerships between donor and recipient Governments. The basic principle, as the report put it, was that "locally-owned country development strategies, according to DAC good practice principles, emerge from an open and collaborative dialogue by local authorities with civil society and with external partners, about shared objectives and their respective contributions to the common enterprise. Each donor's contributions should then operate within the framework of that locally-owned strategy in ways that respect and encourage strong local commitment, participation, capacity development and ownership" (OECD, 1996: 14).

In 1999, the World Bank launched the Comprehensive Development Framework, which was also based on the partnership approach. Ownership was one of the four key principles of this approach. It is clear that "ownership is essential", the World Bank's then-President James Wolfensohn said, adding, "Countries must be in the driver's seat and set the course. They must determine goals and the phasing, timing and sequencing of programs" (Wolfensohn, 1999:9).

PRSPs have become the main operational instrument for implementing the development partnership approach and enhancing national ownership of strategies and policies.

A major practical impetus to these proposals was provided when it was decided in late 1999 that qualification for debt relief under the Enhanced Heavily Indebted Poor Country (HIPC) initiative would be conditional upon a recipient country preparing a PRSP. One of the key principles of the PRSP approach was that these documents would be prepared within the countries and be country-owned, including broad participation of civil society (IMF and World Bank, 1999). Although the PRSP approach was initially linked to debt relief, the application of its basic principles has since widened. As the OECD (2000: 21) insightfully and succinctly put it, "The decision to place the implementation of the Enhanced HIPC into the larger context of the new development partnership paradigm has in effect leveraged political support for debt relief into a reform of the whole concessional financing system". In effect, the PRSPs have become the main operational instrument for implementing the development partnership approach, and enhancing national ownership of strategies and policies.[2]

2. THE PARIS DECLARATION AND THE DRIVE TO IMPROVE AID EFFECTIVENESS

One important reason for the shift to the new approach to development assistance was the realization that both development effectiveness and aid effectiveness had been undermined during the 1980s and 1990s by policy conditionality and all-pervasive coordination failures in the delivery of aid. Traditional policy conditionality did not work well, firstly, because the local commitment to implement the externally-devised policies was low; and secondly, because the policies were inappropriate for the local context.[3] Aid inflows were also very volatile, with conditionality triggering disruptions and uncertainty. On top of this, the dismantling of the institutions and capabilities of development planning, which occurred particularly in sub-Saharan Africa, opened a vacuum in which donors had no national framework into which to fit their assistance. The lack of coordination and integration of the aid system led to a fragmentation of decision-making and a proliferation of projects and procedures, which put increasing pressure on the meager human resources of recipient countries. Moreover, a vicious cycle often began to set in, as the internal brain drain from Government service to donor projects further undermined State capacity and further encouraged donors to set up parallel systems and institutions to ensure effective implementation of their own projects and programmes as a response.

During the 1980s and 1990s development effectiveness and aid effectiveness were undermined by policy conditionality and all-pervasive coordination failures in the delivery of aid.

As analysed in *The Least Developed Countries Report 2000*, many LDCs found themselves during this period in a very complex situation, in which country ownership was very weak. They faced, on the one hand, a budgetary squeeze arising from policy conditionalities which sought to control public expenditure and bring down the domestic budget deficit, and on the other hand, a proliferation of fragmented aid projects, often financed through parallel channels and procedures, sometimes bypassing any government oversight and aligned with donor priorities rather than national priorities. While the projects and programmes being implemented were often controlled by donors, the debt service on aid funds was very much "owned" by the central government budget (UNCTAD, 2000: 171–207).

Strengthening development partnership has been at the heart of the drive to improve aid effectiveness. The development partnership approach was endorsed in 2002 in the Monterrey Consensus on Financing for Development, which states: "Effective partnerships among donors and recipients are based on the recognition of national leadership and ownership of development plans and, within that framework, sound policies and good governance at all levels are necessary to ensure ODA effectiveness" (United Nations, 2002: 14). Important further milestones in this process were the Rome Declaration on Harmonization in 2003 and the Paris Declaration on Aid Effectiveness in 2005 (OECD 2005a), which identified the following key principles for enhanced aid effectiveness:

(a) *Ownership:* Support for developing country leadership on development strategies, plans and policies;

(b) *Alignment:* Linking donor support to developing country strategies, greater use of country systems and capacity-building;

(c) *Harmonization:* Improved donor coordination, rationalized procedures, and common arrangements;

(d) *Managing for results:* Improving management of resources and decision-making in support of development results; and

(e) *Mutual accountability:* Shared accountability for development results (chart 20).

3. THE IMPORTANCE OF COUNTRY OWNERSHIP

As the discussion of the introduction and deepening of the partnership approach to development cooperation shows, it is universally agreed that country

> *Strengthening development partnership has been at the heart of the drive to improve aid effectiveness.*

> *"Effective partnerships among donors and recipients are based on the recognition of national leadership and ownership of development plans and, within that framework, sound policies and good governance at all levels are necessary to ensure ODA effectiveness" (Monterrey Consensus).*

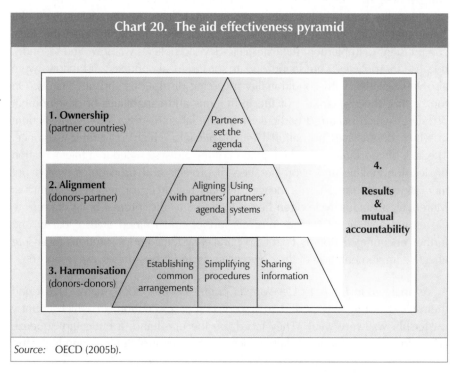

Chart 20. The aid effectiveness pyramid

Source: OECD (2005b).

ownership is the foundation of balanced and effective development partnerships. However, there are many different ways of understanding what country ownership means in practice (box 4).

This chapter is particularly concerned with country ownership in the sense that national Governments have the ability to freely choose the strategies which they design and implement, and to take the lead in both policy formulation and implementation. Assessing country ownership in this sense is very difficult. The degree of ownership of development strategies and policies cannot be solely attributed to the practices of donors *per se*, or to recipients *per se*; rather, it depends on the nature of the aid relationships, involving the practices of both parties. Moreover, the nature of that relationship is an active ongoing process in which the various representatives of each party are constantly negotiating and bargaining in relation to their interests, needs and concerns. These interests, needs and concerns are not necessarily held in common by all participants on each side of the bargaining process. To get at this process requires intense anthropological analysis and access to normally-closed discussions. Nevertheless, it is possible to identify some of the mechanisms by which country ownership is weakened through the nature of the aid relationship. Moreover, it is possible to identify the outcomes of these processes, which are indicative of dysfunctionality within the development partnership.

It must be stressed that whilst this Report identifies mechanisms which are weakening country ownership, it is not arguing that donors or international financial institutions (IFIs) are intentionally undermining country ownership of development strategies and policies. It is clear that there is a strong conviction on the part of IFIs and donors that they should stand back and give country authorities greater policy space for formulating and implementing their own strategies, and strong efforts are being made to do this. However, there is a constant tension between country ownership and the need for IFIs and bilateral donors to be assured that their assistance will be used to support what they regard as credible strategies. Ensuring that high levels of aid dependence do not result in donor domination is a very complex challenge for both aid donors and aid recipients. Understanding how development partnership actually works in a context where there are major inequalities between the parties in terms of resources, capabilities and power can provide the basis for effectively strengthening country ownership, an outcome which all parties wish for and intend through their practices.

The degree of ownership of development strategies and policies cannot be solely attributed to the practices of donors per se, or to recipients per se; rather, it depends on the nature of the aid relationships, involving the practices of both parties.

Whilst there is a conviction on the part of IFIs and donors to give LDCs greater policy space for formulating and implementing their own strategies, there remains a tension between country ownership and what IFIs and donors regard as credible strategies.

C. The transformation of the PRSPs

1. THE EARLY PHASES OF THE PRSP APPROACH

Most LDCs undertook policy reforms financed by the IMF's Enhanced Structural Adjustment Facility (ESAF) in the 1990s (UNCTAD, 2000: 101–134). Borrowers from this facility were required to prepare a Policy Framework Paper which set out the country's overall policy objectives and strategy as a basis for support from the International Monetary Fund (IMF) and World Bank. Although it was supposed to be the country's own document, it was usually prepared in Washington by the staff of the World Bank and IMF, with help from country authorities (Broughton, 2003). In 1999, ESAF was replaced by the Poverty Reduction and Growth Facility (PRGF) and borrowers from that facility were required to prepare a PRSP in the country itself with broad participation from civil society. Concessional lending from the IMF and World Bank were conditional on endorsement of the PRSPs as satisfactory by the boards of the IMF and World Bank.

Ensuring that high levels of aid dependence do not result in donor domination is a very complex challenge for both aid donors and aid recipients.

Box 4. The elusive concept of country ownership

Although almost all analysts agree that country ownership of development strategies and policies is the foundation for effective development partnerships, the concept of country ownership is difficult to define and also to measure.[1] Indeed, behind the consensus that "ownership is essential", there are different interpretations of what country ownership means. It is possible to identify at least five different approaches to defining country ownership within the literature. These are:

(a) The existence of local commitment to the policy reforms of international financial institutions;

(b) The existence of national development strategies which are "operational";

(c) The ability of national Governments to choose freely the strategies and policies which they design and implement;

(d) The ability of national Governments to choose freely these strategies and policies, including consideration of "home-grown" solutions; and

(e) The ability of national Governments to choose freely strategies and policies and the exercise of that choice through a democratic process.

The first approach is exemplified by the definition of national ownership put forward by the IMF Policy Development & Review Department as "a willing assumption of responsibility for an agreed programme of policies, by officials in a borrowing country who have responsibility to formulate and carry out those policies, based on an understanding that the programme is achievable and is in the country's own interest (IMF, 2001:6). This definition follows the critique of policy conditionality in the 1990s which found that it did not work if local agents responsible for implementing policies were not committed to them (see Broughton, 2003). Against this background, country ownership was considered vital for the success of policy reform. But in essence, ownership here is equivalent to the acceptance and assumption of responsibility for programmes and their associated conditionalities.

A second approach is the way in which ownership is monitored in the context of the Paris Declaration. The basic indicator of ownership is that a country is judged to have an operational development strategy. In this approach, evidence of ownership is provided by "a track record of sound policy implementation" (World Bank, 2005: 28). A strategy is defined as operational when it is "a prioritized outcome-oriented national development strategy that is drawn from a long-term vision and shapes a country's public expenditures" (World Bank, 2007: 4). The judgment as to whether a country has such a strategy is made by the World Bank and it is in effect centred on the quality of a country's PRSP (see annex to World Bank, 2007).

The third approach is exemplified by Killick (1998) who defines government ownership as "at its strongest when the political leadership and its advisers, with broad support among agencies of State and civil society, decide of their own volition that policy changes are desirable, choose what these changes should be and when they should be introduced, and where these changes become built into parameters of policy and administration which are generally accepted as desirable" (Killick, 1998: 87). From this perspective, ownership is not necessarily about who designs the programme, with different degrees of ownership related to the level of active participation of nationals and outsiders in programme design. It is rather a question of freedom of choice. In this vein, for example, Johnson (2005) writes that, "ownership is about (i) the right of county representatives to be heard in the process of diagnosis and programme design; and (ii) the freedom and ability of the country to choose the programme to be implemented, without coercion" (Johnson, 2005: 3). This approach to defining country ownership is also closely related to the concerns expressed in the Paris Declaration that countries should "exercise leadership" in policy design, policy implementation and aid coordination.

The fourth and fifth approaches accept this view of ownership, but go further. In the fourth approach, it is argued that local ownership must be based on "home-grown solutions". This approach is founded on the view that the sound policies are locally-specific rather than universal, and that local actors are best situated to mobilize indigenous knowledge effectively. From this perspective, home-grown solutions "mean the generation, by local actors, of knowledge and policy interventions that are specific to the local environment" and ownership is defined as "acceptance of, commitment to and responsibility for the implementation of home-grown solutions" (Girvan, 2007: 2). Such ownership is evident in a wide degree of policy heterodoxy vis-à-vis the role of the State as well as a trial-and-error approach to development policy which adapts best practices to local circumstances though policy learning.

Finally, in the fifth approach, the process of policy choice must be democratic to be fully owned. This approach is adopted by some NGOs that criticize the degree of participation in the PRSP process. ActionAid International (2006: 9) argues that "to be truly owned, government policies should be adopted through democratic means involving a wide range of stakeholders in society, and Governments should be accountable to citizens when implementing policies". The emphasis in the Paris Declaration on the importance of developing and implementing development strategies through broad consultative processes also relates to this democratic view of ownership.

This chapter focuses on the third approach.

[1] See Buiter (2004) for a critical deconstruction which argues that it is simply too difficult to be meaningful.

As of 7 May 2008, 39 LDCs had prepared some kind of PRSP document and presented it to the boards of the World Bank and IMF. Only four of these countries — Comoros, Liberia, the Maldives and Togo — are at the earliest stage of the process, having presented interim PRSPs. Moreover, of the 35 LDCs that have prepared full PRSPs, 17 have now finalized a second PRSP document (table 33).

Table 33. Progress in preparation of PRSPs in LDCs[a]				
Country	Region	I-PRSP	PRSP	PRSP II
Afghanistan	Asia	25 May 2006	9 May 2008	
Angola	Africa			
Bangladesh	Asia	19 June 2003	26 January 2006	
Benin	Africa	13July 2000	20 March 2003	28 June 2007
Bhutan	Asia	08 February 2005		
Burkina Faso	Africa		30 June 2000	05 May 2005
Burundi	Africa	22 January 2004	13 March 2007	
Cambodia	Asia	18 January 2001	20 February 20003	17 July 2007
Cape Verde	Island	09 April 2002	25 January 2005	
Central African Republic	Africa	18 January 2001	17 November 2006	
Chad	Africa	25 July 2000	13 November 2003	
Comoros	Island	16 May 2006		
Dem. Rep. of the Congo	Africa	11 June 2002	31-May-07	
Djibouti	Africa	27 November 2001	08 June 2004	
Equatorial Guinea	Africa			
Eritrea	Africa			
Ethiopia	Africa	20 March 2001	17 September 2002	28 August 2007
Gambia	Africa	14 December 2000	16 July 2002	19 July 2007
Guinea	Africa	22 December 2000	25 July 2002	21 December 2007
Guinea-Bissau	Africa	14 December 2000	10 May 2007	
Haiti	Island	21 November 2006	01 March 2008	
Kiribati	Island			
Lao People's Dem. Republic	Asia	24 April 2001	30 Novermber 2004	
Lesotho	Africa	6 March 2001	12 September 2005	
Liberia	Africa	12 February 2007		
Madagascar	Africa	19 December 2000	18 November 2003	06 March 2007
Malawi	Africa	21 December 2000	29 August 2002	16 January 2007
Maldives	Island		23 January 2008	
Mali	Africa	7 September 2000	06 March 2003	03 April 2008
Mauritania	Africa		06 February 2001	16 January 2007
Mozambique	Africa	06 April 2000	25 September 2001	19 December 2006
Myanmar	Asia			
Nepal	Asia		18 November 2003	
Niger	Africa	20 December 2000	07 February 2002	05 May 2008
Rwanda	Africa	21 December 2000	08 August 2002	06 March 08
Samoa	Island			
Sao Tome and Principe	Island	27 April 2000	25 April 2005	
Senegal	Africa	20 June 2000	23 December 2002	30 January 2007
Sierra Leone	Africa	25 September 2001	06 May 2005	
Solomon Islands	Island			
Somalia	Africa			
Sudan	Africa			
Togo	Africa	25 April 2008		
Tuvalu	Island			
Uganda	Africa		02 May 2000	28 July 2005
United Rep. of Tanzania	Africa	04 April 2000	30 November 2000	09 May 2006
Vanuatu	Island			
Yemen	Asia	27 February 2001	01 August 2002	
Zambia	Africa	04 August 2000	23 May 2002	21 August 2007

Source: World Bank and IMF, online.

Note: The date indicates when the PRSP was presented to the Boards of the IMF and the World Bank.
I-PRSP is an interim PRSP. PRSP II is a second-generation PRSP.
a As of May 2008.

To date, 35 LDCs have prepared full PRSPs, and 17 have finalized a second PRSP document.

In the initial phases of the process, even though IFIs and donor countries stepped back somewhat from the policy formulation process, it proved difficult to promote country ownership. As *The Least Developed Countries Report 2002* put it, the PRSP process was "a compulsory process in which Governments that need concessional assistance and debt relief from the IFIs find out through the endorsement process... the limits of what is acceptable policy. In such a situation, it is very difficult for governments to take the risks which would enable the full potential of the PRSP approach to be realized. Even if there is no outside interference in the PRSP preparation process, and also no sign of threat to interfere in the process, the mere awareness of dependence on the Joint Staff Assessment and on endorsement by the Boards of the IMF and World Bank places constraints on freedom of action of those designing the PRSPs. In effect, the country owns the technical process of policy formulation, but it still lacks the freedom which would release the creative potential of the approach" (UNCTAD, 2002: 193). Moreover, the report went on to state that, unless the international financial institutions have total open-mindedness as to what is regarded as a credible strategy, "the consequences for governance will be adverse as politicians and policymakers will feel inhibited from saying and doing certain things, and thus the political qualities of a free-thinking society, which are meant to be encouraged through the PRSP process, will atrophy" (ibid.: 193).

The initial PRSPs thus just added a social dimension to the structural adjustment programmes of the 1990s by focusing on increasing public expenditure in social sectors (UNCTAD, 2000 and 2002). However, after mid-2002, there has been a significant shift towards growth-oriented PRSPs. As *The Least Developed Countries Report 2004* put it, "the PRSPs are evolving away from the old structural adjustment programmes towards new growth strategies which seek to include the poor" (UNCTAD, 2004: 273). But the transition at that time was still incomplete. The first batch of the later PRSPs tended to have a common template with four basic pillars: (a) ensuring strong and sustainable growth; (b) developing human resources; (c) improving the living conditions of the poor; and (d) ensuring good governance.

2. THE SECOND-GENERATION PRSPS

The evolution of the PRSP approach has gone even further now in many of those countries which have prepared a second full PRSP. With these second-generation PRSPs, many LDCs are striving to transform their poverty reduction strategies into national development strategies.

With second-generation PRSPs, many LDCs are striving to transform their poverty reduction strategies into national development strategies.

The shift towards a development orientation is signaled in the names, the time-horizon and the policy content of the second-generation PRSPs. Of the 17 which have been prepared, only five still name themselves "Poverty Reduction Strategies" — those of Burkina Faso, Gambia, Guinea, Mauritania and Senegal. Mozambique and Uganda call their strategies "an Action Plan for the Reduction of Absolute Poverty", and "a Poverty Eradication Action Plan", respectively. The other countries describe their PRSPs as development plans, growth strategies or development and poverty reduction strategies.[4]

The second-generation PRSPs also have a different time-horizon than the earlier PRSPs. Of the 17 which have been prepared, only five now retain the three-year planning horizon of the first generation PRSPs. The rest have five-year planning horizons. These documents appear to be a return to five-year development planning in a new guise. This is explicitly expressed in the Zambian PRSP, where it is argued that "the resurgence of planning to tackle wealth creation and poverty reduction is both timely and imperative"; and that "one of the important lessons learnt from the 1990s was the realization that, in a liberalized economy, development planning is necessary for guiding priority setting and resource allocation" (Republic of Zambia, 2007:1).

The policy content of the second-generation PRSPs is also evolving. All the second-generation PRSPs are based on a balance between economic and social pillars, and they also all give priority to improved governance as a third basic strategic pillar. The economic pillar is concerned with promoting macroeconomic stability and accelerating economic growth and development. The social pillar is concerned with human resource development and social service provision. Good governance is included as the third pillar, including public administration reforms as well as the institutionalization of the rule of law.

Second-generation PRSPs appear to be a return to five-year development planning in a new guise.

In effect, the second-generation PRSPs are seeking to place poverty reduction and the achievement of the MDGs within a broad economic development framework. Most of the PRSPs now include actions for the development of productive sectors and economic infrastructure. Agricultural development is identified as critical in all the PRSPs. But other sectors are also referred to. Increased investment in economic infrastructure, particularly power and transport, is also a ubiquitous priority. Some also identify building science, technology and innovation capabilities as important concerns. Employment generation is identified as a key challenge for poverty reduction in some of these documents. Moreover, local development initiatives are often identified as a key mechanism to promote employment and also link economy-wide growth to household-level poverty reduction.

The second-generation PRSPs are seeking to place poverty reduction and the achievement of the MDGs within a broad economic development framework.

This shift in the policy content of the recent PRSPs is indicative that countries have been emphasizing country ownership and seeking to take a greater lead in the design of their poverty reduction strategies. This has also been encouraged by shifts by the IFIs. Following the review of the poverty reduction strategy process in 2004, the Joint Staff Assessment assumed a lower profile advisory status and the PRSPs are now less formally received by the two institutions (Marshall, 2008). Moreover, international financial institutions have also been signaling their willingness and desire to work with more ambitious and less one-size-fits-all strategies. This is particularly evident in the *2005 Review of the Poverty Reduction Strategy* approach (IMF and World Bank 2005). The review argues that (a) the poverty reduction strategy approach provides a framework for countries to elaborate comprehensive medium-term development programmes (p. 31); (b) they should be incorporate productive sectors as well as social sectors (pp. 77–78); (c) they should include growth diagnostics as well as poverty diagnostics (p. 79); and (d) overall, they should support "ambitious development plans" (p. 79) and provide a framework for scaling up aid, using alternative scenarios (p. 81) and discussing macroeconomic policy options (p. 49).

Most of the PRSPs now include actions for the development of productive sectors and economic infrastructure.

3. THE CHALLENGE OF REINVENTING DEVELOPMENT GOVERNANCE

As the PRSPs evolve into national development strategies, major policy and institutional challenges arise. These go far beyond poverty-oriented public expenditure and budgeting, which were critical for the early PRSPs, and concern the role of the State in national development. Seeking to put poverty reduction and the achievement of the MDGs in a broad economic development framework, the second-generation PRSPs are in effect a return to development planning. But what is required now is not a return to the past; rather, it is necessary to devise new modes of development governance which do not repeat the weaknesses of old forms of development planning. These should also be tailored to the context of weak State capacities which is prevalent in LDCs.

The term "development governance" is used here to refer to refer to the political processes and institutional arrangements which are dedicated and devoted to the purposeful promotion of economic development, poverty reduction and the achievement of internationally-agreed development goals. Development governance occurs whenever people and their organizations interact to solve development problems and create new development opportunities. It involves defining problems, setting goals, choosing strategies, identifying appropriate policy instruments, creating institutions and allocating resources. The State must play an active role in this process, and in particular seek to animate and channel the energies of the private sector, driven by the search for private profits, towards the achievement of publicly-agreed national development goals.

This is a major challenge. But, in general, the second-generation PRSPs are only just beginning to address the complex policy issues involved in the shift from poverty reduction strategies to development strategies. Three weaknesses in meeting the challenge seem to characterize most second-generation PRSPs.

Firstly, there is little discussion in the second-generation PRSPs of the question of choice of development strategy. This is a critical issue which affects the priorities given to different sectors and courses of action. It was a central issue of the old development planning, and gave rise to discussions on the role of agriculture, relative importance of domestic and external sources of growth, intersectoral dynamics and sequencing of global integration (Lewis, 1986). But this is absent in the second-generation PRSPs. Discussion of the relationship between short-term macroeconomic stabilization goals and long-term development goals is also absent.

Secondly, the rebalancing of the poverty reduction strategies to cover not only social sectors but also economic infrastructure, private sector development and productive sectors has major implications for development governance. It is no longer possible to envisage this process solely in terms of public expenditure allocation. It is also necessary to focus on the policies which will shape the incentives and capabilities of private sector actors in order to achieve the objective and targets of the strategy. But the current strategies still largely rely on privatization and liberalization as major tools for productive sector development, and are founded on the expectation that, even in LDC-type economies, the reduction of fiscal deficits and low rates of inflation will "crowd in" the private sector. There is no discussion of the validity and relevance of this development model in circumstances where private sector capabilities are very weak and the majority of the population is very poor.

Thirdly, there is weak analytical discussion of the relationship between growth, poverty and the achievement of the MDGs in general. Instead, more emphasis is generally placed on description of poverty profiles. Placing poverty reduction and the achievement of the MDGs into a broader economic development framework is proving difficult to accomplish.

To sum up, the increasing diversity of the second-generation PRSPs is an indication of increased ownership of the formulation of the documents. However, the generally weak treatment of the complex issues of development governance listed above raises questions as to how much progress towards country ownership has been made and what processes are impeding such progress.

D. The Paris Declaration assessment of progress towards ownership

One source of evidence for assessing progress toward country ownership in the LDCs is the systematic appraisal that is conducted as part of the monitoring of the Paris Declaration. In this context, country ownership is assessed according to whether aid recipients have an "operational national development strategy". Their national development strategy (including poverty reduction strategy) is operational when it has "strategic priorities linked to a medium-term expenditure framework (MTEF) and annual budgets". This involves: (a) having "a long-term vision and medium-term strategy derived from that vision which is common reference point for policy makers, nationally, locally and at the sector level"; (b) "the long-term vision and medium-term strategy identify objectives and targets linked to MDGs but tailored, with some specificity to local circumstances" and "the medium-term strategy focuses on a prioritized set of targets" and "adequately addresses cross-cutting issues such as gender, HIV/AIDS, environment and governance"; (c) "the government is progressing towards performance-oriented budgeting to facilitate a link of the strategy with the medium-term fiscal framework", and (d) "institutionalized participation of national stakeholders in strategy formulation and implementation (World Bank, 2007: A5). The results of the World Bank's evaluation of country ownership for 37 LDCs on the first three of these assessment criteria are summarized in table 34. Progress is graded according to (a) whether little action has been taken; (b) elements for progress exist; (c) action has been taken and some progress, though not enough, is being made; (d) significant action is being taken and so progress on the criteria is largely developed; and (e) significant progress has been made and it is sustainable.

According to the World Bank's evaluation, no LDC yet has a "sustainable" operational development strategy and only six of the 37 LDCs have "largely developed" operational development strategies (World Bank, 2007). These countries are Burkina Faso, Ethiopia, Rwanda, Uganda, the United Republic of Tanzania and Zambia. However, some action to develop operational development strategies has been taken in 23 of the 37 LDCs, and there are elements to build on in the remaining eight LDCs in which progress is least advanced. These countries are all designated as fragile states by the World Bank assessment and include Afghanistan, Central African Republic, Democratic Republic of the Congo, Guinea-Bissau, Haiti, Liberia, Sao Tome and Principe, and Sudan. In terms of the three criteria used to assess the status of operational development strategies, more progress has been made in terms of elaborating a unified strategic framework and prioritization rather than making a strategic link to the budget. The weak progress on the latter criteria is particularly evident in countries which are described as fragile States. Nevertheless, a number of LDCs are identified by the World Bank as examples of best practices in the elaboration of operational development strategies according to the Paris targets. These countries are Burkina Faso, Ethiopia, Mozambique, United Republic of Tanzania, Uganda and Zambia (box 5).

The finding by the World Bank that none of the current PRSPs for LDCs can be described as "operational development strategies" is very important in itself. It indicates the very weak State capacities of most LDCs. However, the current approach to assessing ownership within the framework of the Paris Declaration is limited. The evaluation and judgments reflect a particular view of what constitutes an operational national development strategy. It is striking, for example, that Bangladesh is not assessed as having an operational development strategy, even though its strategic approach has been one of the most successful of all the LDCs and its PRSP is amongst the most technically sophisticated of the PRSPs

According to the World Bank's evaluation, no LDC yet has a "sustainable" operational development strategy.

The finding that none of the current PRSPs for LDCs can be described as "operational development strategies" indicates the very weak State capacities of most LDCs.

The current approach to assessing ownership within the framework of the Paris Declaration is limited.

Table 34. Progress of LDCs towards operational national development strategies: The Paris Declaration assessment

	Overall score	Unified strategic framework	Priorization	Strategic link to budget
PRSP II countries:[a]				
Benin	3	3	3	3
Burkina Faso	2	2	2	3
Cambodia	3	3	2	3
Ethiopia	2	2	2	3
Gambia	3	3	3	4
Guinea	3	3	3	3
Madagascar	3	2	3	3
Malawi	3	3	3	3
Mali	3	3	3	3
Mauritania	3	3	2	3
Mozambique	3	3	2	3
Niger	3	3	3	3
Rwanda	2	2	2	2
Senegal	3	3	2	3
Uganda	2	2	2	2
United Rep. of Tanzania	2	2	3	2
Zambia	2	2	2	2
Other countries:				
Afghanistan	4	4	4	4
Bangladesh	3	3	3	3
Bhutan	3	2	2	4
Burundi	3	3	3	4
Cape Verde	3	3	3	3
Central African Republic	4	4	4	4
Chad	3	3	3	3
Dem. Republic of Congo	4	3	4	4
Djibouti	3	3	3	4
Guinea-Bissau	4	3	4	4
Haiti	4	4	4	4
Lao People's Dem. Republic	3	3	3	4
Lesotho	3	3	3	3
Liberia	4	4	3	4
Nepal	3	3	3	3
Sao Tome and Principe	4	4	4	4
Sierra Leone	3	3	3	4
Sudan	4	4	4	4
Timor-Leste	3	3	3	3
Yemen	3	2	2	4

Source: World Bank (2007).

Key: **Level 1:** sustainable, **Level 2:** developed, **Level 3:** actions taken, **Level 4:** elements exist, and **Level 5:** little action.

a   These countries have prepared two PRSPs.

A major aspect of what is being monitored is the actions which recipient countries should take in order to increase the confidence of donors that their financial aid will be well-managed.

produced by LDCs. The evaluation and judgement also reflect a particular view of ownership.

In the current approach, a major aspect of what is being monitored is the actions which recipient countries should take in order to increase the confidence of donors that their financial aid will be well-managed. Such confidence is of course critical for country ownership in the sense that, if donors think that aid will be mismanaged they will set up parallel implementation systems which may not be well-aligned with country priorities. But, in effect, what ownership

---

Box 5. Paris Declaration review of operational development strategies in LDCs: Examples of best practices

In the latest World Bank review, six LDCs — Burkina Faso, Ethiopia, Rwanda, the United Republic of Tanzania, Uganda and Zambia — are identified as having "largely developed" operational development strategies.

Burkina Faso has used the medium-term strategy to achieve the goals identified in an existing vision and long-term sectoral plans. It has conducted yearly reviews to adjust strategy targets in accordance with lessons learned and resource availability.

Ethiopia has merged multiple strategies into a unified strategic framework that builds on MDG needs assessments to base its objectives on country reality.

Rwanda has used existing sector strategies to inform its medium-term strategy. This has facilitated linking the strategy to the budget, on the basis of sector strategies, line ministries prepare sectoral MTEFs.

United Republic of Tanzania has shifted toward an outcome-oriented strategy that includes cluster strategies as the road map to achieve development objective. This shift is promoting greater use of performance data in the budget process, requiring sectors to justify their bids in terms of the relevant cluster strtegies. Sector policymakers thus have a material incentive to develop outcome-oriented rationales for their budget submissions.

Uganda has built strongly on a well established planning tradition to move incrementally toward a stronger focus on results. It has progressively improved its development data set, complementing this with participatory poverty assessments that have brought the perspective of the poor into planning. Better and more comprehensive data have in turn fed into strategy revision, making the strategy more balanced and focused, and have helped to inform budgetary allocations.

Zambia has used MDG needs assessments to fine-tune the focus and balance of the strategy and better cost it. This in turn has created a stronger basis to move toward a closer link between the budget and the strategy.

In addition the following countries are identified as examples of good practices in relation to relation to (a) developing a consolidated strategic framework; (b) prioritization; and (c) linking strategies and budgets:

Unified Strategic Framework:

Bhutan, Burkina Faso, Ethiopia, Rwanda, United Republic of Tanzania and Uganda have built on existing long-term vision studies to guide the preparation of a medium-term strategy linked to the country's long-term goals. **Madagascar** has built on the revision of their medium-term strategy to align it with existing the long-term vision. **Ethiopia, Yemen and Zambia** have consolidated parallel medium-term strategies into a single national development strategy. **Ethiopia** has build on sector strategies under implementation to revise the medium-term strategy.

Prioritization:

Zambia has built on MDG needs assessment and MDG progress reports to help improve costing and financial projections for its second PRSP. **Bhutan, Ethiopia, Mauritania and Yemen** have used information on progress toward meting the MDGs to better tailor MDG targets to country circumstances. **Ethiopia** has it has built strongly on sector strategies under implementation to revise their medium-term strategy. In **Cambodia**, detailed assessments of challenges toward meeting the MDGs have shaped the choice of country-specific goals and medium-term targets that inform the medium-term strategy. Clarity on the country objectives has in turn made it easier to prioritize strategy in line with expected resources. **Burkina, Faso, Ethiopia, Mauritania, Mozambique, Rwanda, Senegal, Uganda and Zambia** have taken into account implementation progress and lessons learned to achieve a better balance within their medium-term goals and short-term priorities, focusing on sectors and themes relevant for country development, including productive sectors, governance, gender , HIV/AIDS and the environment.

Link to budget:

Rwanda has conducted bi-annual review assessing expenditures against planned outputs and future budget allocation. **Tanzania** has introduced a Strategic Budget Allocation System that, when combined with timely information on outturns, shows some promise to link strategy to budget. The government has developed a Local Government Planning and Reporting Database to allow local governments to formulate MTEF plans and budgets linked to the national strategy and better monitor local expenditures. **Uganda** has established a clearer link between budget ceilings and strategy objectives, with sector working groups identifying sectoral outcomes, outputs, and targets based on the medium-term strategy, to justify budget ceilings. **Zambia** has introduced an activity-based budget classification, which informs summary tables presented to the National Assembly during the budget submission.

Source: World Bank (2007).

---

means here is local commitment to a process conditionality in relation to how a country undertakes development planning. In equating ownership with whether a development strategy is deemed operational, and specifying the meaning of an operational development strategy in a particular way, the monitoring of ownership has become a way in which process conditionality in relation to financial governance is being reinforced. At the same time, the deeper issues of freedom of choice of national Government, as well as the exercise of leadership, are sidelined.

This approach to monitoring ownership ignores the other important aspects of ownership which are identified in the Paris Declaration. In the Declaration, under the principle of ownership, aid recipients committed to:

Some LDCs are beginning to exercise leadership in the policy formulation process and establishing complex institutional mechanisms to get inputs to the process from national stakeholders...

- Exercise leadership in developing and implementing their national development strategies through broad consultative processes;

- Translate these national development strategies into prioritized results-oriented programmes as expressed in medium-term expenditure frameworks and annual budgets; and

- Take the lead in coordinating aid at all levels in conjunction with other development resources in dialogue with donors and encouraging the participation of civil society and the private sector.

Donors also agreed to "respect country leadership and help strengthen their capacity to exercise it" (OECD 2005a: 3). The systematic monitoring of progress towards country-led development strategies now examines only the second of the aid recipient's commitments.

... however, weak national technical capacities undermine the ability of LDCs to exercise leadership in designing and implementing their national development strategies.

The rest of this chapter focuses on the extent to which LDCs are exercising – and, given the complex nature of the aid relationship, are able to exercise – leadership in the design and implementation of their development strategies, as well as the extent to which they are taking the lead in coordinating assistance at the country level. It also identifies factors which weaken country ownership, as well as some adverse consequences for meeting the new challenges of development governance.

E. Processes weakening country ownership — policy formulation

Evidence from the case studies referred to at the start of this chapter show that some LDCs are certainly beginning to exercise leadership in the policy formulation process and establishing complex institutional mechanisms to get inputs to the process from national stakeholders. This has progressed to a different extent in different countries. However, AFRODAD (2007e: 28), in its synthesis of African case studies, notes that "recipient Governments have particularly demonstrated greater realism and assertiveness about national objectives and priorities" and "have shown encouraging progress in assuring the realization of ownership and leadership within the context of the Paris Declaration". It exemplifies this with the cases of Malawi, Mozambique, Uganda and United Republic of Tanzania. It also indicates that participation in policy dialogue has broadened and is becoming institutionalized, although "participation by the mass media and the parliament are not sufficiently developed" (AFRODAD, 2007e: 29).

LDCs still rely heavily on donor support in the design of the national strategy.

This overall picture of progress must be tempered by two factors which weaken country ownership. Firstly, weak national technical capacities continue to undermine the ability of countries to exercise leadership in designing and implementing their national development strategies, meaning that countries have to rely heavily on donor support in the design of the national strategy. EURODAD (2008b: 17), for example, reports the case of one LDC where, following the request from the national PRSP secretariat for help from donors, 15 Government representatives from the LDCs were flown to Washington, D.C., where they met officials from the World Bank, United Nations Development Programme (UNDP), European Commission, Belgium and IMF for a working session to draft their second PRSP. Following this, the World Bank contacted a consultant from a neighbouring country who had worked on his own country's PRSP to help finalize the PRSP. In another country, it was observed that — although the PRSP unit had benefited from increased financial, material and human resources — there was a "chronic problem of weak capacity in macroeconomic and strategic development planning" (Bergamaschi, 2007: 10). The PRSP unit has no macroeconomist and the Ministry of Finance has no capacity to undertake macroeconomic planning. The second-generation PRSP's growth model was elaborated by a consultant hired by the German cooperation agency (ibid.: 10). The general weakness of national technical capacities means that donors can exercise an important influence on the design and implementation of national development strategies through the technical cooperation which they provide.

Freedom of action in policy design is also constrained by the need to mobilize aid inflows, and the sense that signs of lack of commitment to policies favoured by donors and IFIs can work against aid mobilization.

Secondly, even for countries that take the lead in formulating their strategies, the content of those strategies can be influenced through the inequality of power and resources, as well as the potential sanctions which donors can bring to bear if the recipients stray away from what donors regard as a realistic and credible strategy. Studies in three LDCs in which country ownership is generally regarded as quite well developed and where Governments have reached a general policy consensus with donors — but at the same time have publicly disagreed with the donors — have found that the formulation of the policy agenda is still influenced by the high level of reliance on assistance and the past history of continual oversight of policies.[5] In effect, freedom of action in policy design is constrained by the need to mobilize aid inflows, and the sense, justifiable or not, that signs of lack of commitment to the types of policies which donors and IFIs believe are the best ones, can work against aid mobilization.

One area where these factors seem particularly important is in the design of the macroeconomic framework.

One area where these factors seem particularly important is in the design of the macroeconomic framework. In most PRSPs, the macroeconomic framework conforms to that of the IMF's PRGF (AFRODAD, 2007a, b, c, and d). AFRODAD (2006) reports how the first-generation PRSPs which were tightly linked to the HIPC Initiative were rushed and "there was no evidence that the PRSP fed into the PRGF realistically" (AFRODAD, 2006: 11). But the relationship between the PRGF and PRSPs in the second-generation PRSPs remains ambiguous. For example, AFRODAD notes that, in the case of Mozambique — because access to IMF resources requires the Government to comply with macroeconomic conditions in the PRGF which are binding commitments — these commitments are reflected in government plans which then feed into the PRSP. Whatever the case, the macroeconomic framework is usually "owned" at the country level, but only by a narrow circle of officials who are concerned with such policies (Working Group on IMF Programmes and Health Spending, 2007). There is often strong opposition from civil society to the macroeconomic framework, and the limited exploration of macroeconomic policy options means that there is limited scope for choice and political debate.[6]

One important tendency show is that donors increasingly demand to have representation and a voice in forums taking decisions on the utilization of aid.

One important tendency which the case studies show is that donors increasingly demand to have representation and a voice in forums where decisions regarding the utilization of aid are made. This tendency is observed in both Liberia, which has little experience in elaborating a poverty reduction strategy, and Uganda, from which the very idea of a poverty reduction strategy was originally derived (AFRODAD, 2007e: 26–27). In one country, which is regarded as a demonstration case for how an aid-dependent country can negotiate and create space for pursuing its own policy agenda, government officials and donors have increasingly come together "to negotiate and plan development activities from macroeconomic management to specific thematic initiatives" (Hayman, 2007: 20). This is regarded as one of the "the perverse outcomes of an aid system which aims at increasing local ownership but which leads to heightened external entanglement in internal policy processes" (ibid.: 20).

It should be noted that these interactions do not necessarily infringe upon domestic interests.[7] However, an outcome of this involvement is that the PRSPs can be seen as an amalgam of policy elements that include some strongly related to a donor development agenda and others that are related to a national development agenda. With this view, Furtado and Smith (2007) have proposed that the overall policy agenda of a PRSP can be conceptualized as having three spheres: (a) a core policy agenda which is strongly owned by the national Government; (b) a policy agenda which is directly or indirectly negotiated with donors and around which there is broad consensus and agreement; and (c) a part of the policy agenda which is donor-originated and donor-driven and which enjoys very little or very narrow country ownership (see chart 21). In effect, there is an ownership frontier within the PRSPs.

Their broad scope is one of the key features of the second-generation PRSPs. The location of ownership frontier — and the size of the area of strong country ownership — may be expected to vary between countries according to their technical capacity and also leadership in designing the PRSPs. The issues which are matters of dispute also vary between countries. But it is notable that, in the case studies where it is possible to identify areas of disagreement, primary areas of disagreement often related to productive sector development. In Mozambique, areas of disagreement in 2006 were related to land privatization, the creation of a development bank and governance (De Renzio and Hanlon, 2007). In Ethiopia, the areas embraced by donors but enjoying little government support were liberalization of the fertilizer distribution system, financial sectors and telecommunications, whilst the areas which the Government supported but the donors did not share the same view were approaches to the financial sector, industrial development and support for agriculture. In all these cases, Government believed in a more proactive role for the State (Furtado and Smith, 2007).

The overall policy agenda of a PRSP has a core policy agenda which is strongly owned by the national Government; a policy agenda which is negotiated with donors, around which there is broad consensus and agreement; and a part of the policy agenda which is donor-originated and donor-driven.

There is an ownership frontier within the PRSPs.

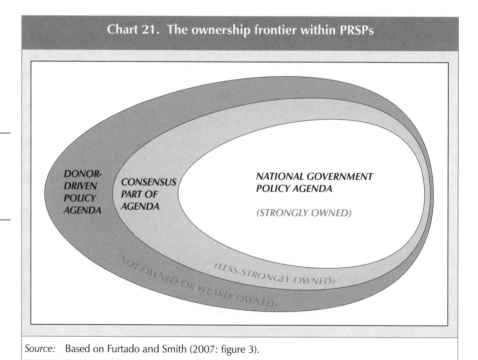

Chart 21. The ownership frontier within PRSPs

DONOR-DRIVEN POLICY AGENDA

CONSENSUS PART OF AGENDA

NATIONAL GOVERNMENT POLICY AGENDA

(STRONGLY OWNED)

(NOT OWNED OR WEAKLY OWNED)

(LESS-STRONGLY OWNED)

Source: Based on Furtado and Smith (2007: figure 3).

F. Processes weakening country ownership — policy implementation

The fact that the new PRSPs cover a very broad policy agenda and include an ownership frontier within them is a critical feature of how ownership is now working in LDCs. Even though the strategies contain priorities which are expressed in their key pillars, these now cover so many issues that it is possible for conditionalities to be drawn from the strategy and for donors to allocate aid in ways which are aligned and harmonized with their priorities but focus more on the donor priorities within the national agenda. Policy implementation is thus critical to how ownership works in practice.

1. POLICY CONDITIONALITY

In the past, policy conditionality was a principal mechanism through which country ownership was undermined. However, both the World Bank and IMF have made major efforts in the last few years to reduce the intrusive and negative effects of policy conditionality. The IMF issued new Guidelines on Conditionality in 2002 which reaffirmed that the key purpose of conditionality is to ensure that fund resources are used to assist a member resolve its balance of payments problems. The design of conditionality should be formulated through a mutually acceptable process led by the country itself and programmes supported by the PRGF should normally be based on the PRSP. Policy conditionality should be parsimonious, focusing on conditions that are critical to the achievement of programme goals, and should be integrated within a coherent country-led framework. Since 2000, the World Bank has sought to streamline conditionality and exercise more selectivity by focusing its support on countries which were committed to the policies it was advocating. In 2006, following an extensive review of conditionality, the World Bank adopted five "Good Practice Principles" that are intended to govern the way Bank staff apply conditionality, namely: (a) reinforce country ownership; (b) agree up-front with the Government and other financial partners on a coordinated accountability framework (harmonization); (c) customize the accountability framework and modalities of bank support to country circumstances; (d) choose only action critical for achieving results as conditions for disbursement; and (e) conduct transparent progress reviews conducive to predictable and performance-based financial support.

There is only limited evidence of how the switch from the old-style conditionality, which was applied in the 1980s and 1990s, to the new-style conditionality is working out in practice. The IMF Independent Evaluation Office (IEO) (IMF, 2007a) evaluation of progress found that "there is no evidence of a reduction in the number of structural conditions following the introduction of the streamlining initiative" (p. 24) and "arrangements continued to include conditions that do not appear to have been 'critical to programme objectives'" (p. 26). A sectoral analysis shows that "programmes contained a large number of structural conditions dealing with many aspects of policymaking" and "often these conditions were quite detailed, even when they covered areas over which the Fund had little expertise and that were outside its core areas of responsibility" (p. 14). It also found that the use of specific structural conditions in the period 2004–2005 were no better justified than in 1999–2003, and that "well-specified medium-term roadmaps were present in PRGFs only in those countries whose Poverty Reduction Strategy Paper contained a well-developed medium-term policy assessment" (p. 26). Mozambique was the only example which the evaluation found in the countries it studied.

That the new PRSPs cover a very broad policy agenda and include an ownership frontier within them is a critical feature of how ownership is now working in LDCs.

Policy implementation is critical to how ownership works in practice.

In the past, policy conditionality was a principal mechanism through which country ownership was undermined...

... however, both the World Bank and IMF have made major efforts in the last few years to reduce the intrusive and negative effects of policy conditionality.

The Review of World Bank Conditionality found that, in the early 2000s, there was a drop in the number of binding conditionalities but a rise in the number of indicative benchmarks which guide rather than compel policy action. Public sector governance was the fastest-growing conditionality theme in IDA loans, with half of public sector governance conditions relating to public expenditure management, financial management and procurement-related conditions. The share of social sector conditionality is also growing and public expenditure management conditions are used more in countries with lower social sector spending, lower social conditions, and higher poverty. Compared with the 1990s, there has also been a shift to tailor conditionality in ways more appropriate for very poor countries (World Bank, 2005a).

Compliance with IMF macroeconomic conditions is still of major importance for bilateral donors.

From the country cases studies within the published literature, a number of tendencies associated with new-style conditionality can be discerned in LDCs. Firstly, compliance with IMF macroeconomic conditions is still of major importance for bilateral donors. ODA inflows to both Malawi and Zambia were cut in 2003, owing to failure to meet macroeconomic targets (AFRODAD, 2006: 13) and the same thing occurred in Sierra Leone in 2007 (EURODAD, 2008a). Compliance with the conditions within the PRGF is also becoming an entry-level condition for budget support, as the Sierra Leone case shows.

ODA inflows to both Malawi and Zambia were cut in 2003, owing to failure to meet macroeconomic targets, and the same occurred in Sierra Leone in 2007.

Secondly, IMF macroeconomic conditionality is strongly oriented towards achieving macroeconomic stability and, with this in view, it has been targeting low financial deficits and inflation lower than 5 per cent, and also setting wage bill ceilings. These policies are often vigorously opposed by civil society groups. They are usually strongly supported by a narrow circle of officials. But the scope for choice and political debate about the costs and risks of alterative macroeconomic frameworks has been limited because of the limited exploration of more expansionary but feasible policy options (Working Group on IMF Programmes and Health Spending, 2007).

Thirdly, there is a greater division of labour between the World Bank and IMF, and together they continue to recommend privatization and liberalization. AFRODAD (2006) reports that, in Ethiopia, conditionalities under PRGF are greater than under ESAF and encompass (a) liberalization of the external sector and interest rates; (b) the reorientation of spending to poverty alleviation; and (c) the speeding up of tax reform, privatization and the strengthening of the private sector, including removing barriers to foreign bank entry. EURODAD (2007) found that the overall number of conditions the World Bank is attaching to its development finance (including legally binding conditions and structural benchmarks) is falling in poor countries. However, this is related to the practice of bundling a number of policy actions related to one objective as one condition. Moreover, "more than two thirds of loans and grants (71 per cent) from the IDA still have sensitive policy reforms attached to them" (ibid.: 3). In this context, privatization and liberalization remain important themes, often now classified as part of public sector reform. The research found that, on average, loans contained six privatization-related conditions each (ibid.: 17). Examples are Bangladesh (privatization of health), Rwanda (privatization of tea plantations), Burkina Faso (private management of electricity sector) and Afghanistan (privatization of State-owned enterprises).

For LDCs there has been a very slight decline in the number of structural conditions attached per IMF programme between 2003–2004 and 2005–2007.

Using a broad definition of policy conditionality, Molina and Pereira (2008) show that there has been an increase in IMF structural conditionality recently. But for the LDCs in their sample of countries, their data indicate there has been a very slight decline in the number of structural conditions attached per IMF programme between the periods 2003–2004 and 2005–2007 — from 13.5 to 13 per programme. This analysis includes prior actions (policy reforms that have to be acted upon prior to receiving funds), performance criteria (policy reforms that have to be acted upon during a PRGF in order to gain access to subsequent disbursements) and structural benchmarks (which are not legally binding but are used to assess performance of a loan). The total number of binding conditions per loan has stayed almost constant at seven per programme. Nevertheless, a third of all structural conditions attached to PRGFs approved for LDCs since 2005 focus on "sensitive" policy reforms. "Sensitive" policy reforms are defined as reforms which limit fiscal space conditions, increase regressive taxation conditions, or require public sector restructuring, banking and financial sector privatization and liberalization, or other kinds of privatization and liberalization. The share of sensitive reforms is significantly down from a half in 2003–2004. But the share is higher in some countries. For example, in Benin, 7 of 13 conditions in 2005 required privatizing State-owned enterprises in the infrastructure, telecommunications and cotton sectors (Molina and Pereira, 2008). Both privatization and liberalization of the banking and financial sectors remain key conditionalities for LDCs (table 35).

A third of all structural conditions attached to PRGFs approved in LDCs since 2005 focus on "sensitive" policy reforms.

Fourthly, there is a tendency for policy conditionality to be increasingly drawn from Government documents. But the tensions between conditionality and ownership still remain. The IMF IEO interviews with national authorities found that some LDCs saw IMF structural conditionality as being imposed on them and not adapted to the country's institutional circumstances, implementation capacity or political constraints, whilst others saw it as excessive and inflexible in the face of shocks (IMF, 2007a: 20). Case studies of conditionality in relation to privatization and liberalization in Bangladesh, Mozambique, Uganda and Zambia found a range of interactions (Bull, Jerve and Sigvaldsen, 2006). In Zambia, pressure was put on the Government to privatize State-owned banks and utilities. In Bangladesh, privatization of parts of the energy sector was viewed as aligned with governmental priorities and earlier reviews of the sector. However, the World Bank was heavily involved with those reviews, and some government officials said that the policy agendas did not reflect government priorities and pressure was

Macroeconomic stabilization, privatization and liberalization are still important types of conditionality, and these are now being complemented with more governance conditionalities.

Table 35. Structural conditionality[a] attached to PRGF loans in LDCs: 2003–2004 and 2005–2007

	2003/2004	2005/2007
Number of programmes	**11**	**15**
Total conditions	**149**	**196**
of which:		
Binding	77	104
Non-binding	72	92
Total non-sensitive	100	139
Total sensitive	49	57
of which:		
Banking and financial sector liberalisation	19	19
Limiting fiscal space	0	8
Regressive taxation	2	3
Privatisation related	18	15
Public enterprise restructuring	3	7
Liberalisation related	7	5
Total sensitive privatization and liberalisation conditions	44	38
by sector:		
Bank and financial sector	20	19
Trade and prices	7	4
Natural resources	6	4
Telecommunications	1	3
Energy and water utilities	1	2
Infrastructures and transport	0	5
Other	9	1

Source: Personal communication with EURODAD, based on database of Molina and Pereira (2008).

a   Includes prior actions, performance criteria and structural benchmarks.

applied to implement the policies. In Mozambique, the World Bank was a major proponent of privatization of the energy sector, but moved away from this when government priorities shifted away from privatization. In Uganda, privatization and liberalization are not major elements of current reforms and all Poverty Reduction Strategy Credit (PRSC) conditionalities are jointly decided by government and donors. AFRODAD (2007b:22) states that in Mozambique, some privatizations which are conditionalities are not clearly spelt out in the PRSP but, nevertheless, are being implemented. These are private concession for management of the major port, private management of water in five cities and private concessions on energy, telecommunications and transport services.

There have been major shifts in the practice of policy conditionality including a greater shift towards administrative guidance through benchmarks rather than legally binding conditionality. But much less shift in its content.

To sum up, it can be said that there have been major shifts in the practice of policy conditionality but much less shift in its content. There is little clear public evidence that conditionalities are imposed on countries and there is an increasing tendency for policy conditionalities to be negotiated based on government documents. There is also a greater shift towards administrative guidance through benchmarks rather than legally binding conditionality related to clearly-specified variables and measures which, in case of non-observance, lead to the interruption of disbursements. Macroeconomic stabilization, privatization and liberalization are still important types of policy conditionality, and these are now being complemented with more governance conditionalities.

Policy conditionality has not been conducive to policy pluralism. The degree of detail of conditionality is also a problem. The effect of conditionality is to focus the tempo and content of policy actions.

Policy conditionality has not been conducive to policy pluralism. One effect of the content of policy conditionality is to ensure that the strategic thrust at the heart of the national development strategies of LDCs is still liberalization and privatization within a tight fiscal and monetary policy. As indicated in the last chapter, in an LDC context, this development model has not been leading to sustainable and inclusive growth.

The degree of detail of conditionality is also a problem. For example, the structural conditionality attached to the PRGF in Sierra Leone included the introduction of a photo verification system for civil servants and teachers as part of structural measures to strengthen wage bill policies (Fedelino et al., 2006: Appendix 3). Whatever the merits of this as a measure to eliminate ghost workers, the example illustrates the level of detail of conditionality and raises the question of whether or not such actions should be a major priority for development planning in Sierra Leone. The effect of conditionality is to focus the tempo and content of policy actions. In the process of policy implementation, what happens is that the task of meeting the conditions must take precedence over the promotion of development.

2. Donor financing choices

Given the broad policy agenda contained in the PRSPs, donor financing choices are an important determinant of which programmes within the PRSP get financed.

Given the broad policy agenda contained in the PRSPs, donor financing choices are an important determinant of which programmes within the PRSP get financed. In one case study, it is suggested that because of the broad nature of the PRSP, any aid money can be aligned to the PRSP and thus "donors select and fund their own priorities from the PRSP as they narrow down what they will focus their spending on" (EURODAD 2008a). In another case, it is reported that the PRSP involves "a vastness of areas and activities, to such as degree that almost all donor areas and activities find a place" (IPAM, 2008: 35).

Donor involvement in what gets financed occurs even when donors commit to general budget support. In that case, performance assessment frameworks are negotiated to set priorities in the way in which budget money is spent. In the best case, this involves mutual commitments, as they have in Mozambique (Castel-

Branco, 2007). However, in another country, one donor official is reported as stating that "initially the donors do a draft to agree on the conditions and then these are taken to the Government to be discussed" (EURODAD, 2008a: 17). In that country, the targets in the Performance Assessment Framework (PAF) priorities were extremely wide-ranging, including (a) specified targets for rural feeder roads in good condition; (b) number of bed nets with long-lasting insecticide distributed annually; (c) improvement in primary school pass rate; (d) civil service reform; (e) implementation of decentralization; (f) the submission of legislation on financial sector reform; and (g) procurement reform to increase international competitive bidding. These are not necessarily undesirable *per se*, but they orient the direction and pace of national development planning in the same way the policy conditionality does.

There are various processes through which the financing of productive sectors is currently getting neglected in the implementation process.

One of the hallmarks of the PRSPs written since mid-2002 is that they are no longer narrowly focused on increased social expenditure, but also include the development of productive sectors. However, there are various processes through which the financing of productive sectors is currently getting neglected in the implementation process.

Firstly, although productive sectors often appear among the priority policy objectives, they do not receive the necessary attention in the action matrices which focus policy actions. This has been observed for science and technology intervention in Mozambique and also on rural productive development in Malawi (Warren-Rodriguez, 2007; Cabral, 2006). In the case of Malawi, the outcome is related to the difficulty of achieving a policy consensus on agriculture and rural development. In the case of Mozambique, the marginalization of science and technology is related to the low priority given by donor agencies to science and technology as well as "the fragmented nature of development aid in Mozambique, with a plethora of donor agencies, non-governmental organizations (NGOs) and international development organizations operating in the country, each using a variety of funding and technical assistance mechanisms and most aid funds, as well as associated technical assistance, being disbursed directly to sectoral ministries or, even, specific projects in priority sectors" (Warren-Rodriguez, 2007:31). Such fragmentation makes it difficult to treat cross-sectoral issues such as science and technology in the action matrix, even though they are identified as central in the plan.

Although productive sectors often appear among the priority policy objectives, they do not receive the necessary attention in action matrices which focus policy actions.

Active policies to promote productive sector development are often on the wrong side of the ownership frontier.

Secondly, as noted above, active policies to promote productive sector development are often on the wrong side of the ownership frontier. In the case of Malawi, strategy disagreements over agricultural development meant it was difficult to get donor support. A lack of policy pluralism in relation to private sector development is also weakening discussion of alternatives. Box 6 illustrates how private sector development and the promotion of structural change were marginalized in the preparation of Mozambique's second-generation poverty reduction strategy.

Thirdly, donor efforts to support productive sector development are sometimes misaligned. Shepherd and Fritz (2005) reported that large shares of donor funds for rural productive sectors were made available through off-budget projects and programmes. They quote a World Bank review of alignment of its PRSC and the rural priority activities in the action matrices of the PRSPs of 12 countries published in 2005 which found that there was very low alignment. Out of 189 rural priority activities, only 38 per cent were taken up in the PRSC.

Donor efforts to support productive sector development are sometimes misaligned.

Fourthly, even where aid is aligned with government priorities through budget support, the allocation of aid is oriented towards social sectors. In Mozambique, for example, the crucial role of small-scale agriculture for income generation

---

Box 6. The treatment of private sector development, technology issues and manufacturing in Mozambique's second-generation PRSP

Mozambique's second-generation PRSP, PARPA II, has made some progress in incorporating productive considerations in the Government's poverty reduction efforts, including those related to private sector development, especially when compared to Mozambique's first PRSP. But the discussions on private sector development — in which representatives of the Government, the business community and aid agencies participated — essentially focused on investment climate issues, largely leaving aside other considerations. Questions relating to international trade and investment policy, infrastructure development, industrial capacity-building or institutional reform — which could have provided an opportunity to address issues relating to science and technology development — were, for the most part, absent in these discussions. As a result, the document put forward by the PARPA II private sector working group basically consisted of some key measures relating to major investment climate constraints, plus an amalgamation of initiatives put forward by the various ministries involved in these discussions — tourism, agriculture, mineral resources, energy, fisheries, and trade and industry. These initiatives not only did not respond to any coordinated effort to formulate a consistent strategy for private sector development; in addition, their quality was considerably impaired by the weak institutional and — in particular — planning and policy formulation capacities that exist in many of these ministries.

Furthermore, the organization of the PARPA II preparation process into working groups of a sectoral nature, together with lack of effective intersectoral coordination mechanisms prior and during the preparation of PARPA II, made it difficult to address issues cutting across the various policy spheres intervening in the promotion of private sector development. For instance, the private sector's concerns on the lack and cost of investment finance in Mozambique were not incorporated, or even taken into account, in the PARPA II discussions regarding macroeconomic policy considerations, an issue which is largely driven by the Government's PRGF negotiations with the IMF. Similarly, the discussion and definition of initiatives in the spheres of TVET or infrastructure development undertaken by the PARPA II working groups dealing with education and infrastructures did not include the participation of members of the private sector working group, nor explicitly incorporate the private sector's concerns in each of these areas. The same was the case with the incorporation in the PARPA II private sector development strategy of the recommendations made by the science and technology working group, which were generally not explicitly addressed during this process.

The PARPA II strategy for private sector development largely neglects technical capacity and technology upgrading considerations, essentially focusing on investment climate issues. Despite several references in the text to the need to "promote the creation of a strong, dynamic, competitive and innovative private sector", measures to do this are largely absent in the matrix of strategic initiatives included at the end of the PARPA II document, against which the implementation of this strategy is monitored and assessed. The overall outcome reflects the little clout that issues relating to industrial technological development currently hold in the Mozambican policy agenda, as well as the predominance of privatization and liberalization, together with an improved investment climate, as the key policy mechanisms to promote productive development.

Source: Warren-Rodriguez (2007).

In Mozambique, while agriculture and rural development are identified as priority poverty-reducing sectors in the budget, only 3.3 per cent went to agriculture and rural development.

and survival of the majority of the population is widely recognized, but public investments in agriculture and rural development are marginal. Agriculture and rural development are identified as priority poverty-reducing sectors in the budget. But in 2006, amongst the priority poverty-reducing sectors, 20 per cent of the budget went to education, 15 per cent to health, 16 per cent to infrastructure, 13 per cent to governance and the judicial system, and only 3.3 per cent went to agriculture and rural development (IPAM, 2008: table 2). The annual average share of the budget going to agriculture and rural development between 2004 and 2005 was 3.9 per cent. To what extent this is a government preference is unclear. AFRODAD (2007f) notes that in Mozambique some sectors get more assisted than others and the education and health sectors appear to be "donor sectors" (p.23).

Finally, "there are often serious capacity constraints at the sector level that affect the quality of policy development and analysis, planning, costing, budgeting, implementation and M&E" (AFRODAD, 2007e: 28).

G. Processes weakening country ownership — the continuing problem of aid misalignment

In the 1990s, as indicated above, country ownership was undermined by a combination of traditional policy conditionality, the misalignment of aid with national priorities and government processes, and all-pervasive coordination failures in the delivery of aid. These problems are being addressed through the Paris Declaration and the most recent progress will be assessed later this year. However, the OECD/Development Assistance Committee (DAC) *2006 Survey on Monitoring the Paris Declaration* summarized its chief finding with the judgement that, "in half of the developing countries signing on to the Paris Declaration, partners and donors have a long road ahead to meet the commitments they have undertaken" (OECD/DAC, 2006:9). The report also notes "a strong disconnect between headquarters policies and in-country (donor) practices" (ibid.: 10). A recent civil society report, financed by DFID to increase the perspectives of southern civil society on the aid effectiveness process, finds that donors are progressing in some areas but: (a) too little aid is still provided through national systems; (b) parallel management systems continue to proliferate; (c) aid disbursements are still unpredictable, disrupting development planning and implementation; and (d) even though some positive actions are being taken, an accountable aid system is still a distant prospect (EURODAD, 2008b: 7). Similarly, the synthesis study of cases studies of aid effectiveness in Africa found that "there is a clear difference between the structure of central government budget allocation and aid allocation, particularly when off-budget aid flows are included" (AFRODAD, 2007e: 28).

The degree to which assistance to LDCs remains off-budget, off-plan and uncounted varies between countries. Box 7 illustrates the situation in Afghanistan between 2003 and 2006, a case in which the national Government made strenuous efforts to ensure that aid was well-aligned with government priorities. This is obviously a special case given the security situation. But it is not necessarily untypical of what happens in other LDCs.

In one country, for example, donors provided $361.3 million in 2006, funding 265 different projects at an average of approximately $1 million per project (EURODAD, 2008a). This aid is meant to support the work of ministries, departments and agencies. But the vast majority of this money does not appear in the government budget and is not managed by any government body. Rather, it is spent through separate projects, so-called project implementation units. It is estimated that two thirds of donor project aid is not reflected in the budget. The Government also has incomplete information of how much aid has been spent and on what. Moreover, donors disbursed less than half of the aid that they had committed to the country in 2006. In this country, only 18 per cent of aid is provided as budget support. But access to budget support is conditional upon (a) continued good macroeconomic performance, as evidenced by satisfactory progress under an IMF programme; (b) satisfactory progress in PRSP implementation; and (c) continuous improvements in public finance management, as well as in implementing actions agreed in the PAF. Overall, the authors of this case study argue that the current situation reflects high levels of aid dependence, together with a major Government capacity gap after years of conflict and brain drain. The Government has made some progress in improving aid coordination and information through the establishment of the Development Assistance Coordination Office. But owing to mutual distrust, donors continue the practice of "heavily conditioning their aid, setting up parallel project units to control their aid and trying to mould policymaking" (EURODAD, 2008a: 4).

The OECD/DAC 2006 survey found that in half of the developing countries signing on to the Paris Declaration, partners and donors have a long road ahead to meet the commitments they have undertaken.

The degree to which assistance to LDCs remains off-budget, off-plan and uncounted varies between countries.

Box 7. Aid delivery in Afghanistan, 2001–2006

The Government formulated a national development strategy, identified priority programmes, established a set of principles and rules for donor interaction and set up a number of institutional mechanisms for managing donors (including the Afghanistan Development Forum and consultative group process). Its approach to aid implementation had the following characteristics:

(a) Pooling of financing to the budget, either directly or through trust fund or common programming mechanism. The Afghanistan Reconstruction Trust Fund was established to pool donor financing behind a single set of policies and implementation mechanisms, creating cost-effective modalities and policy coherence;

(b) Alignment behind the Government's strategy and policy agenda, most notably through the adoption of the National Development Framework and the budget as the policy basis;

(c) Programme implementation through Government-managed national projects and programmes, tendered through transparent mechanisms to the most effective organization for the job, whether private sector, NGO or international organization;

(d) Reporting on implementation of the budget through a single annual report that was shared with the population, Parliament, media and international community (Lockhart, 2007: 18–19).

Some international organizations and donors aligned behind this approach. But the largest bilateral donors and United Nations agencies, and the humanitarian funding system, did not follow this model. Instead, they adopted a project-based, donor-managed approach whose key characteristics were that:

(a) Financing flows went directly from each donor agency to the respective implementation agency, and not through the Government of Afghanistan;

(b) Strategy and policy for the financing programme was determined by the donor, usually in national or international headquarters, and is not included in the Afghanistan budget process;

(c) Implementation (procurement, accounting, management) took place through projects managed by international staff and project units outside the Government of Afghanistan; and

(d) Reporting took place from the implementing agency to the donor agency and is not incorporated in the national annual report (Lockhart, 2007: 19).

A number of donors provided part of their assistance through the Government's preferred modality but continued to finance "a significant proportion of their assistance through parallel mechanisms" (Lockhart, 2007: 20).

That the Government approach was followed at all depended on: (a) the leadership and vision of the Government of Afghanistan; (b) the quality of the programmes prepared by the Government and consistent progress in implementing them; and (c) trust between national leaders and international counterparts. Donors who did not have a record of channeling money through donor support mechanisms and who met core costs through percentages from projects were more likely to use parallel mechanisms. Those that had experience with budget support, were interested in the cost-effectiveness of aid and which recognized the links between aid for security, humanitarian assistance and economic development were more willing to support the government-led approach. In 2004, it is estimated that international actors spent $15 billion on security and $2 billion on economic and humanitarian assistance; of the latter, $200 million was directed to the Government.

This case shows the high cost to the Government of donor practices. For aid delivered through the second donor-managed approach, it is estimated that "anything between 40 and 90 per cent of a project cost is spent on overheads abroad" and "given the long contractual chain of many donor-managed projects, the resources that were available for a project on the ground would often be a fraction of that allocated to a particular project" (Lockhart, 2007: 25). Technical assistance is also very expensive. In 2005, Afghanistan received $600 million a year in technical assistance, which outweighed the costs of the entire civil service of 260,000 people. There is also a high cost in terms of the effectiveness of state institutions. Firstly, international staff deployed in the country required drivers, translators, secretaries and guards. Because of the high salaries which the Government could not match, these were often recruited from the civil service, where they had previously worked as teachers, doctors and managers. Secondly, the hundreds of different projects each came with specific internal rules for procurement, managing and reporting, and this undermined the coherence of laws and procedures in the country (ibid.:26). Thirdly, government authorities could not focus on formulating and implementing their own policy agenda. "To try to limit the negative impact of one of the parallel processes put into effect in competition with the national budget process, eight senior managers of the Afghanistan Coordination Assistance Authority had to spend six weeks during budget preparation time to review $1.8 billion projects prepared by United Nations agencies, instead of using their time to prepare and implement the national budget. Sixty per cent of these projects were subsequently rejected on the basis of World Bank rules" (Lockhart, 2007: 28).

Source: Lockhart (2007).

This situation is illustrative of what OECD (2003) calls "the low ownership trap". This arises when there is low capacity of the Government in a recipient country and donors fear aid will not be well-managed by the Government, either because of inadequate policies or inadequate management. Donors reduce this risk by bypassing Government and setting up parallel structures, for example, management units run by consultants. The Government has low ownership of what is happening and does not participate. This reduces trust on the part of donors, which reinforces their orientation not to integrate their activities with those of the Government. The parallel implementation units also pull scarce skills away from Government, and this further undermines capacity and reinforces the tendency of donors to seek to bypass government systems.

Some LDCs are caught in a low ownership trap but the problems of poor integration of aid with government plans and budgets are not simply confined to such countries.

However, the problems of poor integration of aid with government plans and budgets are not simply confined to countries which could be described as being caught in a low ownership trap. This is evident in the overview to the Rwanda Aid Policy, published in 2006, which lists the following problems in terms of the way in which aid was being delivered in Rwanda:

(a) "Excessive conditionality arises and this may result in problems of predictability;

(b) "High transactions costs lower the real value of assistance — donors continue to place significant demands on Government in terms of time, reporting needs, and use of other resources through numerous missions and meetings;

(c) "Incomplete reporting of ODA to the Government reduces transparency, and hinders the ability of Government to monitor and manage the assistance Rwanda receives. This information is critical to the planning and budgeting process, as well as the execution of the development budget. It is difficult to obtain a complete picture of external assistance to Rwanda, as some donors are unwilling or unable to meet the Government's request for information;

Although progress is being made, the slow alignment of aid with recipient countries' priorities, systems and procedures remains a problem which weakens ownership in a range of LDCs.

(d) "Too frequently donors continue to promote their own, often political objectives at the expense of Government ownership. Much assistance remains off-plan and off-budget, reflecting a lack of alignment with Government priorities and systems;

(e) "The existence of large vertical funds, while beneficial to development in some areas, may have a distortionary effect in the allocation of resources across sectors and subsectors; and

(f) "Technical assistance is not always effective, and in some instances is perceived to undermine local capacities rather than improving them" (Government of Rwanda, 2006: 1–2).

However, the document also acknowledges that the Government itself has major capacity problems, which result in poor coordination and implementation, and that "the lack of clear process in some cases leads line ministries and decentralized entities to negotiate directly with donors" and that the Government may also put unstructured demands for information on their development partners" (ibid.: 1–2).

To sum up, it is clear that, although progress is being made, the slow alignment of aid with recipient countries' priorities, systems and procedures remains a problem which weakens ownership in a range of LDCs.

H. Adverse consequences of weak country ownership

Weak country ownership has adverse consequences for the effectiveness of the poverty reduction strategies in promoting economic growth, reducing poverty and achieving the MDGs.

Weak country ownership has adverse consequences for the effectiveness of the poverty reduction strategies in promoting economic growth, reducing poverty and achieving the MDGs. There are in particular three features of their design and implementation which can be related to weak ownership but which undermine their effectiveness. These are related to (a) the weak integration of the macroeconomic framework with sectoral and trade policies; (b) the downscaling of ambition in relation to increased aid inflows; and (c) the inadequate level of financing for productive sector development.

1. The weak integration of the macroeconomic framework with sectoral and trade policies

It is widely recognized that the macroeconomic frameworks which LDCs have agreed with the IMF have helped to promote macroeconomic stability, in particular to bring down inflation. However, there is much more controversy about the effects of the macroeconomic framework on economic growth, poverty reduction and the achievement of the MDGs. Results from an IMF survey of views on PRGF design in sub-Saharan Africa found that only 55 per cent of IMF respondents and only 20 per cent of World Bank respondents agreed or strongly agreed that the programmes focused on economic growth (IMF, 2007b). Still fewer IMF respondents believed that they focused on poverty reduction or the MDGs (38 per cent and 13 per cent, respectively), and the numbers were still fewer for World Bank respondents (12 per cent and 3 per cent, respectively). Respondents from national authorities held more or less the same views as the IMF respondents, but a slightly higher proportion agreed or strongly agreed that they were focused on growth and 26 per cent believed that they were focused on MDGs (table 36).

Only 20 per cent of World Bank respondents agreed or strongly agreed that IMF PRGF programmes in Africa focused on growth.

Fiscal and monetary policies generally target low fiscal deficits and inflation at 5 per cent of below. The evidence from African countries indicates that there has been increasing flexibility with the shift from ESAF to PRGF programmes. The PRGF programmes since 2003 have targeted a small (1 per cent) increase in the fiscal deficit before grants, whereas the ESAF programmes targeted substantial cuts (by 3 per cent of GDP over the three-year programme period). But a number of qualified analysts believe that despite the looser policy stance, these targets are still too conservative in relation to economic growth, poverty reduction and the achievement of the MDGs.[8]

An important adverse consequence of the narrow ownership of the macroeconomic policies is that there is a lack of integration between macroeconomic policies and sectoral policies, and also with trade policies.

Wherever one stands in relation to these economic debates, an important adverse consequence of the narrow ownership of the macroeconomic policies is that there is a lack of integration between macroeconomic policies and sectoral policies, and also with trade policies. The lack of integration between

Table 36. The design of IMF's Poverty Reduction and Growth Facility in sub-Saharan Africa: Survey views on growth and poverty orientation

Design of PRGF programmes focused on:	Percentage of respondents "Agreeing" or "Strongly Agreeing":			
	IMF	National Authorities	World Bank	Donors
Macro stability	100	98	98	97
Growth	55	57	20	53
Poverty reduction	38	36	12	23
MDGs	13	26	3	13

Source: Adapted from IMF (2007b), table A5.3.

the macroeconomic policies and sectoral policies means that different policy options cannot be adequately explored. For example, the impact of different spending choices on domestic prices depends on sectoral parameters (such as the composition of spending, the extent of spare capacity, and the ability of public spending to crowd in private investment). In assessing the potential for public spending, it is necessary to integrate sector-level information on costs and consequences (Working Group on IMF Programs and Health Spending, 2007).

The lack of integration of the macroeconomic framework with the trade policies is a further adverse consequence of the narrow ownership of the macroeconomic policies. In this regard, it was proposed in *The Least Developed Countries Report 2004* that the key to integrating trade into poverty reduction policies was through the export and import forecasts which are part of the macroeconomic framework. The detailed trade policies need to be realistically related to these forecasts and export and import policies geared to achieving these goals. However, in practice, despite the increase in trade policy content in the PRSPs, the trade objectives in the macroeconomic framework float freely, having no connection with the more detailed trade objectives and policy measures contained in the main text of the PRSP. This disarticulation is related to weak integration of the macroeconomic framework with the rest of the document.

2. THE DOWNSCALING OF AMBITION IN RELATION TO INCREASED AID INFLOWS

A second adverse consequence of weak ownership is the downscaling of ambition in relation to increased aid inflows. It is clear that most LDC Governments want increased aid inflows. But there is a fundamental mismatch between this desire and the way in which PRSPs are written. This arises once again because the macroeconomic framework is usually based on projections of future aid inflows which dampen expectations of both donor and recipient countries in the scaling up of aid. This results in minimalist poverty reduction strategies rather than poverty reduction strategies which explore the effects of the scaling-up of aid.

In general terms, it is possible to project future aid inflows on the basis of (a) the minimum requirements for viable macroeconomic programmes; (b) past aid trends; (c) normative financing requirements to achieve growth, poverty reduction or MDG targets; or (d) the third approach adjusted for absorptive capacity constraints. In general, IMF (2007b) finds that, in African countries with PRGF programmes, the first and second approaches have been followed. Moreover, in general, very modest short-term projections of aid inflows are made because aid inflows are volatile, because there is past experience of actual disbursements falling short of commitments and because the major concern is to ensure that programmes are not underfinanced.

Where the forecasts come from is not entirely clear. IMF (2007b) says that IMF staff generally took the forecast of the authorities for the programme year, validated through discussion with donors. But in post-conflict countries where government capacity was limited, IMF staff played a more active role in working with authorities to aggregate donor plans in the context of the programme's macroeconomic framework. Interviewed staff said that the authorities were in many cases very conservative about future aid flows and, for medium-term forecasts, staff often triangulated between the authorities' forecasts, to which they added a premium, and indications from donors.

The consequence of the general approach to forecasting aid inflows is that development strategies are downscaled to be realistic in terms of past aid inflows rather than upscaled to explore how increased aid inflows can be effectively used

An adverse consequence of weak ownership is the downscaling of ambition in relation to increased aid inflows.

The general approach to forecasting aid inflows is that development strategies are downscaled to be realistic in terms of past aid inflows, rather than upscaled to explore how increased aid inflows can be effectively used to promote economic growth, poverty reduction and the achievement of the MDGs.

to promote economic growth, poverty reduction and the achievement of the MDGs. Recently, the IMF has undertaken some in-depth analyses of alternative scenarios to scale up aid in some countries – Ethiopia, Madagascar, Mozambique, Rwanda and Zambia (Goldsbrough and Elberger, 2007). However, in general, Governments are placed in a very difficult dilemma in drafting their PRSPs. To be realistic in terms of expected aid inflows, a development strategy cannot draw attention to the vast needs of the LDCs in pursuing MDGs, which is necessary to catalyse the extra flows. This catch-22 leads to a downscaling of ambition by both LDC Governments and their development partners.

Donors will only disburse aid if the macroeconomic framework is certified to be sound by the IMF. But the macroeconomic framework, through its aid projections, may at the same time discourage aid scale-up.

The Working Group on IMF Programs and Health Spending (2007) argues that the projections have also risked sending confused signals to donors. The case studies of Rwanda, Mozambique and Zambia also indicate that the notion that an increase in aid levels is undesirable may also have influenced the projections. When only conservative projections are presented, donors may conclude that this means that more resources cannot be usefully absorbed from a macroeconomic perspective. Donors will only disburse aid if the macroeconomic framework is certified to be sound by the IMF. But the macroeconomic framework, through its aid projections, may at the same time discourage the scale-up of aid. Goldbrough and Elberger (2007: 19) state that "the IMF initially sent signals that tended to discourage a substantial increase in aid. Of the 27 IMF programmes and reviews in sub-Saharan Africa that were completed in the 18 months after the Gleneagles Summit, aid projections in only two were as optimistic as the Gleneagles commitments".

The discouragement of aid scale-up is also apparent in the practices which have been adopted in relation to how actually increasing aid inflows are dealt with and what happens to aid windfalls when forecasts are not right (box 8).

Box 8. The use of increased aid inflows in African countries with PRGF programmes

A recent IMF Independent Evaluation Office Report on how aid is used in African countries which have PRGF programmes indicates that macroeconomic policies have tended to favour using additional aid to reduce domestic debt or rebuild external reserves rather than to increase public spending (IMF 2007b). The IEO study found that (a) if external reserves are less than 2.5 months of imports, virtually all aid is programmed to be saved in the form of higher reserves; (b) if reserves are above this level but inflation is above 5 per cent, 85 cents in every extra dollar of aid is channeled into reducing domestic debt; and (c) if reserves are above the 2.5-month threshold and inflation below 5 per cent, most additional aid is programmed for higher public spending.

The consequence of these rules of thumb have been that, across all countries experiencing aid increases during the PRGF programme period, only 27 cents of each dollar of the anticipated aid increases were programmed to be used for expansion of public expenditure. Some adjustments are made during the programme. But for the period 2004–2006, 91 cents of each additional dollar of aid over the level of the pre-programme year was "saved" in international reserves in Mozambique and 47 cents of each additional dollar of aid was "saved" in Zambia over the same period. Between 13 and 20 per cent of all aid which was received in these countries over this period went into international reserves, and 19 per cent of all aid was saved in that way in Rwanda in 2002–2004 (Working Group on IMF and Health Spending, 2007).

Recommendations concerning how unanticipated aid inflows are dealt with further reduce the pass-through of aid inflows to increased public expenditures. This is important because aid projections are often wrong, particularly given the unpredictability of aid inflows. The case studies of Mozambique, Rwanda and Zambia show that the IMF programmes initially required that in the short term, higher-than-projected aid was saved while public expenditure was cut if aid fell short. However, there is some evidence of increasing flexibility in these countries (ibid.: 39). Similarly, a study of eight African countries found that episodes of lower-than-programmed budget aid led to lower public investment, while higher-than-projected aid did not lead to high investment but instead was saved (Celasun and Walliser, 2005).

These practices in dealing with aid inflows at the country level are a major reason for the increase in international reserves in LDCs noted in chapter 1. Whether or not they are the right policy is an economic judgement. But these practices may work to discourage commitments to scale up aid, reinforcing the signaling effect of the unambitious macroeconomic forecasts.

3. THE INADEQUATE LEVEL OF FINANCING OF PRODUCTIVE SECTORS AND ECONOMIC INFRASTRUCTURE

A final adverse consequence of weak ownership is that there is now a growing disconnect between the content of the PRSPs, which are emphasizing the importance of productive sectors and economic infrastructure, and the composition of aid disbursements which, as analyzed in chapter 1 of this Report, are still focused on social sectors and social infrastructure. This mismatch between the changes in the policy content of the PRSPs without a change in the composition of aid is a primary indicator of weak country ownership of national development strategies as they are implemented.

This pattern of allocation is related to donor preference for financing social sectors. These financing choices, coupled with the thrust of policy conditionality, mean that the strategic orientation of the PRSPs in practice is basically a combination of policies promoting stabilization, privatization and liberalization, together with increased donor financing for social sectors. The inadequate financing of productive sectors and economic infrastructure implies that, although the PRSPs aspire to place poverty reduction and the achievement of the MDGs within a broad economic development framework, in practice they do not succeed. Moreover, as discussed in chapter 2 of this Report, it is unlikely that this development model can result in sustained and inclusive development.

The inadequate financing of productive sectors and economic infrastructure implies that, although the PRSPs aspire to place poverty reduction and the achievement of the MDGs within a broad economic development framework, in practice they do not succeed.

I. Practical policy mechanisms to enhance country ownership

Increasing country ownership of national development strategies should be a major priority for improving development and aid effectiveness in LDCs. This is a complex issue which depends on changing relations between donors and recipients. This section focuses on the potential of recipient-led aid management policies and identifies some elements for a broader agenda to enhance country ownership.

One first step which can be made to increase country ownership is the adoption of an aid management policy within LDCs.

1. THE POTENTIAL OF RECIPIENT-LED AID MANAGEMENT POLICIES

One first step which can be made to increase country ownership is the adoption of an aid management policy within LDCs. This can play an important role in reducing the multiple ways in which aid delivery is undermining ownership through being unaccounted, off-budget or unaligned with the Government priorities.

An aid management policy is different from a national development strategy. The national development strategy identifies goals, objective and targets, and the actions needed to achieve them. The aid management policy does not cover this ground. Rather "it is designed and used to ensure that assistance received is of such a type, and is so deployed, as to maximize its contribution to the priorities set out in the country's statements of development strategy" (Killick, 2008: 5). As we have seen, the PRSPs were actually introduced initially as a debt relief management policy instrument, and they still may be used as an instrument for attracting and channeling aid. By adopting an aid management policy, it is possible to separate, but interrelate the role of the development strategy and the aid management policy.

An aid management policy is designed and used to ensure that assistance received is of such a type, and is so deployed, as to maximize its contribution to the priorities set out in the country's statements of development strategy.

Significantly, the Paris Declaration encourages recipient countries "to take the lead in coordinating aid at all levels in conjunction with other development resources in dialogue with donors and encouraging the participation of civil society and the private sector" (OECD 2005a: 3). LDC Governments should seize the opportunity of the Paris Declaration and seek to elaborate aid management policies. The Declaration also seeks to promote mutual accountability. This idea is an essential element of more equal development partnership, and it directly seeks to address the imbalance of bargaining strength of donors and recipients. As the Declaration puts it, "[b]ecause demonstrating real progress at the country level is critical, under the leadership of the partner country we will periodically assess, qualitatively as well as quantitatively, our mutual progress at country level in implementing agreed commitments on aid effectiveness. In doing so, we will make use of appropriate country level mechanisms" (ibid.: 3). The Paris Declaration thus encourages countries to take the lead in developing locally appropriate mechanisms to ensure mutual, rather than one-sided accountability.

The evaluation of the process of country-led aid coordination in the United Republic of Tanzania indicates a number of positive developments in the nature of the aid relationship.

Following Killick (2008), a well-working aid management policy should:

(a) Improve the coordination of assistance and reduce uncertainties about actual and prospective aid inflows;

(b) Avoid or reduce the proliferation of sources of assistance and of discrete donor initiatives;

(c) By this and other means, increase the policy space of Governments, reduce the proliferation of conditionalities and raise the predictability of receipts;

(d) As a result of improved Government–donor relations and better harmonization and alignment, reduce transactions costs;

(e) Provide a platform for greater mutual accountability; and

(f) Provide a framework through which technical assistance can become increasingly demand-driven and oriented to recipient capacity development needs.

Some developing countries have taken the lead in elaborating aid management policies. Indeed, a few LDCs are global leaders in the adoption of such policies. The countries which have done so include Rwanda, Uganda and the United Republic of Tanzania, whose experience is summarized in box 9, as well as Afghanistan and Mozambique.

The introduction of jointly agreed monitoring indicators at the country level in relation to donor practices seems to be a particularly powerful way to reduce transaction costs and promote alignment and harmonization.

From the experiences of LDCs thus far, it is apparent that aid management policies can offer a powerful bottom-up approach to better aid coordination (Menocal and Mulley, 2006; De Renzio and Mulley, 2006). The evaluation of the process of country-led aid coordination in the United Republic of Tanzania indicates a number of positive developments in the nature of the aid relationship. These include (a) better data on aid inflows; (b) increased levels of trust; (c) increasing assertiveness on the part of the Government in expressing its preferences; (d) greater rationalization and harmonization of processes and procedures amongst donors; (e) increased predictability of aid, with donors making multi-year aid commitments; (f) reduced transaction costs as donors support a joint assistance strategy; and (g) increased mutual accountability, as performance indicators not only relate to Government actions but also donor actions in relation to aid disbursements (Wangwe et al. 2005). The introduction of jointly agreed monitoring indicators at the country level in relation to donor practices seems to be a particularly powerful way to reduce transaction costs and promote alignment and harmonization.

Box 9. Aid management policies in Rwanda, Uganda and the United Republic of Tanzania

Rwanda:

The Government formally adopted its Rwanda Aid Policy in 2006. However, this was the culmination of a number of prior steps, including the creation of a central machinery for aid coordination, the preparation of a PRSP and sector development strategies, and the establishment of a development partners coordination group. In preparation for the drafting of the aid policy, in 2005 it initiated an independent "Baseline Survey of Donor Alignment and Harmonization" to provide a necessary factual base. Although the aid policy document is clearly a statement of government positions, the manner of its preparation was designed to build consensus. It was the outcome of several rounds of consultation, both within the Government and with its principal donors. Designed to give local effect to the Paris Declaration, its goals are stated to be to increase aid effectiveness and to provide a basis for mobilizing the additional assistance sought by the Government. There is a special unit within the Ministry of Finance responsible for implementation of the policy and one of its first steps was to request donors to undertake a systematic self-assessment of the extent to which their existing policies and practices were in line with the aid policy guidelines.

Uganda:

In the late 1980s and early 1990s, public investment in Uganda was characterized by a large number of donor-driven projects, which resulted in significant duplication and chronic recurrent expenditure shortfalls. Thus, the Government of Uganda progressively developed sector strategies that set a coherent framework and established clear priorities for donor support. This facilitated "first-order" harmonization efforts among donors (e.g. common reporting, disbursement and auditing arrangements for basket funds). Sector strategies were then integrated into the PRSP and unified in a medium-term expenditure framework. The Government also centralized donor coordination in one ministry and in 2003 developed a set of "Partnership Principles" as a framework for coordination and dialogue. This included undertakings by the Government on such matters as corruption and public service reform, set out clear preferences for the types of aid it wished to receive, and proposed a variety of other changes to raise aid effectiveness and lower transactions costs. Both the existence of a strong, competent central ministry driving the process forward and sustained support by development partners have been crucial for the Government's ability to play a strong role in managing relations with its donors. In 2005, the Government and several major donors took what they saw as a logical next step and agreed to a Joint Assistance Strategy for 2005–2009. This built on the principles of the Paris Declaration, committed partners to important changes in behaviour intended to raise aid effectiveness and further aligned donors' support with the country's poverty reduction strategy.

United Republic of Tanzania:

In 1994, the Government of the United Republic of Tanzania commissioned an independent group of advisers to investigate the crisis that then existed between the Government and donors, and to propose solutions. Its report facilitated the definition of specific commitments on both sides to improve aid outcomes. Progress against these commitments has been regularly monitored through a formally constituted independent monitoring group. In 2002 the Government's strategy for managing its aid was formalized in the form of the United Republic of Tanzania Assistance Strategy. The strategy was a government initiative "aimed at restoring local ownership and leadership by promoting partnership in the design and execution of development programmes" and outlined the undertakings of the Government and its donors. There were annual implementation reports and it was subsequently used as the basis for the development of a Joint Assistance Strategy. Finalized in 2006, this is viewed as providing a more inclusive set of principles to which donors and the Government can be held accountable. It aims to further improve donor coordination, including through the identification of donors' comparative advantages and the introduction of a single review cycle. It is intended to replace individual donor assistance strategies.

Source: Killick (2008).

Nevertheless, there are limits to improvements. The case of Afghanistan shows that, even where a country implements a strong aid management policy, success is not necessarily assured (box 7). In both Uganda and the United Republic of Tanzania, a number of donors remain outside the joint assistance strategies and, in Mozambique, the aid management policy only covers aid which is provided through budget support. Experience also suggests that country-level efforts to improve aid management are very time-consuming and thus could crowd out thinking and action on effective development strategies. It might be added that aid recipients have no sanctions to bring to bear when donors underperform in relation to agreed goals; this means that there may be an asymmetry in accountability, even when performance indicators are mutually agreed. The main sanctions which recipient countries can use to influence donor behaviour seem to be the donors' sense of reputation and also peer pressure, whilst the recipient is always facing the possibility that aid will be withdrawn. Recipients may have greater leverage in the aid relationship if they have access to multiple sources of aid and also historical relationships with like-minded donors (De Renzio and Mulley, 2006).

There is a need to rebuild State capacity in relation to the broader agenda of growth and development to which the latest PRSPs aspire.

Despite these caveats, the introduction of an aid management policy can offer a practical way to reduce those processes weakening country ownership which are arising from aid being off-budget, unaccounted, unpredictable and unaligned with government priorities. It can also be a keystone to building trust and mutual understanding between donors and recipients which are essential to tackle the other processes which are weakening the ability of countries to take the lead in the design and implementation of their national development strategy. The annex to this chapter thus includes a roadmap for LDCs to set up an aid management policy.

The content of policy conditionality needs to be tempered by its possible negative effects on country ownership and tailored to its underlying rationale.

2. Elements of a broader agenda

Whilst it is possible to make some progress at the country level, there remain systemic issues which must be addressed in a full approach to enhance country ownership. Elements of a broader agenda would include: (a) technical cooperation to rebuild State capacity to formulate and implement national development strategies; (b) further thinking on policy conditionality; (c) enhanced systemic efforts to increase the predictability of aid; (d) addressing systemic biases against aid for productive sectors; and (e) the enhancing of alternative voices, and particularly developing country and LDC perspectives and local knowledge, in the production of knowledge about development processes and practices.

(a) Rebuilding State capacity

Establishing capable States is essential for enhanced country ownership of national development strategies. There is a need to rebuild State capacity in relation to the broader agenda of growth and development to which the latest PRSPs aspire. This involves major questions of development governance, which should encompass both the formulation and the implementation of development strategies and, in particular, new forms of development planning. At the same time, sound financial governance is needed to assure donors that aid money is used effectively.

Increasing the predictability of aid is a key goal to improve country ownership, as the unpredictability of aid makes it very difficult to plan and programme activities in countries which are highly aid-dependent.

(b) Policy conditionality

Although there has been a major shift in practices related to policy conditionality, there is a need for further debate on its rationale and effectiveness, and how donors' legitimate concerns about how money is spent are balanced with recipients' legitimate concerns that policy conditionality is still over-detailed and sometimes intrusive, effectively setting the pace and strategic direction of the policy agenda, and doing so in ways which ensure the implementation of what IFIs consider the best policies. The content of policy conditionality needs to be tempered by its possible negative effects on country ownership and tailored to its underlying rationale. The original purpose of IMF conditionality was to ensure that IMF resources are used to assist a member resolve its balance of payments problems, and do so in a way which ensures repayment and thus does not threaten the collective interest. This has also been reaffirmed recently. The question is: what implications does this have for the content of conditionality? Moreover, if aid is provided in the form of grants, what is the rationale for conditionality and how can its scope be focused on that rationale?

(c) Aid predictability and volatility

Increasing the predictability of aid is a key goal to improve country ownership, as the unpredictability of aid makes it very difficult to plan and programme activities in countries which are highly aid-dependent. Aid volatility and the unpredictability of aid inflows contribute to macroeconomic instability, undermine effective financial management and reduce aid effectiveness. The central issue for Governments is how to prepare effective development strategies with a meaningful financial resource envelope when they are highly dependent on aid, yet ignorant of future aid flows, which are highly volatile. Recent research shows that this remains a significant problem and the disconnect between aid commitments and disbursements is particularly strong in poor countries (Bulir and Hamann, 2006). Although an aid management policy can help to alleviate these problems, there is a need for systemic measures as well, in particular the exploration of ways and means to have more long-term aid commitments. This should also address legitimate constraints on donors, such as their own budget cycles, which make it difficult for them to make forward commitments.

The whole aid system is geared to a model of aid based on Government–to–Government transfers, which are particularly appropriate for using aid to increase public expenditure.

(d) Addressing systemic bias against aid for productive sectors

The shift in aid allocation away from productive sectors raises the question of whether there is a systemic bias in current aid practices which is leading to this. It is possible to suggest a number of ways such a systemic bias could arise. Firstly, a higher proportion of aid for economic infrastructure and production sectors is financed by loans rather than grants (UNCTAD, 2006: 18–20). With the shift from loans to grants, there has been an implicit shift towards social infrastructure and services. Secondly, tied aid was often associated with aid for economic infrastructure and production sectors, and shift away from tied aid has similarly led to an implicit shift away from aid to production sectors and economic infrastructure. Thirdly, the MDGs are leading to specific focus on a few sectors which are deemed particularly important for their realization — education, health, population programmes, water supply and sanitation. Fourthly, the whole aid system is geared to a model of aid based on Government–to–Government transfers, which are particularly appropriate for using aid to increase public expenditure.

Rebalancing the composition of aid may actually need a radical shift in aid practices towards a different paradigm in which aid is not seen as Government–to–Government transfers but as a catalyst for a development process which involves a broad range of stakeholders.

Rebalancing the composition of aid may actually need a radical shift in aid practices towards a different paradigm in which it is not seen as Government–to–Government transfers but as a catalyst for a development process which involves a broad range of stakeholders and is animated in a particular by the private sector (Cohen, Jaquet and Reisen 2005). Such a new approach to aid would not necessarily involve budget support, but would nevertheless have to be well-aligned with Government priorities.

(e) The production of development knowledge

Finally, enhanced country ownership does not simply depend on improved technical capacities, but also the deeper exploration of theoretical and policy alternatives for development. In this regard, the way in which knowledge is produced is crucial (Zimmerman and McDonald, 2008). A growing number of eminent scholars from developing countries argue that ownership requires independent thought based on the interplay between local knowledge, experimentation, and trial and error (Girvan, 2007). Country ownership of development policies needs to reflect the local realities and conditions. But these perspectives are marginalized by the current way in which the production of development knowledge is dominated by research carried out in developed countries and also IFIs (Wilks and Lefrancois, 2002; Utting, 2006).

Enhanced country ownership does not simply depend on improved technical capacities, but also the deeper exploration of theoretical and policy alternatives for development.

The way in which knowledge is produced is crucial.

A major goal of development assistance which seeks to enhance country ownership should thus be to support and the accumulation of indigenous capabilities in developing countries, particularly LDCs. Independent policy approaches require capacities that most developing countries do not yet possess

This capacity of developing countries needs to be strengthened through acceptance of intellectual pluralism and critical debate.

The processes weakening country ownership come into play at the level of policy formulation or at the level of policy implementation.

Country ownership may be weakened because donors deliver part of their aid in ways which are off-plan, off-budget or simply unknown, or because the way in which PRSPs are implemented is strongly influenced by policy conditionality, monitoring benchmarks or donor financing choices.

in abundance. This capacity of developing countries needs to be strengthened through acceptance of intellectual pluralism and critical debate. International agencies and donors need to support the evolution of stronger domestic knowledge systems and promote networking to share experiences. This will provide a sound basis for greater policy pluralism.

J. Conclusions

All parties agree that country ownership of development strategies is essential for development effectiveness and aid effectiveness. Since the late 1990s, there have been significant changes in the nature of the aid relationship between LDCs and their development partners. In the context of the PRSP approach, significant steps have been taken to enhance country ownership. But this chapter shows that various processes continue to weaken country ownership in LDCs and this is having adverse consequences for development effectiveness.

The processes weakening country ownership come into play at the level of policy formulation or at the level of policy implementation. The latter may arise because donors deliver part of their aid in ways which are off-plan, off-budget or simply unknown. Alternatively, it may also arise because, even when aid is integrated with Government priorities, processes and systems, the way in which PRSPs are implemented is strongly influenced by policy conditionality, monitoring benchmarks or donor financing choices.

Although progress is being made in the context of the drive to improve aid effectiveness, the case studies reviewed in this chapter show a continuing problem of poor alignment and harmonization of aid with government plans and budgets. In the process of policy formulation, weak technical capacities undermine the ability of countries to exercise effective leadership, meaning that countries sometimes have to rely heavily on donor support in the design of national strategies. Freedom of action in policy design is also constrained by the need to mobilize aid inflows and the sense, justifiable or not, that signs of lack of commitment to the types of policies which donors and IFIs believe are the best ones can work against aid mobilization. The second-generation PRSPS are now very broad documents with an amalgam of elements which include (a) a core policy agenda strongly owned by the national Government; (b) a policy agenda which is directly or indirectly negotiated with donors, and around which there is broad consensus and agreement; and (c) a policy agenda which is more closely aligned with donor preferences and which enjoys very little or very narrow country ownership. There is thus an ownership frontier *within* the PRSPs. It is possible, therefore, for aid to be aligned and harmonized with the document but to do so in a way which is more oriented to donor priorities within the national plan.

A consequence of this is that processes of policy implementation are now a very important mechanism through which country ownership can be strengthened or weakened. This chapter shows that there have been major shifts in the practice of policy conditionality. There is an increasing tendency for policy conditionalities to be drawn from Government documents and there has also been a shift towards administrative benchmarks rather than legally binding conditionality. However, macroeconomic stabilization, privatization and liberalization are still important types of conditionality. Policy conditionality is not conducive to policy pluralism and the degree of detail is also a problem. The effect of conditionality is to focus the tempo and content of policy actions.

Given the broad policy agenda contained in PRSPs, donor financing choices are also an important determinant of how PRSPs work out in practice. This happens even when donors give budget support, as this usually involves performance assessment framework negotiated to set priorities. Donors are particularly oriented to financing social sectors and social infrastructure.

The second-generation poverty reduction strategies in LDCs are seeking to place poverty reduction and the achievement of MDGs within a broad economic development framework. In many LDCs, these strategies have the potential to become effective development strategies. However, realizing this potential depends on broader development governance challenges than merely focusing on poverty-oriented public expenditure and budgeting, which have been the key concerns in the first generation poverty reduction strategies up to now. The weak country ownership is having negative consequences for addressing these challenges and also for development effectiveness.

There are three major adverse consequences of weak ownership. Firstly, the macroeconomic frameworks of the poverty reduction strategies are weakly integrated with sectoral policies and trade policies. Secondly, despite the desire on the part of LDC Governments to receive more aid, the PRSPs are devised in a way which is failing to encourage aid scale-up and explore its possibilities. Thirdly, there is a mismatch between the new emphasis on productive sectors and economic infrastructure in the latest PRSPs and the composition of aid to support the building of productive capacities. The strategic thrust of the PRSPs reflects the combination of policy conditionality focused on stabilization, liberalization and privatization, together with donor financing choices oriented to social sectors. As discussed in chapter 2 of this Report, it is unlikely that this development model can result in sustained and inclusive development.

One positive feature of the current situation is that aid management policies are being adopted in a few LDCs as part of the process of elaborating new development partnerships. These policies are designed and used to ensure that foreign financial and technical assistance is of such a type and is so deployed that it maximizes its contribution to the priorities set out in a country's statements of its national development strategy. Initial experience with these innovative practices suggests that they can be an effective tool to tackle some dysfunctional features of the way in which aid is currently delivered, notably donor coordination failures and lack of alignment with national priorities, and to improve aid effectiveness through mutual rather than one-sided accountability. LDC Governments are therefore encouraged to adopt such policies.

However, in the end, enhanced country ownership will depend on systemic measures, as well as country-level action. It is necessary to rebuild State capacities for promoting growth and development. Renewed attention needs to be given to the nature of policy conditionality and the problem of aid predictability and volatility. It is also necessary to assess whether there are systemic biases against using aid in a catalytic way to develop productive sectors. Action to promote alternative perspectives — especially from developing-country and LDC voices — in the production of knowledge about development will also be important in order to promote policy pluralism.

In many LDCs, the second-generation poverty reduction strategies have the potential to become effective development strategies. However, realizing this potential depends on broader development governance challenges than merely focusing on poverty-oriented public expenditure and budgeting.

Weak country ownership is having negative consequences for addressing development governance challenges and for development effectiveness.

One positive feature is that aid management policies are being adopted in a few LDCs as part of the process of elaborating new development partnerships.

In the end, enhanced country ownership will depend on systemic measures, as well as country-level action.

Annex:
A roadmap for devising aid management policies in LDCs

This annex sets out a roadmap for devising aid management policies in LDCs. This roadmap includes a structured checklist of the parameters which could be included in a statement and the initial steps which could be taken to devise an aid management policy. Overall, it is stressed that the policy should be formed through a consultative process with donors and with strong domestic political leadership if it is to be successful. Constructing an aid management policy is not simply a technocratic exercise undertaken by a small coterie of officials and advisers; it is also the result of a process of building greater institutional trust, transparency and capacity through effective negotiation and political commitment.

1. Elements of the policy statement

The following sets out a possible structure and set of guidelines that might go into a policy statement: (a) background and rationale; (b) objectives and guiding principles; (c) a statement of mutual commitments and obligations; (d) a statement of specific policies relating to volume and effectiveness of aid; (e) the organization of aid mobilization and management; and (f) implementation.

(a) Background and rationale

This should include the need for a brief history of aid and assessment of the current situation in an LDC as a first step, as well as an inventory of recent and ongoing initiatives and an assessment of impact and sustainability.

(b) Objectives and guiding principles

This could include a restatement of the objectives and principles of the Paris Declaration as they relate to the country. The policy statement could be viewed as a 'living' document, to be reviewed periodically.

(c) Statement of mutual commitments and obligations

This would be comprised of two key components: (i) commitments by Government; and (ii) Government expectations concerning the contribution of its donor partners to more effective aid. Regarding the former, this might involve a restatement of the commitments outlined in the Paris Declaration and governance transparency, the pursuit of poverty reduction and other development goals, greater mobilization of domestic resources, Government leadership in promoting aid harmonization and institutional capacity-building. Regarding Government expectations concerning the contribution of its donor partners to more effective aid, this could be based on local agreements with donors and include institutional provisions for the conduct of dialogue between Government and its development partners.

(d) Statement of specific policies relating to volume and effectiveness of aid

This would be comprised of four key components: (i) the volume of assistance; (ii) donor numbers and specialization; (iii) inclusivity and concessionality; (iv) aid modalities; (v) technical assistance; and (vi) transaction costs.

Regarding the volume of assistance, LDC Governments will need to consider factors regarding the macroeconomic management of large increases in aid inflows in developing their approach to aid volumes. A statement on donor numbers and specialization is recommended to improve donor coordination by limiting the number of donors and channels of assistance. As previously noted, it could also specify an appropriate division of labour between donors. Inclusivity requires that all donors (whether new or traditional) should be subject to the same procedures and machinery of dialogue with Government. Similarly, a statement of minimum acceptable levels of concessionality should be included. This should be consistent with external debt sustainability policies where relevant. A statement on Government preferences regarding aid modalities (budget support, technical assistance, etc.) is clearly a very important aspect of any aid management policy. Technical assistance in LDCs needs to be nationally owned, demand-driven and oriented around Government priorities. The aid management policy will also need to specify mechanisms for reducing transaction costs, as outlined in the Paris Declaration.

(e) The organization of aid mobilization and management

It is clear that greater inter-ministerial coordination in terms of streamlining aid management within LDC Governments to avoid fragmentation and unclear divisions of responsibility will be necessary. This may require Government tasking a particular ministry or department with drafting an agreed protocol setting out the roles and responsibilities of the ministries involved. A further possibility might consist of creating small secretariats supported by consultative forums and structured around key sub-themes of the aid management policy. Thematic bodies and forums are especially relevant in contexts where problems and opportunities cut across subsectors, or ministries.

(f) Implementation

This would be comprised of two key components: (i) dealing with matters of mutual concern to both Government and donors; and (ii) dealing with how Government intends to implement the content of the aid management policy. The former concerns matters of mutual accountability such as (a) improving the provision of information on aid flows and plans to strengthen partnerships and efficacy; (b) measures to strengthen monitoring and evaluation through the use of joint accounting and national reporting procedures, which also reduce the transaction costs of aid management; and (c) the policy statement, which should specify how monitoring and evaluation of both donor performance and Government in a given LDC will be organized and managed. This may take the form of periodic independent monitoring and evaluation reviews as in Mozambique and the United Republic of Tanzania. In terms of the execution of the policy, this should outline initial implementation stages or steps as part of an implementation action plan. Potential components of an action plan elaborated to give this effect might include the following: (a) the administration of a donor self-assessment questionnaire outlining the extent to which they conform to the content of the policy; (b) shared dissemination strategies; (c) an evaluation of the adequacy of the resources of the agency/unit responsible for the implementation of the policy; and (d) proposals for enhancing local ownership and effectiveness of technical assistance.

2. Steps to an aid management policy – preparing the policy statement

It is possible to envisage a five-stage process for the preparation of an aid management policy statement:

(a) *Stage 1:* Prepare and distribute a consultation document by Government outlining the policy objectives, process to be followed and a statement of initial issues to be addressed through the aid management policy;

(b) *Stage 2:* Schedule and hold stakeholder (e.g. Government ministries, agencies, NGOs and donors) workshops to solicit reactions to the consultation document. These workshops could be convened jointly by Government with wider stakeholder groups, or solely within Government (involving only ministries and agencies of the State);

(c) *Stage 3:* The responsible executing unit or authority within Government should revise the consultation document in the light of feedback received and then shared with stakeholders;

(d) *Stage 4:* A second round of consultation meetings, which should also include a politically mandated resolution within Government of the division of labour amongst ministries and agencies. At this stage, the implications of this policy for resources, training and location of the agency/body responsible for its implementation should be considered; and

(e) *Stage 5:* The aid management policy is finalized and approved by Government through the preparation of an action plan for its implementation.

This process is vital for building greater trust and transparency. The Government must retain control over what is finally put into the policy, but there is a need to convince donors as far as possible of the desirability of its provisions. It should also be based on a realistic understanding of donor perspectives. The responsibilities of different stakeholders also need to be negotiated.

Source: Killick (2008).

Notes

1   The main country studies on which this chapter draws are: Afghanistan (Lockhart, 2007); Burkina Faso (AFRODAD, 2007a); Ethiopia (AFRODAD, 2006; Furtado and Smith, 2007); Malawi (Cromwell et al., 2005); Mali (Bergamaschi, 2007); Mozambique (De Renzio and Hanlon, 2007; IPAM, 2008; Warren-Rodrigues, 2007); Rwanda (Hayman, 2007); Senegal (AFRODAD, 2007b); Sierra Leone (EURODAD, 2008a); Uganda (AFRODAD, 2007c); United Republic of Tanzania (AFRODAD, 2006 and 2007d; Harrison and Mulley, 2007); Zambia (AFRODAD, 2006; Fraser, 2007); as well as AFRODAD (2007e), which synthesizes the findings of case studies of aid effectiveness which include: Mozambique, Malawi, Tanzania, Liberia, Uganda and Senegal. EURODAD (2008b) synthesizes the findings of case studies of aid effectiveness which include Cambodia, Mali and Niger, as well as IPAM (2008) and EURODAD (2008a). The chapter also draws on De Renzio and Goldsbrough (2007), Goldsbrough and Cheelo (2007) and Goldsbrough et al. (2007), which are case studies of IMF practices in Mozambique, Zambia and Rwanda respectively; and Bull et al. (2006), which examines conditionality related on privatization and liberalization in Bangladesh, Mozambique, Uganda and Zambia. The sources are listed in the references at the end of this chapter.

2   In some ways, this was a return to the past. The Report of the Secretary-General of UNCTAD to UNCTAD II in 1968, entitled "A Global Strategy for Development", not only introduced the target of 0.7 per cent of gross domestic product (GDP) but also argued that finance should be provided to those developing countries which showed the willingness and discipline to promote their own development. A "development plan" which increased their domestic resource mobilization and decreased their aid dependence and external economic vulnerability was seen as "the expression of the primary responsibility of the peripheral countries to solve their own problems" (UNCTAD, 1968: 66). Moreover, "the granting of international finance should closely be linked to the way in which a development plan proposes to achieve these aims" (ibid.: 60). But in the current partnership framework, the focus has shifted from economic development to poverty reduction and human development, a change which raises many important questions about how the one is related to the other.

3   For an extensive review of the debates surrounding conditionality, including the deficiencies of traditional policy conditionality, see the background papers in World Bank (2005) and IMF (2007a).

4   The specific titles are: Benin: Growth Strategy for Poverty Reduction; Burkina Faso: Growth and Poverty Reduction Strategy Paper; Cambodia: National Strategic Development Plan; Ethiopia: A Plan for Accelerated and Sustained Development to End Poverty; Gambia: Growth and Poverty Reduction Strategy Paper; Madagascar: Madagascar Action Plan; Malawi: Malawi Growth and Development Strategy; Mali: Growth and Poverty Reduction Strategy; Niger: Accelerated Development and Poverty Reduction Strategy; Rwanda: Economic Development and Poverty Reduction Strategy; United Republic of Tanzania: National Strategy for Growth and Reduction of Poverty; Zambia: Fifth National Development Plan.

5   In one case, it is noted that high levels of aid dependence make the Government reluctant to insist on its own priorities (Killick et al., 2005: 50). In the other case, "government technicians and planners know very well what kinds of development management discourse appeal to donors and they evoke these terms in order to increase their chances of gaining approval and access to credit" (Harrison and Mulley, 2007: 24). In both these cases, effective partnership depends on some level of strategic ambiguity in terms of agreed priorities. In the final case, it is noted, "[T]he Government needs to keep donors on board, which it does by committing itself to the international norms of development and reminding the international community of its responsibilities… Real policy freedom is therefore constrained by the need to appeal to external financiers" (Hayman, 2007: 20).

6   The relationship between the PRSP and PRGF is also evolving since the introduction by the IMF of the Policy Support Instrument in October 2005. This is designed as a complement to the PRGF for countries which are mature stabilizers, and which may not want or need Fund financial support but still seek IMF policy support and signaling. Uganda (2006), Cape Verde (2006), Tanzania (2006) and Mozambique (2007) have used this facility.

7   In this regard, it is worth recalling that in the consultation with low-income countries on policy conditionality, organized by the World Bank on 22 April 2005, whilst some country representatives wanted no World Bank or IMF role, others "stressed that their Governments welcomed bank and fund participation in helping prepare their PRSPs and welcomed the positive role being played by budget support groups of donors". Moreover, in some cases, they stressed that "close Fund involvement was needed as donors wanted a positive signal from the Bank and the Fund" (World Bank, 2005b:15–16).

8   Case studies of Mozambique, Rwanda and Zambia show that "programmes did not sufficiently explore more expansionary but still feasible spending options, although recent programmes are more flexible in this regard" (Center for Global Development, 2007: 28–29).

References

ActionAid (2006). What progress? A shadow review of World Bank conditionality. ActionAid, London.

AFRODAD (2006). Assessing the impact of the PRGF on social services in selected African countries: A synthesis report on Ethiopia, Malawi, Zambia and the United Republic of Tanzania. African Forum and Network on Debt and Development, Harare.

AFRODAD (2007a). The second-generation poverty reduction strategy papers (PRSPs II): The case of Burkina Faso. African Forum and Network on Debt and Development, Harare.

AFRODAD (2007b). The second-generation poverty reduction strategy papers (PRSPs II): The case of Senegal. African Forum and Network on Debt and Development, Harare.

AFRODAD (2007c). The second-generation poverty reduction strategy papers (PRSPs II): The case of the United Republic of Tanzania. African Forum and Network on Debt and Development, Harare.

AFRODAD (2007d). The second-generation poverty reduction strategy papers (PRSPs II): The case of Uganda. African Forum and Network on Debt and Development, Harare.

AFRODAD (2007e). Aid effectiveness in Africa: A synthesis. African Forum and Network on Debt and Development, Harare.

AFRODAD (2007f). A critical assessment of aid management and donor harmonization: The case of Mozambique. African Forum and Network on Debt and Development, Harare.

Bergamaschi, I. (2007). Mali: Patterns and limits of donor-driven ownership. Managing Aid Dependency Programme: Global Economic Governance (GEG) Working Paper No. 2007/31, The University of Oxford and University College, Oxford.

Buiter, W. (2005). Country ownership: A term whose time has gone. In Koeberle, S., Bedoya, H., Silarszky, P., and Verheyen, G. (Eds), Conditionality Revisited: Concepts, Experiences and Lessons. World Bank, Washington, DC.

Bulir, A. and Hamann, A.J. (2006). Volatility of development aid: From the frying pan into the fire? IMF Working Paper No. WP/06/65, International Monetary Fund, Washington, DC.

Bull, B., Jerve, A. M. and Sigvaldsen, E. (2006). The World Bank's and the IMF's use of conditionality to encourage privatization and liberalization: Current issues and practices. Sum Report No. 13, prepared for the Norwegian Ministry of Foreign Affairs as background for the Oslo Conditionality Conference, Oslo.

Broughton, J.M. (2003). Who's in charge? Ownership and conditionality in IMF-supported programs. IMF Working Paper No. WP/03/191, International Monetary Fund, Washington DC.

Cabral, L. (2006). Poverty reduction strategies and the rural productive sectors: What have we learnt, what else do we need to ask? ODI Natural Resource Perspectives No. 100, Overseas Development Institute, London.

Castel-Branco, C.N. (2007). The Mozambique performance assessment framework for donors: Lessons learned. Paper presented at the High-level Symposium "County-level experiences in coordinating and managing development cooperation". United Nations, 19–20 April, Vienna.

Celasun, O. and Walliser, J. (2005). Predictability of budget aid: Experiences in eight African countries. Paper prepared for the World Bank practitioners' forum on budget support, 5-6 May, Cape Town. http://www.cgdev.org/doc/event%20docs/Predictability%20 of20budget%20Aid%20revised.pdf.

Cohen, D., Jacquet, P. and Reisen, H. (2005). Beyond "grants versus loans": How to use ODA and debt for development. Paper prepared for the AFD/EUDN international conference, 15 December, Paris. http://www.eudnet/download/Jacquet.pdf

Cromwell, E., Luttrell, C., Shepherd, A. and Wiggins, S. (2005). Poverty reduction strategies and the rural productive sectors: Insights from Malawi, Nicaragua and Viet Nam. ODI Working Paper No. 258, Overseas Development Institute, London.

De Renzio, P. and Goldsbrough, D. (2007). IMF programs and health spending: Case study of Mozambique. Background paper prepared by the working group on IMF programs and health expenditures, Centre for Global Development, Washington, DC.

De Renzio, P. and Mulley, S. (2006). Donor coordination and good governance: Donor-led and recipient-led approaches. Managing Aid Dependency Project, the University of Oxford and University College, Oxford.

De Renzio, P. and Hanlon, J. (2007). Contested sovereignty in Mozambique: The dilemmas of aid dependence. Global Economic Governance (GEG) Working Paper No. 2007/25, The University of Oxford and University College Oxford, Oxford.

EURODAD (2007). Untying the knots: How the World Bank is failing to deliver real change on conditionality. The European Network on Debt and Development, Brussels.

EURODAD (2008a). Old habits die hard: Aid and accountability in Sierra Leone. The European Network on Debt and Development, Brussels.

EURODAD (2008b). Turning the tables: Aid and accountability under the Paris Framework. The European Network on Debt and Development, Brussels.

Fedelino, A., Schwartz, G. and Verhoeven, M. (2006). Aid scaling up: Do wage bill ceilings stand in the way? IMF Working Paper No. WP/06/106, International Monetary Fund, Washington, DC.

Fraser, A. (2007). Zambia: Back to the future? Managing aid dependency programme. Global Economic Governance (GEG) Working Paper No. 2007/30, The University of Oxford and University College Oxford, Oxford.

Furtado, X. and Smith, J. (2007). Ethiopia: Aid, ownership and sovereignty. Managing Aid Dependency Programme: Global Economic Governance (GEG) Working Paper No. 2007/28, The University of Oxford and University College, Oxford.

G8 (2005). Signed version of the Gleneagles communiqué on Africa, climate change, energy and sustainable development. Document from the G8 Summit, 6–8 July, Gleneagles.

Girvan, N. (2007). Home-grown solutions and ownership. Paper prepared for OECD Development Forum Informal Experts' Workshop on Ownership in Practice, 27–28 September, Paris.

Goldsbrough, D. and Cheelo, C. (2007). IMF programs and health spending: Case study of Zambia. Background paper prepared by the Working Group on IMF Programs and Health Expenditures, Centre for Global Development, Washington, DC.

Goldsbrough, D., Leeming, T. and Christiansen, K. (2007). IMF programs and health spending: Case study of Rwanda. Background paper prepared by the Working Group on IMF Programs and Health Expenditures, Centre for Global Development, Washington, DC.

Goldsbrough, D. and Elberger, B. (2007). The IMF and spending for the MDGs. *IPC Poverty in Focus*, October 2007: 18–19.

Government of Rwanda (2006). Rwanda aid policy, as endorsed by the Cabinet. 26 July, Kigali.

Harrison, G. and Mulley, S. (2007). The United Republic of Tanzania: A genuine case of recipient leadership in the aid system? Managing Aid Dependency Programme: Global Economic Governance (GEG) Working Paper No. 2007/29, The University of Oxford and University College, Oxford.

Hayman, R. (2007). "Milking the cow": Negotiating ownership and aid and policy in Rwanda. Managing Aid Dependency Programme: Global Economic Governance (GEG) Working Paper No. 2007/26, The University of Oxford and University College, Oxford.

IMF (2001). "Strengthening Country Ownership of Fund-Supported Programs" (December 5). http://www.imf.org/external/np/pdr/cond/2001/eng/collab/071701.pdf

IMF (2007a). An IEO evaluation of structural conditionality in IMF-supported programmes. Independent Evaluation Office of the IMF. International Monetary Fund, Washington, DC.

IMF (2007b). The IMF and aid to sub-Saharan Africa. Independent Evaluation Office of the International Monetary Fund, Washington, DC.

IMF and World Bank (1999). Poverty reduction strategy papers: Operational issues. Paper prepared by the staffs of the International Monetary Fund and World Bank, Washington, DC.

IMF and World Bank (2005). 2005 Review of the poverty reduction strategy approach: Balancing accountabilities and scaling up results. Paper prepared by the staffs of the International Monetary Fund and World Bank, Washington, DC.

IPAM (2008). Mozambique: An independent analysis of ownership and accountability in the development aid system. Paper submitted to EURODAD, TROCAIRE and CAFOD.

Johnson, O.E.G. (2005). Country ownership of reform programmes and the implications for conditionality. G-24 Discussion Paper Series No. 35, United Nations, New York and Geneva.

Killick, T., Gunatilaka, R. and Marr, A. (1998). *Aid and the Political Economy of Political Change*. Routledge, London and New York.

Killick, T., Castel-Branco, C.N. and Gerster, R. (2005). Perfect partners? The performance of programme aid partners in Mozambique, 2004. A report to the programme aid partners and Government of Mozambique.

Killick, T. (2008). Aid management policies in least developed countries. Study prepared for UNCTAD as a background paper for *The Least Developed Countries Report 2008,* Geneva and New York.

Lewis, J.P. (1986). *Development Strategies Reconsidered.* Transaction Publishers, Piscataway.

Lockhart, C. (2007). The aid relationship in Afghanistan: Struggling for government leadership. Managing Aid Dependency Project, The University of Oxford and University College, Oxford.

Marshall, R. (2008). Seizing the opportunity of the millennium: Harnessing scaled up aid for the expansion of productive capacities in the least developed countries. Study prepared for UNCTAD as a background paper for *The Least Developed Countries Report 2008.*

Menocal, A.R. and Mulley, S. (2006). Learning from experience? A review of recipient–Government efforts to manage donor relations and improve the quality of aid. ODI Working Paper No. 268, Overseas Development Institute. London.

Molina, N. and Pereira, J. (2008). Critical conditions: The IMF maintains its grip on low-income governments. EURODAD, Brussels.

OECD (1996). *Shaping the Twenty-First century: The Contribution of Development Co-operation.* Organisation for Economic Co-operation and Development, Paris.

OECD (2000). *Development Cooperation Report 1999.* Organisation for Economic Co-operation and Development, Paris.

OECD (2003). Harmonising donor practices for effective aid delivery — good practice papers. DAC Guideline and Reference Series, Organisation for Economic Co-operation and Development, Paris.

OECD (2005a). Paris Declaration on aid effectiveness: Ownership, harmonization, alignment, results and mutual accountability. Development Co-operation Directorate – Development Assistance Committee, Organisation for Economic Co-operation and Development, Paris.

OECD (2005b) *Development Cooperation Report 2005.* Organisation for Economic Co-operation and Development, Paris.

OECD (2006). Aid effectiveness: 2006 survey on monitoring the Paris Declaration – Country chapters. Organisation for Economic Co-operation and Development, Paris.

Republic of Zambia (2007). *Fifth National Development Plan, 2006–2010.* IMF Country Report no. 07/276, International Monetary Fund, Washington, DC.

Shepherd, A. and Fritz, V. (2005). Key issues in sharpening the rural production focus of Poverty Reduction Strategy processes: Literature review for IFAD. ODI Issues paper, Overseas Development Institute, London.

United Nations (2002). Monterrey Consensus of the International Conference on Financing for Development. The final text of agreements and commitments adopted at Conference, 18–22 March, Monterrey.

UNCTAD (1968). Resolution 25 (II). 78th plenary meeting, 27 March. In: *Proceeding of the United Nations Conference on Trade and Development: Volume I – Final Act and Report,* TD/97, Geneva.

UNCTAD (2000). *The Least Developed Countries Report 2000: Aid, Private Capital Flows and External Debt: The Challenge of Financing Development in LDCs.* United Nations publication, sales no. E.00.II.D.21, Geneva and New York.

UNCTAD (2002). *The Least Developed Countries Report 2002: Escaping the Poverty Trap.* United Nations publication, sales no. E.02.II.D.13, Geneva and New York.

UNCTAD (2004). *The Least Developed Countries Report 2004: Linking International Trade with Poverty Reduction.* United Nations publication, sales no. E.04.II.D.27, Geneva and New York.

UNCTAD (2006). *The Least Developed Countries Report 2006: Developing Productive Capacities.* United Nations publication, sales no. E.06.II.D.9, Geneva and New York.

Utting, P. (ed.) (2006). *Reclaiming Development Agendas: Knowledge, Power and International Policy Making.* Palgrave MacMillian and UNRISD, Basingstoke and Geneva.

Wangwe, S., Aarnes, D., Amani, H. and Evans, A. (2005). Enhancing aid relationships in the United Republic of Tanzania. Report of the Independent Monitoring Group, Economic and Social Research Foundation, Dar Es Salaam.

Warren-Rodriguez, A. (2007). Science and technology and the PRSP process: A survey of recent country experiences. Study prepared for UNCTAD as a background paper for *The Least Developed Countries Report 2007,* Geneva and New York.

Wilks, A. and Lefrancois, F. (2002). Blinding with science or encouraging debate? How World Bank analysis determines PRSP policies. Bretton Woods Project and World Vision, London.

Wolfensohn, J. (1999). A proposal for a comprehensive development framework. Mimeo, World Bank, Washington, DC.

Working Group on IMF Programmes and Health Spending (2007). Does the IMF constrain health spending in poor countries? Evidence and an agenda for action. Centre for Global Development, Washington, DC.

World Bank (2005a). Review of World Bank Conditionality. Prepared by Operations Policy and Country Services. World Bank, Washington, DC.

World Bank (2005b). Summary of external consultations. Background paper no. 7 in "Review of World Bank Conditionality." Prepared by Operations Policy and Country Services. World Bank, Washington, DC.

World Bank (2007). Results-based national development strategies: Assessment and challenges ahead. World Bank, Washington, DC.

Zimmermann, F. and McDonnell, I. (2008). Broadening ownership for development. In OECD Development Centre, *Financing Development 2008: Whose Ownership?* OECD Development Centre, Paris.

Statistical Annex:
DATA ON THE
LEAST DEVELOPED COUNTRIES

Contents

Explanatory Notes

Definition of country groupings

Least developed countries[1]

The United Nations has designated 50 countries as least developed: Afghanistan, Angola, Bangladesh, Benin, Bhutan, Burkina Faso, Burundi, Cambodia, Cape Verde, Central African Republic, Chad, Comoros, Democratic Republic of the Congo, Djibouti, Equatorial Guinea, Eritrea, Ethiopia, Gambia, Guinea, Guinea-Bissau, Haiti, Kiribati, Lao People's Democratic Republic, Lesotho, Liberia, Madagascar, Malawi, Maldives, Mali, Mauritania, Mozambique, Myanmar, Nepal, Niger, Rwanda, Samoa, Sao Tome and Principe, Senegal, Sierra Leone, Solomon Islands, Somalia, Sudan, Timor-Leste, Togo, Tuvalu, Uganda, United Republic of Tanzania, Vanuatu, Yemen, Zambia.

LDCs geographical classification

African LDCs (and Haiti): Angola, Benin, Burkina Faso, Burundi, Central African Republic, Chad, Democratic Republic of the Congo, Djibouti, Equatorial Guinea, Eritrea, Ethiopia, Gambia, Guinea, Guinea-Bissau, Haiti, Lesotho, Liberia, Madagascar, Malawi, Mali, Mauritania, Mozambique, Niger, Rwanda, Senegal, Sierra Leone, Somalia, Sudan, Togo, Uganda, United Republic of Tanzania, Zambia (32).

Asian LDCs: Afghanistan, Bangladesh, Bhutan, Cambodia, Lao People's Democratic Republic, Myanmar, Nepal and Yemen (8).

Island LDCs: Cape Verde, Comoros, Kiribati, Maldives, Samoa, Sao Tome and Principe, Solomon islands, Timor-Leste, Tuvalu and Vanuatu (10).

Major economic areas

The classification of countries and territories according to main economic areas used in this document has been adopted for purposes of statistical convenience only and follows that in UNCTAD, *Handbook of International Trade and Development Statistics 2007*.[2] Countries and territories are classified according to main economic areas as follows:

Developed economies: Andorra, Australia, Austria, Belgium, Bermuda, Canada, Cyprus, Czech Republic, Denmark, Estonia, Faeroe Islands, Finland, France, Germany, Gibraltar, Greece, Greenland, Holy See, Hungary, Iceland, Ireland, Italy, Israel, Japan, Latvia, Lithuania, Luxembourg, Malta, Netherlands, New Zealand, Norway, Poland, Portugal, Saint Pierre and Miquelon, San Marino, Slovakia, Slovenia, Spain, Sweden, Switzerland, United Kingdom, United States.

Transition economies: Albania, Armenia, Azerbaijan, Belarus, Bosnia and Herzegovina, Bulgaria, Croatia, Georgia, Kazakhstan, Kyrgyzstan, Moldova, Montenegro, Romania, Russian Federation, Serbia, Tajikistan, The former Yugoslav Republic of Macedonia, Turkmenistan, Ukraine, Uzbekistan.

All developing countries: All other countries, territories and areas in Africa, Asia, America, Europe and Oceania not specified above.

Other developing countries: All developing countries excluding LDCs.

Major petroleum exporters: Algeria, Angola, Bahrain, Brunei Darussalam, Congo, Gabon, Antilles, Indonesia, Iran (Islamic Republic of), Iraq, Kuwait, Libyan Arab Jamahiriya, Netherlands, Nigeria, Oman, Qatar, Saudia Arabia, Syrian Arab Republic, United Arab Emirates, Venezuela (Bolivarian Republic of), Yemen.

Newly industrialized economies: 1st tier: Hong Kong (Special Administrative Region of China), Republic of Korea, Singapore, Taiwan Province of China.

Newly industrialized economies: 2nd tier: Indonesia, Malaysia, Philippines, Thailand.

Other country groupings

DAC member countries: The countries of the OECD Development Assistance Committee are Australia, Austria, Belgium, Canada, Denmark, Finland, France, Germany, Greece, Ireland, Italy, Japan, Luxembourg, Netherlands, New Zealand, Norway, Portugal, Spain, Sweden, Switzerland, United Kingdom, United States.

Non-DAC member countries: Czech Republic, Hungary, Iceland, Rep. of Korea, Mexico, Poland, Slovak Rep. Turkey, Thailand and Arab Countries (Algeria, Iran Islamic Republic of, Kuwait, Libyan Arab Jamahiriya, Qatar, Saudi Arabia, United Arab Emirates).

Other notes

Calculation of annual average growth rates. In general, they are defined as the coefficient b in the exponential trend function $y^t = ae^{bt}$ where t stands for time. This method takes all observations in a period into account. Therefore, the resulting growth rates reflect trends that are not unduly influenced by exceptional values.

Population growth rates are calculated as exponential growth rates.

The term "dollars" ($) refers to United States dollars, unless otherwise stated.

Details and percentages in tables do not necessarily add to totals because of rounding.
The following symbols have been used:
    A hyphen (-) indicates that the item is not applicable.
    Two dots (..) indicate that the data are not available or are not separately reported.
    A zero (0) means that the amount is nil or negligible.
    Use of a dash (–) between dates representing years, e.g. 1980–1990, signifies the full period involved, including the initial and final years.

---

[1] Cape Verde is included in spite of its graduation from the LDC group on 21 December 2007 (see box on p.xii).
[2] United Nations Publication, Sales No. E/F.07.II.D.19.

Abbreviations

AfDF	African Development Fund
AsDF	Asian Development Fund
DAC	Development Assistance Committee
EC	European Commission
EIA	Energy Information Administration
ESAF	Enhanced Structural Adjustment Facility
EU	European Union
FAO	Food and Agriculture Organization of the United Nations
FAOSTAT	FAO statistical database
GDP	gross domestic product
GEF	Global Environment Facility
GNI	gross national income
IDA	International Development Association
IDB	Inter-American Development Bank
IEA	International Energy Agency
IFAD	International Fund for Agricultural Development
ILO	International Labour Organization
IMF	International Monetary Fund
IPU	Inter-parliamentary Union
ITU	International Telecommunication Union
LDC	least developed country
ODA	official development assistance
OECD	Organisation for Economic Co-operation and Development
OPEC	Organization of the Petroleum Exporting Countries
PASS.	Passengers
PRGF	Poverty Reduction and Growth Facility
SAF	Structural Adjustment Facility
SITC	Standard International Trade Classification
UN DATA	United Nations Data Access System
UN DESA	United Nations Department of Economic and Social Affairs
UNCTAD	United Nations Conference on Trade and Development
UNDP	United Nations Development Programme
UNESCO	United Nations Educational, Scientific and Cultural Organization
UNFPA	United Nations Population Fund
UIS	UNESCO Institute for Statistics
UNHCR	United Nations High Commissioner for Refugees
UNICEF	United Nations Children's Fund
UNTA	United Nations Technical Assistance
UPU	Universal Postal Union
USAID	United States Agency for International Development
WFP	World Food Programme
WHO	World Health Organization

1. GDP per capita and population: Levels and growth									
Country	Real GDP per capita			Annual average growth rates of real GDP per capita			Population			
	(2006 dollars)[a]			(%)			Level (million)	Annual average growth rates (%)		
	1980	1990	2006	1980–1990	1990–2000	2000–2006	2006	1980–1990	1990–2000	2000–2006
Afghanistan	496	466	319	-0.2	-5.9	9.8	26.1	-1.4	5.1	3.9
Angola	2 371	2 115	2 855	-0.1	-0.6	7.9	16.6	3.0	2.8	2.9
Bangladesh	233	267	437	1.4	2.8	3.8	156.0	2.4	2.1	1.9
Benin	448	460	536	-0.1	1.2	0.6	8.8	3.4	3.4	3.3
Bhutan	316	644	1 422	7.6	5.5	5.0	0.6	2.8	0.0	2.6
Burkina Faso	286	298	416	-0.1	2.4	2.9	14.4	2.7	3.0	3.2
Burundi	152	164	114	0.7	-4.0	-1.0	8.2	3.3	1.5	3.5
Cambodia	175	207	453	2.6	3.5	7.4	14.2	3.9	2.8	1.8
Cape Verde	883	1 198	2 153	3.2	4.6	2.7	0.5	2.1	2.4	2.4
Central African Republic	499	428	333	-1.2	-1.3	-2.4	4.3	2.6	2.6	1.6
Chad	299	373	634	3.1	0.1	10.4	10.5	2.9	3.3	3.6
Comoros	603	576	486	-0.4	-1.6	-0.5	0.8	3.1	2.9	2.7
Dem. Republic of the Congo	370	299	136	-1.4	-7.6	1.8	60.6	3.0	2.9	3.1
Djibouti	1 493	998	925	-4.5	-1.2	1.2	0.8	5.3	2.6	1.9
Equatorial Guinea	1 738	1 324	19 166	-2.7	20.8	17.7	0.5	4.9	2.4	2.4
Eritrea	..	..	249	..	2.1	-0.7	4.7	0.0	0.0	4.2
Ethiopia	..	..	164	..	1.5	3.2	81.0	0.0	0.0	2.6
Gambia	268	293	307	0.1	-0.5	0.9	1.7	3.7	3.7	3.1
Guinea	253	260	311	0.5	1.2	1.2	9.2	2.8	3.1	1.9
Guinea-Bissau	211	269	196	1.8	-1.9	-2.6	1.6	2.4	3.0	3.1
Haiti	907	723	489	-2.0	-2.7	-1.9	9.4	2.3	1.9	1.6
Kiribati	676	552	801	-1.9	3.7	0.4	0.1	2.8	1.5	1.8
Lao People's Dem. Republic	233	316	599	2.2	3.9	4.8	5.8	2.8	2.5	1.6
Lesotho	435	547	725	2.3	2.2	1.9	2.0	2.1	1.7	0.9
Liberia	1 067	304	192	-6.3	-0.2	-7.0	3.6	1.4	4.1	2.3
Madagascar	408	329	287	-1.6	-1.0	-0.2	19.2	2.9	3.0	2.8
Malawi	127	110	164	-1.2	4.9	1.2	13.6	4.5	2.0	2.6
Maldives	599	1 306	3 020	8.4	5.3	5.5	0.3	3.2	2.4	1.6
Mali	322	366	498	1.4	2.0	2.6	12.0	2.4	2.7	3.0
Mauritania	852	753	899	-1.0	0.2	2.3	3.0	2.6	2.8	2.9
Mozambique	218	198	349	-1.0	2.7	5.6	21.0	1.0	3.1	2.4
Myanmar	93	87	281	-1.3	5.6	11.4	48.4	1.9	1.3	0.9
Nepal	173	218	290	2.2	2.4	0.6	27.6	2.3	2.5	2.1
Niger	367	268	247	-3.1	-0.7	0.5	13.7	3.0	3.6	3.6
Rwanda	265	226	242	-1.9	-0.9	2.4	9.5	3.8	1.1	2.3
Samoa	1 788	1 694	2 348	0.6	1.6	3.0	0.2	0.4	1.0	0.7
Sao Tome and Principe	557	419	480	-2.4	-0.1	2.2	0.2	2.0	1.9	1.7
Senegal	647	653	768	0.1	0.9	1.9	12.1	3.0	2.7	2.6
Sierra Leone	344	356	318	0.2	-8.0	7.4	5.7	2.5	0.8	4.2
Solomon Islands	1 086	1 044	860	-0.9	-0.7	0.4	0.5	3.2	2.9	2.6
Somalia	369	395	283	0.9	-3.5	-0.3	8.4	0.2	0.4	3.0
Sudan	598	472	934	-2.6	3.5	5.2	37.7	2.8	2.6	2.0
Timor-Leste	..	453	319	..	0.6	-5.9	1.1	2.6	0.8	5.5
Togo	574	464	356	-1.8	-1.7	-0.5	6.4	3.7	3.2	2.9
Tuvalu	1 747	1 599	2 441	-0.4	2.7	4.0	0.0	1.6	0.8	0.5
Uganda	197	209	346	0.0	4.0	2.6	29.9	3.5	3.3	3.2
United Rep. of Tanzania	247	236	335	-0.3	0.8	4.1	39.5	3.1	2.9	2.6
Vanuatu	1 242	1 576	1 635	2.1	1.4	-1.4	0.2	2.4	2.4	2.6
Yemen	..	636	853	0.0	2.7	0.9	21.7	0.0	4.0	3.0
Zambia	1 163	944	938	-2.1	-2.0	3.0	11.7	3.2	2.6	1.9
LDCs	**336**	**322**	**454**	**-0.4**	**1.3**	**4.0**	**785.4**	**2.6**	**2.6**	**2.4**
African LDCs and Haiti	*403*	*367*	*468*	*-1.0*	*0.6*	*3.6*	*481.1*	*2.9*	*2.8*	*2.7*
Asian LDCs	*242*	*252*	*424*	*0.7*	*2.6*	*4.8*	*300.4*	*2.2*	*2.4*	*2.0*
Island LDCs	*641*	*833*	*1 068*	*0.5*	*2.3*	*0.9*	*3.9*	*2.6*	*2.0*	*3.1*
Other developing countries	**1 243**	**1 464**	**2 580**	**1.8**	**3.4**	**4.3**	**4 499.6**	**2.0**	**1.6**	**1.3**
All developing countries	**1 134**	**1 317**	**2 264**	**1.7**	**3.2**	**4.2**	**5 285.1**	**2.1**	**1.8**	**1.5**

Source: UNCTAD secretariat calculations based on data from United Nations/DESA/Statistics and Population Divisions, January 2008.

a Real GDP data has been rebased using an implicit GDP deflator.

2. Real GDP, total and per capita: Annual average growth rates
(Per cent)

Country	Real GDP							Real GDP per capita						
	1980–1990	1990–2000	2000–2006	2003	2004	2005	2006	1980–1990	1990–2000	2000–2006	2003	2004	2005	2006
Afghanistan	-1.6	-1.1	14.1	14.3	9.4	14.5	11.1	-0.2	-5.9	9.8	9.9	5.1	10.0	6.8
Angola	2.9	2.2	11.1	3.3	11.2	20.6	14.3	-0.1	-0.6	7.9	0.3	7.9	17.2	11.1
Bangladesh	3.9	4.9	5.8	6.3	5.4	6.7	6.5	1.4	2.8	3.8	4.3	3.4	4.8	4.7
Benin	3.3	4.6	3.9	3.9	3.1	2.9	3.6	-0.1	1.2	0.6	0.5	-0.2	-0.4	0.4
Bhutan	10.6	5.5	7.7	7.6	6.8	6.5	8.5	7.6	5.5	5.0	4.6	4.1	4.2	6.5
Burkina Faso	2.5	5.4	6.3	7.9	6.6	5.9	5.9	-0.1	2.4	2.9	4.5	3.2	2.6	2.7
Burundi	4.0	-2.6	2.5	-1.2	4.4	0.9	6.1	0.7	-4.0	-1.0	-4.5	0.6	-2.9	2.0
Cambodia	6.6	6.4	9.3	7.0	14.9	13.4	7.2	2.6	3.5	7.4	5.2	12.9	11.5	5.4
Cape Verde	5.4	7.1	5.2	4.7	4.4	5.8	5.5	3.2	4.6	2.7	2.2	2.0	3.3	3.1
Central African Republic	1.4	1.3	-0.8	-7.6	1.3	2.2	3.2	-1.2	-1.3	-2.4	-9.0	-0.2	0.5	1.4
Chad	6.0	3.4	14.4	14.3	33.7	8.6	2.9	3.1	0.1	10.4	10.1	29.0	5.0	-0.3
Comoros	2.7	1.2	2.2	2.1	1.9	2.8	1.2	-0.4	-1.6	-0.5	-0.6	-0.7	0.2	-1.3
Dem. Rep. of the Congo	1.6	-4.9	4.9	5.8	6.6	6.5	6.5	-1.4	-7.6	1.8	2.7	3.4	3.2	3.2
Djibouti	0.5	1.3	3.1	3.5	3.0	3.2	4.2	-4.5	-1.2	1.2	1.6	1.2	1.4	2.4
Equatorial Guinea	2.0	23.7	20.5	13.6	30.0	9.3	-1.0	-2.7	20.8	17.7	11.0	27.0	6.8	-3.3
Eritrea	..	4.3a	3.4	3.9	2.0	4.8	2.0	..	2.1a	-0.7	-0.5	-2.2	0.8	-1.6
Ethiopia	3.4b	4.4	5.9	-3.5	13.1	10.3	10.6	0.1b	1.5	3.2	-6.0	10.3	7.5	7.9
Gambia	3.8	3.2	4.0	6.9	5.1	5.0	5.6	0.1	-0.5	0.9	3.6	1.9	2.0	2.7
Guinea	3.2	4.4	3.1	1.2	2.7	3.3	5.0	0.5	1.2	1.2	-0.6	0.8	1.4	3.0
Guinea-Bissau	4.3	1.1	0.4	0.6	2.2	3.5	4.6	1.8	-1.9	-2.6	-2.5	-0.9	0.4	1.5
Haiti	0.2	-0.8	-0.3	0.4	-3.5	1.8	2.3	-2.0	-2.7	-1.9	-1.2	-5.0	0.2	0.7
Kiribati	0.8	5.3	2.2	0.9	-2.0	3.6	0.8	-1.9	3.7	0.4	-0.9	-3.8	1.8	-0.9
Lao People's Dem. Rep.	5.1	6.5	6.5	5.8	6.9	7.3	7.3	2.2	3.9	4.8	4.1	5.3	5.6	5.5
Lesotho	4.5	3.9	2.9	2.7	4.0	2.9	1.6	2.3	2.2	1.9	1.7	3.2	2.2	0.9
Liberia	-5.0	3.9	-4.8	-31.3	2.6	5.3	7.0	-6.3	-0.2	-7.0	-32.2	0.8	2.4	2.9
Madagascar	1.2	2.0	2.6	9.8	5.3	4.6	4.7	-1.6	-1.0	-0.2	6.7	2.4	1.7	1.9
Malawi	3.2	7.0	3.9	6.1	6.7	1.9	8.5	-1.2	4.9	1.2	3.4	4.1	-0.7	5.8
Maldives	11.9	7.8	7.2	9.2	11.3	-4.0	21.7	8.4	5.3	5.5	7.6	9.6	-5.6	19.7
Mali	3.8	4.7	5.7	7.6	2.3	6.1	4.6	1.4	2.0	2.6	4.4	-0.8	3.0	1.5
Mauritania	1.6	3.0	5.2	5.6	5.2	5.4	14.1	-1.0	0.2	2.3	2.5	2.2	2.5	11.1
Mozambique	-0.1	5.9	8.2	7.9	7.5	6.2	8.5	-1.0	2.7	5.6	5.3	5.0	3.8	6.3
Myanmar	0.6	7.0	12.3	13.8	13.6	13.2	7.0	-1.3	5.6	11.4	12.9	12.6	12.3	6.1
Nepal	4.6	4.9	2.7	3.3	3.8	2.7	1.9	2.2	2.4	0.6	1.2	1.7	0.7	-0.1
Niger	-0.1	2.9	4.0	3.8	-0.6	7.1	3.5	-3.1	-0.7	0.5	0.2	-4.0	3.4	0.0
Rwanda	1.8	0.1	4.7	0.7	3.8	6.0	3.0	-1.9	-0.9	2.4	-1.0	2.2	3.9	0.5
Samoa	1.0	2.6	3.7	3.5	3.7	5.1	4.0	0.6	1.6	3.0	2.8	3.1	4.4	3.1
Sao Tome and Principe	-0.4	1.8	4.0	4.1	3.9	3.0	5.5	-2.4	-0.1	2.2	2.3	2.2	1.3	3.8
Senegal	3.1	3.6	4.6	6.7	5.6	5.5	4.0	0.1	0.9	1.9	3.9	2.9	2.8	1.4
Sierra Leone	2.6	-7.2	11.9	10.7	9.6	7.5	9.7	0.2	-8.0	7.4	5.6	5.0	3.7	6.8
Solomon Islands	2.3	2.1	3.0	6.5	8.0	5.0	5.0	-0.9	-0.7	0.4	3.8	5.3	2.4	2.5
Somalia	1.1	-3.2	2.7	2.1	2.8	2.4	2.4	0.9	-3.5	-0.3	-0.9	-0.2	-0.6	-0.6
Sudan	0.1	6.2	7.4	6.1	7.2	7.9	12.1	-2.6	3.5	5.2	4.1	5.1	5.7	9.7
Timor-Leste	0.0	1.4	-0.7	-6.2	0.4	2.2	-1.6	0.0	0.6	-5.9	-11.9	-5.5	-2.9	-5.7
Togo	1.8	1.4	2.4	1.9	3.0	0.8	4.2	-1.8	-1.7	-0.5	-0.9	0.2	-1.9	1.4
Tuvalu	1.2	3.5	4.5	4.0	4.0	2.0	1.0	-0.4	2.7	4.0	3.5	3.5	1.6	0.6
Uganda	3.5	7.4	5.9	6.5	5.6	6.5	6.2	0.0	4.0	2.6	3.1	2.2	3.1	2.8
United Rep. of Tanzania	2.8	3.7	6.8	7.1	6.7	6.9	5.9	-0.3	0.8	4.1	4.3	4.0	4.3	3.3
Vanuatu	4.5	3.8	1.1	2.4	4.2	3.1	3.4	2.1	1.4	-1.4	-0.2	1.5	0.5	0.9
Yemen	..	6.8	4.0	3.7	3.8	4.6	3.9	..	2.7	0.9	0.7	0.8	1.5	0.9
Zambia	1.0	0.5	4.9	4.3	6.2	5.1	6.0	-2.1	-2.0	3.0	2.4	4.3	3.2	4.1
LDCs	**2.2**	**4.0**	**6.5**	**5.5**	**7.3**	**7.9**	**7.5**	**-0.4**	**1.3**	**4.0**	**3.0**	**4.7**	**5.3**	**5.0**
African LDCs and Haiti	*1.9*	*3.4*	*6.4*	*4.5*	*7.6*	*7.9*	*8.2*	*-1.0*	*0.6*	*3.6*	*1.7*	*4.7*	*5.0*	*5.3*
Asian LDCs	*2.7*	*5.1*	*6.8*	*7.2*	*6.9*	*7.9*	*6.4*	*0.7*	*2.6*	*4.8*	*5.1*	*4.8*	*5.8*	*4.3*
Island LDCs	*4.6*	*4.3*	*4.0*	*4.2*	*5.4*	*2.4*	*7.5*	*0.5*	*2.3*	*0.9*	*0.8*	*2.0*	*-0.6*	*4.6*
Other developing countries	**3.9**	**5.0**	**5.7**	**5.6**	**7.1**	**6.5**	**6.9**	**1.8**	**3.4**	**4.3**	**4.3**	**5.8**	**5.2**	**5.6**
All developing countries	**3.9**	**5.0**	**5.7**	**5.6**	**7.1**	**6.5**	**7.0**	**1.7**	**3.2**	**4.2**	**4.1**	**5.6**	**5.1**	**5.5**

Source: UNCTAD Secretariat calculations based on UN/DESA Statistics and Population Divisions, January 2008.
Note: Data refers to real GDP and real GDP per capita (1990 dollars).
      a 1993–2000 for Eritrea and Ethiopia. *b* Data for Ethiopia prior to 1992 include Eritrea.

3. Agricultural production: Total and per capita
(Per cent)

Country	Percentage share of agriculture in:				Total agricultural production[a]					Per capita agricultural production[a]				
	Total Labour force		Share of GDP		*(Annual average growth rates)*					*(Annual average growth rates)*				
	1990	2004	1990	2006	1990–1996	2000–2006	2004	2005	2006	1990–1996	2000–2006	2004	2005	2006
Afghanistan	70.3	65.6	35.7	42.4	..	..	..	..	..	..	..	..	..	..
Angola	74.5	70.8	18.0	8.0	4.3	7.1	7.1	6.2	2.3	1.1	4.0	4.0	3.2	-0.6
Bangladesh	65.2	51.8	30.8	20.2	0.9	2.2	-2.1	8.8	5.5	-1.3	0.3	-3.9	6.8	3.6
Benin	63.6	50.0	35.4	37.3	7.1	1.2	5.1	-4.0	-9.8	3.3	-2.0	1.7	-7.0	-12.6
Bhutan	94.1	93.6	39.0	22.2	2.8	1.4[b]	2.6	0.0	..	1.3	-1.5[b]	-0.3	-2.8	..
Burkina Faso	92.4	92.2	28.6	26.1	3.7	7.5	-6.1	15.3	5.2	0.7	4.1	-9.0	11.8	2.1
Burundi	91.6	89.7	52.4	38.4	-2.0	0.3	-0.3	-3.7	3.1	-3.7	-3.0	-3.8	-7.3	-0.6
Cambodia	73.9	68.5	50.1	29.6	4.7	6.6	-7.5	30.3	3.7	1.5	4.7	-9.0	28.1	2.0
Cape Verde	30.9	20.4	15.2	11.5	3.1	-1.2[b]	-2.9	0.3	..	0.8	-3.2[b]	-4.9	-1.5	..
Central African Republic	80.2	69.2	43.0	51.8	4.2	0.5	4.9	1.0	-3.2	1.4	-1.1	3.3	-0.6	-4.8
Chad	83.2	71.4	39.2	21.3	3.0	3.9	-0.1	9.2	2.3	-0.2	0.2	-3.6	5.6	-1.0
Comoros	77.6	71.8	40.4	49.1	2.3	-0.1	0.6	-5.2	-1.5	-0.5	-2.7	-2.0	-7.6	-4.0
Dem. Rep. of the Congo	67.8	61.3	28.6	51.2	-2.0	-0.6	-0.2	0.2	-1.3	-5.3	-3.5	-3.3	-2.9	-4.2
Djibouti	82	76.8	3.1	3.7	2.4	0.1	0.1	0.4	0.0	0.2	-1.7	-1.6	-1.3	-1.7
Equatorial Guinea	74.8	68.4	61.9	4.4	-0.9	-1.5[b]	-1.3	0.0	..	-2.6	-3.6[b]	-0.8	-2.7	..
Eritrea	..	76.3	..	17.1	4.3 [c]	0.4[b]	-1.0	17.4	..	10.8[c]	-3.2[b]	-4.5	13.3	..
Ethiopia	..	80.7	..	47.5	8.5[c]	5.2	6.3	10.4	0.9	2.4[c]	2.5	3.6	7.7	-1.5
Gambia	82	77.7	22.2	32.4	-1.7	-0.1	25.1	-13.7	4.5	-5.3	-3.1	21.4	-16.2	1.6
Guinea	87.2	82.3	23.8	25.2	3.8	3.1	4.2	1.2	7.3	-0.1	1.2	2.3	-0.7	5.3
Guinea-Bissau	85.4	81.8	44.6	60.8	2.2	2.7	9.7	6.8	-2.4	-1.0	-0.4	6.3	3.6	-5.3
Haiti	67.8	60.2	35.8	30.8	-1.4	-0.1	-1.1	-0.5	-0.2	-3.3	-1.7	-2.7	-2.1	-1.7
Kiribati	30	25.6	18.6	9.7	4.3	2.6	6.8	3.3	0.0	2.9	0.7	4.9	1.5	-1.7
Lao People's Dem. Rep.	78.2	75.8	61.2	46.8	1.1	1.8[b]	4.6	-1.2	..	-0.5	0.0[b]	0.8	-3.9	..
Lesotho	41.3	38.4	20.8	16.2	2.4	0.9[b]	8.6	0.0	..	0.8	0.8[b]	9.2	0.2	..
Liberia	72.4	65.5	53.4	65.2	-2.5	0.3	3.3	-0.6	2.8	-3.3	-1.9	1.5	-3.3	0.1
Madagascar	78.1	72.5	28.6	27.6	0.9	2.7	7.1	4.4	2.7	-2.1	-0.2	4.2	1.6	0.0
Malawi	86.6	81.3	45.0	38.3	4.0	-2.0	14.7	-12.5	5.2	2.7	-4.5	11.8	-14.7	2.7
Maldives	32.6	19.1	14.9	8.4	2.5	-1.8	-17.7	-9.3	-1.9	-0.2	-3.3	-18.9	-10.7	-3.4
Mali	85.8	78.7	47.8	38.3	3.5	5.0[b]	-1.1	0.5	..	-0.1	0.3[b]	-2.1	-2.4	..
Mauritania	55.2	51.8	37.5	25.6	1.1	1.3[b]	-0.6	-2.4	..	-1.4	-1.6[b]	-3.4	-5.3	..
Mozambique	83.4	80.3	37.1	21.5	3.0	7.7	5.0	27.3	-0.5	-0.4	5.1	2.5	24.5	-2.7
Myanmar	73.3	68.9	57.3	52.6	6.0	5.3	6.8	3.9	0.0	4.5	4.4	5.9	3.0	-0.9
Nepal	93.6	92.8	50.6	38.1	2.3	3.1	3.8	2.1	1.8	-0.2	1.0	1.7	0.1	-0.1
Niger	89.8	86.8	35.3	43.2	2.7	5.2	-19.9	18.6	7.7	-0.7	1.6	-22.6	14.5	4.2
Rwanda	91.7	90.1	43.6	41.8	-8.3	2.8	-0.5	6.4	1.1	-4.1	0.6	-2.0	4.3	-0.8
Samoa	42.1	30.8	20.5	13.0	1.1	1.3	2.9	1.7	0.0	0.2	0.6	2.3	0.9	-0.7
Sao Tome and Principe	71.4	61.8	27.6	17.7	6.6	1.5	1.1	0.3	0.0	4.6	-0.2	-0.6	-1.4	-1.6
Senegal	76.8	72.4	19.4	16.3	1.2	-0.3	2.3	16.1	-16.6	-1.5	-2.9	-0.3	13.1	-18.6
Sierra Leone	67.5	60.1	39.6	47.2	-1.0	11.8	7.8	12.7	17.4	-1.2	7.2	3.3	8.8	13.4
Solomon Islands	76.7	71.5	45.5	44.5	3.7	3.1	8.8	4.4	0.0	0.8	0.5	6.1	1.9	-2.4
Somalia	75.3	69.3	69.3	60.1	..	..	..	..	..	..	..	..	..	..
Sudan	69.5	57.4	33.8	45.8	7.7	2.6	-3.9	2.5	1.5	4.9	0.5	-5.8	0.4	-0.6
Timor-Leste	83.6	81.2	29.5	32.2	2.8	2.9[b]	4.8	0.0	..	0.4	-1.0[b]	0.3	-4.2	..
Togo	65.5	57.3	36.6	43.1	4.6	3.4	0.9	3.9	0.9	1.8	0.5	-1.8	1.1	-1.7
Tuvalu	..	..	25.6	16.7	..	..	..	..	..	..	..	..	..	..
Uganda	84.5	78.1	52.8	32.2	2.0	0.8	0.2	-0.9	-1.3	-1.4	-2.4	-3.0	-4.0	-4.3
United Rep. of Tanzania	84.4	78.7	44.2	44.5	0.8	1.9	7.6	7.3	-3.4	-2.3	-0.7	4.9	4.6	-5.8
Vanuatu	42.9	34.0	20.0	14.4	-0.6	2.5	14.7	0.8	-0.1	-3.3	-0.1	11.7	-1.7	-2.6
Yemen	60.1	46.4	25.7	12.6	2.1	3.8	0.9	2.5	8.3	-2.4	0.8	-2.1	-0.5	5.2
Zambia	74.4	67.0	20.6	21.8	2.0	2.6	3.8	-1.6	1.2	-0.6	0.7	2.0	-3.4	-0.6
LDCs	**74.9**	**68.4**	**35.7**	**28.0**	**4.0**	**3.1**	**1.6**	**5.8**	**1.5**	**-1.0**	**0.7**	**-0.7**	**3.4**	**-0.8**
All developing countries	**61.1**	**53.0**	**14.8**	**10.3**	**1.3**	**3.4**	**4.2**	**3.3**	**2.4**	**0.5**	**2.0**	**2.8**	**1.9**	**1.1**

Source: UNCTAD secretariat calculations based on FAO, FAOSTAT online data, January 2008; UNCTAD, *Handbook of Statistics 2007.*
   a Index, base year 1999–2001.
   b 2000–2005 for Bhutan, Cape verde, Equatorial Guinea, Eritrea, Lao People's Dem. Rep., Lesotho, Mali, Mauritania and Timor-Leste.
   c 1993–1996 for Eritrea and Ethiopia.

4. Food production, total and per capita: Average annual growth rates
(Per cent)

Country	Total Food Production[a]					Net per capita food Production[a]				
	1990–1996	2000–2006	2004	2005	2006	1990–1996	2000–2006	2004	2005	2006
Afghanistan	..	..	..	..	..	..	..	..	..	..
Angola	4.5	7.2	7.1	6.3	2.3	1.3	4.2	4.0	3.3	-0.5
Bangladesh	1.0	2.3	-2.2	9.1	5.7	-1.2	0.4	-4.0	7.1	3.8
Benin	5.1	2.7	5.7	-1.5	-6.2	1.4	-0.6	2.3	-4.6	-9.0
Bhutan	2.8	1.4[b]	2.6	0.0	..	1.3	-1.5[b]	-0.3	-2.8	..
Burkina Faso	4.1	5.3	-12.0	14.3	2.5	1.1	2.0	-14.8	10.8	-0.6
Burundi	-1.8	0.2	-4.2	-0.2	0.1	-3.5	-3.2	-7.6	-3.9	-3.5
Cambodia	4.8	6.7	-6.8	29.5	3.8	1.5	4.8	-8.4	27.3	2.0
Cape Verde	3.1	-1.2[b]	-2.9	0.3	..	0.8	-3.2[b]	-4.9	-1.5	..
Central African Republic	4.2	1.3	5.2	1.2	-3.2	1.4	-0.3	3.5	-0.5	-4.7
Chad	2.9	3.7	-5.0	11.3	1.2	-0.3	0.0	-8.3	7.6	-2.1
Comoros	2.3	-0.1	0.6	-5.2	-1.5	-0.5	-2.7	-2.0	-7.6	-4.0
Dem. Rep. of the Congo	-2.0	-0.6	-0.2	0.2	-1.3	-5.3	-3.5	-3.3	-2.9	-4.3
Djibouti	2.4	0.1	0.1	0.4	0.0	0.2	-1.7	-1.6	-1.3	-1.7
Equatorial Guinea	-0.1	-1.0[b]	1.8	0.0	..	-2.6	-3.6[b]	-0.8	-2.7	..
Eritrea	4.3[c]	0.4[b]	-1.0	17.6	..	3.1[c]	-3.2[b]	-4.5	13.3	..
Ethiopia	8.6[c]	5.5	7.7	10.5	-0.2	5.2[c]	2.8	5.0	7.7	-2.7
Gambia	-1.7	-0.1	25.2	-13.8	4.5	-5.3	-3.2	21.5	-16.2	1.6
Guinea	3.9	3.5	4.4	1.1	7.8	0.1	1.6	2.5	-0.8	5.8
Guinea-Bissau	2.2	2.7	9.8	6.9	-2.5	-0.9	-0.4	6.5	3.7	-5.3
Haiti	-1.2	0.1	-1.1	-0.4	-0.1	-3.1	-1.5	-2.7	-2.0	-1.7
Kiribati	4.3	2.6	6.8	3.3	0.0	2.9	0.7	4.9	1.5	-1.7
Lao People's Dem. Republic	2.0	2.3[b]	3.3	-1.8	..	-0.5	0.0[b]	0.8	-3.9	..
Lesotho	2.3	0.9[b]	9.1	0.0	..	0.8	0.8[b]	9.2	0.2	..
Liberia	-2.0	-0.1	2.1	0.1	3.5	-2.8	-2.3	0.4	-2.6	0.7
Madagascar	1.0	2.7	7.3	5.1	1.9	-1.9	-0.1	4.4	2.2	-0.8
Malawi	4.3	-1.9	15.9	-13.6	6.2	2.9	-4.4	13.0	-15.7	3.6
Maldives	2.5	-1.8	-17.7	-9.3	-1.9	-0.2	-3.3	-18.9	-10.7	-3.4
Mali	2.6	3.4[b]	1.0	0.6	..	-0.1	0.3[b]	-2.1	-2.4	..
Mauritania	1.1	1.3[b]	-0.6	-2.4	..	-1.4	-1.6[b]	-3.4	-5.3	..
Mozambique	3.0	7.8	4.4	28.9	-0.5	-0.4	5.2	1.9	26.1	-2.6
Myanmar	6.0	5.5	6.9	4.0	0.0	4.5	4.6	6.1	3.1	-0.9
Nepal	2.4	3.1	3.7	2.2	1.8	-0.2	1.0	1.6	0.1	-0.2
Niger	2.7	5.3	-19.9	18.7	7.8	-0.8	1.7	-22.6	14.6	4.2
Rwanda	-8.1	2.8	-0.8	6.5	1.0	-4.0	0.6	-2.4	4.4	-0.9
Samoa	1.1	1.3	3.0	1.7	0.0	0.2	0.6	2.3	0.9	-0.7
Sao Tome and Principe	6.6	1.5	1.1	0.3	0.0	4.6	-0.2	-0.6	-1.4	-1.6
Senegal	1.3	-0.6	2.4	17.2	-17.1	-1.4	-3.1	-0.2	14.3	-19.2
Sierra Leone	-1.0	12.3	8.5	13.4	17.9	-1.3	7.7	3.9	9.4	13.9
Solomon Islands	3.7	3.1	8.9	4.4	0.0	0.8	0.5	6.2	1.9	-2.4
Somalia	..	..	..	..	..	..	..	..	..	..
Sudan	8.1	2.4	-4.4	1.9	1.5	5.4	0.4	-6.2	-0.2	-0.5
Timor-Leste	2.4	3.2[b]	5.7	0.0	..	0.4	-1.0[b]	0.3	-4.2	..
Togo	4.6	3.9	1.2	6.5	5.9	1.8	1.0	-1.5	3.7	3.1
Tuvalu	..	..	..	..	..	..	..	..	..	..
Uganda	1.5	0.7	-0.3	-1.2	-0.7	-1.9	-2.5	-3.5	-4.3	-3.7
United Republic of Tanzania	0.7	1.3	5.2	6.3	-2.4	-2.4	-1.3	2.5	3.7	-4.8
Vanuatu	-0.6	2.5	14.7	0.8	-0.1	-3.3	-0.1	11.7	-1.7	-2.5
Yemen	1.9	3.8	0.5	2.3	7.8	-2.6	0.7	-2.4	-0.7	4.7
Zambia	2.5	1.8	3.4	-5.3	1.4	-0.1	-0.1	1.5	-7.1	-0.4
LDCs	**4.0**	**3.1**	**1.3**	**5.9**	**1.5**	**-1.1**	**0.8**	**-1.0**	**3.5**	**-0.8**
All developing countries	**1.4**	**3.3**	**3.7**	**3.6**	**2.3**	**0.6**	**1.9**	**2.2**	**2.2**	**1.0**

Source: UNCTAD secretariat calculations based on FAO, FAOSTAT online data, January 2008.
   a   Index, base year 1999–2001.
   b   2000–2005 for Bhutan, Cape Verde, Equatorial Guinea, Eritrea, Lao People's Dem. Rep., Lesotho, Mali, Mauritania and Timor-Leste.
   c   1993–1996 for Eritrea and Ethiopia.

5. The manufacturing sector: Shares in GDP and average annual growth rates
(Per cent)

Country	Share in GDP			Annual average growth rates						
	1980	1990	2006	1980–1990	1990–2000	2000–2006	2003	2004	2005	2006
Afghanistan	21.7	20.6	14.7	1.1	-5.8	9.2	-2.9	21.7	19.5	4.5
Angola	9.4	4.9	3.8	-1.7	-2.8	13.5	10.5	7.3	19.1	17.1
Bangladesh	16.6	13.4	16.6	3.2	6.9	7.3	7.1	8.4	10.5	3.1
Benin	8.4	7.5	8.3	3.7	5.6	2.2	0.7	-2.1	5.3	-4.6
Bhutan	2.9	8.4	7.6	12.9	8.9	4.0	2.1	5.6	4.4	5.0
Burkina Faso	11.4	14.2	13.3	5.1	3.5	9.6	10.5	9.9	8.8	7.8
Burundi	9.0	16.8	13.2	5.7	-8.1	-4.1	-6.2	-6.2	-6.3	15.8
Cambodia	3.5	7.3	20.9	7.0	13.8	13.9	12.1	17.8	9.7	14.2
Cape Verde	4.9	7.9	4.6	8.2	7.9	1.5	0.0	10.1	5.8	5.5
Central African Republic	8.8	9.8	11.2	2.6	-0.1	2.1	2.2	2.0	-2.7	1.4
Chad	13.4	14.6	6.7	7.9	0.2	8.0	0.5	-11.5	17.3	17.7
Comoros	3.9	4.1	4.2	4.8	1.2	1.5	2.1	3.1	1.4	1.8
Dem. Rep. of the Congo	8.7	9.5	5.4	2.7	-5.2	4.5	9.4	9.4	4.3	4.6
Djibouti	9.7	3.6	2.8	2.1	-1.0	0.6	-1.0	-5.4	3.9	6.8
Equatorial Guinea	1.3	1.6	5.0	2.8	4.7	70.6	6.4	19.3	-8.0	17.9
Eritrea	..	..	10.4	..	8.9[a]	0.1	3.6	-2.2	-21.6	26.9
Ethiopia	..	..	4.6	..	5.8[a]	4.4	0.8	6.5	8.0	8.1
Gambia	6.6	5.6	5.3	4.2	1.4	7.0	6.4	5.9	7.4	6.6
Guinea	4.5	4.6	4.1	3.2	4.5	2.8	-4.0	3.0	5.8	4.1
Guinea-Bissau	11.7	..	..	..	..	..	..	..	..	..
Haiti	19.1	15.5	7.8	-1.6	-6.3	0.3	0.4	-2.5	1.6	1.4
Kiribati	1.2	1.2	0.8	..	..	..	..	..	..	..
Lao People's Dem. Republic	9.6	10.0	20.1	3.7	11.7	9.9	6.3	13.7	9.0	4.0
Lesotho	6.3	12.2	17.4	13.6	6.6	3.3	5.7	2.1	-8.0	10.3
Liberia	9.5	11.2	10.2	-2.2	-6.8	6.1	-11.7	97.5	7.7	-11.4
Madagascar	17.2	11.6	15.4	-1.7	2.5	1.9	14.6	6.5	3.1	4.6
Malawi	17.6	19.5	11.6	3.6	0.2	2.7	3.2	6.9	11.9	1.9
Maldives	7.6	7.5	6.6	11.8	8.0	3.8	4.5	2.7	-9.9	8.8
Mali	4.3	8.1	9.0	8.8	7.5	5.3	-5.6	19.0	0.3	3.5
Mauritania	5.6	9.0	5.7	4.3	5.0	-1.1	-0.6	10.4	-11.6	26.7
Mozambique	22.0	11.7	13.0	-5.3	8.2	12.9	15.4	10.2	10.7	4.7
Myanmar	9.5	7.8	9.3	-0.1	7.9	14.7	22.1	3.9	17.5	7.6
Nepal	4.3	6.0	7.5	9.3	8.9	0.0	2.0	1.7	2.6	2.2
Niger	3.8	7.3	6.5	-1.1	0.5	5.0	6.4	6.5	3.3	3.6
Rwanda	15.8	15.8	9.2	1.3	-2.4	4.5	1.5	6.2	4.4	3.3
Samoa	19.2	19.2	15.2	0.9	-1.1	2.7	8.7	-6.0	-0.9	12.1
Sao Tome and Principe	5.4	4.3	3.9	-0.5	1.7	4.0	3.8	3.7	3.2	5.5
Senegal	12.4	15.0	16.2	4.3	3.7	4.6	4.0	2.7	8.4	3.1
Sierra Leone	4.3	3.7	2.5	-4.0	-7.3	6.7	-5.1	-1.2	23.8	-7.9
Solomon Islands	4.1	3.7	5.9	3.1	5.9	1.3	7.9	7.3	5.4	4.8
Somalia	4.7	2.0	2.5	-0.2	0.0	2.7	2.8	2.8	2.2	2.6
Sudan	7.4	8.7	8.3	2.9	4.7	8.8	10.0	7.0	6.7	12.9
Timor-Leste	..	2.9	2.6	..	0.9	-0.1	0.0	1.8	0.0	-25.0
Togo	8.0	6.6	6.1	-0.3	-1.4	7.6	23.9	6.6	3.6	-6.7
Tuvalu	1.3	3.1	3.4	13.2	-2.3	5.2	-0.3	5.4	2.5	0.2
Uganda	7.0	6.4	9.0	2.8	13.4	6.0	2.6	11.7	4.6	5.5
United Republic of Tanzania	9.9	8.3	6.9	-0.7	3.7	7.6	8.7	8.3	8.9	4.1
Vanuatu	4.1	5.9	3.5	11.8	-2.6	-1.5	0.7	9.7	0.2	3.6
Yemen	..	8.3	6.4	..	8.6	4.9	3.9	6.8	8.8	0.3
Zambia	18.3	36.1	11.2	4.1	0.8	5.5	6.3	5.9	3.7	7.1
LDCs	**11.8**	**10.5**	**9.8**	**2.3**	**4.2**	**7.4**	**7.3**	**7.6**	**8.5**	**5.9**
African LDCs and Haiti	*10.7*	*9.7*	*7.5*	*1.9*	*2.4*	*6.8*	*6.5*	*6.8*	*6.1*	*7.8*
Asian LDCs	*13.9*	*12.1*	*13.8*	*2.9*	*6.6*	*8.0*	*8.1*	*8.6*	*11.0*	*4.1*
Island LDCs	*7.4*	*6.4*	*5.9*	*5.7*	*4.0*	*2.1*	*3.7*	*3.5*	*-1.2*	*5.7*
Other developing countries	**22.1**	**22.5**	**24.0**	**5.3**	**6.8**	**7.4**	**7.8**	**9.8**	**8.0**	**8.3**
All developing countries	**21.7**	**22.0**	**23.6**	**5.2**	**6.8**	**7.4**	**7.8**	**9.7**	**8.0**	**8.3**

Source: UNCTAD secretariat calculations based on data from United Nations/DESA Statistics Division.
a 1993–2000 for Eritrea and Ethiopia.

6. Gross capital formation: Shares in GDP and average annual growth rates
(Per cent)

Country	Share in GDP			Annual average growth rate						
	1980	1990	2006	1980–1990	1990–2000	2000–2005	2003	2004	2005	2006
Afghanistan	13.2	13.4	17.3	-1.6	-1.4	23.0	29.0	45.5	39.7	-9.8
Angola	20.4	11.7	13.1	-6.5	9.5	3.8	4.1	-20.0	-0.2	98.5
Bangladesh	23.2	16.4	25.6	2.7	9.8	8.6	9.2	9.2	7.8	9.4
Benin	22.2	14.2	21.0	-3.0	5.3	6.0	15.6	8.9	-16.1	32.0
Bhutan	31.2	36.3	53.5	11.8	6.9	7.4	-0.9	14.8	-12.0	15.5
Burkina Faso	26.6	18.8	24.5	5.2	6.6	4.1	4.1	8.6	-0.8	10.8
Burundi	13.9	15.8	23.2	4.1	-11.5	22.5	5.4	9.7	39.0	58.3
Cambodia	9.3	8.3	19.3	5.5	15.2	10.7	41.7	-22.9	29.0	-8.0
Cape Verde	41.9	43.6	38.7	4.3	6.3	12.5	1.1	23.7	8.9	12.1
Central African Republic	7.0	12.3	5.7	10.0	-1.3	-3.1	-37.9	2.9	48.0	-2.7
Chad	8.2	7.2	23.6	5.9	5.5	24.0	-6.8	-11.2	19.1	12.6
Comoros	33.2	20.2	13.8	-3.9	-2.5	-0.9	1.1	-11.9	-3.8	29.0
Dem. Republic of the Congo	24.9	25.0	16.7	-1.9	-5.5	-0.1	7.9	8.7	10.5	10.0
Djibouti	14.4	27.1	19.7	1.4	-4.8	4.2	-8.3	3.5	7.3	1.4
Equatorial Guinea	11.9	54.4	33.2	10.0	55.0	15.0	101.7	-1.2	40.7	-7.9
Eritrea	..	..	18.1	..	8.7a	-1.5	-0.2	-13.9	-6.8	-2.7
Ethiopia	..	..	19.8	..	7.9a	7.4	-6.2	4.0	32.1	1.2
Gambia	14.5	17.9	24.1	9.1	2.4	9.2	-2.3	50.3	-0.5	-1.9
Guinea	13.4	17.0	21.5	5.2	2.5	-1.0	-23.6	13.9	27.6	15.8
Guinea-Bissau	28.2	14.7	15.7	6.2	-3.0	-2.7	5.4	9.0	14.5	-4.0
Haiti	17.9	14.3	28.6	-0.1	3.4	2.3	3.1	-3.2	1.4	17.9
Kiribati	44.0	93.1	43.6	5.6	-0.4	1.7	0.0	-4.3	4.5	0.0
Lao People's Dem. Republic	7.4	11.3	30.7	10.7	6.1	25.5	39.6	32.1	8.0	3.2
Lesotho	42.5	53.2	41.1	6.1	1.5	0.3	0.0	-8.6	1.3	19.0
Liberia	26.8	10.8	12.3	-15.6	2.7	13.9	28.0	41.8	37.0	-17.1
Madagascar	23.5	17.0	21.7	-2.0	1.0	14.9	61.5	22.0	0.0	18.0
Malawi	22.2	17.1	10.5	-3.5	0.9	-5.5	3.5	-4.2	-11.9	1.9
Maldives	31.5	31.5	55.6	11.9	8.0	21.4	45.2	23.2	36.1	13.1
Mali	18.5	22.2	22.5	6.0	0.5	11.1	55.7	-32.6	42.0	7.5
Mauritania	26.8	19.5	29.0	-5.9	7.6	18.3	29.6	77.4	1.4	-25.6
Mozambique	10.2	19.7	24.8	-2.9	12.1	19.8	3.2	34.6	25.8	31.8
Myanmar	21.5	13.4	15.2	-4.0	15.3	19.6	6.9	25.8	24.6	26.0
Nepal	18.3	18.4	30.3	5.9	7.0	6.8	10.5	5.9	12.5	6.8
Niger	31.5	12.8	22.8	-7.3	11.0	10.8	6.6	-14.1	52.2	-13.1
Rwanda	19.6	13.9	20.8	3.0	1.1	0.0	-35.0	18.0	16.3	6.3
Samoa	27.6	22.9	9.8	0.2	-4.7	-3.0	-2.9	-5.0	-2.6	-2.2
Sao Tome and Principe	16.8	29.5	67.6	-4.7	2.6	11.6	14.6	1.8	1.6	107.0
Senegal	9.3	11.4	25.6	5.1	4.6	8.5	46.6	-0.5	12.3	3.5
Sierra Leone	16.1	10.0	16.5	-0.3	-20.7	..	..	63.9	38.4	-7.3
Solomon Islands	22.0	20.1	19.6	3.1	1.9	3.0	6.4	8.0	5.0	5.0
Somalia	9.1	23.6	20.3	3.5	-4.9	2.7	2.1	2.8	2.4	2.4
Sudan	23.1	7.3	23.8	-4.0	13.0	11.9	22.3	-7.0	13.4	13.9
Timor-Leste	-	35.0	19.0	..	0.3	-7.9	-17.8	-8.5	2.4	-2.3
Togo	36.3	25.1	20.8	-2.7	0.7	6.7	5.3	2.8	5.5	10.4
Tuvalu	33.1	93.1	55.7	7.1	1.4	4.7	3.7	4.9	1.5	1.0
Uganda	6.2	14.7	24.8	10.9	9.1	12.8	13.7	17.4	13.0	16.1
United Republic of Tanzania	19.1	35.0	22.5	5.6	-1.8	10.1	6.0	9.1	9.5	4.2
Vanuatu	28.9	43.2	20.2	7.1	-2.3	0.1	-4.0	6.8	3.7	2.2
Yemen	-	15.2	21.5	..	9.0	4.6	13.4	1.0	-14.8	26.4
Zambia	23.3	17.3	25.9	-4.3	5.1	9.6	18.9	-1.6	2.1	11.0
LDCs	**20.5**	**15.6**	**22.2**	**-0.4**	**7.5**	**10.0**	**14.5**	**5.4**	**13.3**	**13.0**
African LDCs and Haiti	*19.3*	*15.3*	*21.2*	*-0.8*	*6.1*	*9.6*	*17.8*	*1.1*	*15.8*	*13.9*
Asian LDCs	*22.4*	*15.7*	*23.7*	*0.3*	*9.7*	*10.6*	*11.0*	*10.5*	*10.5*	*11.9*
Island LDCs	*30.3*	*33.0*	*32.5*	*3.8*	*3.0*	*9.9*	*8.0*	*14.5*	*14.4*	*13.1*
Other developing countries	**26.9**	**26.1**	**27.5**	**2.7**	**5.5**	**8.2**	**9.2**	**12.3**	**9.9**	**9.3**
All developing countries	**27.3**	**25.7**	**27.3**	**2.6**	**5.5**	**8.2**	**9.3**	**12.1**	**10.0**	**9.4**

Source: UNCTAD secretariat calculations based on data from United Nations/DESA Statistics Division.
　a　1993–2000 for Eritrea and Ethiopia.

Country	Area			Population					
	Land area[a] (000km²)	% of arable land and land under permanent crops	% of land area covered by forest	Density (pop/km²)	Total (million)	Urban (%)	Activity rate[c] (2006) (%)		
	2006	2005[b]	2005[b]	2006	2006	2006	Male	Female	Total
Afghanistan	652.1	12.3	1.3	40	26.1	29.6	88	39	64
Angola	1 246.7	2.9	47.4	13	16.6	37.6	92	74	82
Bangladesh	130.2	64.6	6.7	1109	156.0	23.5	86	53	70
Benin	110.6	27.3	21.3	79	8.8	46.6	86	54	70
Bhutan	47.0	3.8	68.0	14	0.6	32.1	79	49	64
Burkina Faso	273.8	17.9	24.8	50	14.4	18.0	89	78	83
Burundi	25.7	52.0	5.9	305	8.2	10.5	93	92	93
Cambodia	176.5	21.8	59.2	81	14.2	20.6	80	74	77
Cape Verde	4.0	12.2	20.7	129	0.5	58.4	76	34	54
Central African Republic	623.0	3.2	36.5	7	4.3	42.5	89	70	79
Chad	1 259.2	3.4	9.5	8	10.5	25.1	77	66	71
Comoros	1.9	71.5	3.0	275	0.8	36.9	87	58	72
Dem. Rep. of the Congo	2 267.1	3.4	58.9	26	60.6	32.6	..	..	..
Djibouti	23.2	0.0	0.2	35	0.8	83.7	83	53	68
Equatorial Guinea	28.1	7.8	58.2	18	0.5	52.9	91	51	70
Eritrea	101.0	6.3	15.4	45	4.7	20.7	90	58	74
Ethiopia	1 096.3	12.7	11.9	73	81.0	16.1	89	71	80
Gambia	11.3	35.5	47.1	155	1.7	24.5	86	59	72
Guinea	245.7	7.6	27.4	37	9.2	39.0	87	79	83
Guinea-Bissau	28.1	19.6	73.7	58	1.6	36.1	93	61	77
Haiti	27.6	39.9	3.8	314	9.4	36.1	83	56	69
Kiribati	0.7	45.7	2.7	138	0.1	..	..	..	..
Lao People's Dem. Rep.	230.8	4.7	69.9	25	5.8	23.3	81	54	67
Lesotho	30.4	11.0	0.3	59	2.0	16.5	72	45	57
Liberia	96.3	6.3	32.7	35	3.6	45.5	83	55	69
Madagascar	581.5	6.1	22.1	33	19.2	27.2	86	79	83
Malawi	94.1	29.1	36.2	140	13.6	17.1	89	86	87
Maldives	0.3	43.3	3.0	1 123	0.3	33.9	72	50	61
Mali	1 220.2	4.0	10.3	11	12.0	40.0	83	73	78
Mauritania	1 025.2	0.5	0.3	3	3.0	67.9	84	54	69
Mozambique	784.1	5.9	24.5	26	21.0	37.6	83	84	84
Myanmar	657.6	16.7	49.0	78	48.4	32.9	86	68	77
Nepal	143.0	17.4	25.4	193	27.6	16.3	78	50	64
Niger	1 266.7	11.4	1.0	11	13.7	25.0	95	71	84
Rwanda	24.7	59.8	19.5	375	9.5	23.0	84	80	82
Samoa	2.8	31.8	60.4	66	0.2	22.7	77	39	59
Sao Tome and Principe	1.0	58.3	28.5	167	0.2	39.3	75	30	52
Senegal	192.5	13.5	45.0	62	12.1	51.2	82	56	68
Sierra Leone	71.6	9.5	38.5	79	5.7	40.5	94	56	75
Solomon Islands	28.0	2.8	77.6	17	0.5	17.6	82	54	69
Somalia	627.3	2.2	11.4	14	8.4	36.7	95	59	77
Sudan	2 376.0	8.3	28.4	16	37.7	40.9	72	24	48
Timor-Leste	14.9	12.8	53.7	69	1.1	7.1	83	55	70
Togo	54.4	48.4	7.1	116	6.4	36.4	90	50	70
Tuvalu	0.0	66.7	33.3	403	0.0	..	..	..	..
Uganda	197.1	38.6	18.4	152	29.9	12.5	86	80	83
United Republic of Tanzania	883.6	11.7	39.8	45	39.5	38.1	..	..	..
Vanuatu	12.2	8.6	36.1	18	0.2	23.5	88	80	84
Yemen	528.0	3.1	1.0	41	21.7	26.6	..	..	..
Zambia	743.4	7.1	57.1	16	11.7	37.4	91	66	78
LDCs	**20 267.3**	**8.2**	**27.4**	**38**	**785.4**	**27.9**	**85**	**61**	**73.3**
African LDCs and Haiti	*17 636.2*	*7.3*	*27.4*	*27*	*481.1*	*29.8*	*86*	*66*	*75.9*
Asian LDCs	*2 565.1*	*14.3*	*26.5*	*117*	*300.4*	*25.0*	*85*	*56*	*70.3*
Island LDCs	*66.2*	*11.4*	*56.2*	*59*	*3.9*	*26.3*	*81*	*51*	*66.5*
Other developing countries	**56 622.6**	**13.7**	**27.5**	**79**	**4 499.6**	**45.9**	**82**	**51**	**66.6**
All developing countries	**76 888.9**	**12.2**	**27.5**	**69**	**5 285.1**	**43.2**	**82**	**52.4**	**67.3**

Source: UNCTAD secretariat calculations based on FAO, FAOSTAT online data, January 2008; UNCTAD, *Handbook of Statistics, 2007*; United Nations/DESA Population Division; ILO, online data, December 2007.

a Country area excluding inland water;
b Latest year available;
c Economically active population, aged 15 years and older as percentage of total population aged 15 years and older.

8. Indicators on demography

Country	Under 5 mortality rate		Infant mortality rate		Average life expectancy at birth						Crude birth rate		Crude death rate	
	Per 1 000 live births				Years						Per 1 000 population			
	1990	2006	1990	2006	1990	2005	1990	2005	1990	2005	1990	2006	1990	2006
					Female		Male		Total					
Afghanistan	260	257	168	165	..	..	..	..	46.0	46.0	52	49	23	21
Angola	260	260	154	154	41.6	42.9	38.1	40.0	39.8	41.4	53	48	24	21
Bangladesh	149	69	100	52	55.4	64.8	54.7	63.0	55.1	63.9	35	26	12	8
Benin	185	148	111	88	54.3	55.8	51.7	54.2	53.0	55.0	47	41	15	12
Bhutan	166	70	107	63	..	65.2[a]	..	61.8[a]	55.9	63.5[a]	38	20	14	8
Burkina Faso	206	204	123	122	49.2	49.3	45.9	47.7	47.5	48.5	49	45	17	15
Burundi	190	181	114	109	46.4	45.7	42.5	43.7	44.4	44.7	47	46	19	16
Cambodia	116	82	85	65	56.4	60.6	52.4	53.6	54.3	57.0	43	27	12	10
Cape Verde	60	34	45	25	68.0	73.9	62.7	67.7	65.3	70.7	39	30	8	5
Central African Republic	173	175	114	115	50.7	40.1	45.1	38.8	47.8	39.4	42	37	16	19
Chad	201	209	120	124	47.9	45.1	44.1	43.0	46.0	44.0	48	46	16	16
Comoros	120	68	88	51	57.4	64.0	54.6	61.3	56.0	62.6	41	35	11	7
Dem. Republic of the Congo	205	205	129	129	47.3	45.1	43.8	43.0	45.5	44.0	49	50	18	19
Djibouti	175	130	116	86	52.3	54.6	49.2	52.3	50.8	53.4	42	30	14	12
Equatorial Guinea	170	206	103	124	47.5	42.6	43.8	42.0	45.6	42.3	42	39	19	16
Eritrea	147	74	88	48	50.6	56.8	46.0	53.1	48.2	54.9	41	40	16	10
Ethiopia	204	123	122	77	46.5	43.4	43.5	41.9	45.0	42.7	47	39	18	14
Gambia	153	113	103	84	51.5	58.2	48.5	55.5	50.0	56.8	43	37	15	11
Guinea	235	161	139	98	48.1	54.3	46.9	53.8	47.5	54.1	47	41	19	13
Guinea-Bissau	240	200	142	119	44.1	46.5	40.7	43.8	42.3	45.1	50	50	23	19
Haiti	152	80	105	60	51.1	53.3	46.8	52.0	48.9	52.6	37	29	13	10
Kiribati	88	64	65	47	59.1	66.0[a]	54.6	59.8[a]	56.8	62.8[a]	36	25	9	6
Lao People's Dem. Republic	163	75	120	59	..	63.1[a]	..	60.6[a]	..	61.9[a]	43	28	13	8
Lesotho	101	132	81	102	59.5	35.9	55.4	34.5	57.4	35.2	37	30	11	18
Liberia	235	235	157	157	44.1	43.3	41.3	41.7	42.7	42.5	50	50	21	19
Madagascar	168	115	103	72	52.2	57.1	49.8	54.6	51.0	55.8	44	38	15	10
Malawi	221	120	131	76	47.3	40.2	44.1	40.8	45.7	40.5	50	42	18	16
Maldives	111	30	78	26	59.2	67.4	61.8	67.9	60.5	67.6	39	23	9	6
Mali	250	217	140	119	46.9	49.3	45.1	48.0	46.0	48.6	52	48	20	16
Mauritania	133	125	85	78	50.7	55.3	47.5	52.1	49.1	53.7	40	34	11	8
Mozambique	235	138	158	96	44.9	42.3	41.6	41.4	43.2	41.8	44	42	20	19
Myanmar	130	104	91	74	58.2	64.1	54.1	58.3	56.1	61.1	27	19	11	10
Nepal	142	59	99	46	54.3	63.2	54.8	62.2	54.6	62.7	38	29	13	8
Niger	320	253	191	148	40.2	45.0	40.0	44.9	40.1	44.9	56	50	22	15
Rwanda	176	160	106	98	33.4	45.7	29.0	42.6	31.2	44.1	49	43	31	18
Samoa	50	28	40	23	67.9	73.9	64.7	67.7	66.3	70.7	34	27	7	6
Sao Tome and Principe	100	96	65	63	62.5	64.6	60.7	62.4	61.6	63.5	38	34	10	8
Senegal	149	116	72	60	54.3	57.7	51.9	55.2	53.1	56.5	43	36	13	9
Sierra Leone	290	270	169	159	40.2	42.8	37.4	40.0	38.8	41.4	48	47	26	23
Solomon Islands	121	73	86	55	61.5	63.7	60.3	62.2	60.9	62.9	40	32	11	8
Somalia	203	145	121	90	43.3	49.0	40.0	46.5	41.6	47.7	46	44	22	18
Sudan	120	89	74	61	54.3	58.1	51.2	55.3	52.7	56.7	41	32	14	11
Timor-Leste	177	55	133	47	47.0	57.9	45.3	55.6	46.1	56.7	43	42	18	10
Togo	149	108	88	69	59.6	57.0	55.3	53.3	57.4	55.1	44	38	12	10
Tuvalu	54	38	42	31	..	..	..	..	..	..	28	23	10	9
Uganda	160	134	93	78	47.7	50.6	43.9	49.3	45.7	50.0	49	47	16	14
United Republic of Tanzania	161	118	102	74	55.8	46.7	51.3	46.0	53.5	46.3	44	41	15	14
Vanuatu	62	36	48	30	65.0	71.4	62.0	67.7	63.5	69.5	37	30	7	5
Yemen	139	100	98	75	55.3	63.2	53.8	60.4	54.5	61.7	51	39	13	8
Zambia	180	182	101	102	47.5	37.9	44.1	38.9	45.8	38.4	44	41	16	20
LDCs	**180**	**142**	**113**	**90**	**51.1**	**53.5**	**48.6**	**51.6**	**49.8**	**52.5**	**42**	**36**	**16**	**13**
All Developing countries	**103**	**79**	**70**	**54**	**63.4**	**64.7**	**59.4**	**61.2**	**61.3**	**62.9**	**29**	**23**	**9**	**8**

Source: UNICEF, *The State of the World's Children 2008*, February 2008; World Bank, *World Development Indicators*, online, February 2008.
   a   2002 for Bhutan, Kiribati and Lao's People's Democratic Republic.

9. Indicators on health

Country	Low birthweight infant[a] (%)	Skilled attendant at delivery (%)	Percentage of 1-year-old children immunized against: (%)			Estimated number of children living with HIV (thousands)	Estimated number of people living with HIV (thousands)	Estimated adult HIV prevalence rate (%)
			TB	DPT3[b]	Measles	(0-14 years)	(0+ years)	(15+ years)
	2006[c]	2006[c]	2006			2005	2005	end 2005
Afghanistan	..	14	90	77	68	..	<1.0	<0.1
Angola	12	45	65	44	48	35	320	3.7
Bangladesh	22	20	96	88	81	..	11	<0.1
Benin	16	78	99	93	89	9.8	87	1.8
Bhutan	15	56	92	95	90	..	<0.5	<0.1
Burkina Faso	16	54	99	95	88	17	150	2
Burundi	11	34	84	74	75	20	150	3.3
Cambodia	11	44	87	80	78	..	130	1.6
Cape Verde	13	89	70	72	65	..	..	..
Central African Republic	13	53	70	40	35	24	250	10.7
Chad	22	14	40	20	23	16	180	3.5
Comoros	25	62	84	69	66	<0.1	<0.5	<0.1
Dem. Rep. of the Congo	12	61	87	77	73	120	1 000	3.2
Djibouti	10	61	88	72	67	1.2	15	3.1
Equatorial Guinea	13	65	73	33	51	<1.0	8.9	3.2
Eritrea	14	28	99	97	95	6.6	59	2.4
Ethiopia	20	6	72	72	63	..	..	..
Gambia	20	57	99	95	95	1.2	20	2.4
Guinea	12	38	90	71	67	7	85	1.5
Guinea-Bissau	24	39	87	77	60	3.2	32	3.8
Haiti	25	26	75	53	58	17	190	3.8
Kiribati	5	85	99	86	61	..	..	..
Lao People's Dem. Republic	14	19	61	57	48	..	3.7	0.1
Lesotho	13	55	96	83	85	18	270	23.2
Liberia	..	51	89	88	94	..	..	..
Madagascar	17	51	72	61	59	1.6	49	0.5
Malawi	13	54	99	99	85	91	940	14.1
Maldives	22	84	99	98	97	..	..	..
Mali	23	41	85	85	86	16	130	1.7
Mauritania	..	57	86	68	62	1.1	12	0.7
Mozambique	15	48	87	72	77	140	1 800	16.1
Myanmar	15	57	85	82	78	..	360	1.3
Nepal	21	19	93	89	85	..	75	0.5
Niger	13	33	64	39	47	8.9	79	1.1
Rwanda	6	39	98	99	95	27	190	3.1
Samoa	4	100	84	56	54	..	..	..
Sao Tome and Principe	8	81	98	99	85	..	..	..
Senegal	19	52	99	89	80	5	61	0.9
Sierra Leone	24	43	82	64	67	5.2	48	1.6
Solomon Islands	13	85	84	91	84	..	..	..
Somalia	11	33	50	35	35	4.5	44	0.9
Sudan	31	87	77	78	73	30	350	1.6
Timor-Leste	12	18	72	67	64	..	..	..
Togo	12	62	96	87	83	9.7	110	3.2
Tuvalu	5	100	99	97	84	..	..	..
Uganda	12	42	85	80	89	110	1 000	6.7
United Republic of Tanzania	10	43	99	90	93	110	1 400	6.5
Vanuatu	6	88	92	85	99	..	..	..
Yemen	32	27	70	85	80	..	..	..
Zambia	12	43	94	80	84	130	1 100	17
LDCs	**17**	**38**	**85**	**77**	**74**	**1 100**	**11 700**	**2.7**
All developing countries	**16**	**59**	**86**	**78**	**78**	**2 300**	**35 100**	**1.1**

Source: UNICEF, *The State of World's Children 2008*; UNAIDS, *2006 Global Report*.

a Less than 2,500 grams. b Diphteria, Pertussis and Tetanus. c 2006 or latest year available.

10. Indicators on nutrition and sanitation

Country	Total food supply (Kcal/capita/day)		% of population using improved drinking water sources			% of population using adequate sanitation facilities		
	1990	2005[a]	2004[a]			2004[a]		
			Total	Urban	Rural	Total	Urban	Rural
Afghanistan	..	..	39	63	31	34	49	29
Angola	1 861	2 672	53	75	40	31	56	16
Bangladesh	2 037	2 194	74	82	72	39	51	35
Benin	2 232	2 592	67	78	57	33	59	11
Bhutan	..	..	62	86	60	70	65	70
Burkina Faso	2 471	2 467	61	94	54	13	42	6
Burundi	2 006	1 691	79	92	77	36	47	35
Cambodia	1 881	2 501	41	64	35	17	53	8
Cape Verde	..	..	80	86	73	43	61	19
Central African Republic	1 954	2 040	75	93	61	27	47	12
Chad	1 707	1 828	42	41	43	9	24	4
Comoros	2 065	2 076	86	92	82	33	41	29
Dem. Rep. of the Congo	2 229	1 367	46	82	29	30	42	25
Djibouti	1 887	3 080	73	76	59	82	88	50
Equatorial Guinea	..	..	43	45	42	53	60	46
Eritrea	..	..	60	74	57	9	32	3
Ethiopia	..	1 846	22	81	11	13	44	7
Gambia	2 511	2 400	82	95	77	53	72	46
Guinea	2 233	2 612	50	78	35	18	31	11
Guinea-Bissau	2 194	1 902	59	79	49	35	57	23
Haiti	1 794	1 863	54	52	56	30	57	14
Kiribati	2 643	2 818	65	77	53	40	59	22
Lao People's Dem. Rep.	..	..	51	79	43	30	67	20
Lesotho	..	..	79	92	76	37	61	32
Liberia	2 340	2 078	61	72	52	27	49	7
Madagascar	2 201	2 046	50	77	35	34	48	26
Malawi	1 972	2 231	73	98	68	61	62	61
Maldives	2 680	3 327	83	98	76	59	100	42
Mali	..	..	50	78	36	46	59	39
Mauritania	..	..	53	59	44	34	49	8
Mozambique	1 818	2 288	43	72	26	32	53	19
Myanmar	2 559	3 619	78	80	77	77	88	72
Nepal	2 358	2 503	90	96	89	35	62	30
Niger	2 122	2 061	46	80	36	13	43	4
Rwanda	1 854	1 936	74	92	69	42	56	38
Samoa	2 751	3 592	88	90	87	100	100	100
Sao Tome and Principe	2 454	3 418	79	89	73	25	32	20
Senegal	2 352	2 513	76	92	60	57	79	34
Sierra Leone	2 116	1 874	57	75	46	39	53	30
Solomon Islands	2 185	2 056	70	94	65	31	98	18
Somalia	..	..	29	32	27	26	48	14
Sudan	2 051	2 351	70	78	64	34	50	24
Timor-Leste	..	..	58	77	56	36	66	33
Togo	2 287	2 123	52	80	36	35	71	15
Tuvalu	..	..	100	94	92	90	93	84
Uganda	2 362	2 333	60	87	56	43	54	41
United Republic of Tanzania	2 175	2 230	62	85	49	47	53	43
Vanuatu	2 478	2 025	60	86	52	50	78	42
Yemen	1 950	1 926	67	71	65	43	86	28
Zambia	2 020	1 642	58	90	40	55	59	52
LDCs	**2 127**	**2 251**	**59**	**79**	**51**	**36**	**55**	**29**
All developing countries	**2 571**	**2 772**	**80**	**92**	**70**	**50**	**73**	**33**

Source: FAO, FAOSTAT online data, January 2008; UNICEF, *The State of World's Children 2008*.
    a   Latest year available.

11. Indicators on education and literacy, 2005[a]
(Per cent)

Country	Adult literacy rate			Youth literacy rate			School enrolment ratio								
							Primary[b]			Secondary[c]			Tertiary[d]		
	Male	Female	Total	Male	Female	Total	Male	Female	Total	Male	Female	Total	Male	Female	Total
Afghanistan	43.1	12.6	28.0	50.8	18.4	34.3	..	..	..	..	..	..	1.9	0.5	1.3
Angola	82.9	54.2	67.4	83.7	63.2	72.2	..	..	..	..	..	..	1.0	0.7	2.9
Bangladesh	53.9	40.8	47.5	67.2	60.3	63.6	87.4	90.5	88.9	40.2	41.8	41.0	7.7	4.1	6.0
Benin	47.9	23.3	34.7	59.2	33.2	45.3	85.7	69.4	77.7	22.8	11.3	17.1	4.8	1.2	3.0
Bhutan	..	..	..	..	..	..	74.0	73.8	73.9	35.5	35.6	35.5	4.0	2.1	3.1
Burkina Faso	31.4	16.6	23.6	40.4	26.5	33.0	49.0	39.0	44.1	12.9	9.1	11.0	3.0	1.4	2.2
Burundi	67.3	52.2	59.3	76.8	70.4	73.3	61.1	55.5	58.3	..	..	..	3.4	1.3	2.3
Cambodia	84.7	64.1	73.6	87.9	78.9	83.4	97.1	95.9	96.5	26.0	21.9	23.9	4.8	2.3	3.6
Cape Verde	87.8	75.5	81.2	95.8	96.7	96.3	90.8	89.4	90.1	55.0	60.0	57.5	6.8	7.1	6.9
Central African Republic	64.8	33.5	48.6	70.3	46.9	58.5	..	..	..	..	..	..	3.0	0.6	1.6
Chad	40.8	12.8	25.7	55.7	23.2	37.6	70.9	49.5	60.2	15.7	5.2	10.5	2.0	..	1.2
Comoros	63.0	49.0	56.0	..	..	..	59.5	50.5	55.1	..	..	..	2.6	2.0	2.3
Dem. Rep. of the Congo	80.9	54.1	67.2	78.0	63.1	70.4	..	..	..	..	..	..	..	..	..
Djibouti	..	..	70.3	..	..	..	37.9	30.9	34.4	25.9	17.0	21.5	2.5	1.8	2.2
Equatorial Guinea	93.4	80.5	87.0	94.8	94.9	94.9	91.4	82.7	87.1	..	..	25.3	3.8	1.7	2.7
Eritrea	..	..	60.5	..	..	..	52.4	44.8	48.6	28.9	19.2	24.1	1.8	..	1.0
Ethiopia	50.0	22.8	35.9	62.2	38.5	49.9	62.6	57.4	60.0	33.4	21.6	27.5	4.0	1.3	2.7
Gambia	..	..	42.5	..	..	..	72.3	72.5	72.4	47.2	39.5	43.3	1.8	..	1.1
Guinea	42.6	18.1	29.5	58.7	33.7	46.6	75.3	63.3	69.4	32.1	17.2	24.8	4.8	1.1	3.0
Guinea-Bissau	..	..	44.8	..	..	..	52.9	37.4	45.1	11.2	6.2	8.7	0.6	..	..
Haiti	54.0	50.0	52.0	..	..	..	..	..	..	..	..	..	..	..	..
Kiribati	..	..	..	..	..	..	..	..	97.4	64.6	70.8	67.6	..	..	..
Lao People's Dem. Rep.	77.0	60.9	68.7	82.6	74.7	78.5	85.0	80.3	82.7	38.4	32.7	35.6	9.2	6.6	7.9
Lesotho	73.7	90.3	82.2	..	..	..	73.1	77.4	75.2	18.8	29.2	24.0	3.0	3.8	3.4
Liberia	58.3	45.7	51.9	65.3	69.5	67.4	74.5	57.9	66.2	21.7	12.5	17.1	17.7	13.4	15.6
Madagascar	76.5	65.3	70.7	72.7	68.2	70.2	93.1	92.8	92.9	..	..	..	2.8	2.5	2.6
Malawi	75.0	54.0	64.5	82.0	71.0	76.5	90.5	95.1	92.8	24.4	21.7	23.1	0.5	..	..
Maldives	96.2	96.4	96.3	98.0	98.3	98.2	97.5	97.7	97.6	61.2	67.1	64.1	..	..	..
Mali	32.7	15.9	24.0	32.0	17.0	24.5	66.5	51.7	59.1	..	..	..	4.2	1.9	3.0
Mauritania	59.5	43.4	51.2	67.7	55.5	61.3	74.7	78.8	76.7	16.4	14.6	15.6	4.7	1.6	3.2
Mozambique	62.0	31.0	46.5	60.0	37.0	48.5	80.3	72.9	76.6	7.8	6.1	7.0	1.9	1.0	1.5
Myanmar	93.9	86.4	89.9	95.7	93.4	94.5	98.0	100.0	99.0	43.3	42.8	43.0	8.7	15.4	11.9
Nepal	62.7	34.9	48.6	81.0	60.0	70.0	84.3	73.8	79.2	..	..	..	7.9	3.2	5.6
Niger	42.9	15.1	28.7	52.4	23.2	36.5	49.0	35.6	42.5	10.4	6.9	8.6	1.8	0.6	1.1
Rwanda	71.4	59.8	64.9	78.5	76.9	77.6	71.7	74.9	73.3	..	..	..	3.2	2.0	2.6
Samoa	98.9	98.3	98.6	99.3	99.4	99.3	90.2	90.6	90.4	62.0	70.5	66.0	7.7	7.2	7.5
Sao Tome and Principe	92.2	77.9	84.9	96.0	94.9	95.4	97.1	95.3	96.2	30.9	34.3	32.6	..	..	..
Senegal	51.1	29.2	39.3	58.5	41.0	49.1	71.0	68.3	69.6	19.9	15.0	17.5	..	..	5.5
Sierra Leone	46.7	24.2	34.8	59.6	37.4	47.9	..	..	..	..	..	..	3.0	1.2	2.1
Solomon Islands	..	..	..	..	..	..	64.2	62.2	63.3	29.1	25.2	27.3	..	..	..
Somalia	..	..	..	..	..	..	..	..	..	..	..	..	..	..	..
Sudan	71.1	51.8	60.9	84.6	71.4	77.2	44.9	37.2	41.2	..	..	..	6.4	5.9	6.2
Timor-Leste	..	..	..	..	..	..	69.5	66.6	68.1	..	..	22.8	8.6	10.8	9.6
Togo	68.7	38.5	53.2	83.7	63.6	74.4	83.4	71.6	77.5	30.0	14.4	22.2	6.0	1.2	3.6
Tuvalu	..	..	..	..	..	..	..	..	..	..	..	..	..	..	..
Uganda	76.8	57.7	66.8	82.7	71.2	76.6	..	..	..	15.6	14.0	14.8	4.3	2.7	3.5
United Republic of Tanzania	77.5	62.2	69.4	80.9	76.2	78.4	93.4	91.7	92.5	..	..	..	2.0	0.9	1.4
Vanuatu	..	..	..	..	..	..	92.9	92.1	92.5	40.7	35.3	38.1	5.9	3.5	4.8
Yemen	73.1	34.7	54.1	90.7	58.9	75.2	85.2	62.0	73.8	45.6	20.7	33.5	13.5	5.0	9.4
Zambia	76.0	60.0	68.0	73.0	66.0	69.5	91.2	92.9	92.0	31.2	24.9	28.1	3.2	1.5	2.3
LDCs	**70.0**	**50.0**	**60.0**	**74.0**	**59.0**	**66.5**	..	..	..	..	..	..	..	..	..
All developing countries	**85.0**	**72.0**	**79.0**	**90.0**	**84.0**	**87.0**	..	..	..	..	..	..	..	..	..

Source: UNESCO Institute for Statistics (UIS), online data, February 2008; UNICEF, *The State of the World's Children 2008*; UNDP, *Human Development Report 2007–2008*.

a 2005 or latest year available. b Net primary school enrolment. c Net secondary school enrolment. d Gross tertiary school enrolment.

12. Indicators on communication and media, 2006[a]						
Country	Post offices open to the public	Radio receivers	Television sets	Telephone mainlines	Mobile users	Personal computers	Internet users
	Per 100 000 inhabitants	Per 1 000 inhabitants					
Afghanistan	1.8	128	80	5	81	3	17
Angola	0.3	85	21	6	143	7	5
Bangladesh	6.3	64	106	8	132	24	3
Benin	2.0	358	107	9	121	4	80
Bhutan	13.9	321	32	40	47	16	31
Burkina Faso	0.5	106	13	7	75	2	6
Burundi	0.5	162	36	4	20	7	8
Cambodia	0.6	127	8	2	79	3	3
Cape Verde	6.9	184	105	138	210	116	61
Central African Republic	0.6	109	10	2	25	3	3
Chad	0.4	116	9	1	46	2	6
Comoros	2.9	154	31	21	20	7	26
Dem. Rep. of the Congo	0.2	379	5	0	74	0	3
Djibouti	1.4	107	77	16	64	27	14
Equatorial Guinea	4.2	429	12	20	193	18	16
Eritrea	1.4	466	68	8	14	6	22
Ethiopia	1.0	184	8	9	11	4	2
Gambia	0.6	155	15	34	260	16	38
Guinea	0.9	93	18	3	24	6	5
Guinea-Bissau	1.3	47	45	8	71	2	23
Haiti	0.6	55	63	17	59	2	75
Kiribati	..	96	44	51	7	11	22
Lao People's Dem. Rep.	7.6	150	57	13	108	17	4
Lesotho	7.7	75	44	27	139	1	29
Liberia	0.5	274	28	2	49	0	0
Madagascar	3.1	121	21	7	55	5	5
Malawi	2.4	310	7	8	33	2	5
Maldives	71.6	110	143	109	879	110	58
Mali	0.8	153	36	6	109	4	5
Mauritania	0.9	138	41	11	336	26	32
Mozambique	0.5	255	21	3	116	14	9
Myanmar	2.8	59	7	9	4	7	2
Nepal	..	39	11	22	38	5	9
Niger	0.3	66	12	2	23	1	3
Rwanda	0.2	151	8	2	34	2	7
Samoa	19.6	1 030	126	109	134	20	45
Sao Tome and Principe	6.0	312	127	47	115	38	181
Senegal	1.2	117	45	24	250	21	54
Sierra Leone	0.8	278	13	5	22	..	2
Solomon Islands	4.2	126	12	15	13	46	16
Somalia	..	65	26	12	61	9	11
Sudan	0.5	461	387	17	127	115	95
Timor-Leste	..	..	..	..	..	..	..
Togo	0.9	410	26	13	112	36	59
Tuvalu	..	..	..	85	124	80	162
Uganda	1.0	155	22	4	67	17	25
United Republic of Tanzania	1.1	398	41	4	148	9	10
Vanuatu	21.7	351	12	32	58	14	35
Yemen	1.3	64	337	46	95	19	12
Zambia	2.1	145	64	8	140	11	42

Source: UPU, online data, February 2008; ITU, online data, February 2008.
   a   Or latest year available.

13. Indicators on transport and transport network

Country	Road networks 2004[a]			Railways 2005[a]				Civil Aviation 2005[a]	
	Total	Paved	Density	Network	Density	Freight	Passenger	Freight	Passenger
	km	%	km/ 1000km²	km	km/ 1000km²	million tons per km	million pass. per km	million tons per km	thousands
Afghanistan	34 782	23.7	53.3	..	..	..	..	7.8	150
Angola	51 429	10.4	41.3	2 761	2.2	..	..	68.1	240
Bangladesh	239 226	9.5	1 837.8	2 855	21.9	896	4340	183.5	1 635
Benin	19 000	9.5	171.8	578	5.2	86	66	..	..
Bhutan	8 050	62.0	171.3	..	..	..	..	0.3	49
Burkina Faso	15 272	31.2	55.8	622	2.3	..	..	..	66
Burundi	12 322	10.4	479.8	..	..	..	..	..	..
Cambodia	38 257	6.3	216.7	650	3.7	92	45	1.2	169
Cape Verde	1 350	69.0	335.0	..	..	..	..	1.5	690
Central African Republic	23 810	2.7	38.2	..	..	..	..	..	..
Chad	33 400	0.8	26.5	..	..	..	..	..	..
Comoros	880	76.5	473.1	..	..	..	..	..	..
Dem. Rep. of the Congo	153 497	1.8	67.7	3 641	1.6	444	140	7.4	95
Djibouti	2 890	12.6	124.7	781	33.7	97	82	..	..
Equatorial Guinea	2 880	..	102.7	..	..	..	..	..	..
Eritrea	4 010	21.8	39.7	306	3.0	..	..	..	..
Ethiopia	36 469	19.1	33.3	..	..	..	..	132.6	1 667
Gambia	3 742	19.3	331.2	..	..	..	..	..	..
Guinea	44 348	9.8	180.5	1 115	4.5	..	..	..	59
Guinea-Bissau	3 455	27.9	122.9	..	..	..	..	..	..
Haiti	4 160	24.3	150.9	..	..	..	..	..	..
Kiribati	670	..	917.8	..	..	..	..	..	28
Lao People's Dem. Rep.	31 210	14.4	135.2	..	..	..	..	2.5	293
Lesotho	5 940	18.3	195.7	..	..	..	..	..	..
Liberia	10 600	6.2	110.0	490	5.1	..	..	..	..
Madagascar	49 827	11.6	85.7	732	1.3	12	10	15.4	575
Malawi	15 451	45.0	164.2	710	7.5	87.9	25.03	1.4	132
Maldives	..	..	..	..	..	..	..	0.0	82
Mali	18 709	18.0	15.3	733	0.6	189	196	..	..
Mauritania	7 660	11.3	7.5	717	0.7	..	..	0.1	139
Mozambique	30 400	18.7	38.8	3 070	3.9	768	172	4.9	347
Myanmar	27 966	11.4	42.5	..	..	..	..	2.7	1 504
Nepal	17 380	30.3	121.5	59	0.4	..	..	6.9	480
Niger	14 565	25.0	11.5	..	..	..	..	..	..
Rwanda	14 008	19.0	567.8	..	..	..	..	..	..
Samoa	2 337	14.2	825.8	..	..	..	..	1.8	267
Sao Tome and Principe	320	68.1	333.3	..	..	..	..	0.1	43
Senegal	13 576	29.3	70.5	906	4.7	371	138	..	450
Sierra Leone	11 300	8.0	157.8	..	..	..	..	8.1	17
Solomon Islands	1 391	2.4	49.7	..	..	..	..	0.8	92
Somalia	22 100	11.8	35.2	..	..	..	..	..	..
Sudan	11 900	36.3	5.0	5478	2.3	766	40	43.1	511
Timor-Leste	..	..	..	..	..	..	..	..	..
Togo	7 520	31.6	138.3	568	10.4	..	..	..	..
Tuvalu	..	..	..	..	..	..	..	..	..
Uganda	70 746	23.0	358.9	259	1.3	218	..	28.6	49
United Rep. of Tanzania	78 891	8.6	89.3	2 600	2.9	1 196	628	2.4	263
Vanuatu	1 070	23.9	87.8	..	..	..	..	1.8	112
Yemen	65 144	15.5	123.4	..	..	..	..	66.8	1 083
Zambia	91 440	22.0	123.0	1 273	1.7	554	186	0.0	54

Source: World Bank, *World Development Indicators 2007*, online data, February 2008.

a or latest year available.

14. Indicators on energy and the environment

Country	Electrifi-cation rate (%)	Electricity consumption per capita (Kilowatt-hour)			Net installed electricity capacity (Kilowatt/1000 inhabitants)			Coal, oil, gas and electricity (Consumption per capita in kg of oil equivalent)			Carbon dioxide emissions per capita (Metric tons of carbon dioxide)		
	2005[a]	1990	2000	2005	1990	2000	2005	1990	2000	2004[b]	1990	2000	2005
Afghanistan	7.0	89	28	42	39	20	20	63	17	12	0.5	0.1	0.0
Angola	15.0	80	104	165	44	36	33	68	124	238	0.7	0.9	1.3
Bangladesh	32.0	71	113	148	22	26	28	55	80	108	0.1	0.2	0.3
Benin	22.0	43	63	83	5	7	7	33	74	100	0.1	0.2	0.3
Bhutan	..	314	752	794	645	627	549	35	235	65	0.2	0.5	0.5
Burkina Faso	7.0	21	27	30	8	7	6	20	29	28	0.1	0.1	0.1
Burundi	2.0	22	20	22	6	5	4	14	15	12	0.0	0.1	0.1
Cambodia	20.1	17	36	61	5	10	14	18	14	13	0.0	0.0	0.0
Cape Verde	..	118	324	468	51	104	158	82	102	219	0.3	0.4	0.6
Central African Republic	..	32	28	26	14	11	10	25	25	22	0.1	0.1	0.1
Chad	2.0	15	11	10	5	3	3	8	5	4	0.1	0.0	0.0
Comoros	29.0	30	27	25	9	7	6	41	40	46	0.1	0.1	0.1
Dem. Republic of the Congo	5.8	149	94	96	75	49	44	45	24	19	0.1	0.1	0.0
Djibouti	..	319	247	317	152	151	147	226	175	158	3.1	2.5	2.4
Equatorial Guinea	..	53	53	56	32	28	27	108	125	957	0.4	4.8	10.1
Eritrea	20.2	..	57	64	..	45	37	..	53	57	..	0.2	0.2
Ethiopia	15.0	23	24	36	9	7	7	22	17	27	0.1	0.0	0.1
Gambia	..	73	95	93	18	21	19	69	66	62	0.2	0.2	0.2
Guinea	16.0	86	94	89	31	24	23	60	50	46	0.2	0.2	0.1
Guinea-Bissau	..	39	42	38	11	15	13	70	61	65	0.3	0.3	0.2
Haiti	34.0	67	64	60	22	28	24	47	55	62	0.1	0.2	0.2
Kiribati	..	97	119	109	28	36	33	97	131	92	0.3	0.3	0.3
Lao People's Dem. Republic	..	71	90	129	53	54	81	23	65	65	0.1	0.2	0.2
Lesotho	11.0	..	..	..	..	..	..	..	..	..	0.1	0.1	0.1
Liberia	..	264	101	97	155	61	55	65	48	53	0.3	0.1	0.2
Madagascar	15.0	109	114	124	18	14	12	26	40	38	0.1	0.1	0.1
Malawi	7.0	76	92	96	20	13	14	26	27	34	0.1	0.1	0.1
Maldives	..	111	381	542	23	132	166	139	608	809	0.5	1.8	2.6
Mali	11.0	32	41	40	11	11	10	17	20	19	0.1	0.1	0.1
Mauritania	22.0	72	102	141	54	57	58	411	315	269	0.5	1.3	0.9
Mozambique	6.3	60	72	529	174	130	115	24	28	80	0.1	0.1	0.1
Myanmar	11.0	62	112	125	27	25	25	39	71	74	0.1	0.2	0.3
Nepal	33.0	40	72	87	14	24	23	13	45	42	0.0	0.1	0.1
Niger	7.0	45	41	35	8	9	8	43	34	32	0.1	0.1	0.1
Rwanda	6.0	25	25	27	5	5	4	27	24	22	0.1	0.1	0.1
Samoa	..	310	513	604	118	146	158	272	276	304	0.8	0.8	0.9
Sao Tome and Principe	..	129	128	124	52	36	33	193	221	174	0.6	0.7	0.6
Senegal	33.0	112	162	220	29	27	48	120	106	120	0.3	0.4	0.5
Sierra Leone	..	55	21	15	31	12	9	26	33	44	0.3	0.2	0.2
Solomon Islands	..	96	149	142	38	34	30	169	132	111	0.6	0.4	0.4
Somalia	..	39	35	35	10	9	7	..	..	..	0.1	0.1	0.1
Sudan	30.0	51	73	112	19	23	30	46	54	95	0.1	0.2	0.3
Timor-Leste	..	..	..	281	..	..	42	..	..	57	..	..	..
Togo	17.0	88	103	108	9	9	8	54	87	113	0.1	0.3	0.4
Tuvalu	..	..	..	..	..	..	..	..	..	..	..	..	..
Uganda	8.9	37	57	58	9	11	11	19	23	24	0.0	0.1	0.1
United Republic of Tanzania	11.0	64	75	82	20	13	14	28	27	39	0.1	0.1	0.1
Vanuatu	..	167	216	209	74	63	56	148	142	139	0.9	0.4	0.4
Yemen	36.2	67	188	225	43	48	52	..	201	261	0.9	0.5	0.8
Zambia	19.0	775	569	758	280	216	197	146	99	117	0.3	0.2	0.2
LDCs	..	**76**	**89**	**120**	**33**	**29**	**29**	**45**	**55**	**67**	**0.2**	**0.2**	**0.2**
All developing countries	**68.3**	**388**	**653**	**1304**	**88**	**160**	**295**	**498**	**575**	**718**	**1.5**	**1.9**	**2.4**

Source: OECD/IEA, *World Energy Outlook, 2006*; UNCTAD Secretariat calculations based on United Nations, *Energy Statistics Yearbook 1993, 2003, 2004*; UN, *Energy Statistics*, March 2008, and EIA, *International Energy Annual 2005*, October 2007.
   a   Or latest year available. b   Latest year available.

15. Status of women in LDCs

Country	Education, training and literacy: female-male gaps [a]				Health, fertility and mortality		Economic activity, employment				Political participation (% of total)	
	Adult literacy rate	School enrolment ratio			Fertility rate	Maternal mortality)	Labour force	Employees	Own account workers	Female labour force: Agriculture/ Total labour force	Women in governments	Women in parliaments
		Primary school net enrolment ratio	Secondary school net enrolment ratio	Tertiary gross enrolment ratio	Births per woman	Maternal deaths per 100 000 live births						
	2005[b]				2006	2005	2005	2004[b]	2004[b]	2005	2005	end-Dec. 2007
Afghanistan	29.2	..	..	27.9	7.2	1 800	37.8	..	..	82.7	..	27.7
Angola	65.4	..	..	65.5	6.5	1 400	47.7	..	..	81.9	5.7	15.0
Bangladesh	75.7	103.6	103.9	53.3	2.9	570	43.6	13.3	24.5	61.8	8.3	15.1
Benin	48.7	81.0	49.3	25.2	5.6	840	48.0	..	..	48.6	19.0	10.8
Bhutan	..	99.8	100.3	52.8	2.3	440	40.6	..	..	97.7	0	2.7
Burkina Faso	52.9	79.7	70.6	45.6	6.1	700	47.5	0.9	10.0	93.3	14.8	15.3
Burundi	77.6	90.8	..	37.6	6.8	1 100	50.9	..	..	97.4	10.7	30.5
Cambodia	75.6	98.7	84.2	46.8	3.3	540	53.7	13.6	32.9	72.1	7.1	19.5
Cape Verde	86.1	98.5	109.2	103.8	3.5	210	39.5	..	..	20.3	18.8	18.1
Central African Republic	51.7	..	..	18.7	4.7	980	46.7	..	..	75.4	10.0	10.5
Chad	31.3	69.8	33.2	..	6.3	1 500	46.6	..	..	81.0	11.5	5.2
Comoros	77.8	84.8	..	77.0	4.5	400	43.9	..	..	85.2	..	3.0
Dem. Rep. of the Congo	66.8	..	..	..	6.7	1 100	44.3	..	..	74.9	12.5	8.4
Djibouti	..	81.3	65.7	72.7	4.1	650	46.2	78.7	15.3	82.0	5.3	13.8
Equatorial Guinea	86.2	90.5	..	43.1	5.4	680	36.5	..	..	87.7	4.5	18.0
Eritrea	..	85.5	66.5	..	5.2	450	50.6	..	..	80.3	17.6	22.0
Ethiopia	45.6	91.7	64.7	32.2	5.4	720	42.9	45.9	43.2	77.1	5.9	21.9
Gambia	..	100.2	83.7	..	4.8	690	46.3	..	..	88.2	20.0	9.4
Guinea	42.6	84.1	53.5	23.8	5.6	910	46.8	..	..	86.5	15.4	19.3
Guinea-Bissau	..	70.8	55.4	..	7.1	1 100	42.1	..	..	94.9	37.5	14.0
Haiti	92.6	..	..	..	3.7	670	43.7	..	..	47.3	25.0	4.1
Kiribati	..	..	109.6	..	-	-	41.3	..	..	15.8	..	4.3
Lao People's Dem. Rep.	79.1	94.5	85.1	71.1	3.3	660	48.0	5.4	57.0	78.6	0	25.2
Lesotho	122.5	105.8	155.7	127.0	3.5	960	42.2	43.7	52.7	52.8	27.8	23.5
Liberia	78.5	77.7	57.3	76.0	6.8	1 200	40.8	..	..	73.0	..	12.5
Madagascar	85.8	99.7	..	88.9	4.9	510	45.9	12.0	33.7	80.0	5.9	7.9
Malawi	72.0	105.0	88.7	..	5.7	1 100	49.2	4.8	93.0	94.4	14.3	13.0
Maldives	100.2	100.2	109.5	..	2.6	120	45.0	28.8	35.1	15.9	11.8	12.0
Mali	48.6	77.8	..	45.3	6.6	970	47.2	..	..	78.5	18.5	10.2
Mauritania	72.9	105.5	89.1	34.4	4.5	820	45.0	..	..	62.5	9.1	22.1
Mozambique	50.0	90.7	78.3	49.4	5.2	520	51.3	..	..	94.5	13.0	34.8
Myanmar	92.0	102.0	98.8	177.4	2.1	380	44.4	..	..	72.0	..	..
Nepal	55.6	87.5	..	40.3	3.4	830	43.1	..	..	97.8	7.4	17.3
Niger	35.1	72.5	66.2	33.9	7.3	1 800	44.0	..	..	97.2	23.1	12.4
Rwanda	83.7	104.5	..	61.6	6	1 300	51.2	3.3	65.5	96.6	35.7	48.8
Samoa	99.4	100.5	113.7	93.3	4.1	-	34.8	..	..	30.4	7.7	8.2
Sao Tome and Principe	84.5	98.1	110.7	..	4	-	45.1	..	..	71.9	14.3	1.8
Senegal	57.3	96.1	75.1	..	4.9	980	45.5	..	..	79.6	20.6	22.0
Sierra Leone	51.8	..	..	40.1	6.5	2 100	38.5	..	..	74.7	13.0	13.2
Solomon Islands	..	96.9	86.7	..	4	220	47.5	..	..	82.8	0	0.0
Somalia	..	..	..	..	6.2	1 400	44.7	..	..	80.0	..	8.2
Sudan	72.8	82.9	..	92.0	4.4	450	31.5	..	..	70.8	2.6	18.1
Timor-Leste	..	95.8	..	126.3	6.7	380	46.4	..	..	89.6	22.2	29.2
Togo	56.0	85.8	48.0	20.2	5	510	41.4	..	..	59.5	20.0	11.1
Tuvalu	..	..	..	..	-	-	50.0	..	..	0.0	..	0.0
Uganda	75.1	..	89.8	62.5	6.6	550	48.7	7.5	51.9	80.7	23.4	30.7
United Republic of Tanzania	80.2	98.2	..	47.9	5.3	950	49.6	4.0	...	86.1	15.4	30.4
Vanuatu	..	99.1	86.7	59.4	3.9	-	46.2	..	..	34.9	8.3	3.8
Yemen	47.4	72.7	45.5	37.1	5.6	430	29.6	13.8	23.6	70.2	2.9	0.3
Zambia	78.9	101.9	79.9	46.3	5.3	830	43.8	..	..	72.3	25.0	15.2
LDCs	..	..	..	..	4.7	870	43.3	..	..	76.3	..	16.9

Source: UNESCO, Institute for Statistics (UIS), online data, February 2008; UNICEF, The State of the World's Children 2008; Maternal Mortality Estimates developed by WHO, UNICEF and UNFPA and the World Bank, Maternal Mortality in 2005; IPU database, February 2008.

a Females as percentage of males; b Or latest year available.

16. LDCs refugees population by country or territory of asylum or residence, end-2006

Country[a]	Refugees Population[b]		Asylum seekers[c]	Returned refugees[d]	Internally displaced[e]	Returned IDPs[f]	Stateless persons[g]	Others[h]	Total
	begin year	end year							
Afghanistan	32	35	5	387 917	129 310	10 443	0	0	527 710
Angola	13 984	13 090	1 588	47 017	0	0	0	0	61 695
Bangladesh	21 098	26 311	79	0	0	0	300 000	0	326 390
Benin	30 294	10 797	1 349	0	0	0	0	0	12 146
Bhutan	-	-	-	-	-	-	-	-	-
Burkina Faso	511	511	756	0	0	0	0	0	1 267
Burundi	20 681	13 176	7 137	48 144	13 850	0	0	0	82 307
Cambodia	127	99	127	9	0	0	0	60	295
Cape Verde	-	-	-	-	-	-	-	-	-
Central African Republic	24 569	12 357	1 907	51	147 000	0	0	0	161 315
Chad	275 412	286 743	8	20	112 686	0	0	0	399 457
Comoros	1	1	0	1	0	0	0	0	2
Dem. Rep. of the Congo	204 341	208 371	94	41 228	1 075 297	490 000	0	0	1 814 990
Djibouti	10 456	9 259	19	0	0	0	0	0	9 278
Equatorial Guinea	-	-	0	0	0	0	0	0	0
Eritrea	4 418	4 621	2 004	0	0	0	0	32	6 657
Ethiopia	100 817	96 980	323	23	0	0	0	0	97 326
Gambia	7 331	13 761	602	0	0	0	0	0	14 363
Guinea	63 525	31 468	3 887	1	0	0	0	0	35 356
Guinea-Bissau	7 616	7 804	317	0	0	0	0	0	8 121
Haiti	-	-	0	1	0	0	0	0	1
Kiribati	-	-	-	-	-	-	-	-	-
Lao People's Dem. Rep.	-	-	0	0	0	0	0	0	0
Lesotho	0	0	0	0	0	0	0	0	0
Liberia	10 168	16 185	53	107 954	0	237 822	0	8	362 022
Madagascar	-	-	0	0	0	0	0	0	0
Malawi	4 240	3 943	5 245	0	0	0	0	0	9 188
Maldives	-	-	-	-	-	-	-	-	-
Mali	11 233	10 585	1 884	0	0	0	0	0	12 469
Mauritania	632	770	91	1	0	0	0	29 500	30 362
Mozambique	1 954	2 558	4 316	0	0	0	0	0	6 874
Myanmar	-	-	0	0	58 500	0	669 500	0	728 000
Nepal	126 436	128 175	1 481	0	100 000	0	3 400 000	10 387	3 640 043
Niger	301	317	20	0	0	0	0	0	337
Rwanda	45 206	49 192	3 945	5 971	0	0	0	0	59 108
Samoa	-	-	-	-	-	-	-	-	-
Sao Tome and Principe	-	-	-	-	-	-	-	-	-
Senegal	20 712	20 591	2 634	1	0	0	0	0	23 226
Sierra Leone	59 965	27 365	228	134	0	0	0	0	27 727
Solomon Islands	-	-	-	-	-	-	-	-	-
Somalia	558	669	1 221	1 845	400 000	0	0	0	403 735
Sudan	147 256	196 200	4 460	42 258	1 325 235	11 955	0	42 114	1 622 222
Timor-Leste	3	3	3	0	155 231	11 727	0	0	166 964
Togo	9 287	6 328	442	7 917	0	3 000	0	0	17 687
Tuvalu	-	-	-	-	-	-	-	-	-
Uganda	257 256	272 007	5 812	5 035	1 586 174	300 000	0	0	2 169 028
United Rep. of Tanzania	548 824	485 295	380	4	0	0	0	0	485 679
Vanuatu	-	-	-	-	-	-	-	-	-
Yemen	81 937	95 794	859	2	0	0	0	0	96 655
Zambia	155 718	120 253	215	0	0	0	0	0	120 468

Source: UNHCR, *Global Refugee Trends 2006*.

Note: The data are generally provided by Governments, based on their own definitions and methods of data collection.

   a Country of asylum or residence.

   b Persons recognized as refugees under the 1951 UN convention/1967 Protocol, the 1969 OAU Convention, in accordance with the UNHCR Statute, persons granted a complementary form of protection and those granted temporary protection.

   c Persons whose application for asylum or refugee status is pending at any stage in the procedure or who are otherwise registered as asylum-seekers.

   d Refugees who have returned to their place of origin during the year.

   e Persons who are displaced within their country and to whom UNHCR extends protection and/or assistance.

   f Internally Displaced Persons protected /assisted by UNHCR who have returned to their place of origin during the year.

   g Persons who are not considered nationals by any State under the operation of its laws.

   h Persons of concern to UNHCR not included in the previous columns.

	17. Leading exports of the LDCs, 2004–2006				
SITC Rev.3	Item	Value ($ millions)	As percentage of:		
			LDCs total exports	Developing countries	World
	Total all commodities	77 229	100.00	2.06	0.74
333	Petroleum oils, crude and crude oils obtained from bituminous minerals	30 375	39.33	5.87	4.22
334	Petroleum products, refined	5 954	7.71	2.55	1.39
845	Articles of apparel, of textile fabrics	4 546	5.89	7.31	4.83
841	Men's or boy's clothing of textile fabrics, not knitted	3 124	4.04	9.43	6.03
343	Natural gas, whether or not liquefied	1 989	2.58	4.02	1.31
971	Gold, non-monetary (excluding gold ores & concentrates)	1 769	2.29	7.32	3.86
682	Copper	1 757	2.28	4.95	2.35
842	Women's clothing, of textile fabrics, not knitted	1 692	2.19	3.99	2.56
667	Pearls, precious & semi-precious stones	1 554	2.01	4.55	1.74
844	Women's clothing, of textile, knitted or crocheted	1 390	1.80	6.82	5.01
843	Men's or boy's clothing, of textile, knitted or crocheted	1 329	1.72	10.69	8.51
263	Cotton	1 298	1.68	32.76	11.77
684	Aluminium	1 130	1.46	5.59	1.38
034	Fish, fresh (live or dead), chilled or frozen	978	1.27	7.30	2.90
036	Crustaceans, mollusks and aquatic invertebrates	937	1.21	7.65	4.71
247	Wood in the rough or roughly squared	785	1.02	31.48	7.55
071	Coffee and coffee substitutes	747	0.97	7.72	4.88
054	Vegetables	638	0.83	5.70	1.93
121	Tobacco, unmanufactured	585	0.76	14.18	8.37
285	Aluminium ores and concentrates	506	0.66	13.70	4.68

Source: UNCTAD secretariat estimates and calculations based on United Nations Statistics Division, COMTRADE database, March 2008.

18. Total merchandise exports: Levels and annual average growth rates

Country	Total merchandise exports ($ million)					Annual average growth rates (%)				
	1995	2000	2004	2005	2006	1995–2000	2000–2006	2004	2005	2006
Afghanistan	107.1	140.1	159.3	199.8	179.6	4.1	18.0	-8.5	25.4	-10.1
Angola	3 723.0	7 702.0	12 974.0	23 213.0	33 795.0	10.4	41.1	40.5	78.9	45.6
Bangladesh	3 407.2	5 493.2	8 267.5	9 427.0	11 962.6	8.7	18.4	29.1	14.0	26.9
Benin	332.8	188.4	298.3	288.2	283.1	-12.9	6.3	9.9	-3.4	-1.8
Bhutan	103.0	103.0	154.0	217.2	348.2	1.0	25.9	15.8	41.0	60.3
Burkina Faso	170.9	184.0	393.5	384.1	482.9	2.9	24.7	23.2	-2.4	25.7
Burundi	178.9	42.8	82.7	117.1	120.1	-19.8	32.8	25.5	41.6	2.6
Cambodia	301.8	1 389.5	2 797.5	3 144.4	3 990.5	41.7	20.9	32.1	12.4	26.9
Cape Verde	31.5	49.3	15.2	89.4	110.3	5.2	70.7	21.9	488.4	23.3
Central African Republic	119.5	79.3	101.0	116.4	144.3	-5.9	16.3	53.8	15.2	24.0
Chad	116.2	89.4	1 258.1	1 961.8	2 274.7	-4.4	135.0	1 293.3	55.9	16.0
Comoros	11.0	6.9	14.0	9.0	7.5	-9.7	-6.6	16.6	-35.5	-17.4
Democratic Rep. of the Congo	1 563.0	824.1	1 850.1	2 190.2	2 300.2	-13.7	22.0	34.6	18.4	5.0
Djibouti	14.0	13.0	13.0	13.5	18.9	-2.1	5.8	0.0	4.0	39.7
Equatorial Guinea	86.0	1 097.0	1 889.0	2 933.4	3 804.3	61.6	29.4	31.5	55.3	29.7
Eritrea	73.0	18.8	11.0	10.6	11.2	-28.0	-17.9	66.4	-4.2	5.6
Ethiopia	421.9	482.0	614.7	926.2	1 043.0	2.6	23.4	19.9	50.7	12.6
Gambia	18.7	16.2	18.1	5.1	11.5	0.7	15.7	256.3	-71.8	125.0
Guinea	701.9	522.4	787.0	965.4	976.2	-7.9	13.7	3.0	22.7	1.1
Guinea-Bissau	44.0	62.0	80.0	94.6	83.9	8.7	9.8	15.9	18.2	-11.3
Haiti	35.0	313.0	394.0	473.4	522.6	68.4	15.1	13.9	20.2	10.4
Kiribati	7.2	12.0	18.0	3.6	6.3	13.0	-17.5	38.5	-80.1	77.3
Lao People's Dem. Republic	311.0	330.0	361.1	549.6	876.5	0.6	21.0	-4.5	52.2	59.5
Lesotho	-	336.2	657.0	609.1	671.9	-	19.7	36.9	-7.3	10.3
Liberia	864.7	691.5	1 011.7	1 436.6	1 490.2	-7.0	12.1	15.6	42.0	3.7
Madagascar	359.9	861.9	971.2	835.9	1 008.2	10.3	2.8	-0.8	-13.9	20.6
Malawi	433.3	379.3	458.7	495.5	668.4	-2.8	8.0	-8.7	8.0	34.9
Maldives	49.8	76.2	169.7	154.2	135.6	7.1	14.9	50.3	-9.2	-12.0
Mali	443.0	472.7	987.5	1 147.6	1 476.6	3.9	13.8	-2.0	16.2	28.7
Mauritania	509.3	342.8	435.2	556.4	1 258.7	-7.5	27.2	35.7	27.8	126.2
Mozambique	174.3	364.0	1 503.8	1 783.0	2 381.1	12.9	28.7	44.1	18.6	33.5
Myanmar	860.0	1 647.1	2 572.1	4 121.3	4 863.3	14.3	13.8	3.5	60.2	18.0
Nepal	359.2	708.8	756.0	829.7	759.7	13.7	4.2	15.8	9.7	-8.4
Niger	273.4	330.4	278.9	347.7	355.7	0.4	13.7	22.3	24.7	2.3
Rwanda	52.0	52.0	98.0	125.3	135.4	15.2	26.1	94.6	27.8	8.1
Samoa	9.0	14.0	85.4	84.9	84.9	13.0	5.9	-1.9	-0.6	0.0
Sao Tome and Principe	5.0	2.8	3.6	3.4	3.9	-14.5	0.5	-46.4	-3.9	13.4
Senegal	530.8	693.0	1 315.4	1 470.8	1 491.6	6.4	17.4	13.9	11.8	1.4
Sierra Leone	42.0	13.0	139.0	159.0	216.6	-30.9	51.3	51.1	14.4	36.3
Solomon Islands	168.0	65.0	74.0	80.1	91.5	-15.4	32.3	-3.9	8.2	14.3
Somalia	148.7	121.2	87.1	181.0	160.8	-4.8	8.7	-41.1	107.7	-11.1
Sudan	685.2	1 631.0	3 612.0	4 505.8	5 478.7	11.5	26.9	45.6	24.7	21.6
Timor-Leste	34.0	16.0	53.4	78.5	114.1	-9.1	38.5	84.1	47.1	45.3
Togo	382.8	191.7	408.3	359.9	359.7	-10.1	10.0	-17.4	-11.9	-0.1
Tuvalu	1.1	1.0	1.9	1.2	3.5	-2.6	15.1	-24.9	-37.3	194.4
Uganda	575.3	402.8	653.5	812.8	962.2	-7.1	17.6	22.9	24.4	18.4
United Republic of Tanzania	685.0	655.8	1 329.8	1 544.5	1 689.9	-2.2	17.9	17.5	16.1	9.4
Vanuatu	28.0	23.2	37.0	38.0	44.9	-3.9	21.1	37.1	2.6	18.3
Yemen	1 917.5	4 077.8	4 050.8	5 608.9	6 264.0	7.2	16.7	8.5	38.5	11.7
Zambia	1 055.0	892.4	1 575.6	1 809.8	3 770.4	-1.4	29.6	60.7	14.9	108.3
LDCs	**22 525.5**	**34 221.8**	**55 878.0**	**76 513.6**	**99 294.7**	**51.9**	**33.3**	**28.4**	**36.9**	**29.8**
African LDCs and Haiti	*14 813.8*	*20 066.0*	*36 287.5*	*51 873.6*	*69 447.8*	*35.5*	*38.3*	*34.0*	*43.0*	*33.9*
Asian LDCs	*7 367.0*	*13 889.4*	*19 118.3*	*24 097.7*	*29 244.4*	*88.5*	*23.7*	*18.9*	*26.0*	*21.4*
Island LDCs	*344.7*	*266.4*	*472.2*	*542.3*	*602.5*	*-22.7*	*13.0*	*24.4*	*14.8*	*11.1*
Other developing countries	**1 395 076.8**	**1 989 475.9**	**2 989 516.8**	**3 643 340.4**	**4 370 213.2**	**5.7**	**19.9**	**26.4**	**21.9**	**20.0**
All developing countries	**1 417 602.3**	**2 023 697.7**	**3 045 394.8**	**3 719 854.0**	**4 469 507.9**	**5.8**	**20.0**	**26.4**	**22.1**	**20.2**

Source: UNCTAD secretariat estimates based on United Nations Statistics Division, COMTRADE database, March 2008.

19. Total merchandise imports: Levels and annual average growth rates									
Country	Total merchandise imports ($ million)					Annual average growth rates (%)				
	1995	2000	2004	2005	2006	1995–2000	2000–2006	2004	2005	2006
Afghanistan	464.0	796.2	2 088.4	3 909.3	4 130.9	5.4	42.8	10.6	87.2	5.7
Angola	1 468.1	3 040.2	3 573.2	5 118.0	6 908.9	14.3	16.3	4.9	43.2	35.0
Bangladesh	5 438.4	7 611.3	11 372.7	13 107.9	15 279.4	6.9	13.3	12.1	15.3	16.6
Benin	719.0	547.1	893.8	898.7	1 011.3	-3.0	9.7	0.2	0.5	12.5
Bhutan	113.0	175.0	304.0	285.8	310.4	9.7	11.3	22.1	-6.0	8.6
Burkina Faso	483.8	724.5	1 264.0	1 392.1	1 419.1	9.0	24.4	33.8	10.1	1.9
Burundi	270.5	150.2	172.7	257.0	414.4	-7.7	24.7	19.4	48.8	61.2
Cambodia	218.0	1 438.8	2 062.7	2 478.0	2 996.2	51.2	14.6	16.2	20.1	20.9
Cape Verde	326.8	237.3	429.2	438.2	538.2	-6.7	16.3	21.0	2.1	22.8
Central African Republic	265.5	70.5	159.0	186.4	198.7	-21.4	27.8	59.6	17.2	6.6
Chad	179.7	136.3	358.3	420.9	456.4	-6.5	4.0	2.4	17.5	8.4
Comoros	62.4	71.9	76.1	87.8	102.5	4.6	14.8	24.5	15.4	16.8
Dem. Rep. of the Congo	871.1	697.1	1 986.1	2 269.6	2 799.5	-7.4	28.1	24.6	14.3	23.3
Djibouti	177.0	156.1	168.0	178.3	215.8	-2.9	5.4	1.8	6.1	21.1
Equatorial Guinea	50.1	451.1	844.0	1 136.2	1 098.7	41.2	22.1	34.8	34.6	-3.3
Eritrea	434.0	327.8	472.1	486.8	552.7	-5.7	3.3	9.1	3.1	13.5
Ethiopia	1 141.0	1 260.4	2 873.8	4 094.8	5 207.3	2.1	26.3	7.0	42.5	27.2
Gambia	214.5	189.4	236.7	259.6	259.3	-2.9	16.2	45.6	9.7	-0.1
Guinea	818.5	612.4	619.2	735.9	807.7	-5.7	5.3	2.8	18.8	9.8
Guinea-Bissau	56.8	49.1	82.0	104.5	91.4	-7.2	11.5	18.8	27.4	-12.5
Haiti	654.1	1 040.1	1 317.0	1 466.0	1 637.3	11.6	9.8	10.9	11.3	11.7
Kiribati	34.1	39.1	57.0	74.0	61.4	2.1	17.3	21.3	29.8	-17.0
Lao People's Dem. Republic	589.0	535.1	506.1	626.2	752.3	-4.3	8.5	-3.4	23.7	20.1
Lesotho	-	613.3	1 431.1	1 469.5	1 535.3	-	21.7	40.2	2.7	4.5
Liberia	5 592.7	5 416.1	4 263.7	4 933.4	6 446.3	1.1	8.2	8.1	15.7	30.7
Madagascar	549.5	990.7	1 651.9	1 685.9	1 760.3	7.1	20.6	25.3	2.1	4.4
Malawi	500.4	532.1	928.7	1 165.2	1 209.2	2.1	17.2	18.2	25.5	3.8
Maldives	267.9	388.6	641.8	744.9	926.5	8.1	20.7	36.3	16.1	24.4
Mali	774.1	806.4	1 364.4	1 703.3	1 990.3	1.6	16.7	7.3	24.8	16.8
Mauritania	455.2	353.6	1 340.0	1 342.0	1 073.3	-2.9	35.0	246.8	0.2	-20.0
Mozambique	727.0	1 161.6	2 034.7	2 408.2	2 869.3	10.8	20.6	28.8	18.4	19.1
Myanmar	1 348.1	2 401.1	2 254.2	1 977.5	2 155.2	14.5	-5.2	7.8	-12.3	9.0
Nepal	1 292.0	1 557.9	1 870.1	1 859.0	2 098.9	-	7.7	3.8	-0.6	12.9
Niger	344.6	384.6	667.2	735.6	688.0	2.8	14.3	19.1	10.3	-6.5
Rwanda	241.1	211.1	284.0	402.5	496.4	-1.2	13.5	8.8	41.7	23.3
Samoa	95.0	106.1	209.8	238.9	275.0	2.8	17.4	39.5	13.9	15.1
Sao Tome and Principe	29.0	29.8	41.4	49.9	71.1	5.2	18.7	1.5	20.3	42.7
Senegal	1 224.5	1 552.8	2 839.1	3 497.7	3 671.0	0.7	17.3	18.4	23.2	5.0
Sierra Leone	134.1	149.0	286.1	344.3	388.9	-6.5	11.0	-5.6	20.3	13.0
Solomon Islands	154.1	98.0	100.0	151.7	165.3	-9.4	18.2	21.9	51.6	8.9
Somalia	154.5	324.4	284.4	571.5	602.2	17.0	14.9	-28.7	101.0	5.4
Sudan	1 184.9	1 657.4	4 034.8	7 366.8	8 844.5	4.9	37.4	39.2	82.6	20.1
Timor-Leste	112.0	126.0	113.5	101.6	104.6	-2.5	-11.6	-48.7	-10.5	2.9
Togo	556.3	323.6	557.8	592.6	637.4	-7.2	12.3	-1.9	6.2	7.6
Tuvalu	5.2	7.1	16.7	29.0	39.0	9.5	31.6	-3.5	73.5	34.4
Uganda	1 037.6	953.9	1 720.2	2 054.1	2 557.3	0.3	21.6	25.1	19.4	24.5
United Republic of Tanzania	1 653.0	1 586.4	2 551.9	3 274.7	4 439.5	2.2	21.7	17.9	28.3	35.6
Vanuatu	95.0	86.7	128.1	149.4	159.7	-1.3	14.7	21.9	16.7	6.8
Yemen	1 816.7	2 326.5	3 734.0	4 862.7	4 935.1	2.1	15.4	1.6	30.2	1.5
Zambia	708.2	888.0	2 152.1	2 558.0	3 074.3	3.8	25.9	36.7	18.9	20.2
LDCs	**36 102.2**	**45 389.6**	**69 418.1**	**86 282.2**	**100 463.7**	**4.5**	**17.1**	**15.9**	**24.3**	**16.4**
African LDCs and Haiti	*23 641.5*	*27 357.1*	*43 412.2*	*55 110.1*	*65 361.9*	*3.0*	*19.4*	*20.0*	*26.9*	*18.6*
Asian LDCs	*11 279.3*	*16 842.0*	*24 192.1*	*29 106.5*	*32 658.4*	*7.7*	*13.2*	*9.2*	*20.3*	*12.2*
Island LDCs	*1 181.5*	*1 190.5*	*1 813.8*	*2 065.5*	*2 443.4*	*-0.1*	*15.4*	*17.0*	*13.9*	*18.3*
Other developing countries	**1 443 381**	**1 810 939**	**2 745 002**	**3 259 438**	**3 794 455**	**2.8**	**18.3**	**26.8**	**18.7**	**16.4**
All developing countries	**1 479 483**	**1 856 328**	**2 814 421**	**3 345 720**	**3 894 919**	**2.8**	**18.3**	**26.5**	**18.9**	**16.4**

Source: UNCTAD secretariat estimates based on United Nations Statistics Division, COMTRADE database, March 2008.

20. Main markets for exports of LDCs: Percentage share in 2006

Country	Developed economies					Econo-mies in transition	Developing countries						Other Developing economies	Un-allocated
	Total	EU 25	Japan	USA and Canada	Other developed countries		Total	China	India	Major petro-leum exporters	Newly industrialized economies: 1st tier	2nd tier		
Afghanistan	35.8	20.2	0.2	14.9	0.6	6.6	57.6	0.1	22.0	4.5	1.6	0.1	29.4	0.0
Angola	50.7	8.5	1.9	39.9	0.4	0.0	49.3	34.2	0.0	0.5	6.8	0.4	7.4	0.0
Bangladesh	78.0	46.7	1.1	28.7	1.4	0.5	9.1	0.7	1.2	1.3	2.3	0.8	2.9	12.4
Benin	21.1	20.9	0.0	0.1	0.0	0.1	78.9	20.9	7.0	7.2	0.8	10.6	32.5	0.0
Burkina Faso	10.7	8.4	2.0	0.2	0.1	0.0	85.9	41.9	1.1	1.6	16.3	7.1	17.9	3.4
Burundi	51.2	16.1	0.5	0.9	33.7	1.1	26.8	..	0.0	2.1	1.2	..	23.6	20.8
Cambodia	76.3	18.2	1.0	56.6	0.6	0.2	23.4	0.4	0.0	0.1	19.4	0.7	2.8	0.1
Cape Verde	93.1	85.6	..	2.6	2.6	0.0	6.6	..	0.0	0.4	0.1	0.1	6.1	0.2
Central African Rep.	67.4	62.4	1.3	3.6	0.1	0.0	32.5	6.9	0.3	2.9	0.4	8.0	14.0	0.0
Chad	83.0	1.8	0.5	80.6	0.2	0.0	16.9	10.4	0.0	0.0	4.6	1.3	0.6	0.0
Comoros	77.0	71.7	0.2	4.9	0.2	0.5	21.1	..	3.1	3.2	8.3	0.1	6.4	1.4
Dem. Rep. of the Congo	50.8	45.7	0.1	5.0	0.0	0.1	48.8	21.1	0.5	0.4	0.0	0.2	26.5	0.3
Djibouti	3.4	2.4	..	0.9	0.1	..	96.6	0.1	1.1	6.5	0.5	0.1	88.3	0.0
Equatorial Guinea	56.1	26.5	3.9	25.0	0.7	0.0	43.9	30.9	0.0	0.0	10.6	0.0	2.3	0.0
Ethiopia	49.9	30.6	7.8	7.7	3.8	0.6	34.9	11.0	1.0	10.9	0.5	0.6	10.9	14.6
Gambia	38.7	35.3	1.8	0.7	0.3	0.6	60.7	1.1	38.5	0.0	0.6	13.1	7.4	0.0
Guinea	41.8	31.7	0.0	10.0	0.1	27.4	14.4	0.8	1.9	0.0	9.2	0.1	2.3	16.4
Guinea-Bissau	3.0	2.6	0.0	0.3	..	0.0	97.0	..	76.1	18.1	0.9	0.1	1.9	0.0
Haiti	87.4	3.6	0.2	83.0	0.6	0.0	12.4	0.2	0.1	0.9	0.8	0.3	10.1	0.2
Lao People's Dem. Rep.	15.4	10.6	1.0	1.2	2.6	0.1	63.7	4.1	0.0	0.1	4.5	45.1	9.9	20.8
Liberia	71.2	56.0	0.8	12.4	1.6	0.6	28.2	0.1	1.6	0.2	4.1	4.8	17.3	0.0
Madagascar	86.9	57.1	2.6	26.6	0.5	0.1	10.1	2.1	1.5	0.3	2.7	0.4	3.1	2.9
Malawi	43.4	28.3	3.1	9.7	2.3	7.8	48.2	0.1	0.5	1.3	1.1	1.6	43.6	0.6
Maldives	42.5	30.2	10.3	1.5	0.4	0.0	57.5	0.3	0.7	6.2	2.6	33.6	14.2	0.0
Mali	20.4	11.9	0.1	2.6	5.8	0.1	74.3	35.2	2.0	0.6	7.1	12.1	17.4	5.2
Mauritania	53.9	44.3	5.4	3.5	0.7	3.7	41.1	26.3	0.1	3.1	0.2	0.0	11.4	1.3
Mozambique	68.9	66.1	0.3	0.3	2.2	0.4	24.9	1.4	1.3	0.2	0.2	1.1	20.8	5.8
Myanmar	13.2	7.4	5.2	0.2	0.4	0.1	79.6	5.2	12.7	0.7	4.5	51.8	4.7	7.1
Nepal	26.7	12.1	1.0	12.7	0.9	0.1	70.8	0.2	67.9	0.3	0.9	0.1	1.4	2.4
Niger	64.2	35.4	0.0	27.0	1.7	11.3	24.5	0.2	0.2	18.6	0.5	0.1	4.8	0.0
Rwanda	28.3	23.6	0.0	4.4	0.3	2.1	21.0	10.3	0.1	0.8	0.2	2.2	7.4	48.6
Samoa	50.3	0.8	0.7	3.4	45.4	..	44.5	0.0	0.0	0.2	11.4	0.5	32.4	5.1
Sao Tome and Principe	87.2	84.0	0.4	2.5	0.3	0.1	12.6	..	0.2	2.9	0.7	2.2	6.7	0.0
Senegal	28.5	23.5	1.0	0.5	3.4	0.0	54.9	0.7	5.8	3.7	0.9	0.2	43.6	16.6
Sierra Leone	89.3	67.5	0.4	19.9	1.5	0.5	6.9	0.4	1.7	0.4	0.8	0.3	3.2	3.2
Solomon Islands	17.7	5.6	8.9	1.2	2.0	..	73.0	48.0	1.0	0.1	11.0	10.1	2.7	9.3
Somalia	1.0	0.7	0.2	0.1	0.0	0.0	98.9	0.9	4.0	88.2	0.2	1.0	4.6	0.0
Sudan	52.3	2.3	48.0	1.2	0.8	0.1	47.3	31.0	0.7	5.5	4.2	0.9	5.1	0.3
Togo	26.4	23.8	0.0	0.9	1.6	0.4	71.9	3.5	4.6	3.7	1.6	2.6	55.9	1.3
Uganda	53.6	48.0	0.9	3.5	1.2	1.4	35.9	2.3	0.6	8.7	1.9	1.8	20.5	9.1
United Rep. of Tanzania	40.7	23.9	5.3	4.5	4.8	1.9	49.3	8.8	8.8	5.4	2.7	3.8	19.8	8.1
Vanuatu	17.0	3.4	11.4	1.0	1.2	0.1	82.6	0.4	16.7	0.2	1.1	60.4	3.8	0.3
Yemen	14.2	2.4	3.5	6.7	1.5	0.0	85.2	31.4	17.4	9.8	7.6	17.4	1.6	0.5
Zambia	52.3	12.7	0.6	0.5	38.5	0.1	47.6	10.3	0.5	0.0	0.5	0.0	36.3	0.0
LDCs	**51.6**	**20.1**	**4.8**	**24.1**	**2.5**	**0.7**	**44.2**	**19.2**	**3.2**	**2.2**	**5.5**	**4.9**	**9.1**	**3.5**
African LDCs and Haiti	*52.5*	*18.0*	*5.9*	*25.5*	*3.0*	*0.9*	*44.8*	*24.2*	*0.9*	*1.9*	*5.3*	*0.8*	*11.7*	*1.7*
Asian LDCs	*49.9*	*25.1*	*2.2*	*21.4*	*1.2*	*0.3*	*42.4*	*8.2*	*8.4*	*2.9*	*5.9*	*13.7*	*3.4*	*7.4*
Island LDCs	*33.5*	*15.8*	*7.8*	*1.7*	*8.1*	*0.0*	*62.9*	*13.4*	*5.3*	*1.5*	*5.9*	*26.6*	*10.1*	*3.5*
Other developing countries	**50.4**	**17.5**	**8.2**	**22.2**	**2.4**	**1.8**	**45.9**	**9.5**	**1.4**	**4.5**	**14.7**	**5.7**	**10.1**	**1.9**
All developing countries	**50.4**	**17.5**	**8.2**	**22.3**	**2.4**	**1.7**	**45.9**	**9.7**	**1.4**	**4.4**	**14.5**	**5.7**	**10.1**	**2.0**

Source: UNCTAD, *Handbook of Statistics 2007* and UNCTAD secretariat estimates, based on data from IMF, *Direction of Trade Statistics, online data, March 2008.*

21. Main sources of imports of LDCs: Percentage share in 2006

Country	Developed economies					Econo-mies in transition	Developing countries				Newly industrialized economies:		Other Developing economies	Un-allocated
	Total	EU 25	Japan	USA and Canada	Other developed countries		Total	China	India	Major petroleum exporters	1st tier	2nd tier		
Afghanistan	29.9	15.0	1.9	12.1	0.8	13.9	56.3	2.9	5.1	1.2	2.2	2.1	42.8	0.0
Angola	57.5	37.6	1.8	15.8	2.3	0.9	41.4	8.8	1.6	0.2	11.4	1.3	18.1	0.2
Bangladesh	16.7	8.3	3.7	2.8	1.8	3.5	71.3	17.7	12.5	12.6	16.1	7.1	5.2	8.4
Benin	53.4	42.2	1.1	9.0	1.1	0.1	46.5	6.0	0.7	4.7	5.8	5.3	24.0	0.0
Burkina Faso	34.6	32.0	0.6	1.6	0.4	1.8	57.5	1.5	1.9	3.3	0.9	0.8	49.2	6.0
Burundi	29.4	18.4	7.8	2.9	0.3	4.7	43.4	4.4	3.4	12.7	0.2	..	22.7	22.5
Cambodia	10.0	4.1	4.3	0.9	0.7	0.1	89.6	17.5	0.9	0.2	41.0	20.0	10.0	0.2
Cape Verde	75.7	73.2	..	2.4	0.2	0.2	19.9	1.7	0.1	4.6	0.2	0.3	13.1	4.2
Central African Republic	50.5	40.2	0.3	9.3	0.6	0.1	22.7	0.6	0.6	0.7	0.1	0.4	20.2	26.8
Chad	59.0	40.6	0.2	14.8	3.4	2.6	38.4	3.0	1.0	10.6	0.4	0.3	23.1	0.0
Comoros	39.7	37.6	1.4	0.5	0.2	2.0	56.7	4.8	4.4	11.5	2.8	3.0	30.1	1.7
Dem. Rep. of the Congo	44.9	37.5	1.2	4.7	1.4	0.2	54.6	3.6	0.4	1.4	1.1	0.6	47.5	0.2
Djibouti	21.3	14.4	3.2	3.6	0.2	1.2	73.8	11.0	17.9	25.7	3.4	7.1	8.6	3.7
Equatorial Guinea	73.8	33.7	1.1	37.9	1.1	0.8	25.3	2.8	0.5	0.3	6.3	3.9	11.5	0.0
Ethiopia	28.3	20.3	3.1	4.0	1.0	1.9	52.2	11.4	8.1	20.3	1.5	1.5	9.3	17.6
Gambia	25.1	20.7	0.7	3.4	0.3	0.6	74.3	25.2	3.2	3.0	2.2	4.4	36.3	0.0
Guinea	33.4	26.5	2.3	3.5	1.1	1.2	29.4	8.6	3.2	1.6	1.6	1.9	12.5	36.0
Guinea-Bissau	49.8	45.5	0.1	3.2	1.0	0.0	38.4	3.1	0.5	..	0.7	0.9	33.2	11.8
Haiti	62.3	11.5	1.8	48.1	0.9	0.2	37.4	3.4	1.0	1.1	1.1	3.3	27.5	0.1
Lao People's Dem. Rep.	5.8	2.4	1.4	0.5	1.5	0.2	92.1	11.3	0.4	..	5.2	69.4	5.8	1.9
Liberia	25.4	11.2	12.8	1.1	0.3	3.5	71.0	8.2	0.4	0.0	58.3	0.3	3.8	0.0
Madagascar	27.1	23.0	1.1	2.6	0.5	0.1	59.1	12.0	3.0	14.8	8.7	3.2	17.3	13.6
Malawi	26.5	17.9	1.3	7.0	0.2	0.1	72.7	4.3	8.1	..	2.1	1.8	56.4	0.8
Maldives	19.3	10.1	2.6	2.7	3.9	0.0	80.5	1.8	11.1	18.4	24.3	17.4	7.4	0.2
Mali	29.3	26.0	0.2	2.4	0.7	1.2	37.3	3.5	1.4	0.5	0.6	0.4	30.9	32.1
Mauritania	51.6	42.4	1.2	7.1	1.0	1.6	35.8	8.2	3.7	3.9	0.4	4.0	15.7	10.9
Mozambique	29.1	25.1	0.6	2.7	0.7	..	54.3	2.6	3.2	2.1	1.2	2.8	42.4	16.6
Myanmar	7.1	2.9	3.0	0.2	1.0	0.8	91.9	35.1	4.0	0.2	20.6	30.0	2.0	0.2
Nepal	7.9	3.6	1.1	1.4	1.7	0.9	80.1	3.8	61.8	2.5	3.8	6.2	2.0	11.2
Niger	47.2	28.1	0.5	14.6	4.1	0.3	52.5	7.8	2.8	11.0	0.9	1.5	28.5	0.0
Rwanda	30.2	23.5	1.2	2.2	3.3	0.3	43.3	2.2	2.2	3.6	0.3	0.6	34.4	26.2
Samoa	47.7	2.6	8.6	6.4	30.2	..	51.1	4.4	0.5	0.2	17.4	9.6	19.1	1.2
Sao Tome and Principe	86.5	79.5	0.2	5.2	1.7	1.0	12.5	1.7	0.4	3.6	0.3	2.9	3.5	0.0
Senegal	57.4	49.9	2.8	3.6	1.1	2.2	37.8	4.5	2.6	7.4	1.0	5.4	16.9	2.6
Sierra Leone	39.8	30.0	0.3	8.6	0.9	0.9	53.8	7.7	4.3	0.4	2.6	5.5	33.2	5.5
Solomon Islands	45.0	4.1	7.8	2.5	30.6	..	43.3	2.2	0.1	0.0	24.7	7.0	9.3	11.6
Somalia	5.5	2.4	0.0	3.0	0.1	0.5	81.2	3.8	8.2	17.4	0.2	3.1	48.7	12.7
Sudan	32.2	24.1	2.6	2.0	3.6	3.1	63.5	17.7	4.5	19.7	3.6	2.5	15.5	1.2
Togo	67.6	57.0	0.9	8.0	1.6	2.4	30.1	6.4	1.1	1.9	3.8	1.1	15.7	0.0
Uganda	29.2	20.0	4.2	3.1	1.9	1.1	68.7	7.1	5.6	10.4	1.0	1.2	43.4	1.0
United Rep. of Tanzania	28.6	19.3	2.8	4.8	1.7	1.3	65.6	9.4	6.8	13.8	2.4	5.5	27.9	4.5
Vanuatu	56.8	3.7	19.7	3.9	29.4	0.0	40.9	7.4	0.9	..	13.5	3.0	16.0	2.3
Yemen	25.3	14.9	3.2	4.4	2.7	2.9	70.9	12.8	2.4	31.8	2.6	6.7	14.6	0.9
Zambia	21.9	12.2	1.5	2.4	5.8	0.0	78.1	2.7	2.8	10.6	1.4	0.3	60.4	0.0
LDCs	**32.5**	**21.2**	**3.2**	**6.1**	**2.0**	**2.3**	**62.5**	**11.1**	**6.1**	**9.2**	**11.1**	**6.0**	**18.9**	**2.7**
African LDCs and Haiti	*40.7*	*28.0*	*3.1*	*7.8*	*1.8*	*1.6*	*56.1*	*8.7*	*3.5*	*7.9*	*9.6*	*2.4*	*24.0*	*1.6*
Asian LDCs	*17.1*	*8.8*	*3.2*	*3.4*	*1.7*	*3.6*	*74.5*	*15.9*	*10.8*	*11.6*	*13.5*	*12.3*	*10.4*	*4.8*
Island LDCs	*45.9*	*26.7*	*4.8*	*3.1*	*11.2*	*0.2*	*51.3*	*2.9*	*4.3*	*8.3*	*14.7*	*8.6*	*12.4*	*2.7*
Other developing countries	**42.4**	**15.7**	**10.1**	**13.4**	**3.3**	**2.4**	**51.1**	**11.2**	**1.6**	**9.3**	**14.1**	**7.4**	**7.5**	**4.0**
All developing countries	**42.2**	**15.9**	**9.9**	**13.2**	**3.2**	**2.4**	**51.4**	**11.2**	**1.7**	**9.3**	**14.0**	**7.3**	**7.8**	**4.0**

Source: UNCTAD, *Handbook of Statistics 2007* and estimates, based on data from IMF, *Direction of Trade Statistics*, online data, March 2008.

22. Composition of total financial flows to LDCs
(Net disbursements)

	Million current dollars						Million 2006 dollars[e]					
	1990	*1995*	*2000*	*2004*	*2005*	*2006*	*1990*	*1995*	*2000*	*2004*	*2005*	*2006*
Concessional loans and grants[a]	**16 623**	**17 143**	**12 621**	**25 222**	**25 882**	**28 181**	**22 674**	**19 317**	**17 123**	**26 624**	**26 589**	**28 181**
DAC countries	16 047	17 097	12 427	25 028	25 601	27 659	21 894	19 266	16 871	26 406	26 295	27 659
of which:												
Bilateral	9 888	9 344	7 947	15 971	16 151	17 230	13 462	10 634	10 838	16 910	16 613	17 230
Multilateral	6 159	7 753	4 480	9 057	9 450	10 429	8 432	8 632	6 033	9 496	9 682	10 429
Non-DAC countries	577	46	194	194	281	522	781	50	252	217	294	522
ODA grants total	12 223	13 020	10 593	22 156	23 225	52 708	16 769	14 799	14 572	23 282	23 825	52 708
ODA loans total, net	4 401	4 123	2 028	3 066	2 657	-24 527	5 905	4 518	2 551	3 342	2 764	-24 527
Technical cooperation	3 247	3 711	2 682	4 125	5 023	5 439	4 476	4 242	3 552	4 351	5 151	5 439
Other[b]	13 376	13 432	9 939	21 097	20 859	22 743	18 198	15 075	13 571	22 273	21 438	22 743
Non-concessional flows	**740**	**-430**	**1 072**	**1 861**	**115**	**1 720**	**1 018**	**-503**	**1 582**	**1 915**	**119**	**1 720**
Total other official flows, net	723	-133	341	-456	-68	-871	995	-169	589	-529	-69	-871
DAC countries	726	-133	334	-451	-68	-878	726	-133	334	-451	-68	-878
of which:												
Bilateral	692	-38	339	-607	-289	-953	954	-64	574	-687	-296	-953
Multilateral	35	-95	-4	156	221	75	46	-105	6	164	226	75
Non-DAC countries	-3	..	6	-5	1	7	-4	..	8	-5	1	7
Total private flows, net	17	-297	731	2 317	183	2 591	23	-334	993	2 444	188	2 591
of which:												
Export credits, net[c]	-528	-374	63	-242	292	744	-720	-422	86	-255	300	744
Direct investment	250	332	22	1 790	580	661	341	374	30	1 889	596	661
Other[d]	295	-255	646	768	-689	1 186	403	-287	877	811	-708	1 186
Total financial flows	**17 363**	**16 713**	**13 694**	**27 077**	**25 997**	**29 901**	**23 693**	**18 813**	**18 705**	**28 539**	**26 707**	**29 901**

Source: UNCTAD secretariat calculations based on OECD/DAC, *International Development Statistics*, online data, May 2008.

a Total ODA.
b Total ODA excluding technical assistance grants.
c Bank and non-bank export credits. Non-bank export credit from 1995.
d Portfolio investment, corresponds to bonds and equities.
e Data for total net private flows in constant 2006 dollars has been calculated by applying an ad hoc deflator for DAC countries (2006=100).

23. Distribution of financial flows to LDCs and to all developing countries, by type of flow
(Per cent)

Country	To least developed countries						To developing countries					
	1990	*1995*	*2000*	*2004*	*2005*	*2006*	*1990*	*1995*	*2000*	*2004*	*2005*	*2006*
Concessional loans and grants[a]	**95.7**	**102.6**	**92.2**	**93.1**	**99.6**	**94.2**	**73.0**	**33.9**	**40.9**	**45.1**	**36.5**	**34.6**
DAC countries	92.4	102.3	90.8	92.4	98.5	92.5	64.7	33.4	40.1	44.5	35.9	33.9
Of which:												
Bilateral	56.9	55.9	58.0	59.0	62.1	57.6	47.1	22.3	28.1	30.3	28.1	25.1
Multilateral	35.5	46.4	32.7	33.5	36.3	34.9	17.6	11.1	11.9	14.2	7.8	8.8
Non DAC countries	3.3	0.3	1.4	0.7	1.1	1.7	8.3	0.5	0.8	0.6	0.5	0.6
ODA grants total	70.4	77.9	77.4	81.8	89.3	176.3	53.3	24.4	30.8	42.5	34.1	49.2
ODA loans total, net	25.3	24.7	14.8	11.3	10.2	-82.0	19.7	9.5	10.1	2.7	2.4	-14.7
Technical cooperation	18.7	22.2	19.6	15.2	19.3	18.2	15.5	9.6	11.3	11.0	5.7	7.5
Other[b]	77.0	80.4	72.6	77.9	80.2	76.1	57.5	24.2	29.6	34.1	30.8	27.1
Non-concessional flows	**4.3**	**-2.6**	**7.8**	**6.9**	**0.4**	**5.8**	**27.0**	**66.1**	**59.1**	**54.9**	**63.5**	**65.4**
Total other official flows, net	4.2	-2.6	7.8	6.9	0.4	5.8	25.7	66.1	59.1	54.9	63.5	65.4
DAC countries	4.2	-0.8	2.5	-1.7	-0.3	-2.9	25.9	7.2	3.7	-7.4	-0.2	-4.9
Of which:												
Bilateral	4.0	-0.2	2.5	-2.2	-1.1	-3.2	10.8	5.2	-5.8	-4.2	-1.2	-4.8
Multilateral	0.2	-0.6	0.0	0.6	0.8	0.3	15.1	2.0	10.3	-3.5	0.7	-0.4
Non-DAC Countries	0.0	..	0.0	0.0	0.0	0.0	-0.3	..	-0.8	0.2	0.3	0.3
Total private flows, net	0.1	-1.8	5.3	8.6	0.7	8.7	1.3	58.9	55.4	62.3	63.7	70.3
Of which:												
export credits, net[c]	-3.0	-2.2	0.5	-0.9	1.1	2.5	-0.7	4.0	6.4	5.8	5.8	4.1
Direct investment	1.4	2.0	0.2	6.6	2.2	2.2	28.7	34.8	47.0	59.0	37.1	45.9
Other[d]	1.7	-1.5	4.7	2.8	-2.7	4.0	-26.7	20.1	1.9	-2.5	20.7	20.4
Total financial flows	**100.0**	**100.0**	**100.0**	**100.0**	**100.0**	**100.0**	**100.0**	**100.0**	**100.0**	**100.0**	**100.0**	**100.0**

For source and notes, see table 22.

24. Share of LDCs in financial flows to all developing countries, by type of flow
(Per cent)

	1990	1995	2000	2004	2005	2006
Concessional loans and grants[a]	**35.4**	**38.1**	**37.9**	**46.8**	**31.5**	**37.0**
DAC countries	38.6	38.5	38.1	47.1	31.6	37.0
Of which:						
Bilateral	32.7	31.5	34.7	44.1	25.5	31.1
Multilateral	54.4	52.5	46.2	53.6	53.5	53.5
Non DAC countries	10.8	7.4	28.3	25.4	23.3	38.3
ODA grants total	35.7	40.1	42.2	43.7	30.2	48.6
ODA loans total, net	34.8	32.8	24.7	96.7	49.9	75.9
Technical cooperation	32.5	28.9	29.3	31.3	39.0	33.0
Other[b]	36.2	41.7	41.2	51.9	30.1	38.1
Non-concessional flows	**4.3**	**..**	**2.2**	**2.8**	**0.1**	**1.2**
Total other official flows, net	4.4	..	11.2	5.1	18.9	8.1
DAC countries	4.4	..	9.0	4.9	7.0	7.7
Of which:						
Bilateral	9.9	..	..	12.2	11.0	9.1
Multilateral	0.4	..	..	..	13.4	..
Non-DAC Countries	1.8	..	..	..	0.1	1.0
Total private flows, net	2.0	..	1.6	3.1	0.1	1.7
Of which:						
Export credits, net[c]	114.7	..	1.2	..	2.2	8.3
Direct investment	1.4	0.7	0.1	2.5	0.7	0.7
Other[d]	..	..	42.0	..	..	2.6
Total Financial flows	**27.0**	**12.6**	**16.8**	**22.7**	**11.5**	**13.6**

Note: No percentage is shown when either the net flow to all LDCs or the net flow to all developing countries in a particular year is negative. For other notes and sources, see table 22.

25. Net ODA[a] from individual DAC member countries to LDCs

Donor country[b]	% of GNI						$ million						% change
	1990	1995	2000	2004	2005	2006	1990	1995	2000	2004	2005	2006	2006/ 2000
Luxembourg	0.08	0.14	0.27	0.31	0.35	0.38	10	25	46	87	106	123	167.2
Norway	0.52	0.35	0.26	0.33	0.35	0.34	532	502	427	837	1 029	1 129	164.1
Denmark	0.37	0.30	0.34	0.31	0.31	0.32	462	511	537	735	814	878	63.5
Sweden	0.35	0.22	0.24	0.22	0.31	0.30	775	500	532	762	1 101	1 152	116.5
Ireland	0.06	0.12	0.14	0.21	0.21	0.28	21	66	114	322	365	524	358.2
Netherlands	0.30	0.23	0.21	0.27	0.26	0.21	834	933	794	1 541	1 658	1 395	75.7
Belgium	0.19	0.10	0.10	0.18	0.16	0.18	367	274	221	645	609	729	230.5
United Kingdom	0.09	0.07	0.10	0.14	0.12	0.16	834	827	1 426	2 994	2 709	3 827	168.4
Finland	0.24	0.09	0.09	0.09	0.13	0.14	317	106	112	167	245	296	164.4
Portugal	0.17	0.16	0.16	0.53	0.12	0.13	100	165	171	878	210	240	40.7
France	0.19	0.12	0.08	0.15	0.11	0.12	2 286	1 784	1 144	3 169	2 392	2 624	129.4
Switzerland	0.14	0.11	0.10	0.11	0.10	0.11	325	347	270	399	405	453	67.8
Canada	0.13	0.08	0.05	0.07	0.09	0.10	740	444	308	702	1 048	1 244	303.6
Germany	0.12	0.07	0.07	0.08	0.07	0.09	1 769	1 612	1 212	2 312	1 884	2 642	117.9
DAC countries, total	**0.09**	**0.06**	**0.05**	**0.08**	**0.08**	**0.09**	**15 198**	**13 614**	**12 448**	**23 549**	**24 597**	**29 448**	**136.6**
Austria	0.07	0.06	0.06	0.06	0.08	0.08	106	140	113	168	245	252	123.8
New Zealand	0.04	0.05	0.07	0.07	0.07	0.08	18	26	29	65	70	74	152.7
Japan	0.06	0.05	0.04	0.04	0.05	0.07	1 753	2 665	2 159	1 684	2 326	3 340	54.7
Spain	0.04	0.04	0.03	0.04	0.07	0.06	194	221	144	424	817	767	434.0
Australia	0.06	0.06	0.08	0.06	0.06	0.06	171	210	293	350	419	451	53.9
United States	0.04	0.03	0.02	0.04	0.04	0.05	2 199	1 873	1 989	4 504	4 661	6 416	222.6
Italy	0.13	0.04	0.04	0.05	0.08	0.04	1 382	382	389	788	1 407	789	102.6
Greece	-	-	0.02	0.01	0.03	0.03	-	-	19	15	79	103	451.3

Source: UNCTAD secretariat calculations based on OECD/DAC, *International Development Statistics*, online data, May 2008; United Nations/DESA statistics for GNI.

a Net disbursements including imputed flows through multilateral channels.
b Ranked in descending order of the ODA/GNI ratio in 2006.

26. Bilateral ODA from DAC, non-DAC member countries and multilateral agencies to LDCs
($ million)

	Net disbursements						Commitments					
	1990	1995	2000	2004	2005	2006	1990	1995	2000	2004	2005	2006
Bilateral donors: DAC												
Australia	104.5	139.4	205.8	296.5	330.4	280.6	97.0	156.0	217.3	249.7	321.5	280.6
Austria	60.9	72.7	65.0	54.8	114.3	72.8	132.4	72.3	60.4	46.2	127.3	80.9
Belgium	273.5	156.9	154.8	458.9	351.0	481.0	273.5	162.0	159.9	488.6	521.4	561.0
Canada	391.6	252.8	195.0	548.6	722.2	744.4	354.0	233.1	265.3	655.7	780.4	789.1
Denmark	295.1	330.2	373.4	493.5	553.2	592.0	269.2	238.4	598.4	663.2	807.9	533.5
Finland	194.6	66.3	65.6	124.5	138.0	161.6	129.8	45.2	44.6	186.5	206.9	246.9
France	1 857.1	1 425.8	846.1	2 269.3	1 209.9	1 242.1	1 480.3	1 146.5	891.1	2 503.6	1 474.7	1 858.6
Germany	1 160.6	1 100.0	665.0	963.2	1 032.1	1 225.9	1 323.2	1 259.0	496.5	1 009.5	1 130.9	1 462.8
Greece	..	..	1.8	15.3	23.8	17.6	..	..	1.8	15.3	23.8	17.6
Ireland	13.9	55.7	98.3	270.7	288.2	362.3	13.9	..	98.3	270.7	288.2	362.3
Italy	968.8	275.2	240.1	287.6	291.7	261.1	846.0	529.9	269.0	302.2	463.5	218.8
Japan	1 067.2	1 676.0	1 319.2	914.9	1 311.2	1 139.4	1 144.7	1 824.2	1 266.5	1 848.8	2 559.7	1 676.0
Luxembourg	7.9	21.7	40.5	70.8	82.5	92.5	..	..	39.9	70.8	82.5	92.5
Netherlands	592.8	673.7	559.9	1 054.9	1 076.4	951.4	681.7	689.3	609.9	802.1	1 188.3	1 474.9
New Zealand	13.3	20.7	24.7	56.3	57.5	58.4	9.7	..	24.7	57.6	84.8	95.2
Norway	356.7	371.6	310.8	617.4	712.7	790.9	187.0	393.2	249.3	634.2	866.3	773.2
Portugal	99.6	154.6	147.8	824.5	156.8	165.5	..	103.9	293.0	829.1	162.7	171.5
Spain	96.7	122.1	66.8	169.2	404.1	146.6	..	7.3	91.6	195.6	461.6	244.6
Sweden	530.2	356.5	339.0	586.9	638.8	728.7	332.4	190.2	297.7	527.7	683.5	809.1
Switzerland	232.1	243.4	166.1	257.7	244.6	248.7	214.9	151.4	203.5	278.8	207.2	221.2
United Kingdom	473.0	561.0	1 015.4	2 202.0	1 751.3	2 151.6	480.0	573.4	1 026.7	2 204.1	1 749.8	2 193.7
United States	1 098.0	1 268.0	1 046.4	3 433.5	4 661.1	5 315.3	1 152.2	1 482.2	1 223.7	4 421.2	5 751.1	6 185.6
Total	*9 888.0*	*9 344.1*	*7 947.2*	*15 970.7*	*16 151.4*	*17 230.2*	*9 121.7*	*9 257.2*	*8 428.9*	*18 261.0*	*19 944.1*	*20 349.5*
Bilateral donors: non-DAC												
Czech Republic	..	..	0.4	9.5	5.2	9.9	..	..	0.4	..	..	..
Hungary	..	..	..	2.3	20.4	0.5						
Iceland	..	..	2.2	4.7	8.5	13.1						
Korea	0.2	14.4	21.3	86.1	114.9	92.1	0.3	8.7	38.3	84.3	144.8	171.7
Poland	0.3	..	0.8	9.6	0.9	93.9	..	..	..	..	14.0	7.0
Slovak Republic	..	..	..	1.3	21.9	17.2	..	..	..	..	..	..
Thailand	..	..	..	..	..	61.5						
Turkey	..	1.9	0.4	11.3	33.6	80.6	..	..	..	..	..	80.6
Arab countries	571.2	16.3	149.1	42.1	50.0	122.8	541.0	240.1	199.6	175.5	..	125.9
Other bilateral donors	3.9	13.1	19.9	26.6	25.8	30.6	..	..	19.9	26.5	25.6	1.0
Total	*575.6*	*45.7*	*193.9*	*193.6*	*281.0*	*522.2*	*541.3*	*248.8*	*258.1*	*286.3*	*184.4*	*386.1*
Multilateral donors												
AfDF	561.3	452.6	206.6	675.6	709.0	1 282.2	864.4	0.0	398.5	967.0	1 027.8	1 229.8
AsDF	448.2	410.3	388.4	161.8	268.1	461.3	536.4	400.5	589.5	638.8	577.5	708.2
EC	1 168.4	1 565.1	1 013.8	2 642.6	2 909.2	3 124.6	790.8	1 829.5	2 055.1	2 585.8	4 461.3	3 332.2
GEF	..	..	8.1	16.0	25.3	35.2	..	..	..	..	..	..
Global Fund	..	..	..	305.0	604.2	659.5	..	..	..	463.7	638.4	852.3
Nordic Dev. Fund	..	24.3	25.1	43.0	42.5	41.4	..	31.1	30.2	59.5	56.8	23.9
IDA	2 138.0	1 891.8	1 846.4	3 925.7	3 810.9	3 210.0	2 986.0	2 236.6	2 270.4	4 614.7	..	..
IDB Spec. Fund	11.7	67.4	26.4	18.7	59.2	49.9	56.0	181.1	1.8	2.3	204.6	102.5
SAF+ESAF+PRGF(IMF)	297.9	1 383.9	-33.0	-3.7	-361.4	107.0	..	..	..	..	..	..
IFAD	120.6	55.3	78.6	109.4	116.6	113.7	72.1	131.3	152.1	185.6	180.2	185.6
UNDP	366.6	232.0	187.1	220.0	228.9	251.6	..	..	..	..	..	..
UNFPA	46.3	67.8	52.7	114.1	114.4	132.6	..	..	..	..	..	..
UNHCR	197.6	410.1	172.1	164.1	139.4	134.3	..	..	..	..	..	..
UNICEF	232.7	348.0	171.3	202.8	256.0	294.8	..	..	..	..	..	..
UNTA	59.0	149.2	113.4	114.9	142.6	85.5	..	..	..	..	..	..
WFP	501.3	705.9	216.8	179.9	225.5	217.8	..	..	..	..	..	..
Arab agencies	9.4	-10.2	6.6	167.4	159.2	227.5	216.6	..	250.0	204.5	327.2	320.4
Total	*6 158.8*	*7 753.3*	*4 480.3*	*9 057.3*	*9 449.6*	*10 428.9*	*5 522.2*	*4 810.1*	*5 747.6*	*9 721.9*	*7 473.7*	*6 754.9*
Grand total	**16 622.4**	**17 143.1**	**12 621.4**	**25 221.5**	**25 882.0**	**28 181.3**	**15 185.2**	**14 316.2**	**14 434.6**	**28 269.2**	**27 602.2**	**27 490.6**

Source: UNCTAD secretariat calculations based on OECD/DAC, *International Development Statistics*, online, May 2008.

27. Net ODA to LDCs from DAC member countries and multilateral agencies mainly financed by them: Distribution by donor and shares allocated to LDCs in total ODA to all developing countries
(Per cent)

Country	Distribution by donor						Share of LDCs in ODA flows to all developing countries					
	1990	1995	2000	2004	2005	2006	1990	1995	2000	2004	2005	2006
Bilateral donors: DAC												
Australia	0.6	0.8	1.6	1.2	1.3	1.0	15.4	18.2	31.0	32.1	31.3	20.1
Austria	0.4	0.4	0.5	0.2	0.4	0.3	153.1	33.4	37.5	24.0	10.7	8.4
Belgium	1.6	0.9	1.2	1.8	1.4	1.7	72.2	46.3	50.6	71.4	35.9	48.4
Canada	2.4	1.5	1.5	2.2	2.8	2.6	39.5	38.0	42.6	49.5	39.0	49.4
Denmark	1.8	1.9	3.0	2.0	2.1	2.1	61.3	55.6	55.5	57.4	56.6	53.4
Finland	1.2	0.4	0.5	0.5	0.5	0.6	53.1	42.5	51.6	58.6	33.7	55.5
France	11.2	8.3	6.7	9.0	4.7	4.4	38.7	27.8	39.5	54.7	19.5	18.6
Germany	7.0	6.4	5.3	3.8	4.0	4.4	30.3	30.7	37.5	35.9	17.2	23.9
Greece	..	..	0.0	0.1	0.1	0.1	..	..	14.4	31.2	38.7	30.1
Ireland	0.1	0.3	0.8	1.1	1.1	1.3	87.3	78.9	83.0	81.3	76.1	77.2
Italy	5.8	1.6	1.9	1.1	1.1	0.9	54.4	44.8	103.6	64.8	14.4	15.4
Japan	6.4	9.8	10.5	3.6	5.1	4.0	17.2	18.9	17.0	21.3	14.9	19.2
Luxembourg	0.0	0.1	0.3	0.3	0.3	0.3	60.4	56.0	51.2	55.0	57.1	58.8
Netherlands	3.6	3.9	4.4	4.2	4.2	3.4	37.4	44.4	53.7	66.6	45.6	51.0
New Zealand	0.1	0.1	0.2	0.2	0.2	0.2	22.6	28.6	41.1	46.3	37.0	42.5
Norway	2.1	2.2	2.5	2.4	2.8	2.8	62.2	59.0	59.2	66.7	59.0	66.5
Portugal	0.6	0.9	1.2	3.3	0.6	0.6	100.0	96.9	98.0	97.8	93.4	95.0
Spain	0.6	0.7	0.5	0.7	1.6	0.5	19.5	19.5	14.5	15.8	27.3	9.4
Sweden	3.2	2.1	2.7	2.3	2.5	2.6	57.8	45.9	47.3	57.5	56.8	48.6
Switzerland	1.4	1.4	1.3	1.0	0.9	0.9	60.1	52.8	52.6	52.8	33.1	45.7
United Kingdom	2.8	3.3	8.0	8.7	6.8	7.6	44.1	46.3	53.5	55.1	26.4	30.8
United States	6.6	7.4	8.3	13.6	18.0	18.9	20.2	40.5	32.6	34.1	23.7	35.1
Total	*59.5*	*54.5*	*63.0*	*63.3*	*62.4*	*61.1*	*32.7*	*31.5*	*34.7*	*44.1*	*25.5*	*31.1*
Bilateral donors: non-DAC												
Czech Republic	..	..	0.0	0.0	0.0	0.0	..	..	13.4	24.5	17.1	25.7
Hungary	..	..	..	0.0	0.1	0.0	..	..	..	32.6	93.1	0.7
Iceland	..	..	0.0	0.0	0.0	0.0	..	..	67.5	62.8	69.4	71.8
Korea	0.0	0.1	0.2	0.3	0.4	0.3	2.1	26.7	21.2	29.2	26.9	31.5
Poland	0.0	..	0.0	0.0	0.0	0.3	100.0	..	11.7	69.6	9.8	96.5
Slovak Republic	..	..	..	0.0	0.1	0.1	..	..	..	29.2	87.2	92.4
Thailand	..	..	..	..	..	0.2	..	..	..	..	..	95.3
Turkey	..	0.0	0.0	0.0	0.1	0.3	..	7.4	11.8	14.3	12.4	28.1
Arab Countries	3.4	0.1	1.2	0.2	0.2	0.4	10.8	3.5	28.1	16.2	14.2	30.1
Other bilateral donors	0.0	0.1	0.2	0.1	0.1	0.1	19.8	18.3	50.3	46.1	42.1	43.4
Total	*3.5*	*0.3*	*1.5*	*0.8*	*1.1*	*1.9*	*10.8*	*7.4*	*28.3*	*25.4*	*23.3*	*38.3*
Multilateral donors												
AfDF	3.4	2.6	1.6	2.7	2.7	4.5	94.4	80.7	71.5	82.8	86.4	89.4
AsDF	2.7	2.4	3.1	0.6	1.0	1.6	41.3	37.6	43.8	26.2	33.4	49.0
EC	7.0	9.1	8.0	10.5	11.2	11.1	53.0	48.4	40.3	48.4	48.6	46.5
GEF	..	..	0.1	0.1	0.1	0.1	..	..	12.6	15.6	18.5	27.6
Global Fund	..	..	..	1.2	2.3	2.3	..	..	..	54.1	63.4	56.6
Nordic Dev. Fund	..	0.1	0.2	0.2	0.2	0.1	..	49.5	66.5	61.3	67.4	60.9
IDA	12.9	11.0	14.6	15.6	14.7	11.4	54.7	41.5	48.2	60.0	61.6	57.7
IDB Spec. Fund	0.1	0.4	0.2	0.1	0.2	0.2	10.4	27.8	19.1	7.9	29.8	27.0
SAF+ESAF+PRGF(IMF)	1.8	8.1	-0.3	0.0	-1.4	0.4	92.7	89.4	15.4	2.5	57.4	..
IFAD	0.7	0.3	0.6	0.4	0.5	0.4	49.2	62.0	60.1	76.1	63.9	55.2
UN	8.4	11.2	7.2	3.9	4.3	4.0	51.0	55.8	47.7	46.0	42.5	43.5
Other	0.1	-0.1	0.1	0.7	0.6	0.8	9.3	43.5	6.5	48.8	46.9	45.9
Total	*37.0*	*45.2*	*35.5*	*35.9*	*36.5*	*37.0*	*54.4*	*52.5*	*46.2*	*53.6*	*53.5*	*53.5*
Grand total	**100**	**100**	**100**	**100**	**100**	**100**	**35.4**	**38.1**	**37.9**	**46.8**	**31.5**	**37.0**

Source: UNCTAD secretariat calculations based on OECD/DAC, *International Development Statistics*, online, May 2008.

28. Total Financial Flows and ODA from all sources to individual LDCs
($ million, net disbursements)

Country	Total financial flows						of which: ODA					
	1990	1995	2000	2004	2005	2006	1990	1995	2000	2004	2005	2006
Afghanistan	120	213	157	2 207	2 795	3 045	122	213	136	2 171	2 752	3 000
Angola	88	491	118	1 085	1 689	153	266	416	302	1 145	437	171
Bangladesh	2 164	862	1 230	1 531	1 710	1 325	2 093	1 282	1 168	1 412	1 336	1 223
Benin	242	281	227	382	377	370	267	280	238	386	346	375
Bhutan	49	78	44	78	95	93	46	71	53	78	90	94
Burkina Faso	342	486	342	659	710	971	327	490	335	624	681	871
Burundi	253	279	78	353	373	403	263	287	93	362	365	415
Cambodia	41	568	404	321	558	720	41	551	396	483	541	529
Cape Verde	104	162	119	209	260	195	105	116	94	143	162	138
Central African Republic	256	168	50	111	97	138	249	168	75	110	96	134
Chad	312	284	-226	335	385	298	311	235	130	329	382	284
Comoros	44	40	-2	25	43	31	45	42	19	25	25	30
Dem. Rep. of the Congo	1 409	240	192	1 786	1 708	1 202	896	195	177	1 824	1 827	2 056
Djibouti	191	103	91	74	98	185	194	105	71	64	76	117
Equatorial Guinea	62	34	22	848	471	1 132	60	33	21	30	38	27
Eritrea	0	148	183	256	354	136	0	148	176	264	355	129
Ethiopia	982	860	680	1 669	1 919	1 944	1 009	876	686	1 806	1 910	1 947
Gambia	106	43	45	60	68	72	97	45	49	55	61	74
Guinea	283	433	329	223	163	175	292	416	153	272	199	164
Guinea-Bissau	133	116	84	76	77	77	126	118	80	77	79	82
Haiti	153	711	176	260	508	731	167	722	208	260	502	581
Kiribati	20	15	18	17	29	-46	20	15	18	17	28	-45
Lao People's Dem. Rep.	149	309	287	260	355	1 444	149	307	282	270	296	364
Lesotho	145	209	11	89	51	61	139	113	37	96	69	72
Liberia	519	-54	632	1 256	-2 317	312	114	123	67	213	233	269
Madagascar	429	251	318	1 229	721	888	397	299	322	1 248	914	754
Malawi	515	437	431	507	576	677	500	434	446	501	578	669
Maldives	38	44	11	76	128	143	21	58	19	27	77	39
Mali	471	586	385	534	745	833	479	540	359	568	699	825
Mauritania	218	214	211	217	203	173	236	230	211	181	196	188
Mozambique	1 046	1 092	1 146	1 388	1 269	1 623	998	1 062	876	1 235	1 277	1 611
Myanmar	115	177	56	86	130	120	161	150	106	124	145	147
Nepal	426	412	407	416	415	501	423	429	387	428	425	514
Niger	373	198	183	457	385	-532	388	271	208	541	511	401
Rwanda	283	641	318	490	559	548	288	695	321	486	571	585
Samoa	54	47	29	21	74	50	48	43	27	31	44	47
Sao Tome and Principe	53	58	36	32	31	25	54	84	35	33	32	22
Senegal	753	642	474	981	684	841	812	659	423	1 037	672	825
Sierra Leone	63	211	185	355	343	455	59	205	181	354	344	364
Solomon Islands	58	46	55	125	170	216	46	48	68	121	198	205
Somalia	486	188	100	195	237	400	491	188	101	200	237	392
Sudan	730	295	315	1 014	1 856	2 128	813	237	220	992	1 832	2 058
Timor-Leste	-5	9	649	537	186	147	0	0	231	161	185	210
Togo	256	187	60	108	92	155	258	191	70	64	83	79
Tuvalu	5	8	0	8	8	19	5	8	4	8	9	15
Uganda	660	852	792	1 181	1 241	1 569	663	833	817	1 194	1 177	1 551
United Rep. of Tanzania	1 118	872	1 184	1 766	1 659	1 960	1 163	869	1 019	1 751	1 481	1 825
Vanuatu	148	35	71	21	51	79	50	46	46	38	39	49
Yemen	326	119	287	194	324	876	400	167	263	253	336	284
Zambia	578	2 011	701	973	1 332	845	475	2 031	795	1 125	935	1 425
LDCs	**17 363**	**16 713**	**13 694**	**27 077**	**25 997**	**29 901**	**16 623**	**17 143**	**12 621**	**25 222**	**25 882**	**28 181**
All developing countries	**64 246**	**133 017**	**81 386**	**119 286**	**225 548**	**220 545**	**46 898**	**45 048**	**33 286**	**53 852**	**82 290**	**76 202**

Source: UNCTAD secretariat calculations based on OECD/DAC, *International Development Statistics*, online data, May 2008.

29. Bilateral and multilateral net ODA disbursements to individual LDCs

Country	Per capita	Net disburse-ments	of which: technical cooperation	Bilateral ODA[a]	of which: Grants	Multi-lateral ODA	of which: Grants	Per capita	Net disburse-ments	of which: technical cooperation	Bilateral ODA[a]	of which: Grants	Multi-lateral ODA	of which: Grants
	Dollars	$ million	As % of total net ODA					Dollars	$ million	As % of total net ODA				
			1995–1996							2005–2006				
Afghanistan	10.3	191.0	23.5	49.9	49.9	50.1	50.1	112.4	2 875.9	33.3	82.2	82.0	17.8	15.6
Sudan	7.6	227.4	29.6	55.6	57.3	44.4	36.6	52.1	1 945.3	8.9	80.0	78.0	20.0	19.4
Dem.Rep. of the Congo	3.9	180.4	31.2	62.9	71.0	37.1	39.1	32.5	1 941.5	9.8	65.3	56.5	34.7	25.4
Ethiopia *	13.8	846.2	21.0	57.6	52.5	42.4	19.9	24.1	1 928.4	12.0	58.7	56.7	41.3	123.2
United Rep. of Tanzania *	28.7	869.7	29.0	68.7	68.6	31.3	11.1	42.4	1 653.1	11.9	56.4	56.6	43.6	134.6
Mozambique *	60.2	974.1	21.5	64.4	71.1	35.6	12.5	69.6	1 443.8	14.1	59.0	59.7	41.0	70.3
Uganda *	34.9	753.3	18.2	54.0	48.2	46.0	18.9	46.4	1 364.0	17.9	59.9	60.0	40.1	147.2
Bangladesh	9.8	1 254.8	21.9	54.3	58.1	45.7	15.2	8.3	1 279.5	14.2	42.1	58.9	57.9	17.3
Zambia *	140.7	1 319.4	11.4	30.1	29.4	69.9	6.1	101.8	1 179.9	14.9	82.3	111.8	17.7	126.7
Madagascar *	23.1	327.1	36.3	65.0	76.2	35.0	16.1	44.1	834.1	12.5	46.1	58.2	53.9	154.8
Burkina Faso *	43.6	454.4	26.1	58.9	59.6	41.1	19.1	54.8	775.9	14.7	47.9	47.7	52.1	95.2
Mali *	58.1	514.7	24.3	54.5	52.1	45.5	12.6	64.6	762.0	17.5	51.9	54.2	48.1	132.3
Senegal *	67.2	616.6	27.9	66.1	71.9	33.9	13.3	62.8	748.5	39.4	64.5	76.7	35.5	146.1
Malawi *	45.4	462.8	18.7	52.7	48.8	47.3	19.9	46.5	623.0	16.7	59.1	60.8	40.9	206.4
Rwanda *	100.8	580.0	15.4	51.1	51.8	48.9	41.1	61.8	578.0	20.4	52.6	58.2	47.4	126.2
Haiti	68.9	544.8	18.3	60.7	60.2	39.3	19.3	57.8	541.5	30.0	65.0	64.9	35.0	22.9
Cambodia	41.9	483.8	29.2	61.4	61.6	38.6	19.9	38.0	534.8	34.4	69.6	65.6	30.4	13.1
Nepal	18.6	408.5	33.9	61.4	61.6	38.6	10.5	17.2	469.6	27.1	71.0	78.8	29.0	15.2
Niger *	27.6	261.4	36.4	68.6	75.9	31.4	22.7	33.8	456.1	18.6	53.7	56.6	46.3	162.9
Burundi	31.7	198.7	18.4	43.3	48.9	56.7	45.3	48.7	390.1	11.8	51.8	51.6	48.2	39.1
Benin *	45.0	283.9	22.4	62.5	57.4	37.5	12.8	41.8	360.5	28.5	60.4	63.7	39.6	151.3
Sierra Leone *	46.6	193.9	13.6	33.9	31.1	66.1	21.6	62.5	354.0	10.5	46.6	39.7	53.4	43.5
Chad	36.5	265.4	21.8	47.6	47.6	52.4	20.4	32.3	332.9	13.6	48.9	49.9	51.1	33.8
Laos	67.2	319.0	23.0	49.8	55.9	50.2	9.2	57.8	330.0	24.0	62.1	53.1	37.9	14.1
Somalia	22.0	137.9	27.2	57.6	59.9	42.4	43.3	37.8	314.5	4.4	65.6	65.9	34.4	34.4
Yemen	13.0	204.9	28.8	59.7	65.5	40.3	12.5	14.5	310.3	19.8	47.2	48.7	52.8	18.8
Angola	35.1	437.9	19.5	61.3	57.4	38.7	30.9	18.6	303.8	25.9	50.7	86.3	49.3	42.1
Liberia	66.8	147.9	8.4	49.6	26.7	50.4	50.4	71.4	250.6	22.2	66.4	67.1	33.6	33.6
Eritrea	47.2	152.9	33.5	75.4	73.7	24.6	23.7	52.5	242.0	9.1	58.8	55.3	41.2	22.4
Solomon Islands	123.0	45.2	52.4	79.1	83.4	20.9	12.4	421.1	201.4	73.2	87.2	87.4	12.8	11.8
Timor-Leste	..	..	..	..	..	..	..	180.9	197.2	38.7	84.9	84.9	15.1	15.1
Mauritania *	111.1	250.7	18.9	39.4	42.2	60.6	38.4	63.9	191.8	21.7	56.8	59.0	43.2	232.2
Guinea	48.0	356.9	19.3	53.4	52.0	46.6	21.2	19.9	181.2	38.1	67.9	76.0	32.1	35.3
Cape Verde	286.0	116.1	32.7	67.8	66.0	32.2	18.8	293.0	150.2	29.3	69.0	62.7	31.0	10.1
Myanmar	2.2	94.5	39.6	92.2	152.8	7.8	33.2	3.0	145.6	27.2	65.6	63.5	34.4	35.1
Central African Rep.	48.1	168.2	26.5	74.8	81.7	25.2	12.9	27.1	114.8	33.4	55.7	60.7	44.3	69.7
Djibouti	159.2	100.8	42.8	78.6	76.4	21.4	11.6	119.3	96.8	38.6	74.4	75.1	25.6	20.3
Bhutan	126.6	64.3	41.6	76.1	76.2	23.9	16.6	142.9	91.9	25.0	58.8	59.9	41.2	22.2
Togo	37.7	173.4	17.0	61.6	60.0	38.4	12.6	12.8	80.7	40.9	70.9	77.7	29.1	34.0
Guinea-Bissau	123.2	148.9	28.7	70.2	50.6	29.8	14.4	49.8	80.7	19.8	48.9	49.0	51.1	52.5
Lesotho	62.1	107.9	30.6	53.0	50.8	47.0	27.8	35.3	70.2	22.2	54.6	58.5	45.4	30.5
Gambia	34.5	40.7	47.1	48.0	62.0	52.0	22.9	41.3	67.7	16.1	34.0	31.9	66.0	27.0
Maldives	179.3	44.9	20.7	61.1	48.0	38.9	9.9	194.0	57.8	15.1	62.0	51.5	38.0	26.1
Samoa	223.3	37.8	48.9	81.8	82.5	18.2	11.2	246.6	45.5	46.9	75.1	75.2	24.9	14.0
Vanuatu	220.2	38.3	51.6	86.4	86.4	13.6	11.1	202.4	44.1	72.4	84.9	86.2	15.2	18.1
Equatorial Guinea	83.0	32.1	43.7	70.1	72.2	29.9	23.5	66.7	32.7	52.2	73.1	80.6	26.9	35.7
Comoros	65.2	40.2	38.7	54.7	54.6	45.3	25.5	34.2	27.6	48.4	69.1	76.5	31.9	30.7
Sao Tome & Principe *	509.1	65.7	28.2	68.8	48.4	31.2	12.0	173.7	26.7	41.3	68.6	69.0	31.4	39.1
Tuvalu	923.4	9.1	32.5	85.2	85.2	14.8	12.8	1162.1	12.2	25.2	76.8	76.8	23.4	14.8
Kiribati	180.7	14.1	51.1	81.5	81.5	18.5	18.2	-92.2	-8.6	-123.6	170.4	170.4	-70.4	-57.1
LDCs	**25.6**	**15 562.5**	**23.3**	**56.6**	**57.2**	**43.4**	**19.0**	**34.8**	**27 031.6**	**19.3**	**63.2**	**65.8**	**36.8**	**74.7**
All devg. countries	**9.5**	**42 676.3**	**29.0**	**67.1**	**58.7**	**32.9**	**14.1**	**15.1**	**79 246.4**	**19.9**	**76.6**	**78.7**	**23.4**	**38.3**

Source: UNCTAD secretariat calculations based on OECD/DAC, *International Development Statistics*, online, May 2008; United Nations DESA Population Division, January 2006.

Note: The countries have been ranked in descending order of total net ODA disbursements received in 2005–2006.
  a Includes ODA from DAC and non-DAC donors.
  * LDCs that have reached the HIPC completion point (October 2007).

30. Foreign direct investment: Inflows to and outflows from LDCs
($ million)

Country	FDI inflows						FDI outflows					
	1985	1990	2000	2004	2005	2006	1985	1990	2000	2004	2005	2006
Afghanistan	..	..	0.2	0.6	3.6	2.1	..	..	..	..	..	..
Angola	278.0	-334.5	878.5	1,449.2	-1,303.3	-1,140.0	..	0.9	-21.4	35.2	219.4	92.7
Bangladesh	-6.7	3.2	578.7	460.4	692.0	625.0	..	0.5	2.0	5.7	1.9	8.3
Benin	-0.1	62.4	59.7	63.8	53.0	63.0	..	0.3	3.6	-1.3	-0.4	-0.8
Bhutan	..	1.6	0.0	3.5	9.0	6.1	..	..	..	..	..	..
Burkina Faso	-1.4	0.5	23.1	14.3	34.2	25.9	0.0	-0.6	0.2	-8.9	-0.2	-2.4
Burundi	1.6	1.3	11.7	0.0	0.6	290.0	-1.1	0.0	0.0	..	..	..
Cambodia	..	..	148.5	131.4	381.2	483.2	..	..	6.6	10.2	6.3	8.4
Cape Verde	..	0.3	33.5	20.4	75.5	121.7	..	0.3	1.4	0.1	0.1	0.1
Central African Republic	3.0	0.7	0.8	24.8	28.6	24.3	0.6	3.8	0.0	..	..	..
Chad	53.7	9.4	114.8	495.4	612.9	700.0	0.3	0.1	0.0	..	..	..
Comoros	..	0.4	0.1	0.7	1.0	0.8	..	1.1	..	..	..	..
Dem. Rep. of the Congo	69.2	-14.5	23.4	9.9	-78.6	180.0	..	..	-1.8	-0.1	..	..
Djibouti	0.2	0.1	3.3	38.5	22.2	108.3	..	..	..	..	..	..
Equatorial Guinea	2.4	11.1	111.4	1,650.6	1,873.1	1,655.8	..	0.1	-3.6	..	..	..
Eritrea	..	..	27.9	-7.9	-3.0	3.7	..	..	..	..	..	..
Ethiopia	0.2	12.0	134.6	545.1	221.1	364.4	..	..	..	..	..	..
Ethiopia (former)	0.2	12.0	..	..	..	..	..	..	..	..	..	..
Gambia	-0.5	14.1	43.5	49.1	44.7	69.9	..	..	..	..	..	..
Guinea	1.1	17.9	9.9	97.9	102.0	108.0	0.0	0.1	..	-1.0	-5.0	..
Guinea-Bissau	1.4	2.0	0.7	1.7	8.7	42.0	..	..	..	-7.5	0.7	-3.8
Haiti	4.9	8.0	13.3	5.9	26.0	160.0	..	-8.0	..	..	..	..
Kiribati	0.2	0.3	17.6	18.8	0.8	12.0	..	..	..	..	..	..
Lao People's Dem. Rep.	-1.6	6.0	34.0	16.9	27.7	187.4	-0.2	0.2	4.1	..	..	..
Lesotho	4.8	16.1	31.5	53.3	57.3	57.0	..	..	..	0.1	..	..
Liberia	-16.2	225.2	20.8	236.9	-479.5	-81.7	245.0	-3.1	779.9	304.5	436.8	346.4
Madagascar	-0.2	22.4	83.0	95.2	86.0	230.2	..	1.3	..	..	..	..
Malawi	0.5	23.3	39.6	22.0	26.5	29.7	..	..	-0.6	1.6	1.0	0.9
Maldives	1.2	5.6	13.0	14.7	9.5	13.9	..	..	..	..	..	..
Mali	2.9	5.7	82.4	101.0	223.8	185.0	..	0.2	4.0	0.8	-0.9	0.8
Mauritania	7.0	6.7	40.1	391.6	863.6	-3.4	..	..	..	4.0	2.0	..
Mozambique	0.3	9.2	139.2	244.7	107.9	153.7	..	..	0.2	-0.1	0.2	0.4
Myanmar	..	225.1	208.0	251.0	235.8	142.9	..	..	..	..	..	..
Nepal	0.7	5.9	-0.5	-0.4	2.4	-6.6	..	..	..	..	..	..
Niger	-9.4	40.8	8.4	19.7	30.3	20.5	1.9	0.0	-0.6	7.1	-4.4	1.6
Rwanda	14.6	7.7	8.1	7.7	10.5	15.0	0.0	0.0	..	..	..	..
Samoa	0.4	6.6	-1.5	2.2	-3.6	-1.7	..	..	..	0.4	2.0	1.5
Sao Tome and Principe	..	..	3.8	-1.6	-0.6	-0.4	..	..	..	..	..	..
Senegal	-18.9	56.9	62.9	77.0	44.6	58.0	3.1	-9.5	0.6	13.1	-7.7	4.8
Sierra Leone	-31.0	32.4	38.9	61.2	58.6	42.8	..	0.1	..	..	-7.5	2.7
Solomon Islands	0.7	10.4	1.4	5.7	18.6	18.8	..	..	..	0.0	1.6	0.4
Somalia	-0.7	5.6	0.3	-4.8	24.0	96.0	..	..	..	..	..	..
Sudan	-3.0	-31.1	392.2	1 511.1	2 304.6	3 541.4	..	..	..	..	..	8.8
Timor-Leste	..	..	..	2.9	0.1	2.6	..	..	..	..	..	..
Togo	16.3	22.7	41.5	59.4	77.0	56.7	..	4.6	0.4	-12.6	-14.9	-20.3
Tuvalu	..	..	-0.9	0.0	0.0	0.0	..	..	..	..	..	..
Uganda	-4.0	-5.9	180.8	222.2	257.1	306.7	..	..	..	..	..	..
United Rep. of Tanzania	14.5	0.0	216.0	330.6	447.6	376.9	..	..	..	..	..	-0.1
Vanuatu	4.6	13.1	20.3	17.8	13.4	61.3	..	..	..	0.8	0.8	0.8
Yemen	3.2	-130.9	6.4	143.6	-302.1	-384.7	0.5	..	-8.8	21.5	26.0	36.3
Zambia	51.5	202.8	121.7	364.0	380.0	350.4	..	..	..	..	..	..
LDCs	**445.6**	**578.7**	**4 026.4**	**9 319.9**	**7 326.2**	**9 374.5**	**250.2**	**-7.5**	**766.2**	**373.6**	**657.8**	**487.4**
African LDCs and Haiti	*442.8*	*431.7*	*3 001.4*	*8 250.8*	*6 237.9*	*8 212.2*	*249.9*	*-8.2*	*762.3*	*335.0*	*619.1*	*431.8*
Asian LDCs	*-4.4*	*111.0*	*975.3*	*1 009.9*	*1 049.7*	*1 058.0*	*0.3*	*0.7*	*3.9*	*37.4*	*34.2*	*53.0*
Island LDCs	*7.2*	*36.1*	*49.8*	*59.2*	*38.6*	*104.4*	*..*	*..*	*..*	*1.2*	*4.4*	*2.7*
Other developing countries	**13 751.3**	**35 313.4**	**252 061.4**	**273 709.9**	**306 989.5**	**369 696.0**	**3 661.4**	**11 920.8**	**132 574.8**	**116 962.9**	**115 202.6**	**173 901.8**
All developing countries	**14 196.9**	**35 892.1**	**256 087.8**	**283 029.8**	**314 315.7**	**379 070.5**	**3 911.6**	**11 913.3**	**133 341.0**	**117 336.5**	**115 860.4**	**174 389.3**

Source: UNCTAD, FDI/TNC database.

31. External debt and debt service by source of lending
($ million)

	External debt (at year end)[a]						% of total		Debt service						% of total	
	1985	1990	2000	2004	2005	2006	1985	2006	1985	1990	2000	2004	2005	2006	1985	2006
I. Long term	**59 030**	**106 222**	**120 012**	**139 465**	**132 896**	**108 048**	**80.2**	**81.2**	**2 202**	**3 056**	**4 504**	**5 288**	**6 098**	**7 872**	**100.0**	**100.0**
Public and publicly guaranteed	58 544	105 369	117 594	137 342	130 930	107 535	79.5	80.8	2 145	2 975	4 437	5 061	5 810	7 682	97.4	97.6
Official creditors	50 757	90 628	107 746	126 830	119 303	97 602	69.0	73.3	1 510	2 226	2 868	3 587	3 659	4 842	68.6	61.5
A Concessional	38 313	69 379	90 936	112 900	107 176	85 948	52.0	64.6	682	1 243	2 235	2 538	2 655	3 018	31.0	38.3
Of which:																
Bilateral	25 429	39 481	37 143	35 471	31 638	32 942	34.5	24.8	456	756	1 154	1 039	1 181	1 162	20.7	14.8
Multilateral	12 884	29 897	53 792	77 429	75 538	53 006	17.5	39.8	226	488	1 081	1 499	1 474	1 856	10.3	23.6
B. Non-concessional	12 444	21 249	16 810	13 930	12 127	11 653	16.9	8.8	827	983	633	1 049	1 004	1 824		
Private creditors	7 787	14 741	9 848	10 512	11 627	9 933	10.6	7.5	635	749	1 568	1 474	2 151	2 840	28.8	36.1
Bonds	7	10	7	1	1	1			1	1	0	0	1	0	0.1	0.0
Commercial banks	2 491	3 159	5 023	6 389	7 647	6 640	3.4	5.0	227	174	1 273	1 107	1 889	2 024	10.3	25.7
Other private	5 289	11 572	4 818	4 122	3 978	3 292	7.2	2.5	407	574	295	367	261	816	18.5	10.4
Private non-guaranteed	486	852	2 418	2 123	1 967	2 274	0.7	1.7	57	81	67	227	288	199	2.6	2.5
II. Short term	**9 400**	**13 078**	**16 782**	**16 910**	**18 078**	**19 948**	**12.8**	**15.0**	..	..	..	..	..		..	..
III. Use of IMF credit	**5 181**	**5 397**	**5 838**	**6 397**	**5 474**	**3 315**	**7.0**	**2.5**	..	..	..	..	..		..	..
Total external debt	**73 611**	**124 697**	**142 632**	**162 771**	**156 448**	**133 082**	**100.0**	**100.0**	..	..	..	..	..		..	..

Source: UNCTAD secretariat calculations based on data from World Bank, *Global Development Finance*, online, May 2008.
  a Refers to debt stocks.

32. Total external debt and debt service payments of individual LDCs
($ million)

Country	External debt (at year end)[a]						Debt service[b]					
	1985	1990	2000	2004	2005	2006	1985	1990	2000	2004	2005	2006
Afghanistan	..	..	..	..	..	1 771	..	..	..	..	..	9
Angola	..	8 592	9 412	9 347	11 782	9 563	..	283	1 680	1 866	2 541	4 213
Bangladesh	6 658	12 439	15 717	20 129	18 928	20 521	195	495	684	646	769	624
Benin	854	1 292	1 591	1 916	1 855	824	41	33	60	54	60	81
Bhutan	9	84	204	593	649	713	0	5	7	12	7	9
Burkina Faso	513	832	1 422	2 045	2 042	1 142	25	28	38	48	41	50
Burundi	455	907	1 108	1 390	1 322	1 411	21	40	14	59	39	39
Cambodia	7	1 845	2 628	3 439	3 515	3 527	0	29	19	16	20	28
Cape Verde	95	134	326	520	543	601	5	6	16	23	32	30
Central African Republic	344	699	858	1 081	1 016	1 020	12	17	12	11	1	63
Chad	216	529	1 138	1 701	1 633	1 772	12	6	24	32	47	52
Comoros	134	188	237	307	291	282	2	1	2	3	4	3
Dem. Rep. of the Congo	6 183	10 259	11 692	11 434	10 600	11 201	300	137	0	136	209	311
Djibouti	144	205	262	417	412	464	4	11	11	17	14	21
Equatorial Guinea	132	241	248	296	272	278	2	1	2	5	4	4
Eritrea	..	..	311	718	736	800	..	..	3	19	20	12
Ethiopia	5 206	8 630	5 483	6 644	6 261	2 326	111	201	123	89	80	160
Gambia	245	369	483	672	668	725	1	30	19	25	25	28
Guinea	1 465	2 476	3 388	3 538	3 247	3 281	61	149	131	149	131	141
Guinea-Bissau	318	692	804	765	693	711	5	6	19	39	29	30
Haiti	757	890	953	1 044	1 034	1 189	21	15	29	72	45	48
Kiribati	..	..	..	..	..	..	..	..	..	..	..	..
Lao People's Dem. Rep.	619	1 768	2 502	2 524	2 690	2 985	5	8	32	113	165	166
Lesotho	175	396	672	769	664	670	18	23	56	53	80	46
Liberia	1 243	1 849	2 032	2 715	2 576	2 674	19	2	0	0	0	0
Madagascar	2 520	3 689	4 691	3 790	3 466	1 453	94	155	102	75	66	67
Malawi	1 021	1 558	2 705	3 428	3 183	850	76	103	51	49	60	70
Maldives	83	78	206	353	368	459	9	7	19	32	33	33
Mali	1 456	2 468	2 980	3 320	3 025	1 436	34	43	68	79	70	79
Mauritania	1 454	2 113	2 378	2 333	2 316	1 630	76	118	66	45	54	69
Mozambique	2 871	4 650	7 257	4 869	4 637	3 265	57	64	84	62	66	53
Myanmar	3 098	4 695	5 928	7 239	6 645	6 828	185	57	75	105	92	70
Nepal	590	1 627	2 869	3 358	3 197	3 409	13	52	95	115	116	136
Niger	1 195	1 726	1 677	1 973	1 980	805	95	71	22	35	32	67
Rwanda	363	708	1 272	1 661	1 518	419	13	14	21	23	19	30
Samoa	76	92	197	571	656	858	5	4	6	6	6	8
Sao Tome and Principe	63	150	310	366	340	355	3	2	3	6	6	9
Senegal	2 559	3 744	3 607	3 940	3 883	1 984	103	225	185	297	168	198
Sierra Leone	711	1 197	1 226	1 728	1 682	1 428	15	16	19	24	20	27
Solomon Islands	66	120	155	177	166	173	3	10	9	17	14	4
Somalia	1 639	2 370	2 562	2 849	2 750	2 836	5	7	0	0	0	0
Sudan	8 955	14 762	16 411	19 353	18 455	19 158	89	23	185	281	356	265
Timor-Leste	..	..	..	..	..	..	..	..	..	..	..	..
Togo	935	1 281	1 430	1 836	1 708	1 806	90	60	15	4	5	7
Tuvalu	..	..	..	..	..	..	..	..	..	..	..	..
Uganda	1 239	2 606	3 497	4 753	4 427	1 264	56	84	47	70	133	110
United Rep. of Tanzania	9 105	6 454	6 931	7 805	7 796	4 240	140	136	150	86	75	101
Vanuatu	16	38	74	121	82	86	1	2	2	2	2	3
Yemen	3 339	6 352	5 075	5 488	5 363	5 563	94	108	126	175	148	159
Zambia	4 487	6 905	5 722	7 455	5 378	2 325	87	171	177	211	194	147
LDCs	**73 611**	**124 697**	**142 632**	**162 771**	**156 448**	**133 082**	**2 202**	**3 056**	**4 504**	**5 288**	**6 098**	**7 881**

Source: UNCTAD secretariat calculations based on World Bank *Global Development Finance* online data May 2008.
   a External debt cover both long-term and short term debt as well as the use of IMF credit.
   b Debt service cover long term debt only.

33. Debt and debt service ratio
(Per cent)

Country	External Debt[a] / GDP						Debt service[b] / exports[c]					
	1985	1990	2000	2003	2004	2005	1985	1990	2000	2003	2004	2005
Afghanistan	..	..	..	..	..	21.1	..	..	..	..	..	..
Angola	..	83.7	103.1	47.3	38.5	21.2	..	7.1	20.5	10.7	7.7	7.6
Bangladesh	30.8	41.3	33.4	35.5	31.5	33.2	16.3	26.9	10.4	6.7	6.5	6.5
Benin	81.6	70.0	70.6	47.3	43.3	17.3	16.6	12.3	17.5	8.9	9.4	..
Bhutan	5.0	27.5	45.5	83.2	78.3	75.7	0.1	6.2	5.0	3.3	4.1	2.2
Burkina Faso	33.0	26.8	54.5	40.0	36.4	18.5	16.1	8.3	15.9	7.7	8.8	6.2
Burundi	39.6	80.1	156.3	209.2	166.1	156.2	16.7	44.6	25.3	44.1	65.0	39.6
Cambodia	..	165.5	71.9	64.8	56.1	48.6	..	42.3	1.0	0.3	0.4	0.4
Cape Verde	..	39.5	61.4	56.2	54.4	52.5	..	13.1	10.8	14.0	13.4	14.2
Central African Republic	39.7	47.0	89.4	82.7	74.1	68.3	6.5	7.5	6.2	0.1	6.7	0.3
Chad	21.0	30.4	82.2	38.5	27.7	27.1	10.1	2.8	10.2	1.5	1.0	1.2
Comoros	117.2	75.1	117.2	84.7	75.1	69.9	9.7	2.7	5.9	5.6	6.2	8.1
Dem. Rep. of the Congo	85.9	109.7	271.6	174.0	149.2	131.1	15.2	5.0	0.0	7.1	6.1	8.3
Djibouti	42.2	45.4	47.6	62.6	58.2	60.3	..	4.5	5.5	5.5	6.0	4.4
Equatorial Guinea	166.2	182.4	19.8	6.0	3.6	3.2	7.2	2.5	0.2	0.1	0.1	0.0
Eritrea	..	..	49.1	113.1	75.8	73.7	..	..	3.1	13.2	22.2	23.2
Ethiopia	55.3	71.4	69.4	70.0	55.0	17.5	20.1	29.9	12.5	5.5	4.8	3.8
Gambia	108.6	116.5	114.8	167.6	144.9	142.0	0.9	16.0	9.2	10.8	12.1	..
Guinea	9.4	92.9	108.9	89.1	97.5	98.9	1.4	18.0	17.9	13.8	16.1	12.2
Guinea-Bissau	221.3	283.7	373.3	283.4	230.0	233.6	34.7	23.7	27.7	11.9	34.7	22.8
Haiti	37.7	31.1	24.8	27.2	24.0	23.9	6.6	2.9	6.3	6.7	12.0	6.4
Kiribati	..	..	..	..	..	..	0.0	0.0	0.0	0.0	..	..
Lao People's Dem. Rep.	26.1	204.3	144.2	100.6	93.2	86.9	4.9	8.5	6.2	14.6	14.4	13.4
Lesotho	60.5	64.3	78.8	58.3	46.6	44.8	43.9	22.0	21.9	8.4	7.5	10.6
Liberia	132.9	481.0	362.2	590.2	486.9	423.8	4.0	..	0.0	0.0	0.0	0.0
Madagascar	88.2	119.7	121.0	86.9	68.8	26.4	26.8	30.2	8.6	4.5	5.5	4.1
Malawi	90.2	82.9	155.2	130.6	111.5	26.9	27.9	23.0	11.3	5.0	8.1	11.1
Maldives	65.3	36.2	33.0	46.9	49.1	49.5	..	..	3.3	2.9	..	..
Mali	110.8	101.9	123.0	68.1	57.0	24.5	15.6	10.3	10.4	4.5	5.8	3.7
Mauritania	212.8	207.3	219.9	150.7	126.1	61.2	18.5	25.3	13.1	9.3	6.8	3.7
Mozambique	64.4	188.8	170.8	85.5	70.5	47.8	44.4	31.6	11.3	4.0	2.9	2.3
Myanmar	..	..	..	..	..	..	..	..	..	..	..	..
Nepal	22.5	44.8	52.2	46.2	39.1	38.1	4.4	13.6	7.4	9.1	9.7	9.6
Niger	82.9	69.6	93.2	67.1	57.7	22.0	31.9	18.9	7.0	5.6	6.9	..
Rwanda	21.2	27.4	70.2	91.0	70.7	16.8	7.1	9.5	13.9	10.1	10.2	6.7
Samoa	89.4	82.1	85.2	159.6	162.5	202.5	..	..	7.1	..	..	..
Sao Tome and Principe	..	..	..	341.9	302.3	289.7	..	..	..	..	..	..
Senegal	86.4	65.5	76.9	49.6	44.9	21.6	12.5	15.5	14.1	9.7	12.7	7.2
Sierra Leone	82.9	184.2	193.4	161.3	138.6	98.5	12.0	11.3	16.1	9.7	9.1	6.2
Solomon Islands	41.0	57.1	51.9	66.7	55.5	51.5	3.1	10.2	7.6	7.4	..	..
Somalia	187.0	258.5	..	..	..	..	9.1	7.5	..	..	..	..
Sudan	71.9	163.7	132.7	89.3	66.1	51.2	12.5	4.7	9.8	6.4	5.6	5.9
Timor-Leste	..	..	..	..	..	..	..	..	..	..	..	..
Togo	122.7	78.6	107.6	89.1	81.0	81.9	24.4	11.0	3.6	0.2	0.5	..
Tuvalu	..	..	..	..	..	..	..	..	..	..	..	..
Uganda	35.2	60.5	59.0	69.7	50.6	13.4	11.6	26.9	7.1	6.1	6.1	9.4
United Rep. of Tanzania	..	151.5	76.3	68.8	61.9	33.2	..	25.4	9.8	3.0	2.9	2.4
Vanuatu	13.0	25.4	30.5	36.6	22.3	22.2	0.9	2.3	..	1.3	1.7	..
Yemen	..	131.6	53.8	39.6	32.0	29.2	..	15.7	3.2	..	..	..
Zambia	199.2	210.0	176.7	137.0	74.0	21.7	10.5	14.5	20.2	32.8	8.5	4.7
LDCs	**64.9**	**91.3**	**86.3**	**66.7**	**54.3**	**39.6**	**12.1**	**14.4**	**11.1**	**7.4**	**6.4**	**6.1**

Source: UNCTAD secretariat calculations, based on World Bank, *World Development Indicators 2007* and *Global Development Finance 2007*, online data, May 2008.

    a   External debt cover both long-term and short -term debt as well as use of IMF credit.

    b   Debt service cover long term debt only.

    c   Exports of good and services (including non-factor services).

DATE DUE